WORDSWORTH CLASSICS
OF WORLD LITERATURE

General Editor: Tom Griffith

THE VOYAGES OF CAPTAIN COOK

The Voyages of Captain Cook

Edited by Ernest Rhys
With an Introduction by Simon Marshall

WORDSWORTH CLASSICS
OF WORLD LITERATURE

This edition published 1999 by Wordsworth Editions Limited
Cumberland House, Crib Street, Ware, Hertfordshire sg12 9et

isbn 1 84022 100 3

Typeset by Antony Gray
Printed and bound in Great Britain by
Mackays of Chatham, Chatham, Kent

CONTENTS

INTRODUCTION

Why read Captain Cook?

James Cook, like Tennyson's Ulysses, has 'become a name' – Captain Cook – the indefatigable navigator and explorer who tirelessly charted the unknown and perilous regions of the Pacific, who during Britain's great period of colonial expansion was engaged on the more ideologically neutral task of 'discovery' and who died in the service of scientific enquiry. His actual achievements, like the islands he visited, have often been shrouded in some mystery. Did he really discover Australia, New Zealand and Hawaii? Was he responsible for finding a cure for scurvy? How did the unassuming son of a Yorkshire labourer become a model for Victorian imperialists?

It is perhaps the manner of his death which established him as one of the many secular martyrs to the Britannic cause. In the famous painting by Johann Zoffany, Cook is shown lying mortally wounded in the centre of the painting. Around him seethes a swarm of semi-naked warriors overcoming the hopelessly outnumbered marines. Coming in the wake of Benjamin West's picture of General Wolfe's death at Quebec, exhibited at the Royal Academy in 1771, this picture contributed to the newly fashionable demand for stylised portrayals of heroic deaths of British officers. In this way Cook's death at Kealakekua Bay in 1779 can be seen as representing the supposedly selfless sacrifice of the British élite in the noble cause of enlightenment and progress.

It is not just Cook's death and subsequent imperial canonisation which remain as the abiding memorial to the man; the more tangible reminders are to be found in the corners of the globe still named after him and named by him. Mount Cook still looms large

over South Island in New Zealand (despite recent attempts to
return it to its original Maori name), the Cook Islands still dot the
Pacific between the Samoas and French Polynesia, and the most
westerly point of North America still bears the name Cook gave it
in 1778, Cape Prince of Wales.

Such memorials are part of the myth-making which surrounds
James Cook. The recent resurgence of interest in the origins and
creation of the British Empire and the continuing debates in Pacific
studies over the ethnographical significance of Cook's voyages,
discoveries and death all attest to the continuing importance of the
three long voyages into the Pacific. Whether Cook is seen as merely
a part of the process of the European incursion and expansion into
the Pacific or as one of the principal agents in shaping the direction
of that incursion, his significance is immense. Even discarding the
myths, one is left with a man whose expeditions were of immense
importance to botany, anthropology, navigation, medicine and
exploration, and whose contribution towards solving three of the
great puzzles of cartography was significant. If Cook was not the
saint that British imperial hagiography represented him, neither was
he singlehandedly responsible for the exploitation and degradation
of indigenous life in the Pacific. He was perhaps a fine example
from the so-called Age of Enlightenment, an empiricist and a
scientist (in the full eighteenth-century meaning of the word), and
he deserves to be read both for his achievements and his failings.

Background to Cook's life

As a brief biography of Cook introduces the account of the first
voyage, it will perhaps be more useful in this introduction to
contextualise Cook within his period. The fifty or so years from
his birth in 1728 to his death in 1779 saw huge changes in the
fortunes and prosperity of Britain. Cook's career mirrors and is a
product of the transformation of Britain from a land-based, mainly
English-speaking colonial power into a sea-based, polyglot trading
empire. Cook's rise to prominence in the navy came during the
Seven Years War when Britain acquired huge territories in North
America; when he died in 1779 Britain was on the point of losing
these territories in the War of American Independence but, as a
direct consequence of Cook's voyages, was beginning to extend its
trading links with the Pacific and South-East Asia.

Cook's career can also be seen as a model illustration of the career opportunities offered by the navy. Although his promotion was dependent upon the patronage of influential men, it was at least on the basis of personal merit rather than any family influence. Cook provided a pattern for social improvement, and the navy came increasingly to be seen as providing a possible vehicle for meritocratic achievement in a society which was still extremely stratified socially.

In addition Cook's career took place when three of the great puzzles of cartography and navigation were still unsolved; not only was the search for the elusive North-West Passage, that obsession of Elizabethan seafarers, renewed during the eighteenth century, but it was still thought that a southern continent must exist in the southern oceans to balance the land masses of the northern hemisphere. The search for both of these was inhibited by the lack of a solution to the third puzzle, that of determining longitude. The lack of sure means of determining longitude meant that long voyages were liable to errors in navigation and the hazards of shipwreck; in addition, as the voyage of Anson in 1740-44 had illustrated, it also meant that ships became lost, ran out of fresh provisions and were ravaged with scurvy. Cook's contribution towards helping to solve these puzzles was immense, and it was helped by his determination to find a successful method for preventing scurvy.

Origins of the first voyage

The main reason for the voyage to the South Pacific was scientific: to observe the passing of the planet Venus between the earth and the sun. This so-called transit of Venus was thought to give astronomers the opportunity to measure the distance between the earth and the other planets and the sun. Not only would this help in charting the solar system but it might also help towards resolving the problem of determining longitude. Members of the Royal Society had been arguing the case for mounting an expedition to observe the forthcoming transit of Venus in 1769 after an international exercise to observe the transit in 1761 failed. As there were to be no further transits before 1874, the Society was keen to ensure that this opportunity was not missed. It was also decided to try to ensure that the transit was observed in three different places, to guarantee the demands of parallax observation. The committee which was set up to consider this petitioned King George III to provide funds and urged that the navy should provide a ship to be sent to the Pacific.

It was originally planned that Alexander Dalrymple, a well-connected civilian navigator, scientist and traveller, should lead the observation, but his insistence upon having overall management of the ship incurred the wrath of the Admiralty, which insisted upon having one of its ships commanded by a naval officer. Cook was the Admiralty's alternative choice. Not only was he an exceptionally able navigator and surveyor, but his own observations of a solar eclipse had been presented to the Royal Society in 1767. There were, however, other considerations useful both to the navy and to the Royal Society. The British interest in the Pacific was not entirely scientific. Not only were Spanish and Dutch interests advanced in the Pacific but two of the great puzzles of exploration were connected with the region. The first was the North-West Passage, the potentially 'quick' route to India and China, which might avoid the need to sail round either of the perilous and time-consuming extremities of Africa or South America. The second was the rumoured existence of a great southern continent, lying somewhere in the South Pacific; the hope was that such a continent, if it existed, would either provide a useful market for British manufactures or possibly fertile territory to colonise. In the wake of Britain's success in the Seven Years War two expeditions had been sent to try and solve these puzzles. The first, in 1764, commanded by John Byron, achieved little beyond the fastest circumnavigation of the globe to date. The second, in 1766, commanded by Samuel Wallis, reached Tahiti and claimed to have glimpsed the southern continent on the way. Wallis returned to England in 1768 in time for his discoveries to be communicated to Cook. After he had observed the transit in Tahiti, Cook was ordered to go in search of the southern continent. In addition, Cook was ordered to take possession of any vacant lands in the name of the King, and to deal patiently and tolerantly with any natives he might meet and obtain their consent before taking possession of their lands. Such instructions whilst they were commendable in their tolerance still contained sufficient intimations of imperialist intentions to suggest that the Admiralty's support for the expedition was motivated as much by geo-political concerns as by abstract, if potentially useful, scientific questions.

However, the fact that the naturalists Joseph Banks and Daniel Carl Solander were to accompany Cook was a further sign of the curious collaboration between the navy and the Royal Society. The presence of Banks, a wealthy, well-connected twenty-five year old member of the Royal Society, not only added to the scientific thrust of the expedition but also upon its completion added considerably to its publicity value. Although Banks took much of the credit for the journey, he also ensured that its significance was widely publicised. Thus it was with a mixed ensemble of sailors, naturalists, painters, Banks's servants and his two greyhounds that HMS *Endeavour* left Plymouth on 26 August 1768, bound for the Pacific by way of Cape Horn.

Achievements and incidents of the First Voyage: 1768–1771

The main achievements of the first voyage can be enumerated easily: 5,000 miles of previously uncharted coastline were mapped – not only the entire coastline of New Zealand (including the discovery that it comprised two islands), but most of the east coast of New Holland (as Australia was then called). Banks and Solander brought back some 1,000 new species of plant, 500 fish and 500 skins of birds, as well as innumerable insects. In addition Banks's descriptions of Botany Bay in New Holland were later to result in the establishment of the penal colony there in 1788.

The incidents are less objectively assessed: the various encounters with alien cultures, from the Patagonian natives to the fearsome Maoris, reveal some of the preoccupations of the eighteenth-century traveller with status, manners and morals as compared to the nineteenth-century preoccupations with racial stereotypes. Cook's writings, however, tend to gloss over the sexual experiences of the expedition, which for many aboard the ship must have been among their most significant encounters with other cultures. The ever-present dangers of sickness and death are sharply illustrated by the account of the ship's stay at Batavia; it was here that the story of 'Tupia', a priest of the Queen of Tahiti, whom Banks intended to bring back to Britain along with his son, reached its sad conclusion. In addition, the exciting account of the near-shipwreck on the Great Barrier Reef, when the ship was saved only by a piece of coral which partially plugged the hole it had created, serves as a reminder of the extraordinary dangers which attended such an expedition and how close it came to being yet another tale of maritime loss. Finally, Cook's modesty in assessing the worth of his charts in a letter to the Admiralty illustrates his understated sense of achievement in an extraordinary voyage: 'I flatter myself that the latter [his charts, plans and drawings] will be found sufficient to convey tolerable knowledge of the places they are intended to illustrate, and that the discoveries which we have made, though not great, will apologise for the length of the voyage.'

Origins of the Second Voyage

The publicity generated by the success of the voyage, which was for the most part accredited to (and accepted by) Banks, led to him demanding that a second expedition be sent out as soon as possible. The reappointment of Banks's friend, the Earl of Sandwich, as First Lord of the Admiralty provided the necessary authority, and Banks also set about ensuring that Cook was promoted to the rank of captain (or at least ensuring that Cook thought Banks had been influential in securing this) and that he would be the Admiralty's choice as captain (if not leader) on the next voyage. The success and influence which Banks enjoyed somewhat unsettled his judgment, and when the two ships *Resolution* and *Adventure* were being fitted out, Banks insisted that the living quarters of *Resolution* be extended to provide more commodious accommodation for his swelling entourage (now of fifteen people, including two horn players for relaxation). To the dismay of Cook, the Earl of Sandwich acceded to Banks's demands and ordered an extra deck to be fitted to *Resolution*. It was a disaster: the ship was now unbalanced and the pilot who took her out for a sailing test gave up before he reached the open sea. The Admiralty Board acted decisively and the extra deck was removed. Banks was furious and tried as hard as he could to obtain a replacement ship, but he overplayed his influence with the King, and Sandwich, realising that the reputation of the navy was at stake, resisted Banks's bluster. In response, Banks immediately chartered his own ship and headed off to Iceland to botanise free from naval interference.

The absence of Banks left Cook free from any potential challenge to his authority. The purpose of the voyage was to continue the search for the southern continent in the wastes of the southern Pacific, using the two bases of Tahiti and Queen Charlotte's Bay in New Zealand; Cook was also urged to continue surveying any further discoveries in the Pacific. After the experience at Batavia Cook wanted to ensure that the expedition was untroubled by sickness, and made extensive preparations to guard against scurvy. Despite the recent discoveries of Dr James Lind, who had found that lemon juice was effective in preventing scurvy, Cook's measures relied upon a mixture of deterrents, which included taking huge amounts of sauerkraut, brewing a sort of beer with inspissated juice of wort, and ensuring a rigorous cleaning and airing routine on board ship during the voyage. Cook is often represented as the saviour of countless seamen through the efficacy of these measures, but their success meant that the discoveries of Lind were not put into practice for many years.

In keeping with the scientific aims of exploration, Cook took with him a copy made by Larcum Kendall of John Harrison's fourth chronometer, as well as other chronometers. The full story of Harrison's laborious struggle to gain recognition for his efforts can be read in the recent book *Longitude* by Dava Sobel; Cook gave fulsome praise for this method of determining longitude, and it helped him considerably on this voyage. The *Resolution* and *Adventure* left Plymouth on 13 July 1772, laden with anti-scorbutic measures and provisions. This time Cook headed for the Cape of Good Hope and from there commenced the search for the southern continent.

Incidents and achievements of the Second Voyage: 1772–1775

The achievements of the second voyage, whilst not as astounding as the first voyage, were nevertheless remarkable. Cook visited and charted with considerable precision Easter Island, the Marquesas, Tonga, the New Hebrides, the island of Georgia and the (now South) Sandwich Islands; he also searched the empty southern tracts of the Atlantic and Pacific for the southern continent. The two ships became separated on the way to New Zealand in October 1773 and never reunited; the *Adventure* under Captain Furneaux failed to make the rendezvous at Queen Charlotte Sound before December, only to find that Cook had already departed to continue the search for the southern continent. It was near here that Furneaux's men found first-hand evidence of cannibalism when the remains of the eleven men who had been sent to fetch greens to provision the ship were found scattered on the beach at Grass Cove.

In his searches for the southern continent Cook concluded that such a continent certainly did not lie within hospitable latitudes, and that it was probable that it lay within the polar circle and was the source of so much ice in the southern oceans; he was modestly satisfied that he had solved this particular maritime puzzle. In addition, during the whole voyage of the *Resolution* only one crew member died due to sickness; at a time when it was not unusual for the long-distance trading vessels to lose up to a third of their crew to sickness, this was an outstanding achievement.

Origins of the Third Voyage

On his return Cook was promoted to post-captain, made one of the four captains of the Royal Hospital at Greenwich, one of the naval sinecures for successful service, and elected to the Royal Society. He also received news that the Admiralty was planning to send an expedition into the Pacific to search once again for the North-West Passage; such was the perceived strategic and commercial importance of this route that the Admiralty announced a prize of £20,000 for its discovery. To begin with, Cook was consulted in an advisory capacity. Not only had he spent six of the last seven years at sea, but those years had been spent coping with the unremitting pressures of responsibility and the attendant tensions of charting little-known and dangerous waters; however, at a dinner in January 1776 with the First Sea Lord, the Comptroller and the Secretary of the Navy, during which the leadership of this expedition was discussed, Cook suddenly announced that he would undertake the leadership of the expedition if he were commanded. It was a fateful offer.

The expedition consisted of a refitted *Resolution* and a newly-purchased ship, *Discovery*. However, during the refitting of the *Resolution* Cook's time was taken up with recruiting his officers and crew, making his journal ready for publication and having his portrait painted by Sir Nathaniel Dance. This, too, was to have fateful consequences, as repairs at the naval dockyard at Deptford

were both slow and incompetent. A further problem for the
expedition was that the sailing season in the far North Pacific was
extremely short, and in order to meet the proposed plan of
searching for the passage in June 1777 the expedition ought to
have left Britain by April 1776. Cook was also burdened with
another task. As a legacy of Furneaux's voyage, he was to return
Omai, the Tahitian, to the Society Islands, a task which would cost
him much precious time.

In view of the fatal end to the third voyage much has been
written about the state of mind and the health of Cook; as Hough
records in *Captain Cook: A Biography*, Cook's increasing irritability
and impatience, which resulted in his unusually severe punishment
of any malefactor and his increasingly erratic judgment, has led to
various theories that Cook might have been suffering from an
intestinal parasitic infection contracted on one of his earlier voyages. When the expedition finally departed in July 1776, neither
Cook, nor Charles Clerke, the commander of the *Discovery*, would
see England again

Disappointments and failures of the Third Voyage: 1776–1780

Cook's understated achievements of the first two voyages to the
Pacific had been his tolerance, forbearance and comparative fairness when dealing with the inhabitants of the islands he visited,
and the great care he took to ensure the physical wellbeing and
general orderliness of his crew. During the third voyage Cook's
dealings with his crew were characterised by irascibility and mis-
judgment, and his treatment of the inhabitants of the islands he
visited was marked by impatience, frustration and severity. These
changes are barely perceptible from his journal; what is also not
apparent in his journal of the voyage is his seeming disregard for
the ostensible purpose of the expedition. Not only did he miss the
opportunity of searching for the passage during the summer, 1777,
but he nearly missed the chance again the following year.

The visits to the Pacific islands had always been characterised by
the different notions that the inhabitants had towards the property
of the visitors. On his previous journeys Cook had tried to
preserve the ships' stores while maintaining an awareness of the
cultural difference between the British and the inhabitants. By
contrast, during the third voyage Cook frequently punished any

'theft' by flogging, lashing or even by cutting the ears off the offender. When the expedition's goats were stolen by the inhabitants of Eimeo in the Society Islands, Cook insisted on a retributive burning of the inhabitants' boats (a considerable punishment to people without metal tools). Mutiny was even whispered on the voyage – once on the way to Tahiti, when Cook, failing to discover who had committed a theft, halved the crew's rations, and later near the Arctic, when Cook insisted that the crew eat the repulsive meat of the walruses they had killed.

The achievement of being the first Europeans to visit the Hawaiian archipelago, which he named the Sandwich Islands, was offset by the failure to progress further than the appropriately named Icy Cape on the shore of north-western America. However, despite the failure of the actual aim, Cook's voyage into the Bering Strait led to the first detailed maps of the awkward topography of the region and further hopes that a passage might be possible. Cook had planned to return to the west coast of America to reprovision the ships and then head west to Kamchatka. Instead he altered his plans and decided to head south to pass the winter in the warmer Sandwich Islands. After coasting Maui, Cook headed south towards the largest island, Hawai'i, and after a slow circumnavigation of the island, the ships put in at Kealakekua Bay on 16 January 1779.

Events leading to the death of Cook

There has been much scholarly debate over the precise reasons for and significance of Cook's curious death. Captain King's journal, from which the account in this edition is taken, contains his genuine bewilderment and confusion over the exact cause of the incident, but contains only a vague presentiment that the expedition was encountering events which they could not have been able to foresee. When the ships sailed into Kealakekua Bay, no one on them could have known that their arrival coincided eerily with the narratives and rituals which surrounded the worship of the fertility and harvest god Lono (called Orono in this edition). The season was that of *Matahiki*, the festival of Lono, and not only did the ships' masts and sails replicate the emblem of the god, but the temple of the god was situated at Kealakekua Bay; by arriving during *Matahiki*, the expedition managed to fulfil with uncanny precision the various legends and rituals associated with worship of

Lono. Whether the inhabitants actually supposed Cook to be Lono, as Marshall Sahlins argues, or whether they merely regarded him as a human representative of the god, as Gananath Obeyesekere contends, the subsequent reverent treatment of Cook, the help given him in reprovisioning the ships, and the absence of any theft, indicate that this was an incident of huge significance for the inhabitants. The expedition's departure neatly coincided with the correct end to *Matahiki*, the passing of the season of Lono, and if the expedition had not had to return to the bay after the *Resolution* suffered from storm damage, the incident would have resulted in a very different narrative.

If the help and reverence which the expedition had received during their first stay was the result of an extraordinarily fortuitous coincidence, the mood which greeted their unexpected return was due to extreme misfortune. The season was now devoted to the god Ku, a war god inimical to Lono. Cook's return was contradictory, confusing and disturbing to the inhabitants, and the treatment of the expedition now indicated the fear, suspicion and anger at the disruption of the Hawai'ian ritual calendar. If Sahlins is correct then Cook's actions when he decided to confront the loss of a cutter by force were extremely threatening to the inhabitant. Likewise Obeyesekere's argument that Cook's angry actions were sufficient in themselves to merit such a fierce response is useful, as it draws attention to Cook's fatal misreading of the situation. Whatever the inhabitants actually thought of Cook, whether as a god or as the human representative of a god, it is clear that Cook's rash decision to confront the Hawai'ian king Terreeoboo in person, coupled with the fact that news had just arrived that Chief Kalimu had been killed by the British, precipitated his unfortunate death on the beach at Kealakekua Bay.

News of Cook's death took ten months to reach Britain and the controversy it created then has never subsequently been settled. That fatal collision between mutually uncomprehending cultures still serves as an uneasy reminder of the ambiguity which attended the ostensibly high-minded aims of the voyages, and it calls into question the uncritical use of the language of progress, discovery, improvement and civilisation.

SIMON MARSHALL
St Edward's School, Oxford

FURTHER READING

J. C. Beaglehole, *The Journals of Captain Cook*, Cambridge 1955–67

G. Williams (ed.), *Captain Cook's Voyages 1768–1779*, London 1997

R. Hough, *Captain Cook: A Biography*, London 1993

P. O'Brian, *Joseph Banks*, London 1987

M. Sahlins, *Islands of History*, Chicago 1985

M. Sahlins, *How Natives Think – About Captain Cook for Example*, Chicago 1995

G. Obeyesekere, *The Apotheosis of Captain Cook*, Princeton 1992

B. Smith, *European Vision and the South Pacific*, New Haven 1985

D. Sobel, *Longitude*, London 1995

J. Diamond, *Guns, Germs and Steel*, London 1997

This list includes many of the books used in preparing this Introduction; a good starting place would be *Captain Cook: A Biography* by Richard Hough. Not only is it the most recent and accessible biography but it provides an extremely well-written and interesting account of Cook's life.

NOTE ON THE TEXT

This edition reprints the 1906 Everyman edition of *Captain Cook's Voyages of Discovery*. This was edited by Ernest Rhys in a somewhat idiosyncratic manner. For the first two voyages Rhys rewrites his sources to produce a third-person narrative account, and for the final voyage he uses extracts from Cook's Journal and from that of Lieutenant King (for the account of Cook's death) to produce a first-person narrative. Despite the antiquated nature of the prose-style this edition makes available to the general reader the text in which the majority of twentieth-century readers have encountered Cook's travels. The pioneering scholarly edition of Cook's Journals by J. C. Beaglehole is not widely accessible, and the recent selection from his edition of Cook's Journals by Glyndwr Williams is only available to members of the Folio Society.

FIRST VOYAGE

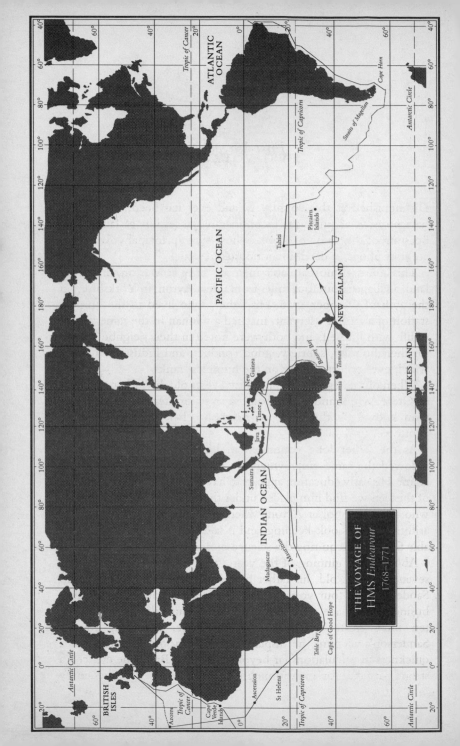

THE VOYAGE OF
HMS *Endeavour*
1768–1771

ATLANTIC OCEAN

PACIFIC OCEAN

INDIAN OCEAN

BRITISH ISLES

Azores

Cape Verde Islands

Ascension

St Helena

Madagascar

Mauritius

Table Bay

Cape of Good Hope

Sumatra

Java

Timor

New Guinea

Tasmania

Tasman Sea

NEW ZEALAND

Botany Bay

WILKES LAND

Tahiti

Pitcairn Islands

Cape Horn

Straits of Magellan

Tropic of Cancer

Tropic of Capricorn

Antarctic Circle

First Voyage

Distinguished as this country is, and ever has been, for its able navigators, it acquires no inconsiderable accession of fame from boasting of the name of Cook, whose three principal voyages we are now about to detail in an unbroken series.

This able and most amiable man was born at Marton, in Cleveland, a village about four miles from Great Ayton, in Yorkshire, on the 27th of October 1728. His father, who lived in the humble station of a farmer's servant, married a woman in the same sphere of life with himself; and both were noted in their neighbourhood for their honesty, sobriety, good conduct, and industry, qualities which ever reflect a lustre on the humblest ranks.

When our navigator was about two years old, his father removed to Great Ayton, and was appointed to superintend a considerable farm known by the name of Airyholm, belonging to Thomas Scottowe, Esq.

As the father long continued in this trust, the son naturally followed the same employment, as far as his tender years would admit. His early education appears to have been slight; but at the age of thirteen we find him placed under the tuition of one Mr Pullen, who taught school at Ayton, where he learned the rudiments of arithmetic and book-keeping, and is said to have shown a remarkable facility in acquiring the science of numbers.

About the beginning of the year 1745, when young Cook was seventeen years old, his father bound him apprentice to William Sanderson, for four years, to learn the grocery and haberdashery business, at a place called Staithes, a populous fishing town about ten miles from Whitby, and while here, according to Mr Sanderson's account, he displayed a maturity of judgment and a quickness in calculations far beyond his years. But as he evinced a strong partiality for a maritime life (a predilection strengthened by the situation of the place, and the company with which, perhaps, he associated), on some trivial disagreement with his master, he obtained a release from his engagements, after a year and a half's servitude, and determined to follow the bent of his own inclination.

In July 1746 he was bound apprentice to Messrs Walker of Whitby, for the term of three years, which he served to the full satisfaction of his employers. His first voyage was on board the ship *Freelove*, of about 450 tons burden, chiefly employed in the coal trade from Newcastle to London.

In May 1748 he was ordered home to assist in rigging and fitting for sea, a fine new ship, named the *Three Brothers*, 600 tons. This was designed to improve him in his profession and to qualify him for a better berth, when his apprenticeship should expire. After two coal voyages in this vessel, she was taken into the service of government, and sent as a transport to Middleburgh, to convey some troops to Dublin. These being landed at their destination, another regiment was taken on board, and brought to Liverpool. Thence the ship proceeded to Deptford, where she was paid off in April 1749. The remaining part of the season, Cook served on board her in the Norway trade.

Being honourably released from his engagements, he next entered on board a ship employed in the Baltic trade, and during the two following years performed several voyages, of no great importance. In 1752 his old master promoted him to be mate of one of his ships, called the *Friendship*, in which capacity he acted for some time, with so much credit to himself and satisfaction to his owners, that it is said he was offered the place of captain. This, however, he declined, and fortunate indeed was it for his country that he did so.

In the spring of 1755 hostilities commenced between Great Britain and France; press-warrants were issued, and Cook, whose ship was then in the river Thames, afraid of being pressed, resolved, if possible, to conceal himself; but afterwards, reflecting on the difficulty of this course, he adopted the resolution of entering as a volunteer in the Royal Navy, 'having a mind', as he expressed himself, 'to try his fortune in that way'.

In pursuance of this design, he repaired to a house of rendezvous at Wapping, and entered on board the *Eagle*, a sixty gun ship, at that time commanded by Captain Hamer. To this ship, Captain, afterwards Sir Hugh Palliser, being appointed in October following, Cook's diligence and attention to the duties of his profession did not escape the notice of that intelligent commander, and he met with every encouragement compatible with his humble station.

Cook's merit having been blazoned among his connections and friends in his native country, some of them generously interested themselves in his behalf, and procured a letter of recommendation to his captain from Mr Osbaldeston, member of parliament for Scarborough, in which it was requested that he would point out in what manner they might possibly contribute to his promotion.

Captain Palliser did full justice to Cook's character, and suggested that a master's warrant might perhaps be procured for him, by which he would be put in a situation suited to his talents, and be enabled to reflect credit on those who honoured him with their patronage.

In consequence of this, interest was made for a master's warrant, which he obtained to the *Grampus* sloop, in May 1759; but this appointment did not take place, as the former master unexpectedly returned. In a few days, however, he was made master of the *Garland*; but here too he was disappointed, for, on inquiry, it was found that the ship had already sailed. At last he was appointed to the *Mercury*, which was destined for North America, under the command of Sir Charles Saunders, who, in conjunction with General Wolfe, was then engaged in the memorable siege of Quebec.

During that signal transaction, it was found necessary to obtain the soundings of the river St Lawrence, directly opposite to the French camp at Montmorency and Beauport. As this was universally esteemed to be a dangerous and very difficult service, Cook's well-known sagacity and intrepidity recommended him to Captain Palliser for the undertaking; and notwithstanding the difficulties of having to take the soundings during the night, to evade observation, Cook executed the task in the most complete manner, and to the entire satisfaction of his superiors. For several successive nights he carried on the work unmolested, but at last he was discovered by the enemy, who sent a number of canoes filled with Indians to surround him, and he had no other alternative but to make for the Isle of Orleans, where he was so closely pursued, that he had scarcely leaped from the bow of the boat, before the Indians entered by the stern, and carried her off in triumph.

There is little or no reason to believe that, before this period, Cook had acquainted himself with the principles of drawing; but such was the vigour of his mind, and his aptitude for the acquisition of knowledge, that he soon mastered every subject to which he applied himself. And notwithstanding the disadvantages under which he laboured, he presented the admiral with as complete a draft of the channel and its soundings as could have been furnished by the most expert surveyor in more favoured circumstances.

Our navigator performed another service, not less important, and which redounds equally to his honour. The navigation of the river St Lawrence is both difficult and dangerous, and was then particularly so to the English, who were strangers in that quarter. The admiral, therefore, who had conceived a very favourable opinion of Mr Cook's abilities, appointed him to survey the river below Quebec, which he also executed with the same diligence and ability that he had displayed on the former occasion.

This chart of the river, when completed, was published, with soundings and sailing directions; and so great was the accuracy observed, that it superseded all other surveys of the period.

After the conquest of Canada, so glorious to every person who had a share in it, Mr Cook was appointed master of the *Northumberland*, under Lord Colvill, on the 2nd of September 1759. In this ship his lordship continued the following winter as commodore at Halifax; and Cook's conduct, in his new station, did not fail, as on former occasions, to gain him the friendship and esteem of his commander.

Sensible that he was now on the road to promotion, he showed a laudable desire to qualify himself to adorn his profession, by devoting his leisure hours to the study of such branches of knowledge as would be serviceable to him in after life. At Halifax he first read Euclid's *Elements*, and studied astronomy. The books he was able to procure were few indeed; but application and perseverance supplied many deficiencies, and enabled him to make a progress, which a man of less genius could not attain under much superior advantages.

He received a commission on the 1st of April 1760, and daily advanced in the career of glory. In September 1762 he assisted at the recapture of Newfoundland, after which the English fleet remained some time at Placentia, in order to put that place into a better state of defence. During this period Mr Cook had another opportunity of displaying his diligence, and manifesting his zeal in the service of his country; he surveyed the harbour and heights of that place, and, by this means, attracted the notice of Captain, afterwards Admiral Graves, who was at that time governor of Newfoundland. Captain Graves having entered into conversation with him, found him possessed of such intelligence and judgment, that he conceived a very favourable opinion of his general abilities, and particularly of his nautical skill; and in cultivating a longer acquaintance with him, he was still more prepossessed in his favour.

Endowed with a vigorous and active mind, and stimulated, perhaps, by the success that had attended his past labours, and the hopes of future promotion, Cook continued to display the most unremitting assiduity to make himself acquainted with the North American coast, and to facilitate its navigation; while the esteem which Captain Graves had justly conceived for him was heightened by the concurrent testimonies of approbation freely paid to him by all the officers under whom he had served.

Towards the close of 1762 Cook returned as lieutenant to England, and on the 21st of December was married at Barking in Essex to a young lady of the name of Batts, whom he tenderly loved, and who had every claim to his warmest affection and esteem. It is said that Cook had been godfather to this lady, and that he declared at that time his wish for their future union. If this anecdote is true, it is a singular instance of the firmness of his character, and the strength of his attachment. His situation in life, however, and the high and important services to which he was called, did not suffer him to enjoy matrimonial felicity without interruption; and like all officers of any worth, his first thoughts were turned to his profession.

On the conclusion of the war in 1763, Captain Graves was again sent out as governor of Newfoundland; and as that island was considered of great commercial importance, and had been a principal object of contention between Great Britain and France, the governor obtained, at his pressing solicitation, an establishment for the survey of its coasts; and Cook was appointed to carry this plan into execution. He therefore went out with his friend the governor; and having surveyed the small islands of St Pierre and Miquelon, which by treaty had been ceded to France, after the business was finished, he returned to England at the close of the season.

In the beginning of the following year, 1764, he was appointed Marine Surveyor of Newfoundland and Labrador, and accompanied his former patron, Sir Hugh Palliser, who had been nominated governor of Labrador and Newfoundland, and prosecuted his surveys of the coasts as before.

For his employment, Cook was, by the unanimous voice of the best judges, deemed extremely well qualified; and the charts which he afterwards published reflect the highest credit on his abilities. He also explored the interior of Newfoundland, in a much more accurate manner than had ever been done before; and by penetrating into the heart of the country, discovered several large lakes, the position of which he exactly ascertained. In this service he appears to have been occasionally engaged till 1767. However, we find him with Sir William Burnaby, on the Jamaica station in 1765; and that officer having occasion to send despatches to the governor of Yucatan, relative to the log cutters in the Bay of Honduras, Lieutenant Cook was selected for that mission, and he performed it in a manner that entitled him to the approbation of the admiral. A relation of this voyage and journey was published in 1769, under the title of 'Remarks on a Passage from the River Balise, in the Bay of Honduras, to Merida, the capital of the Province of Yucatan, in the Spanish West Indies, by Lieutenant Cook'.

That our navigator had by this time made a considerable proficiency in practical astronomy, is evident from a short paper, drawn up by him, which was inserted in the seventh volume of the *Philosophical Transactions*, entitled 'An Observation of an Eclipse of the Sun at the Island of Newfoundland, August 5, 1766, with the Longitude of the Place of Observation deduced from it'. This observation was made at one of the Burgeo islands, near Cape Ray, in latitude 47° 36' 19" on the southwest extremity of Newfoundland; and Cook's paper having been communicated to Mr Witchell, he compared it with an observation made on the same eclipse by Professor Hornsby, and thence computed the difference of longitude of the places of observation, making proper allowance for parallax, and the prolate spheroidal figure of the earth. That Cook was now counted an able mathematician, the admission of this paper into the *Philosophical Transactions*, and the notice that was taken of it, will sufficiently verify.

It was reserved for the reign of George III to carry the spirit of enterprise to its fullest extent, and to direct it to the accomplishment of the noblest purposes. As soon as the return of peace gave an opportunity for promoting the interests of science, by enlarging the bounds of discovery, two voyages were projected by the king, which were performed by Captains Byron, Wallis and Carteret; and before the two latter gentlemen returned, a third was resolved upon, the principal object of which was the improvement of astronomy.

It having been long before calculated that the planet Venus would pass over the sun's disc in 1769, a phenomenon of great importance to astronomy, and which had engaged the attention of men of science, it was judged that the most proper place for observing this phenomenon would be either at the Marquesas, or at one of those islands to which Tasman had given the several appellations of Amsterdam, Rotterdam, and Middleburgh; but which are now better known under the general name of the Friendly Isles. This being a matter of so much importance in the science of astronomy, the Royal Society, with that laudable zeal they have ever shown for its advancement, presented a memorial to his Majesty at the beginning of the previous year, requesting, among other things, that a vessel might be fitted out at the expense of the government, to convey proper persons to observe this transit at one of the places already mentioned.

The petition being readily complied with, and orders having been given by the Admiralty to provide a vessel for that purpose, on the 3rd of April, Mr Stephens, the secretary to the Board, informed the Society that everything was progressing according to their wishes.

Mr Dalrymple was originally fixed upon to superintend this expedition: a man eminent in science, a member of the Royal Society, and who had already greatly distinguished himself respecting the geography of the Southern Ocean. As this gentleman had been regularly bred to the sea, he insisted (very properly too) on having a brevet commission, as captain of the vessel, before he would undertake the employment. Sir Edward Hawke (afterwards Lord Hawke, a naval officer and not a civilian), who then presided at the Admiralty, violently opposed this measure; and being pressed on the subject, declared that nothing could induce him to give his sanction to such a commission.

Both parties were inflexible; and it was therefore thought expedient to look out for some other person to conduct the expedition. Accordingly, Mr Stephens having recommended Lieutenant Cook, and this recommendation being strengthened by the testimony of Sir Hugh Palliser, who was well acquainted with Cook's merit, and abilities for the discharge of this office, he was appointed to this distinguished post by the lords commissioners, and promoted to the rank of lieutenant of the royal navy on the 25th of May 1768. He was now, be it remembered, close upon forty years of age.

This appointment having taken place, Sir Hugh Palliser was commissioned to provide a vessel adapted for such a voyage. After examining a great number then lying in the Thames, in conjunction with Cook, of whose judgment he entertained the highest opinion, they at last fixed upon the *Endeavour*, a barque of 370 tons, which had been built for the coal trade.

In the interim, Captain Wallis having returned from his voyage round the world, and having signified to the Royal Society that Port Royal Harbour, in King George's Island, now called Otaheite, would be the most convenient place for observing the transit, his opinion was adopted, and the observers were ordered to repair thither.

Mr Charles Green, the coadjutor of Dr Bradley, the astronomer royal, was nominated to assist Captain Cook in conducting the astronomical part of the undertaking; and he was accompanied also by Joseph Banks, Esq. (afterwards Sir Joseph, the President of the Royal Society). This friend of science possessed, at an early period of life, an opulent fortune, and being zealous to apply it to the best ends, embarked on this tedious and hazardous enterprise, animated by the wish of improving himself and enlarging the bounds of knowledge. He took two draftsmen with him, and had likewise a secretary and four servants in his retinue.

Dr Solander, an ingenious and learned Swede, who had been appointed one of the librarians in the British Museum, and who was particularly skilled as a disciple of Linnaeus, and distinguished in his knowledge of natural history, likewise joined the expedition. Possessed of the enthusiasm with which Linnaeus inspired his disciples, he braved danger in the prosecution of his favourite studies, and being a man of erudition and capacity, he added no small éclat to the voyage in which he had embarked.

Though the principal intention of this expedition was to observe the transit of Venus, it was thought proper to make it comprehend other objects as well. Captain Cook was therefore directed, after he had accomplished his main business, to proceed in making further discoveries in the South Seas, which now began to be explored with uncommon resolution.

The complement of the *Endeavour* consisted of eighty-four persons. She was victualled for eighteen months, and carried ten carriage and twelve swivel guns, with abundance of ammunition: and all manner of stores were taken on board. The following were the principal officers:

Endeavour Barque [1]

James Cook, appointed Lieutenant Commander, 25th May 1768

Zachary Hicks, lieutenant

John Gore

Robert Molineux, master, died 15th April 1771; succeeded by Richard Pickersgill

Charles Clerke, mate

John Gathray, boatswain, died 4th February 1771; succeeded by Samuel Evans

Stephen Forward, gunner

John Satterley, carpenter, died 12th February 1771; succeeded by George Nowell

William B. Monkhouse, surgeon, died 5th November 1770; succeeded by William Perry

Richard Orton, clerk

Being completely fitted for sea, Captain Cook sailed from Deptford on the 30th of July 1768, and on the 13th of August anchored in Plymouth Sound, from which, after a few days' stay, they proceeded to sea.

The first land they made, after their leaving the Channel, was on the 2nd of September, when Cape Finisterre and Cape Ortegal, in Spain, both came in view. They arrived on the 13th at Madeira, and anchored in Funchal Roads. Here unfortunately they lost Mr Weir,

1 Records, Admiralty, Whitehall.

the master's mate, who, in heaving the anchor, fell overboard and was drowned. This island has a beautiful appearance from the sea, those parts of hills which present themselves being covered with vines. Nature has been very liberal in her gifts to Madeira. The inhabitants are not without ingenuity, but they want industry. The soil is so very rich, and there is such a variety in the climate, that there is scarcely any article, either of the necessaries or luxuries of life, which cannot be cultivated. Pineapples and mangoes grow almost spontaneously, and great variety of fruit upon the hills. Corn is also very large and plentiful.

Funchal is seated at the bottom of a bay; it is indifferently built, and the streets are narrow, and wretchedly paved. In the churches there are great numbers of ornaments, with pictures and images of saints, for the most part indifferently executed.

They sailed from Madeira September 19th, and on the 23rd came in sight of the Peak of Tenerife. This mountain is nearly 15,400 feet high. On the 29th they sighted Bona Vista, one of the Cape de Verd Islands. From Tenerife to Bona Vista flying fish were seen in considerable numbers, which appeared very beautiful, their sides resembling burnished silver. Mr Banks, on the 7th of October, caught what is called a Portuguese man-of-war, together with several marine animals of the Mollusca tribe.

On the 25th of October, they crossed the line with the usual forms. On the 29th, in the evening, the luminous appearance of the sea mentioned by navigators, was observed by them: it emitted rays of light resembling those of lightning. Mr Banks and Dr Solander threw out a casting-net, when a species of the Medusa was caught, resembling a metallic substance greatly heated, emitting a whitish light. Some crabs were also caught at the same time, which were exceeding small, yet gave a very glittering appearance.

Provisions now falling short, it was determined to put into Rio de Janeiro; where they arrived on the 13th of November.

Mr Hicks, the first lieutenant, was sent before in the pinnace to the city, to inform the governor that they put in there for refreshments and a pilot. The pinnace returned without the lieutenant, who was detained till the captain came on shore. Soon after a ten-oared boat, filled with soldiers, came up, and rowed round the ship, without any conversation taking place. A second boat came up, with several of the viceroy's officers; they inquired whence the *Endeavour* came; what she had on board; her number of men, guns, and destination. These, and many other questions, were answered without equivocation; when they apologised for detaining the lieutenant, and other steps they had taken, which they justified on the plea of custom.

Captain Cook went on shore on the 14th, and obtained leave to purchase what he wanted, on condition of employing an inhabitant as a factor. The captain judging that the viceroy imagined they were come to trade, endeavoured to convince him of his mistake, by acquainting him that they were bound to the southward, to observe the transit of Venus; a very interesting object to the advancement of navigation, of which phenomenon, however, he appeared, as might be supposed, to be totally ignorant.

The viceroy having ordered, that only the captain, and such sailors as were necessary to be upon duty, should be suffered to land; they, notwithstanding, attempted to come on shore, but were prevented by the guard-boat. Several of the crew, however, unknown to the sentinel, stole out of the cabin window at midnight, letting themselves down by a rope into the boat; and rowing to some unfrequented part of the shore, made excursions up the country, though not so far as they could have wished. When Captain Cook complained of these restrictions, the only answer he obtained from the viceroy was, that he had acted in conformity to his master's orders. It was now agreed to present two memorials to the viceroy; one was written by the captain, the other by Mr Banks: the answers received were in no way satisfactory. The captain, judging it necessary, in vindication of his compliance, to urge the viceroy to an act of force in the execution of his orders, sent Lieutenant Hicks, with a packet, with directions not to allow a guard in his boat. The officer of the guard-boat did not oppose him by force, but accompanying the lieutenant on shore, went to the viceroy, and acquainted him with what had passed, which induced his excellency to refuse opening the packet, commanding the lieutenant to return. Finding a soldier had been put on board the boat in his absence, as a guard, he insisted upon his quitting it. The officer now seized the boat's crew, and conducted them to prison, under a guard; and the lieutenant was sent back to the ship, guarded likewise. When Mr Hicks had acquainted the captain with these transactions, the latter wrote to the viceroy, demanding his boat and men, and enclosed that very memorial, which he had refused to receive from the lieutenant.

This express was sent by a petty officer, and the viceroy promised to return an answer. In the interim, in a sudden gust of wind, the longboat, with four pipes of rum, went adrift, with a small skiff of Mr Banks's that was fastened to her. The misfortune was still greater, as the pinnace was on shore. The yawl was manned immediately, but did not return till next morning, when she brought all the hands of the longboat on board. From them Captain Cook learnt that the boat having filled with water, they had brought her to a grappling, and quitted her; and falling in with a reef of rocks, on their return, they were compelled to cut adrift the little boat belonging to Mr Banks. In this situation the captain despatched another letter to the viceroy, acquainting him with the accident; at the same time desiring he would assist them with a boat to recover their own: this was accompanied with a fresh demand of the pinnace and her crew. His excellency at length complied both with the request and demand; and the same day they fortunately recovered the longboat and skiff. Mr Banks, on the 26th, artfully eluded the vigilance of the guard, and went on shore. He avoided the town, and passed the day in the fields, where the chief objects of his curiosity lay.

Being prepared for sea, with water and provisions, they took on board a pilot the 1st of December, but the wind being contrary, were prevented getting out. On the 7th, having passed the fort, the pilot was discharged, and the guard-boat quitted them at the same time.

The town of Rio de Janeiro is situated on the west side of the river, from which it extends about three-quarters of a mile. The ground on which it stands is pretty level. Some of its streets run parallel from north to south, and are intersected by others at right angles. The principal street is near a hundred feet in width; the other streets are commonly twenty or thirty feet wide. The houses adjoining to the principal street have three storeys, but in other places they are very irregular, though built after the same manner as in Lisbon. The viceroy's palace formed the right angle of a large square; the palace, mint, stables, jail, etc., composing but one large building, which has two storeys, and is ninety feet from the water.

In the centre of the square is a fountain supplied with water from a spring at the distance of three miles, conveyed by an aqueduct. From this fountain both the shipping and inhabitants are supplied with water. At every corner of the streets was an altar. Negroes were almost the only people employed in selling the different commodities exposed in the market, and they filled up their leisure time in spinning cotton.

The gentry keep their carriages, which were drawn by mules; the ladies, however, used a sedan chair, boarded before and behind, with curtains on each side, which were carried by two negroes.

The apothecaries' shops served the purposes of a coffee-house, people meeting in them to drink capillaire and play at backgammon. Beggars, who infest the streets of most European cities, were not to be found in this.

With regard to the women, it was on all hands agreed, that the females of the Portuguese and Spanish settlements, in South America, are much addicted to gallantry. According to Dr Solander's account, as soon as the evening began, females appeared on all sides in every window, and particularised their favourites, by giving them nosegays.

The climate of Rio de Janeiro is both agreeable and healthy, being free from any inconveniences that are incidental to other tropical countries. The air is but seldom immoderately hot, as the sea breeze constantly begins to blow about ten o'clock in the morning, and continues until night, when it is generally succeeded by a land wind.

The soil produces all the tropical fruits, such as oranges, lemons, limes, melons, mangoes, and coconuts, in great abundance.

The mines are rich, and lie a considerable way up the country. They were kept so private, that any person found upon the road which led to them, was hung upon the next tree, unless he could give a satisfactory account of the cause of his being in that situation. Near forty thousand negroes were annually imported to dig in these mines, which are so pernicious to the human frame, and occasion so great a mortality amongst the poor wretches employed in them, that in the year 1766 twenty thousand more were drafted from the town of Rio, to supply the deficiency of the former number. Who can read this without emotion!

The harbour is safe and commodious, and may be distinguished

by a remarkable hill, in the shape of a cone, at the west point of
the bay.

Thursday, December 8th, 1768, having procured all necessary
supplies, they left Rio. They did not meet with any material
occurrence from this time to the 22nd, when they were surrounded by great numbers of porpoises, of a singular species,
which were about fifteen feet in length, and of an ash colour.

On the 23rd, they observed an eclipse of the moon; and about
seven o'clock in the morning, a small white cloud appeared in the
west, from which a train of fire issued, extending itself westerly;
about two minutes after, they heard two distinct loud explosions,
immediately succeeding each other like cannon; after which the
cloud soon disappeared.

January 4th [1769], they saw an appearance of land, which they
mistook for Pepys' Island; but on standing towards it, it proved to
be what the sailors call a fog bank. On the 14th they entered the
Strait of La Maire; but the tide being against them, they were
driven out with great violence, and the waves ran so high, that the
ship's bowsprit was frequently under water; at length, however,
they got anchorage, at the entrance of a little cove, which Captain
Cook called St Vincent's Bay.

The weeds, which here grow upon rocky ground, are very
remarkable; they appear above the surface in eight and nine
fathoms water; the leaves are four feet in length, and many of the
stalks, though not more than an inch and a half in circumference,
above one hundred. Mr Banks and Dr Solander having been on
shore some hours, returned with more than a hundred different
plants and flowers, hitherto unnoticed by the European botanists.

Sunday, 15th, having anchored in twelve fathoms water, upon
coral rocks, before a small cove, distant from shore about a mile,
two of the natives came down upon the beach in expectation that
they would land; but this situation affording little shelter, the
captain got under sail again and the natives retired.

About two o'clock they anchored in the Bay of Good Success,
and Captain Cook went on shore, accompanied by Mr Banks and
Dr Solander, to search for a watering-place, and confer with the
Indians. They proceeded about a hundred yards in advance, when
two of the Indians, having approached and seated themselves,
immediately rose, upon Mr Banks and the Doctor coming up,

throwing away a small stick (bumerang), which they had before in their hands; this they did in such a direction, that the stick flew both from themselves and the strangers, which they meant as a token of peace. They then returned briskly towards their companions, who had remained at some distance behind, and made signs to the strangers to advance, which they accordingly complied with. The reception was friendly, though the manner was uncouth. The civility was returned, by the distribution of beads and ribbons, with which the Indians were much pleased.

After a mutual confidence had been thus established, the rest of the English party joined, and a general conversation, though of a singular kind, ensued. Three of the Indians now returned with the captain and his friends to the ship, whom they clothed and entertained. They refused to drink rum or brandy, after tasting them, intimating by signs that it burnt their throats. They were of a middle stature, with broad flat faces, low foreheads, high cheeks, noses inclining to flatness, wide nostrils, small black eyes, large mouths, small, but indifferent teeth, and black, straight hair, falling down over their ears and forehead, which was commonly smeared with brown and red paint; and, like all the original natives of America, they were beardless. Their garments were the skins of guanacos and seals, which they wrapped round their shoulders. The women have a small string tied round each ankle, and wear each a flap of skin round the middle.

Mr Banks, Dr Solander, Mr Buchan, and several other gentlemen, accompanied by servants, went a considerable way into the country, where they had marshy ground, and very cold blasts of wind and snow, to contend with. After much fatigue, they attained a considerable eminence, where they found a variety of plants, which gratified their curiosity and repaid them for their toil.

It was now nearly eight o'clock in the evening, and Dr Solander, who knew from experience that extreme cold, when joined which fatigue, occasions a drowsiness that is not easily resisted, entreated his friends to keep in motion, however disagreeable it might be to them; his words were, 'Whoever sits down, will sleep; and whoever sleeps, will wake no more.' Everyone seemed accordingly armed with resolution; but on a sudden the cold became so intense, as to threaten the most direful effects. It was remarkable, that Dr Solander himself, who had so forcibly admonished and alarmed his party, should be the first who insisted upon being suffered to repose. In spite of the most earnest entreaties of his friends, he lay down amidst the snow, and it was with great difficulty that they kept him awake. One of the black servants became also weary and faint, and was upon the point of following the Doctor's example. Mr Buchan was therefore detached with a party to make a fire at the first commodious spot they could meet with. Mr Banks, with four more, remained with the Doctor and Richmond the black, who, with the utmost difficulty, were induced to come on; but after walking a few miles farther, they expressed their inability of proceeding. When the black was informed, that if he remained there he would soon be frozen to death, he replied, that he was so exhausted with fatigue, that death would be a relief to him. Dr Solander said he was not unwilling to go, but that he must first take some sleep.

Thus resolved, they both sat down, supported by bushes, and in a short time fell fast asleep. Intelligence now came from the advanced party, that a fire was kindled about a quarter of a mile farther on the way. Mr Banks then waked the Doctor, who had almost lost the use of his limbs already, though it was but a few minutes since he sat down; he nevertheless consented to go on. Every measure taken to relieve the black proved ineffectual; he remained motionless, and they were obliged to leave him to the care of the other black servant and a sailor, who appeared to have been the least hurt by the cold; and they were to be relieved as soon as two others were sufficiently warmed to supply their places. The Doctor was with much difficulty got to the fire. Those who were sent to relieve the companions of Richmond returned in about half an hour without being able to find them. There was a fall of snow which incessantly continued for nearly two hours, and there remained no hopes of seeing the three absentees alive. About twelve o'clock, however, a great shouting was heard at a distance, which gave inexpressible satisfaction to everyone present. Mr Banks and four others went forth and met the sailor, with just strength enough to walk; he was immediately sent to the fire, and they proceeded to seek for the two others. They found Richmond upon his legs, but incapable of moving them; the other black was lying senseless upon the ground. All endeavours to bring them to the fire were fruitless, nor was it possible to kindle one upon the spot, on account of the snow that was still falling. There was no alternative; they were compelled to leave the two unfortunate negroes to their fate, after covering them very thick with the boughs of trees.

Those who had been employed in endeavouring to move the two blacks to the fire, had been exposed to the cold for nearly an hour and a half; some of them began to be afflicted in the same manner as those they went to relieve. At length, however, they reached the fire, where they passed the night in a very disagreeable manner. The party that set out from the ship consisted of twelve, of whom two were already judged to be dead: it was doubtful whether a third would be able to return on board; and Mr Buchan, a fourth, who had just recovered from fits, seemed threatened with them again. They had wandered so far, that they were now distant a long day's journey from the ship; and they had not provisions left sufficient to afford a single meal.

On the 17th, in the morning at daybreak, nothing presented itself to view but snow all around; and the blasts of wind were so violent and frequent, that their journey was rendered impracticable, and there was much reason to dread perishing with cold and famine. They therefore returned to the ship, which, to their great astonishment and satisfaction, they reached in about three hours.

On the 20th, Mr Banks and Dr Solander made another excursion into the country. After walking for some time, they arrived at a small town, consisting of about a dozen miserable huts, constructed without art or regularity, in the form of a sugar loaf, with a place left open, which answers the double purpose of a door and chimney. Mr Banks observed some European articles amongst them, from whence it was judged that they travelled at times to the north; as no ship had touched at this part of Tierra del Fuego for some years.

These people appeared upon the whole to be the outcasts of human nature; their only food was shellfish; and they were destitute of every convenience arising from the rudest art. Nevertheless they seemed content; so little does refinement or luxury promote happiness!

The generality of writers who have described the island of Tierra del Fuego, have represented it as covered with snow, and destitute of wood. In this, however, they are evidently mistaken, and their error must have arisen from having visited it in the winter season, when it possibly may be covered with snow. The crew of the *Endeavour* perceived trees when they were at a considerable distance from the island, and on their nearer approach, they found the sea coast and the sides of the hills clothed with an agreeable verdure. The summits of the hills are barren, but the valleys are rich, and a brook is to be found at the foot of almost every hill; the water has a reddish tinge, but is not ill tasted, and was found to be some of the best obtained during the whole voyage.

Thursday, January 20th, Captain Cook weighed anchor, and the weather being calm, Mr Banks, from a small boat, shot some shearwaters and albatrosses; the latter proved good eating.

Although the doubling of Cape Horn was represented as a dangerous, and the Strait of Magellan a less perilous course, the *Endeavour* doubled the Cape on this occasion with as much ease as if it had been the North Foreland on the Kentish coast; the heavens were fair, the wind temperate, the weather pleasant; and, being near shore, they had a distinct view of the coast.

About ten o'clock, Tuesday, April 4th, Peter Briscoe, servant to Mr Banks, discovered land to the south, about three or four leagues distant. Captain Cook immediately hauled up for it, and found it to be an island of an oval form, with a lake in the centre, that extended over the greater part of it. The border of land which surrounded the lake was in many places low and narrow, especially towards the south, where the beach consisted of a reef of rocks; three places on the north side had the same appearance. Captain Cook came within a mile on the north side, but though he cast a line of one hundred and thirty fathoms, he found no bottom, and could not meet with any anchorage.

There were several natives visible on shore; they seemed tall, with remarkably large heads, probably increased by the head dress; their hair was black, and their complexions copper colour. Some that were abreast of the ship, had in their hands pikes or poles twice the height of themselves.

Captain Cook saw land again in the afternoon to the north-west. He reached it by sunset, when it appeared to be a low island covered with wood, in circular form, about a mile in circumference. No inhabitants were visible, nor any coconut trees, though the *Endeavour* approached within half a mile of the shore;

yet the land appeared to be covered with verdure of various tinges. This island the officers on board named Thrumb Cap.

On the 10th, upon their looking out for the island to which they were destined, they saw land ahead. The next morning it appeared very high and mountainous, and it was known to be King George III's Island, so named by Captain Wallis, but by the natives called Otaheite. The calms prevented the *Endeavour* from approaching it till the morning of the 12th, when a breeze springing up, several canoes were making towards the ship. Each canoe had in it young plantains, and branches of trees, as tokens of peace and friendship; and they were handed up the sides of the ship by the people in one of the canoes, who made signals in a very expressive manner, intimating that they desired these emblems of pacification should be placed in a conspicuous part of the ship; and they were accordingly stuck amongst the rigging, at which they testified their approbation. Their cargoes consisted of coconuts, bananas, bread-fruit, apples, and figs, which were very acceptable to the crew, and were readily purchased.

On the morning of the 13th the *Endeavour* entered Port Royal harbour, in the island of Otaheite, and anchored within half a mile of the shore. A great number of the natives immediately came off in their canoes, and bartered their commodities for beads and other trinkets.

An elderly man, named Owhaw, who was known to Mr Gore and others, who had visited this island with Captain Wallis, came on board; and as he was considered a useful man, the captain endeavoured to gratify all his inquiries. Captain Cook now drew up several necessary rules for the regulation of traffic with the inhabitants, and ordered that they should be strictly observed.

When the ship was properly secured, the captain went on shore with Mr Banks and Dr Solander, a party under arms, and their friend the old Indian. They were received on shore by some hundreds of the natives, who were struck with such awe, that the first who approached crept almost upon his hands and knees. He also presented to them branches of trees, the usual symbol of peace. This symbol was received, on the part of the English party, with demonstrations of satisfaction and friendship.

They were conducted by the old Indian, accompanied by his countrymen, towards the place where the *Dolphin* had watered.

Here, the ground being cleared, the chiefs of the natives threw down their boughs, and the captain and his companions followed the example, after having drawn up the marines, who, marching in order, dropped their branches upon those of the Indians. When they came to the watering place, the Indians intimated that they had their permission to occupy that ground, but it was not suited to their purpose. In the course of this walk, and a circuit through the woods, the Indians had got rid of their timidity, and became familiarised.

The whole circuit was nearly four miles, through groves of coconut and breadfruit trees; beneath the trees were the habitations of the natives, consisting of only a roof, destitute of walls. The breadfruit is about the size of the horse-chestnut; and the fruit is not unlike the cantaloupe melon in appearance. It is somewhat of the consistency of new bread, and is roasted before it is eaten.

Next morning, before they left the ship, several canoes came about her, filled with people, whose dress denoted them to be of a superior class; two of these came on board, and each of them fixed upon a friend; one of them chose Mr Banks, and the other Captain Cook. The ceremony consisted of taking off their clothes in great part, and putting them upon their adopted friends. This compliment was returned, by presenting them some trinkets. They then made signs for these gentlemen to go with them to the place of their abode; and the captain being desirous of meeting with a more convenient harbour, and knowing more of the people, readily assented.

Accordingly, Captain Cook, Mr Banks, Dr Solander, with the Indians and other friends, got into two boats. About three miles distance they landed among several hundreds of the natives, who conducted them to a large house. Upon their entrance they saw a middle-aged man, named Tootahah, who as soon as they were seated, ordered a cock and hen to be produced, which he presented to Mr Banks and the captain, as well as a piece of perfumed cloth; which compliment was returned by a present from Mr Banks. They were then conducted with great civility to several large houses, constructed in the same manner as those already described; the women, so far from shunning, invited, and even pressed them to be seated. Whilst they were afterwards walking along the shore, they met, accompanied by a great number of natives, another chief, named Tubora Tumaida, with whom they settled a treaty of peace, in the manner before described. Tubora Tumaida intimated he had provisions for them, if they chose to eat, and they accordingly dined heartily upon breadfruit, plantains, and fish.

In the course of this visit, Dr Solander complained to the chief that he had lost an opera glass. The chief appeared much concerned at the accident, and gave him to understand, with an appearance of great sincerity, that he would endeavour if possible to have the glass recovered; but that if this could not be done, he would make the Doctor compensation, by giving him as much new cloth as should be thought equal to its value. Mr Banks, in order to try the effect of a little intimidation, started up, and striking the butt end of his musket on the ground, alarmed the Indians so much that they all precipitately ran out of the house, except the chief, and a few others of the superior class. The case was in a little time brought, and the glass itself soon after. After the amicable termination of this adventure, they returned to the ship about six o'clock in the evening.

Saturday the 15th, the captain, attended by Mr Banks, and some others of the crew, went on shore to fix on a proper spot to erect a small fort for their defence, during their stay on the island; and the ground was accordingly marked out for that purpose, a great number of the natives looking on all the while, and behaving in the most peaceable and friendly manner.

Mr Banks and others, accompanied by several of the natives, having gone out shooting in the woods, some marines and a petty officer were appointed to guard the tent. Before they had gone far they were alarmed by the discharge of two pieces, fired by the tent-guard. Upon their return to the tent, it appeared that an Indian had taken an opportunity to snatch away one of the sentinel's muskets; whereupon the young midshipman in command imprudently ordered the marines to fire, which they did immediately amongst the thickest of the fugitive Indians, several of whom were wounded; but as the criminal did not fall, they pursued and shot him dead.

When Mr Banks heard of the affair, he was greatly displeased with the guard, and used his utmost endeavours to adjust the difference; and through the mediation of an old man, prevailed on many of the natives to come over to them, bringing plantain trees, their usual signal of peace; and clapping their hands on their breasts, they cried 'Tyau', which signifies friendship.

Few of the natives appeared next morning upon the beach; and not one of them came on board. Hence Mr Banks and the other gentlemen concluded, that their apprehensions were not entirely removed, more especially as even Owhaw had forsaken them. The captain, in consequence of these disagreeable appearances, brought the ship nearer to shore, and moored her so as to make her broadside bear on the spot which had been marked for erecting the fort. In the evening he landed with some of the crew, when the Indians assembled round them, and they trafficked together as before.

The fort began to be erected on the 18th. Some of the company were employed in throwing up entrenchments, whilst others were occupied in cutting fascines and pickets, which the Indians of their own accord cheerfully assisted in bringing from the woods. Bread-fruit and coconuts were also brought in such large quantities, that it was necessary to reject them, and to intimate that none would be wanted for two days. Beads were taken in exchange for everything.

Mr Monkhouse, the surgeon, in his evening walk, saw the body of the man who had been shot at the tent. It was deposited in a shed, close to the house where he had resided when alive. The corpse was placed on a bier, the frame of which was wood, with a matted bottom, supported by posts about five feet high. It was covered with a mat, overlaid by a white cloth; by its side lay a wooden mace, and towards the head two coconut shells; towards the feet was a bunch of green leaves and small dried boughs, tied together and stuck in the ground, near which was a stone the size of a coconut: here was also placed a young plantain tree and a stone axe. The natives seemed displeased at his approaching the body.

A specimen of the music of the country was given on the 22nd; some of the natives performed on flutes with only two stops; the performer blew with his nostril instead of his mouth: several accompanied the instrument with a gong, but there was only one tune.

On the 25th, several knives belonging to the officers were missing; upon which Mr Banks, who had lost his among the rest, rashly accused one of the chiefs of the theft, the knife all the while having been mislaid by Mr Banks' servant. The poor chief, who was quite innocent, took the charge very much to heart. The tears started from his eyes, and he made signs with the knife, that if he had ever been guilty of such an action as was imputed to him, he would suffer his throat to be cut. In general, however, these people, from the highest to the lowest, are too much addicted to pilfering.

On the 26th, six swivel guns were mounted upon the fort, which put the natives into great consternation; and caused several fishermen, who lived upon the point, to remove further off, imagining they were to be fired at in a few days.

The next day Tubora Tumaida, with a friend and three of his women, dined at the fort. Soon after his departure he returned in much agitation, to acquaint Mr Banks that the ship's butcher had threatened to cut his wife's throat, upon her refusing to sell him a stone hatchet, which he had taken a fancy to, for a nail. It clearly appeared he had been culpable, and he was flogged on board, in sight of several Indians. As soon as the first stroke was given they interfered, and earnestly entreated that he might be untied. This being refused, they burst into tears, and showed great concern.

During the forenoon of this day, canoes were continually coming in, and the tents at the fort were filled with people of both sexes. Mr Molineux, master of the *Endeavour*, went on shore, and as he had visited the island on a previous voyage, he was the first to recognise and point out Oberea, the queen of the island.

Everyone was now anxious to see her who had made so distinguished a figure in the accounts that had been given by the first discoverers of this island. Queen Oberea was now about forty years of age; her figure was large and tall; her skin white; her eyes had great expression; she had been handsome, but her beauty was now upon the decline. She was soon conducted to the ship, and went on board with some of her family. Many presents were made to her, particularly a child's doll, which seemed the most to engross her attention. Captain Cook accompanied her on shore; and as soon as they landed, she presented him with a hog, and some plantains, which were carried to the fort in procession, Oberea and the captain bringing up the rear. They met Tootahah, who, though not king, seemed to be at this time invested with sovereign authority. He immediately became jealous of the queen's having the doll; which made them feel it necessary to compliment him with one also.

The next day, Sunday the 30th, Tomio came running to the tents, and taking Mr Banks by the arm (to whom they applied in all emergent cases), told him that Tubora Tumaida was dying, owing to something which had been given him to eat by the sailors, and prayed him to go instantly to him. Mr Banks found the Indian very sick. He was told that he had been vomiting, and had thrown up a leaf, which they said contained some of the poison he had taken. Upon examining the leaf, Mr Banks found it to be nothing more than tobacco, which the Indian had begged of some of their people. Mr Banks, now knowing his disorder, ordered him to drink coconut milk, which soon restored him to health; and he was as cheerful as ever.

On the 1st of May, a chief, who had dined on board a few days before, accompanied by some of his women, who used to feed him, came on board by himself; and when dinner was on table, the captain helped him to some victuals, thinking upon this occasion he would condescend to feed himself; but he never attempted to eat, and had not one of the servants fed him, he would certainly have gone without his dinner.

Next day, having occasion to use the quadrant, to their great astonishment and concern it was missing. This was the more extraordinary, as a sentinel had been posted the whole night within a few yards of the tent in which it had been deposited; and it had never been taken out of the case in which it was packed. As the loss of this instrument would have rendered it impossible for them to have made the necessary observations respecting the transit, every possible search was made in the vicinity. At last Mr Banks, accompanied by Mr Green and some others, set out for the woods, where it was thought some intelligence of the robbery might be gained, if it had been committed by the natives. In the course of their journey they met Tubora Tumaida, with a few of the natives, who by signs was made to understand that some of his countrymen had stolen the quadrant, and that it must be produced. The chief immediately made inquiry; and by his interference, the instrument was recovered without any material injury, though it had been taken to pieces.

On Friday the 5th, Captain Cook, accompanied by Mr Banks and Dr Solander, set out in the pinnace, taking one of Tootahah's people with them, to visit that chief. They soon reached Eparre, the place where he lived, which was but a few miles to the west of the tents. Upon their arrival, they were immediately conducted to the chief, whilst the natives shouted round them, '*Taio Tootahah*! Tootahah is your friend!' They found him sitting under a tree, and some old men standing round him. As soon as he had made signs for them to sit down, Captain Cook presented him with a shirt and a broad cloth garment, with which he seemed greatly pleased. and put the garment on. After eating a mouthful together in the boat, they were conducted to a large area, or courtyard, on one side of his house, where an entertainment was provided for them, consisting of wrestling. The chief sat at the upper end of the area, with several of his principal men on each side of him, by way of judges, from whom the conquerors received applause. Ten or twelve combatants entered the area, and after many simple ceremonies of challenging each other, they engaged, endeavouring to throw one another by dint of strength; then seizing hold of each other by the thigh, the hand, the hair, or the clothes, they grappled without the least art, till one was thrown on his back; this conquest was applauded by some words from the old men, and three huzzas.[1]

When this entertainment was over, they were informed that some hogs and a quantity of breadfruit were preparing for their dinner, which intelligence was the more agreeable as their appetites were at this time exceedingly keen. But instead of dining either on shore or on board the boat, they had the mortification of going as far as the ship by the desire of the chief. As soon as the chief was known to be on board the ship, the people brought plenty of breadfruit, coconuts, and other provisions, to the fort.

On Tuesday the 9th, in the forenoon, Oberea paid them a visit, accompanied by her favourite Obadee; she presented them with a hog and some breadfruit.

The forge being now set up, and frequently at work, became not only a new object of admiration to the Indians, but afforded the captain an additional opportunity of conferring obligations on them, by permitting the smith, during his leisure hours, to convert the old iron, which they were supposed to have procured from the *Dolphin*, into different kinds of tools.

---

1 'The conqueror never exulted over the conquered, neither did the conquered repine at his ill-luck, but the whole was carried on with great good humour.' – Extract, Captain Cook's Journal, Admiralty Records.

The natives, after repeated attempts, finding themselves incapable of pronouncing the names of the English gentlemen, had recourse to new ones formed from their own language. Captain Cook was named Toote; Hicks, Hete; Gore, Toura; Solander, Tolano; Banks, Opane; Green, Treene; and so on for the greatest part of the ship's crew.

The next evening Mr Banks was under the disagreeable necessity of reprimanding, in strong terms, Tubora Tumaida, for having the insolence to snatch his gun from him, and firing it in the air – a thing which surprised Mr Banks greatly, as he imagined him totally ignorant of the use of it – and as their safety depended on keeping them in that state, he told him, with threats, that his touching his piece was the greatest of insults. The Indian made no reply, but set off with his family to his house at Eparre. He being a useful man, Mr Banks, accompanied by Mr Molineux, thought fit to go after him, and they found him among a number of people, greatly dejected. However, as Mr Banks judiciously caused all animosity to cease, they brought him back to supper; after which the chief and his wife both slept in his tent. Soon after, Mr Banks suspected Tubora Tumaida of having stolen some nails. Having a good opinion of this chief, he was willing to put his fidelity to the test, and several temptations were thrown in his way – among the rest a basket of nails, which proved irresistible. He confessed the fact; and upon Mr Banks's insisting upon restitution, he declared the nails were at Eparre. This occasioned high words, and at length the Indian produced one of them. He was to have been forgiven upon restoring the rest, but not having resolution to fulfil his engagement, he fled with his furniture and family before night.

On the 27th of May, Tootahah being removed to a place called Atahourou, Mr Banks, Dr Solander, Captain Cook, and some others, set out in the pinnace to pay him another visit; and after making presents of a few trifling articles, they were invited to stay the night. Mr Banks having accepted a place in Oberea's canoe, left his companions in order to retire to rest. Notwithstanding the care Oberea took of his clothes, by having them in her own custody, they were stolen, with his pistols, powder-horn, and many other things that were in his waistcoat pockets. The alarm was given to Tootahah, who slept in the next canoe, and who went with

Oberea in search of the thief, leaving Mr Banks with only his breeches on, and his musket uncharged. They soon returned, but without success, and Mr Banks thought proper to put up with the loss for the present. However, he went to the hut where Captain Cook and three of his associates lay, and began to relate his melancholy tale; but instead of receiving much comfort from them, he was told that they had shared the same fate, having lost their stockings and jackets.

They now began to make preparations for observing the transit of Venus, and from the hints which Captain Cook had received from the Royal Society, he sent out two parties to make observations from different spots, that in case they failed at Otaheite, they might succeed elsewhere. They employed themselves in preparing their instruments, and giving instructions in the use of them. On Thursday, the 1st of June (the next Saturday being the day of the transit), they sent the longboat to Eimayo, having on board Mr Gore, Mr Monkhouse, and Mr Sporing, a friend of Mr Banks, each furnished with necessary instruments by Mr Green. Mr Banks and several of the Indians went out with this party. Others were despatched to find out a convenient spot, at such a distance from their principal station as might suit their purpose.

Those who went to Eimayo in the longboat, after rowing the best part of the night, by the help of some Indians on board a canoe, which they hailed, found a proper situation for their observatory upon a rock, where they fixed their tents, and prepared the apparatus for the following day's observation.

On Saturday the 3rd June, as soon as it was light, Mr Banks left them to go to the island for fresh provisions. As he was trading with the natives who belonged to Tarrao, the king of the island arrived with his sister, whose name was Nuna, in order to pay him a visit. After being seated as is customary, the royal present was brought, consisting of a hog, a dog, some coconuts, breadfruit, etc. A messenger was despatched by Mr Banks for an adze, a shirt, and some beads, which his majesty received with much pleasure. Mr Banks returned to the observatory with his visitors, and showed them the transit of the planet Venus over the sun's disc, informing them that he and his companions had come from their own country solely to view it in that situation.

Both the parties which were sent out made their observation

with great success. They nevertheless differed in the accounts of the times of the contacts more than might have been imagined.[1]

Mr Green's account was as follows:

> The first external contact, or first appearance of Venus on the sun, was 9 hours 25 min. 4 sec.
>
> The first internal contact, or total immersion, was 9 hours 44 min. 4 sec.
>
> The second internal contact, or beginning of the immersion, was 3 hours 14 min. 8 sec.
>
> The second external contact, or total immersion, was 3 hours 32 min. 10 sec.
>
> Latitude of the observatory, 17° 15' 29" S.
>
> Longitude, 149° 32' 30" W. of Greenwich.

There having been a scarcity of breadfruit for some days, it appeared, upon inquiry, that the fruit had been gathered to make a sort of sour paste, called *mahie*, which, after fermentation, will keep a long time, in times of death.

Complaint was made on Monday the 12th to Captain Cook, that the Indians had lost some bows and arrows and strings of plaited hair. The affair was inquired into, and the fact being well attested, two dozen lashes[2] were inflicted upon the sailors who had stolen them.

A variety of articles having been stolen by the natives at different times, the captain wished, if possible, to put an end to these

1 'The day proved as favourable to our purpose as we could wish; not a cloud was to be seen the whole day, and the air was perfectly clear: so that we had every advantage in observing the whole of the passage of the planet Venus over the sun's disc. We very distinctly saw an atmosphere, or dusky shade, round the body of the planet, which very much disturbed the times of the contact, particularly the two internal ones. It was nearly calm the whole day, and the thermometer, exposed to the sun about the middle of the day, rose to a degree of heat we have not before met with.' – Extract, Captain Cook's Journal, Admiralty Records.

2 The justice and humanity of Captain Cook is shown throughout all his dealings, whether with the natives he met with in his several voyages, or with his own men. He never had recourse to the lash except in cases of marked necessity; and even in the grossest cases, he never sanctioned more than two dozen lashes. One seaman of the *Endeavour* was sentenced to 'twelve lashes for refusing to come on deck when all hands were called, and afterwards refusing to comply with the orders of his officer'; another 'with twelve for getting drunk, grossly assaulting the officer of the watch, and beating some of the sick'.

practices by making it their common interest to prevent them. Accordingly, he ordered a number of their canoes to be seized till restitution was made, but at last was prevailed on to release them.

About this time another event had nearly involved the English in a quarrel with the Indians. Captain Cook having sent a boat on shore to get ballast, the officer not meeting immediately with what he wanted, began to pull down one of their sepulchral buildings. This measure was strenuously opposed by the Indians. Mr Banks, having received intelligence of the affair, repaired to the spot, and the matter was soon amicably terminated, there being stones sufficient found elsewhere.

On the 19th, in the evening, soon after dark, while the canoes were detained by the captain, Queen Oberea presented the crew with a hog, breadfruit, and other presents, among which was a dog. Dogs are esteemed here more delicate eating than pork, as those bred to be eaten taste no animal food, but live entirely upon vegetables, and the experiment was tried. Tupia undertook to kill and dress one, which he did by making a hole in the ground and baking it. It was deemed a very good dish.

Many of the natives brought various kinds of presents to the party at the fort. Among the party was Oamo, a chief of several districts on the island, whom they had never before seen, and who brought with him a hog. The chief was treated with great respect by the natives and was accompanied by a boy and a young woman. The boy, though able to walk, was carried upon a man's back. Oberea, and some other of the Indians, went out of the fort to meet them, their heads and bodies being first uncovered as low as the waist. This was considered as a mark of respect they had not noticed it before, but judged that it was usually shown to persons of distinguished rank among them. Oamo entered the tent, but the young woman, who was about sixteen, could not be prevailed upon to accompany him, though she seemed to combat with her curiosity and inclination. Dr Solander took the youth by the hand, and conducted him in; but the natives without, who had prevented the girl's entrance, soon found means to get him out again.

The curiosity of Mr Banks, and the other gentlemen, being excited from these circumstances, they made inquiry who these strangers were, and were informed, that Oamo was Oberea's husband, but that by mutual consent they had been for a considerable time separated; and that the youth and girl were their off-spring. The boy was named Terridiri, and was heir apparent to the sovereignty of the island; and was to espouse his sister as soon as he had attained the proper age.

Monday, June 26th, early in the morning, Captain Cook set out in the pinnace, accompanied by Mr Banks, to circumnavigate the island. They sailed to the eastward, and in the forenoon went on shore, in a part of the island under the government of Ahio, a young chief, who had often visited them at their tents. They also found here some other natives of their acquaintance.

Having taken a survey of the harbour, and a large bay, near to which it is situated, they proposed going to the opposite side of the bay; but Titubaola, who was their conductor, not only refused to accompany them, but endeavoured to dissuade Captain Cook and Mr Banks, saying, that 'the country was inhabited by people who were not subjects to Tootahah, and who would destroy them all.' This information did not, however, prevent the execution of their design; and upon loading their pieces with ball, Titubaola took courage to go with them. They rowed till it was dark, when they reached a narrow neck of land that divided the island into two peninsulas, which are distinct governments. As they had not yet reached the hostile part of the country, they agreed to spend the night on shore; where they were provided with supper and lodging by a woman named Ooratooa.

In the morning they pursued their passage, and landed in a district which was governed by a chief, named Maraitata, the burying place of men; and his father was called Pahairade, the stealer of boats. But notwithstanding the ominous nature of their names, they gave Captain Cook and Mr Banks a civil reception, furnished them with provisions, and exchanged them a large hog for a hatchet.

The curiosity of the natives was soon excited, and a crowd gathered round the party of English, but they saw only two people whom they knew. They then advanced till they reached the district, which was under the dominion of the principal chief, or king, named Waheatua. Having continued their journey along the shore for a considerable way, they at last saw the chief, and with him an agreeable young woman, about two-and-twenty, named Toudidde.

In passing through this part of the island, they found it better cultivated, and more improved than any they had hitherto met with; though the houses were but few, and those small, there were a great number of canoes, which excelled any they had seen, both in size and workmanship. Notwithstanding the fertility of the country, provision of every kind was scarce.

Towards the southernmost part of the island they found a good harbour, formed by a reef, and the country around remarkably fruitful.

They landed again a little farther to the east. Mathiabo, the chief, with whom they had no acquaintance, nor had ever seen before, soon came to them, and supplied them with coconuts and bread-fruit. They purchased a hog for a glass bottle, which he took in preference to every other thing that was offered him. They saw here a turkey-cock and a goose, which the *Dolphin* left on the island; they were remarkably fat, and seemed to be greatly admired by the Indians.

A very uncommon sight presented itself in a house near this place; several human jaw-bones were fastened to a board of a semicircular form; they seemed fresh, and had not lost any of their teeth. Mr Banks could obtain no explanation of this mystery. They quitted this place, and arrived in a bay on the north-west side.

Several canoes came off with some beautiful women, who appeared to be desirous of their going on shore, to which they readily assented. They met with a friendly reception from the chief, whose name was Wiverou, at whose house they supped, in company with Mathiabo. Part of the house was allotted for them to sleep in; and soon after supper they retired to rest. Mathiabo having obtained a cloak from Mr Banks, under pretence of using it as a coverlet, immediately made off with it, unperceived by anyone. News of the robbery was soon brought by one of the natives; in consequence of which they set out in pursuit of the thief, but had proceeded a very little way, before they were met by a person bringing back the cloak, which Mathiabo had given up through fear. The house, upon their return, was entirely deserted; and about four in the morning the sentinel gave the alarm that the boat was missing. Their situation was now extremely alarming; the party consisting of four had but a single musket and two pocket pistols, without a spare ball or a charge of powder. After remaining in this distressing state of anxiety for a considerable time, dreading the advantage the Indians might take of it, to their great joy, the boat, which had been driven away by the tide, returned; and they departed.

This place is situated on the north side of Tiarrabou, the south-east peninsula of the island. It is fertile and populous, and the inhabitants everywhere behaved with civility. The last district in Tiarrabou, in which they landed, was governed by a chief named Omoe.

Here they saw one of their *eatuas*, or gods; it was made of wicker work, and resembled the figure of a man; it was nearly seven feet in height, and was covered with black and white feathers; on the head were four protuberances, which the natives called *tate ete*, or little men.

They were now near the district, named Paparra, which was governed by Oamo and Oberea, where they intended to spend the night. Mr Banks and his company landed about an hour before it was dark, and found that they had both set out to pay them a visit at the fort. They, nevertheless, slept at the house of Oberea, which, though not large, was very neat; no inhabitant but her father, who showed them much civility, was now in possession of it. They took this opportunity of walking out to a point, upon which they had observed some trees called *etoa*, which usually grow on the burial-places of these people. These burying grounds are called *morai*, which are also places of worship. They here saw an immense edifice, which they found to be the *morai* of Oamo and Oberea.

It consisted of an enormous pile of stonework, raised in the form of a pyramid, with a flight of steps on each side, and was nearly two hundred and seventy feet long, about one-third as wide, and between forty and fifty feet high. As the Indians were totally destitute of iron utensils to shape their stones, as well as mortar to cement them when they had made them fit for use, a structure of such height and magnitude must have been a work of infinite labour and fatigue.

In the centre of the summit was the representation of a bird, carved in wood; close to this was the figure of a fish, which was in stone. This pyramid made part of one side of a wide court or square, the sides of which were nearly equal; the whole was walled in, and paved with flat stones. At a little distance, to the west of this edifice, was another paved square, which contained several small stages, called by the natives *ewattas*, which appeared to be altars; upon them they place provisions as sacrifices to their gods.

The inhabitants of the island of Otaheite seem in nothing so desirous of excelling each other, as in the grandeur and magnificence of their sepulchres; and the rank and authority of Oberea was forcibly evinced upon this occasion. The crew of the *Endeavour*, it has been observed, did not find Oberea possessed of the same power as when the *Dolphin* was at this place, and they were now informed of the cause. It seemed that, about four or five months before Captain Cook's arrival, the inhabitants of Tiarrabou, the peninsula to the south-east, made a descent here, and slew many of the people; that hereupon Oberea, and Oamo who then held the government for his son, had fled and taken refuge in the mountains; and that the victors destroyed all the houses and pillaged the country. The turkey and goose, which had been seen in the district of Mathiabo, were among the booty; and the jaw-bones, which were discovered there, had likewise been carried off as trophies of victory.

On Friday the 30th, they arrived at Otahourou, where their old acquaintance Tootahah resided; he received them with great civility, and provided for them a good supper and a convenient lodging; and notwithstanding they were so shamefully plundered the last time they slept with this chief, they spent the night in the utmost security, none of their clothes, or any other article, being missing in the morning.

On Saturday, July 1st, they returned to the fort at Port Royal Harbour; having discovered the island, both peninsulas included, to be about one hundred miles in circumference.

Their Indian friends crowded about them upon their return, and none of them came without provisions.

Monday the 3rd, Mr Banks made an excursion, with some Indian guides, to trace the river up the valley to its source, and observe to what extent its banks were inhabited. After meeting with houses for the space of six miles, they came up to one which was said to be the last that could be seen. The master of it presented them with coconuts and other fruits; and after a short visit, they continued their walk. In this tour they often passed under vaults, formed by rocky fragments, in which they were informed that those who were benighted often took refuge. During this tour he had a good opportunity of searching for minerals, but found none. The stones, everywhere resembling those of Madeira, gave manifest signs of having been burnt. There were also evident traces of fire in the clay upon the hills, both of this and the neighbouring islands.

Mr Banks was engaged the 4th in planting on each side of the fort a quantity of the seeds of water melons, oranges, lemons, limes, and other plants and trees which he had brought from Rio de Janeiro. He gave these seeds to the Indians in great plenty, and planted many of them in the woods: some of the melon-seeds which had been planted soon after his arrival, had already produced plants, which appeared to be in a very flourishing state.

Preparations were now made for departing; and Captain Cook hoped to quit the island, without any further misunderstanding with the natives; but in this he was mistaken. Two foreign sailors having been out, one of them was robbed of his knife, and striving to recover it, the Indians attacked and wounded him in a dangerous manner with a stone; his companion also received a slight wound in the head. As Captain Cook would have been unwilling to have taken further notice of the transaction, he was not sorry the offenders had made their escape.

Another affair, equally disagreeable, soon after happened. Between the 8th and 9th, in the evening, two young marines retired secretly from the fort, and in the morning were not to be met with. Notice having been given for all the company to go on board the next day, and that the ship would sail on that or the ensuing day, Captain Cook began to fear that the marines intended to remain on shore. He was apprised that no effectual steps could be taken to recover them, without risking the harmony and good fellowship which, at present, subsisted between the English and the natives; and, therefore, resolved to wait a day in hopes of their returning.

The 10th in the morning, the marines not having returned, an inquiry was made after them, when the Indians declared that they did not propose returning, having taken refuge in the mountains, where it was impossible to discover them; and that each had taken a wife. In consequence of which it was intimated to several chiefs, who were in the fort with their women, among whom were Tubora Tumaida, Tomio, and Oberea, that they would not be suffered to quit it till the deserters were produced. They received the intimation with very little signs either of fear or discontent, assuring the captain that the marines should be sent back; but night coming on, Captain Cook judged it was not prudent to let the hostages remain at the fort; and he therefore ordered them to be brought on board. This gave an unusual alarm; and several of them, especially the females, testified their apprehensions with great agitation of mind, and floods of tears.

One of the marines was brought back in the evening by some of the Indians, who reported that the other and the two people who were sent to fetch them back, would be detained till Tootahah, who was one of the confined, should be liberated. Mr Hicks was immediately despatched, in the longboat, with several men, to rescue the English prisoners; at the same time, Captain Cook told Tootahah, that it was incumbent on him to assist them with some of his people, and to give orders in his name that the men should be set at liberty, for that he should expect him to answer for the event. Tootahah immediately complied, and this party recovered the men without any opposition.

At the time the chiefs were set on shore from the ship, those at the fort were also released, and after remaining with Mr Banks about an hour and a half, they all returned to their respective places of residence. When the deserters were examined, it was discovered that the account which the Indians had given was no way false; they had become attached to women, and it was their design to keep themselves concealed till the ship had set sail, and to continue upon the island.

Tupia, who had been prime minister of Oberea, when she was at the pinnacle of her authority, and was also the principal priest of the island, and, therefore, intimately acquainted with the religion of the country, having often testified a desire to go with them, on Wednesday the 12th, in the morning, came on board, with a boy about twelve years of age, his servant, named Taiyota, and requested permission to sail with them. This was unanimously agreed to. Tupia then went on shore, for the last time, to see his friends, and took with him several baubles, to give as parting tokens of remembrance.

Thursday the 13th of July, the ship was visited by a multitude of friends, and surrounded by numberless canoes, which contained the inferior natives. They weighed anchor about twelve, and the Indians took leave of the crew, weeping in a friendly and affecting manner. Tupia supported himself in this scene with a becoming fortitude; tears flowed from his eyes, it is true, but the effort that he made to conceal them did him additional honour. He went with Mr Banks to the masthead, where he continued waving his hand to the canoes, as long as they remained visible.

According to Tupia's account, the island could furnish above six thousand fighting men, whereby a computation of the number of inhabitants may easily be made.

They have no European fruits, garden stuff, or pulse, nor grain of any species, but many valuable vegetable productions of their own. Their tame animals are hogs, dogs, and poultry; there is not a wild animal in the island, except ducks, pigeons, parrots, and a few other birds – rats being the only quadruped; and there are no serpents. The sea, however, supplies them with a variety of excellent fish.

With regard to the people, they are in general rather of a larger make than Europeans. The males are tall, robust, and finely shaped. The females, of the superior class, are likewise generally above our common size, but those of the lower rank are rather below it, and some of them are remarkably little.

Their natural complexion is a fine clear olive, or what we call brunette; their skin delicately smooth, and agreeably soft. The shape of their faces is in general handsome, and their eyes are full of sensibility and expression: their teeth are likewise remarkably white and regular, and their breath entirely free from any disagreeable smell; their hair is, for the most part, black. Their motions are easy and graceful, but not vigorous; their deportment is generous and open, and their behaviour affable and courteous.

Both sexes frequently wear a piece of cloth, of the manufacture of the island, tied round their heads in the form of a turban; and the women take no little pains in plaiting hair into long strings, which being folded into branches, are tied on their foreheads by way of ornament.

They stain their bodies by indenting or pricking the flesh with a small instrument made of bone, cut into short teeth; which indentures they fill with a dark blue or blackish mixture, prepared from the smoke of an oily nut – used by them instead of candles – and water; this operation of tattooing, as it is called by them, is exceedingly painful, and leaves an indelible mark on the skin. It is usually performed when they are about ten or twelve years of age, and on different parts of the body.

They clothe themselves in cloth and matting of various kinds; the first they wear in fair, the latter in wet weather. They are in different forms, no shape being preserved, nor are the pieces sewed together. The women of a superior class wear three or four pieces; one, which is of considerable length, they wrap several times round their waist, which falls down to the middle of the leg. Two or three other short pieces, with a hole cut in the middle of each, are placed on one another, and their heads coming through the holes, the long ends hang before and behind, both sides being open, by which means they have the free use of their arms.

The men's dress is very similar, differing only in one instance, which is that part of the garment, instead of falling below the knees, is brought between the legs. This dress is worn by all ranks of people, the only distinction being quantity in the superior class. At noon both sexes appear almost naked, wearing only the piece of cloth that is tied round the waist.

The boys and girls go naked – the first till they are seven or eight years old, the latter till they are about five. Their houses they seldom use but to sleep in, or to avoid the rain, as they eat in the open air, under the shade of a tree. Their clothes serve them at night for covering, and there are no divisions or apartments. The master and his wife repose in the middle; then the married people; next to these the unmarried females, and at a small distance the men who are unmarried.

The houses of the chiefs, however, differ in some degree; there are some very small, and so built as to be carried in canoes; all sides of them are enclosed with the leaves of the coconut; the air, nevertheless, penetrates; in these the chief and his wife alone sleep. There are also houses which are general receptacles for the inhabitants of a district. These are much larger.

If a chief kills a hog, which is but seldom, he divides it equally among his vassals; dogs and fowls, however, are more common.

When the breadfruit is not in season, they are supplied by coconuts, bananas, plantains, etc.

Their cookery is confined to baking, and their drink is generally water, or the milk of the coconut, though there were instances in which some of them drank so freely of the English liquors, as to become intoxicated; this, however, seemed to proceed more from ignorance than design, as they were never known to repeat a debauch of this kind a second time. They were told, indeed, that the chiefs sometimes became inebriated by drinking the juice of a plant called *ava*, but of this they saw no instance during the time they remained on the island.

The chiefs generally eat alone, unless when visited by a stranger, who is sometimes permitted to become a second in their mess; leaves of trees serve as a tablecloth; and their attendants, who are numerous, having placed a basket before the chiefs, containing their provisions, and a coconut shell of flesh and salt water, seat themselves round them. They then begin by washing their mouth and hands, after which they eat a mouthful of breadfruit and fish, dipped in salt water alternately, till the whole is consumed, taking a sup of salt water likewise between almost every morsel. The breadfruit and fish being all eaten, they next have either plantains or apples, which they never eat without being pared. During this time a soft paste is prepared from the breadfruit, which they sup out of a coconut shell; this finishes the meal, and the hands and mouth are again washed, as at the beginning. They devour vast quantities of food at a meal.

It is not a little surprising, that the inhabitants of this island, who seemed exceedingly sensible of the pleasures of society, should have an universal aversion to the least intercourse with each other at their meals; and so rigid are they in the observance of this unusual custom, that even brothers and sisters have their separate baskets to contain their provisions, and generally sit some yards apart when they eat, with their backs turned towards each other, not exchanging a single word during the whole time of their repast. The middle-aged of superior rank usually betake themselves to sleep after dinner, but what is remarkable, the older people are not so lazy; music, dancing, wrestling, and shooting with the bow, or throwing a lance, constitute the chief part of their diversions.

Flutes, which have been mentioned before, and drums, are the only musical instruments among them; their drums are formed of a circular piece of wood, hollow at one end only, which is covered with the skin of a shark, and they are beaten with the hand instead of a stick. Their songs are extempore, and frequently in rhyme, but consist of only two lines.

Among their other amusements they have a dance, which is performed by ten or a dozen young females, who put themselves into the most unbecoming attitudes that can possibly be imagined, keeping time, during the performance, with the greatest nicety and exactness.

Their personal cleanliness is an object that merits peculiar attention. Independently of their washing their mouths and hands before and after meals, as already stated, both sexes never omit to wash with water three times a day — when they rise, at noon, and before they go to rest. They also keep their clothes extremely clean; so that in the largest communities no disagreeable effluvia ever arises, nor is there any other inconvenience than heat.

The chief manufacture of Otaheite is cloth; of this cloth there are three different sorts, which are made of the bark of as many different trees, viz., the mulberry, the breadfruit, and a tree not unlike the wild fig-tree, which is found in some parts of the West Indies. The mulberry-tree, which the Indians call *aouta*, produces the finest cloth, which is seldom worn but by those of the first rank. The next sort, which is worn by the lower class of people, is made of the breadfruit tree, and the coarsest of the tree resembling the fig-tree. This last sort, though more useful than the two former, on account of its keeping out water, which neither of the others will, is exceedingly scarce, being manufactured but in small quantities.

The cloth becomes quite white by bleaching, and is dyed of a red, yellow, brown, or black colour; the first of which is very beautiful, and equal, if not superior, to any in Europe.

Matting of various kinds is another considerable manufacture, in which, in many respects, they excel the Europeans. They make use of the coarser sort to sleep on, and in wet weather they wear the finer.

They greatly excel in the basket and wicker work; both men and women employ themselves at it, and can make it of a variety of patterns.

Their fishing-lines are esteemed the best in the world, made of the bark of the *erowa*, a kind of nettle which grows on the mountains; they are strong enough to hold the heaviest and most vigorous fish, such as bonitas and albicores; in short, they are extremely ingenious in every expedient for taking all kinds of fish.

The tools which these people make use of for building houses, constructing canoes, hewing stone, and for felling, cleaving, carving, and polishing timber, consist of nothing more than an adze of stone, and a chisel of bone, most commonly that of a man's arm; and for a file, or polisher, they make use of a rasp of coral, and coral sand.

Some of their smaller boats are made of the breadfruit tree, which is wrought with much difficulty, being of a light, spongy nature. Their canoes are all shaped with the hand, the Indians not being acquainted with the method of warping a plank.

Their language is soft and musical, abounding in vowels, and is easy to be pronounced. But whether it is copious, Mr Banks and Dr Solander were not sufficiently acquainted with it to know. As few either of their nouns or verbs are declinable, it must consequently be very imperfect. They found means, however, to be mutually understood without much difficulty.

The management of the sick falls to the lot of the priests; and their method of cure consists chiefly of prayers and ceremonies, which are repeated till the patients recover or die.

The religion of these people appeared to be exceedingly mysterious. They emphatically style the Supreme Being the causer of earthquakes; but their prayers are more generally addressed to Tane, supposed to be a son of the first progenitors of nature.

They believe in the existence of the soul in a separate state; and that there are two situations, differing in their degrees of happiness, which they consider as receptacles for different ranks, but not as places of reward and punishment. They suppose that their chiefs and principal people will have the preference to those of inferior rank, as they imagine their actions no way influence their future state, and that their deities take no cognisance of them whatsoever.

The office of priest is hereditary; there are several of them, and of all ranks; the chief is respected next to their kings; and they are superior to the rest of the natives, not only in point of divine knowledge, but also in that of navigation and astronomy.

They are no way concerned with the ceremony of marriage, which is a simple agreement between the man and woman; and when they choose to separate, it is done with as little ceremony as that of their marriage.

Slings, with which they are dexterous, pikes headed with stone, and long clubs made of wood, remarkably hard and heavy, constitute their weapons. With these they fight with great obstinacy and cruelty, giving no quarter to either man, woman, or child, if they fall into their hands in time of battle.

July the 13th, after leaving the island of Otaheite, they sailed with a gentle breeze and clear weather; and were informed by Tupia, that four islands, which he called Huaheine, Ulietea, Otaha, and Bolabola, were at the distance of about one or two days' sail; and that hogs, fowls, and other refreshments, which had lately been scarce, were to be got there in abundance. They accordingly steered their course in search of these islands, and on the 15th discovered the island of Huaheine, and next morning, they sounded near the north-west part of the island, but found no bottom with seventy fathoms.

Several canoes immediately put off, but they appeared afraid of coming near the ship, till they saw Tupia, who totally removed their apprehensions, and upon assurances of friendship, the king of Huaheine and his queen went on board. Astonishment was testified by their majesties at everything that was shown to them; yet they made no researches, and appeared satisfied with what was presented to their observation, making no inquiry after any other objects, though it was reasonable to suppose that a building of such novelty and extent as the ship, must have afforded many curiosities. The king, whose name was Oree, made a proposal to exchange names with Captain Cook, which was readily assented to. The custom of exchanging names is very prevalent in this island, and is considered as a mark of friendship. They found the people here nearly similar to those of Otaheite in almost every circumstance, except, if Tupia may be credited, they were not addicted to thieving.

Having come to an anchor in a small but fine harbour, on the west side of the island, Captain Cook went ashore, accompanied by Mr Banks and some other gentlemen, with Tupia and the king. The instant they landed, Tupia uncovered himself as low as his waist, and desired Mr Monkhouse to follow his example. Being seated, he now began a speech, which lasted about twenty minutes; the king, who stood opposite to him, answered in what seemed to be set replies. During this discourse he delivered at different times, a handkerchief, a black silk neckcloth, some beads and plantains, as presents to their *eatua*, or deity. He received in return, for the *eatua* of the English, a hog, some young plantains, and two bunches of feathers, which were carried on board. These ceremonies were considered as a kind of ratification of a treaty between the English and the king of Huaheine.

Wednesday, the 19th, they went ashore, and carried some hatchets with them, with which they procured three large hogs. As they proposed to sail in the afternoon, the king, accompanied by some others of the natives, came on board to take his leave, when his majesty received from Captain Cook a small pewter plate, with the following inscription: 'His Britannic Majesty's ship *Endeavour*, Lieutenant Cook commander, 16th July, 1769'. He also was presented with some medals, or counters, resembling the coin of England, and a few other trifles.

This island is distant from Otaheite about thirty leagues, and is about twenty miles in circumference. The people are of a lazy disposition, though they are stouter and larger made than those of Otaheite.

From Huaheine they sailed for the island of Ulietea, and in the afternoon came within a league or two of the shore. They anchored in a bay, which is formed by a reef, on the north side of the island. Two canoes of natives soon came off from the shore, and brought with them two small hogs, which they exchanged for some nails and beads. On the 20th, Mr Banks, the Captain, and others, went on shore, accompanied by Tupia, who introduced them with the same kind of ceremonies that had taken place on their landing at Huaheine; after which, Captain Cook took possession of this and the adjacent islands, in the name of the King of Great Britain.

On the 24th they got under sail, and steered to the northward within the reef, towards an opening five or six leagues distant. In effecting this, they were in the greatest danger of striking on a rock; the man who sounded, crying out on a sudden, two fathoms, at which they were much alarmed, but happily got clear without receiving any damage.

On the 25th, they were within a league or two of the island of Otaha, but the wind continuing contrary, they could not get near enough to land till the 28th, in the morning, when Mr Banks and Dr Solander went in the longboat, with the master, to sound a harbour on the east side of the island, which they found safe and convenient, with good anchorage. They then went on shore, and purchased some hogs and fowls, and a large quantity of yams and plantains.

This island appeared to be more barren than Ulietea, but the produce was much the same.

On the 29th they sailed to the northward; and in the afternoon, finding themselves to windward of some harbours that lay on the west side of Ulietea, they intended to put into one of them, in order to stop a leak which they had sprung in the powder room, and to take in some additional ballast.

On the 2nd of August they anchored in twenty-eight fathoms water, in a convenient harbour. In the interim many of the natives came off, and brought hogs, fowls, and plantains, which were purchased upon moderate terms.

Mr Banks and Dr Solander now went on shore, and spent the day agreeably; the natives showing them great respect. In one house they observed some young girls, dressed in the neatest manner, waiting for the strangers to accost them; these girls were the most beautiful the gentlemen had ever seen.

Before their departure they were entertained with a dance, different from any they had seen before. The performer put upon his head a large piece of wicker work, about four feet long, of a cylindrical form, covered with feathers, and edged round with shark's teeth. Having this head-dress on, which is called a *whou*, he began to dance with a slow motion, frequently moving his head so as to describe a circle with the top of his wicker cap, and sometimes throwing it so near the faces of the bystanders, as to make them jump back; this they considered as an excellent piece of humour; and it always produced a hearty laugh, when practised upon any of the English gentlemen.

On the 3rd they saw another company of dancers, consisting of some of the principal females of the island. They advanced side-ways, keeping time, with great exactness, to the drums, which beat quick and loud; soon after, they began to shake themselves, in a very whimsical manner, and put their bodies into a variety of strange postures; sometimes standing in a row one behind another; sometimes sitting down; and at others falling with their faces to the ground, and resting on their knees and elbows, accompanied with many other unbecoming attitudes; moving their fingers at the same time with a quickness scarcely to be credited.

On the 5th, some hogs and fowls, and several large pieces of cloth, many of them being fifty or sixty yards in length, together with a quantity of plantains and coconuts, were sent to Captain Cook as a present, from the *earee rahie* of a neighbouring island called Bolabola, accompanied with a message, that he was then on the island, and intended waiting on the captain the next day.

The king, however, did not visit them agreeably to his promise; but his absence was not in the least regretted, as he sent three agreeable young women to demand something in return for his present. After dinner they set out to pay his majesty a visit on shore, as he did not think proper to come on board. As this man was the *earee rahie* of the Bolabola men, who had conquered this, and were the dread of all the neighbouring islands, they were greatly disappointed, instead of finding a vigorous, enterprising young chief, to see a poor, feeble, decrepit old dotard, half blind, and sinking under the weight of age and infirmities. He received them without either that state or ceremony which they had hitherto met with among the other chiefs.

They had now plenty of hogs on board; but as these animals could not be brought to eat any sort of European grain, or any provender whatever, that the ship afforded, they were reduced to the necessity of killing them immediately on their leaving those islands; and the fowls all died of a disorder in their head, with which they were seized soon after they were brought on board.

As they were detained longer at Ulietea in repairing the ship than they expected, they did not go on shore at Bolabola; but after giving the general name of the Society Islands to the whole group, which lie between the latitude of 16° 10' and 16° 55' S., they pursued their course, standing southwardly for an island, to which they were directed by Tupia, at above a hundred leagues distant, which they discovered on the 13th, and were informed by him that it was called Ohiteroa, or Rurutu, in 23° 10' S.

The next morning they stood in for land. When they came near the shore, they could perceive that the inhabitants were armed with lances of a considerable length. The appearance of the boat soon drew together a great number of them upon the beach, two of whom leaped into the water and endeavoured to gain the boat, but she soon left them behind; several others made the same attempt, but with as little success.

The boat having doubled the point where they intended to land, rowed towards the shore, and began to make preparations for landing; upon which a canoe, with some of the natives on board, came off towards them. They ordered Tupia to acquaint these people, that they did not intend doing them any injury, but wanted to traffic with them with nails, which they showed them. This information encouraged them to come alongside the boat, and they accepted of some nails, which were given them, with much apparent pleasure and satisfaction. In a few minutes, however, several of them unexpectedly boarded the boat, with an intention of dragging her on shore; some muskets were immediately discharged over their heads, which had the desired effect, all of them leaping directly into the sea, and put back to the shore as fast as they could paddle. This is another proof of Captain Cook's humanity, which is conspicuous throughout. Captain Cook now gave up all hopes of establishing a friendly intercourse with these people, and returned to the ship.

The island Ohiteroa does not shoot up into high peaks, like the others which they visited, but is more level and uniform, and divided into small hillocks, some of which are covered with groves of trees; they saw no breadfruit, and not many coconut trees, but great numbers of the tree called *etoa* were planted all along the shore.

On the 15th, they sailed to the southward, and on the 25th they celebrated the anniversary of their leaving England, from whence they had been absent one year; a large Cheshire cheese, which had been carefully preserved for that purpose, was brought out, and a barrel of porter tapped, which proved to be as good as any they had ever drank in England.

On the 28th of August, the boatswain's mate died. 'His death was occasioned by the boatswain, out of mere good nature, having given him part of a bottle of rum, which it is supposed he drank all at once. He was found to be very much in liquor last night; but as this was no more than what was common with him when he could get any, no farther notice was taken of him, than to put him to bed, where this morning, about eight o'clock, he was found speechless, and past recovery.'[1]

On the 7th of October, they discovered land at west by north, and in the afternoon of the next day, they came to an anchor opposite the mouth of a little river, about a mile and a half from the shore. The Captain, with Mr Banks, Dr Solander, and some other

1 Extract Captain Cook's log – Records, Admiralty, Whitehall.

gentlemen, accompanied by a party of marines, went on shore in the evening, and proceeded to a few small houses which they saw at a little distance. Taking the advantage of their absence from the boat, some of the natives, who had concealed themselves behind the bushes, suddenly rushed out, and ran towards it, brandishing the long wooden lances which they had in their hands in a threatening manner. The coxswain fired a musquetoon over their heads, which did not seem to intimidate them; he then fired a second time over their heads, but with no better effect; alarmed at the situation of the boat, as they were now got near enough to discharge their lances at it, the coxswain levelled his piece at them, and shot one man dead on the spot. Struck with astonishment at the fall of their companion, they retreated to the woods with the utmost precipitation. The report of the gun soon brought the advanced party back, and they immediately returned to the ship.

On Monday the 9th, in the morning, a number of the natives were seen near the place where the gentlemen in the yawl had landed the preceding evening, and the greatest part of them appeared to be unarmed. The longboat, pinnace, and yawl being ordered out, and manned with marines and sailors, Captain Cook, together with Mr Banks, the rest of the gentlemen, and Tupia, went on shore, and landed on the opposite side of the river, over against several Indians who were sitting on the ground.

They started up as soon as the gentlemen began to land, and their intentions appeared hostile, brandishing their weapons in the usual threatening manner; upon which a musket was fired at some distance from them, at the effect of which, the ball happening to strike the water, they appeared rather terrified, and desisted from their menaces. Tupia spoke to them, and informed them, that they wanted to traffic with them for provisions. They readily consented to trade, and requested the English gentlemen to cross the river and come over to them; which was agreed to, upon condition that the natives would quit their weapons; but this, the most solemn assurances of friendship could not prevail upon them to comply with.

The gentlemen, in their turn, entreated the Indians to come over to them, which, after some time, they induced one of them to do; he was presently followed by several others, bringing their weapons with them. They did not appear to set any great value on the beads, iron, etc., which were presented to them, nor would they give anything in return; but proposed to exchange their weapons for those belonging to the English, which being objected to, they endeavoured several times to snatch them out of their hands. Tupia, by direction of the gentlemen, gave them notice, that any further offer of violence would be punished with instant death. One of them had, nevertheless, the audacity to snatch Mr Green's hanger, and retiring a few paces, flourished it over his head; he, however, paid for this temerity with his life; and with great difficulty the hanger was recovered.

This behaviour of the natives, added to the want of fresh water, induced Captain Cook to continue his course round the head of the bay. He was still in hopes of getting some of the Indians on board, and by presents, added to civil usage, convey through them a favourable idea of the English to their fellow countrymen; and thereby settle a good correspondence with them. Soon after, an event occurred, though attended with disagreeable circumstances, that promised to facilitate this design. Two canoes appeared making towards land, and Captain Cook proposed intercepting them with his boats. One of them got clear off, but the Indians in the other, finding it impossible to escape the boats, began to attack them with their paddles: this compelled the *Endeavour's* people to fire upon them, when four of the Indians were killed, and the other three, who were youths, jumped into the water, and endeavoured to swim to shore; they were, however, taken up and brought on board. They were at first greatly terrified, thinking they should be killed; but Tupia, by repeated assurances of friendship, removed their fears, and they afterwards ate very heartily of the ship's provisions. When they retired to rest in the evening, they appeared perfectly easy in their minds, and slept very quietly.[1] The next

1 The following remarks on this untoward event are extracted from Captain Cook's own journal of proceedings, 10th Oct. 1769 – 'I rowed round the head of the bay, but could find no place to land, on account of the great surf which beat everywhere upon the shore. Seeing two boats or canoes coming in from sea, I rowed to one of them in order to seize upon the people, and came so near before they took notice of us, that Tupia called to them to come alongside and we would not hurt them, but instead of doing this they endeavoured to get away, upon which I ordered a musket to be fired over their heads, thinking that this would either make them surrender or jump overboard, but here I was mistaken, for they immediately

morning, they testified much satisfaction, when told they were going to be released. They informed Captain Cook that there was a particular kind of deer upon the island, likewise taro, capes, romara, yams, a kind of long pepper, bald coots, and black-birds.

On the 12th several Indians came off in a canoe; they were disfigured in a strange manner, danced and sung, and appeared at times to be peaceably inclined, at others to menace hostilities; but notwithstanding Tupia strongly invited them to come on board, none of them would quit the canoe. Whilst the *Endeavour* was getting clear of the shambles, five canoes full of Indians came off, and seemed to threaten the people on board, by brandishing their lances, and other hostile gestures; a four pounder, loaded with grape-shot, was therefore ordered to be fired, but not pointed at them. This had the desired effect, and made them drop astern. Next morning nine canoes full of Indians came from the shore, and five of them, after having consulted together, pursued the *Endeavour*, apparently with a hostile design. Tupia was desired to acquaint them, that immediate destruction would ensue, if they persevered in their attempts; but words had no influence, and a four-pounder, with grape-shot, was fired, to give them some notion of the arms of their opponents. They were terrified at this kind of reasoning, and paddled away in precipitation.

The following day, Sunday the 15th, in the afternoon, a large canoe, with a number of armed Indians, came up, and one of them, who was remarkably clothed with a black skin, found means to defraud the Captain of a piece of red baize, under pretence of bartering the skin

---

took to their arms or whatever they had in the boats, and began to attack us. This obliged us to fire upon them, and unfortunately either two or three were killed and one wounded, and three jumped overboard. These last we took up and brought on board, where they were clothed and treated with all imaginable kindness, and, to the surprise of everybody, became at once as cheerful and merry as if they had been with their own friends. They were all three young; the eldest not above twenty years of age, and the youngest about ten or twelve. I am aware that most humane persons who have not experienced things of this nature will censure my conduct in firing upon people in the boat, nor do I myself think that the reason I had for seizing upon them will at all justify me; and had I thought that they would have made the least resistance I would not have come near them, but as they did, I was not to stand still and suffer either myself or those that were with me to be knocked on the head.'
— Extract, Captain Cook's Journal, Records, Admiralty, Whitehall, p. 137.

he had on. As soon as he had got the baize into his possession, instead of giving the skin in return, agreeable to his bargain, he rolled them up together, and ordered the canoe to put off from the ship, turning a deaf ear to the repeated remonstrances of the Captain against his unjust behaviour. After a short time this canoe, together with the fishing boats which had put off at the same time, came back to the ship, and trade was again begun. During this second traffic with the Indians, one of them unexpectedly seized Tupia's little boy, Tayota, and pulling him into his canoe, instantly put off, and paddled away with the utmost speed. Several muskets were immediately discharged at the people in the canoe; and one of them receiving a wound, they all let go the boy, who before was held down in the bottom of the canoe. Tayota taking advantage of their consternation, immediately jumped into the sea, and swam back to the *Endeavour*. In consequence of this attempt to carry off Tayota, Captain Cook called the cape off which it happened Cape Kidnappers.

As every circumstance that tends to elucidate the manners and customs of these people must attract the attention of the curious reader, we cannot omit Tayota's behaviour upon recovering from his fright, occasioned by his being kidnapped. He produced a fish, and acquainted Tupia that he designed to make an offering of it to his God, or *eatua*, as a testimonial of his gratitude for his deliverance. Tupia approved of his intention, and by his direction the fish was cast into the sea. This is an evident proof that even these unenlightened savages, by the mere impulse of nature, believe in the existence of a particular providence.

The *Endeavour* now passed a small island, white and high, supposed to be inhabited only by fishermen, as it appeared quite barren, and was named Bare Island; on the 17th, Captain Cook gave the name of Cape Turnagain to a headland.

The land between this cape and Kidnappers' Bay is unequal and resembles the high downs of England. There appeared numerous inhabitants, and several villages. Wednesday the 18th, the *Endeavour* came abreast of a peninsula in Portland Island, named Terakako, when a canoe, with five Indians, came up to the ship. Two chiefs, who were in this canoe, came on board, where they remained all night, and were treated with great civility. The chiefs would neither eat nor drink, but the servants made up for their masters' abstinence by their voracious appetites. The three boys had given these natives an account of the hospitality and liberality of the English, which had prevailed upon them to pay this visit.

Thursday the 19th, the *Endeavour* passed a remarkable headland, which Captain Cook named Gable End Foreland. Here three canoes came up, and one Indian came on board; he received some small presents, and retired to his companions. He wore a new garment of white silky flax, with a border of black, red, and white.

On the 20th, they anchored in a bay, about two leagues to the north of the Foreland. The natives, in canoes, invited them hither, and behaved very amicably. There appeared to be two chiefs, who came on board. They received presents of linen, which gave them much satisfaction, but they did not hold spike-nails in such estimation as the inhabitants of some of the other islands. Captain Cook, Mr Banks, and Dr Solander went on shore, and were courteously received by the inhabitants, who did not appear in numerous bodies, to avoid giving offence. The captain had the satisfaction to find fresh water in the course of a tour round the bay. They remained on shore all night. Dogs, with small pointed ears, and very ugly, were the only tame animals seen here. They have sweet potatoes, like those of North America, in great quantities; and the cloth plant grows spontaneously. There was plenty of fish in the bay, such as crabs, crawfish, and shipjacks, or horse-mackerel, which were larger than those upon our coasts.

Mr Banks and Dr Solander visited their houses, and were kindly received. Fish constituted their principal food at this time, and the root of a sort of fern served them for bread; which, when roasted upon a fire, and divested of its bark, was sweet and clammy; in taste not disagreeable, but unpleasant, from its number of fibres. Vegetables were, doubtless, at other seasons plentiful. The women paint their faces red, which, so far from increasing, diminishes the very little beauty they have. The men's faces were not, in general, painted, but some were rubbed over with red ochre from head to foot, their apparel not excepted. The women wore a girdle made of the blade of grass, under a petticoat, and to this girdle was tied, in front, a bunch of fragrant leaves. They seemed to hold chastity in little estimation.

The 22nd, in the evening, they sailed from this bay, which, by the natives, is called Tegadoo. The wind being contrary, they put into another bay a little to the south, called by the natives Tolaga, in order to complete their wood and water, and extend their correspondence with the natives.

On the 24th, Mr Gore and the marines were sent on shore to guard the people employed in cutting wood and filling water. Captain Cook, Mr Banks, and the Doctor also went on shore. In their route they found in the vales many houses uninhabited, the natives residing chiefly in slight sheds on the ridges of the hills, which are very steep. In a valley between two very high hills, they saw a curious rock that formed a large arch, opposite to the sea. This cavity was in length above seventy feet, in breadth thirty, and near fifty in height; it commanded a view of the hills and the bay, which had a very happy effect. Indeed, the whole country about the bay is agreeable beyond description, and, if properly cultivated, would be a most fertile spot. Upon their return, they met an old man, who entertained them with the military exercises of the natives, which are performed with the patoo patoo and the lance. The former is used as a battle-axe; the latter is ten or twelve feet in length, made of extreme hard wood, and sharpened at each end. A stake was substituted for their old warrior's supposed enemy; he first attacked him with his lance, when, having pierced him, the patoo patoo was used to demolish his head, and the force with which he struck would, at one blow, have split any man's skull.

At the watering-place, the Indians, by desire, sung their war song, which was a strange medley of shouting, sighing, and grimace, at which the women assisted. The next day Captain Cook and the other gentlemen went upon an island at the entrance of the bay, and met with a canoe that was sixty-seven feet in length, six in breadth, and four in height; her bottom, which was sharp, consisted of three trunks of trees, and the sides and head were curiously carved. Their favourite figure is a volute or spiral, which is sometimes single, double, and triple, and is done with great exactness, though the only instruments the gentlemen saw were an axe made of stone, and a chisel.

There are many beautiful parrots, and great numbers of birds of different kinds, particularly one whose note resembled the European blackbird; but no ground-fowl or poultry, nor were there any quadrupeds, except rats and dogs, and these were not numerous. The dogs are considered as delicate food, and their skins serve for ornaments to their apparel.

October 29th, they set sail from this bay, and sailing to the northward, fell in with a small island, about a mile distant from the north-east point of the main; and this being the most eastern part of it, the captain named it East Cape, and the island East Island; it was but small, and appeared barren. Next morning, about nine, several canoes came off from shore, with a number of armed men, who appeared to have hostile intentions. Before these had reached the ship, another canoe, larger than any that had yet been seen, full of armed Indians, came off, and made towards the *Endeavour* with great expedition. The captain now judging it expedient to prevent, if possible, their attacking him, ordered a gun to be fired over their heads; this not producing the desired effect, another gun was fired with ball, which threw them into such consternation, that they immediately returned much faster than they came. Next morning, at daybreak, they saw between forty and fifty canoes along shore, many of which came off in the manner they had done the day before, shouting and menacing an attack. One of their chiefs, in the largest of the canoes, made several harangues, and by the menacing flourish of his pike, seemed to bid the ship defiance; but the gentlemen continuing to invite them to trade, they at last came close alongside; and the chief who had been declaiming, after uttering a sentence, took up a stone and threw it against the side of the ship, which appeared to be a declaration of hostilities, as they instantly seized their arms. One of them took some linen that was hanging to dry, and made off with it. A musket was fired over his head to make him return, but this did not prevail; and even after another was fired at him with small shot, which hit him in the back, he still persevered in his design. Upon this the rest of the Indians set up their song of defiance. They did not, however, make any preparations for attacking the ship; but Captain Cook judged, that if he suffered them to go off without convincing them of his power of avenging the insult, it might give an unfavourable opinion of the English to the natives on shore. He accordingly fired a four-pounder, which passed over them; and the effect it had in the water terrified them so greatly, that they made to shore with the utmost precipitancy.

The *Endeavour* passed the night under an island about twenty miles from the main, which they named the Mayor. In the morning of the 3rd November, they gave the name of the Court of Aldermen to a number of small islands that lay contiguous. The chief, who governed the district from Cape Turnagain to this coast, was named Teratu.

On the 4th, three canoes came alongside with several Indians. These canoes were built very different from the others, being formed of the trunks of single trees, made hollow by burning: they were not carved, or in any shape ornamented. These Indians were of a darker complexion than the others, but made use of the same modes of defiance, and threw several stones and some of their lances into the ship.

In the morning of the 5th, a great number of canoes, with near two hundred men, armed with spears, lances, and stones, made their appearance; seemingly resolved to attack the ship, and desirous of boarding her, but could not determine at what part, changing their stations, and paddling round her. These motions kept the crew upon the watch, in the rain, whilst Tupia at the request of the captain, used every dissuasive argument he could suggest to prevent their carrying their apparent designs into execution; but his expostulations did not pacify them, till some muskets were fired; they then laid aside their hostile intentions, and began to trade. They sold two of their weapons without fraud; but a third, for which they had received cloth, they would not deliver up; and instead of paying any attention to the demand that was made for it, they only laughed at them, and turned their expostulations into ridicule.

As the captain proposed to stay some days at this place, that he might observe the transit of Mercury, he judged it expedient to chastise these people for their insolence and knavery; accordingly, some small shot were fired upon the principal offender, and a musket ball went through his canoe. His companions left him to his fate, without taking the least notice of him, though he was wounded; and continued to trade without any discomposure. They for some time traded very fairly, but returning to their malpractices, another canoe was fired upon and struck: they soon after paddled away, whilst a round shot was fired over them.

Several of the Indians came off to the ship on the 6th, but behaved much better than they had done the preceding day. They had with them an old man, named Tojava, who had before testified his probity and discretion, and he appeared to be of superior rank to the rest. He came on board with another Indian, when the captain presented them with some nails, and two pieces of cloth of English manufacture. Tojava then acquainted the captain, that they were often visited by freebooters from the north, who stripped them of all they could lay their hands on and often made captives of their children and wives; and that being ignorant who the English were upon their arrival, the natives had taken the alarm upon the ship's appearing off the coast; but were now satisfied of their good intent. Probably, their poverty and misery may be ascribed to the ravages of this banditti, who often strip them of every necessary of life. The assurances of friendship which they had received from the gentlemen on board, seemed to have a proper influence upon the natives, who became tractable and submissive. In a word, the natives now treated the English with great hospitality; a large supply of wood and good water was obtained, and the ship being foul, was heeled, and her bottom scrubbed in the bay.

A variety of plants were collected here by Mr Banks and Dr Solander; they had never observed any of the kind before.

Early in the morning of the 9th, several canoes brought a prodigious quantity of mackerel, one sort of which was no way different from the mackerel caught on our coast. These canoes were succeeded by many others, equally well loaded with the same sort of fish; and the cargoes purchased were so great, that when salted, they might be considered as a month's provision for the whole ship's company.

This being a very clear day, the astronomer (Mr Green) and the other gentlemen landed to observe the transit of Mercury, and whilst the observation was making, a large canoe with various commodities on board came alongside the ship, and the officer who had then the command, being desirous of encouraging traffic, produced a piece of Otaheitan cloth, of more value than any they had yet seen, which was immediately seized by one of the Indians, who obstinately refused either to return it, or to give anything in exchange; he paid dearly, however, for his temerity, being shot dead on the spot.[1]

1 Everyone will admit that this was a merciless and most unjustifiable act committed in a rash moment, and doubtless often repented. The editor finds in Captain Cook's Journal the following entry: 'I must own that it did not meet with my approbation, because I thought the punishment a little too severe for the crime, and we had now been long enough acquainted with these people to know

The death of this young Indian alarmed all the rest: they fled with
great precipitancy, and for the present, could not be induced to
renew their traffic with the English. But when the Indians on shore
heard the particulars related by Tojava, who greatly condemned the
conduct of the deceased, they seemed to think that he merited his
fate. This transaction happened, as has been mentioned, whilst the
observation was making of the transit of Mercury, when the
weather was so favourable, that the whole transit was viewed
without a cloud intervening. Mr Green made the observation of the
ingress, whilst Captain Cook was engaged in ascertaining the time,
by taking the sun's altitude. In consequence of this observation
having been made here, this bay was called Mercury Bay.[1]

The Indians sup before sunset, when they eat fish and birds baked
or roasted. A female mourner was present at one of their suppers;
she was seated upon the ground, and wept incessantly, at the same
time repeating some sentences in a doleful manner, but which
Tupia could not explain; at the termination of each period she cut
herself with a shell upon her breast, her hands or her face; notwithstanding this shocking spectacle greatly affected the gentlemen
present, the Indians viewed it with indifference.

November 11th, oysters were procured in great abundance from
a bed which had been discovered, and they proved exceedingly
good. Next day the ship was visited by two canoes, with unknown
Indians; after some invitation they came on board, and trafficked
without fraud. Captain Cook sailed from this bay, after taking
possession of it in the name of the King of Great Britain, on the
15th. A number of islands, of different sizes, appeared toward the
north-west, which were named Mercury Islands. The inhabitants,
though numerous, have no plantations; their canoes are very
indifferently constructed, and are no way ornamented. Upon this
shore iron sand is in plenty to be found, which proves that there are
mines of that metal up the country, it being brought down by a
rivulet from thence.

---

how to chastise trifling faults like this, without taking away their lives.' – Extract,
Captain Cook's Journal, Records, Admiralty, Whitehall, page 154.
1 Lat. 36° 48' 5½" S. as given in Captain Cook's Journal, the extreme accuracy of
which, as in the generality of his observations, is verified by the subsequent
surveys of New Zealand by Captains Stokes, Drury, and Richards, 1848–55.

On the 18th, in the morning, the *Endeavour* steered between the main and an island, which seemed very fertile, and as extensive as Ulietea. Many canoes, filled with Indians, came alongside, and the Indians sung their war song; the *Endeavour*'s people paying them no attention, they threw a volley of stones, and then paddled away, but they presently returned and renewed their insults. However, upon a musket being fired at one of their boats, they made a precipitate retreat.

In the evening they cast anchor, and early the next morning they sailed up an inlet. The *Endeavour* was now in a bay, called by the natives Ooahaouragee, and Captain Cook, accompanied by Mr Banks, Dr Solander, and others, went in the boats to examine it, and did not return till next morning. At the entrance of a wood they met with a tree ninety-eight feet high from the ground to the first branch, quite straight, and nineteen feet in circumference; and they found still larger trees of the same kind as they advanced into the wood. The captain called this river Thames, being not unlike our river of that name.

The ship, at their departure, was surrounded with canoes, which induced Mr Banks to remain on board, that he might trade with the Indians. Though the traders were honest in their dealing, there was one amongst them who took a fancy to a half-minute glass, but was detected in secreting it, and he was punished with the cat-o'-nine tails. The other Indians endeavoured to save him from this punishment; but being opposed, they got their arms from the canoes, and some of the people in them attempted to get on board. Mr Banks and Tupia now coming upon deck, the Indians applied to Tupia, but he having no influence upon Mr Hicks, the commanding officer, informed them of the nature of the offender's intended punishment, which pacified them, as they imagined he was going to be put to death.

On the 23rd, they tided it down the river, and on the 24th steered along the shore, between the islands and the main, and in the evening anchored in an open bay, in about fourteen fathoms water. Here they caught a large number of fish of the bream kind; from which the captain named this Bream Bay. No inhabitants were visible: but from the fires perceived at night, the gentlemen concluded it was inhabited.

The 26th, Captain Cook continued his course slowly along the shore, to the north. This day two canoes came up, and some of the Indians came on board, when they trafficked very fairly. Two larger canoes soon after followed them, and coming up to the ship, the people in them hailed the others, when they conferred together, and afterwards came alongside of the ship. The last two canoes were finely ornamented with carving, and the people, who appeared to be of higher rank, were armed with various weapons; they held in high estimation their patoo patoos, which were made of stone and whalebone, and they had ribs of whale, with ornaments of dog's hair, which were very curious.

The *Endeavour* passed a remarkable point of land, which the captain called Cape Bret, in honour of the baronet of that name. Within a mile to the north-east by north is a curious rocky island; it is arched, and has a pleasing effect at a distance. The natives call this Cape Motugogogo; it forms a bay to the west, which contains many small islands, and Captain Cook named the point at the north-west entrance Point Pococke. The inhabitants had the same propensity for cheating as the others. One of the midshipmen was so nettled at being imposed upon, that he had recourse to a whimsical expedient by way of revenge; taking a fishing line, he threw the lead with so much dexterity that the hook caught the Indian who had imposed upon him by the buttocks, when the line breaking, the hook remained there. These Indians were strong and well-proportioned; their hair was black, and tied up in a bunch, stuck with feathers; the chiefs among them had garments made of fine cloth, ornamented with dog's skin; and they were also tattooed.

On the 27th, the *Endeavour* was among a number of small islands, from which several canoes came off; but the Indians, from their frantic gestures, seemed disordered in their minds; they threw their fish into the ship by handfuls, without demanding anything by way of barter. Some other canoes also came up, who saluted the ship with stones. It was then judged time to bring them to reason; and a musket, with small shot, being fired, a general terror was now spread amongst them, and they all made a precipitate retreat. Among the fish obtained from these canoes were cavelles in great plenty, and for this reason the captain called these islands by the same name.

For several days the wind was so unfavourable, that the vessel rather lost than gained ground. On the 29th, they got into a large bay, where they anchored on the south-west side of several islands; after which the ship was surrounded by thirty-three large canoes, containing nearly three hundred Indians, all armed. Some of them were admitted on board; and Captain Cook gave a piece of broad cloth to one of the chiefs, and some small presents to the others. They traded peaceably for some time, being terrified at the fire-arms, the effect of which they were not unacquainted with; but whilst the captain was at dinner, on a signal given by one of their chiefs, all the Indians quitted the ship, and they attempted to tow away the buoy. A musket was now fired over them, but it produced no effect; small shot was then fired at them, but it did not reach them. A musket loaded with ball was, therefore, ordered to be fired, and the son of one of the chiefs was wounded in the thigh, which induced them immediately to throw the buoy overboard. If these Indians had been under any kind of military discipline, they might have proved a much more formidable enemy; but acting thus, without any plan or regulation, they only exposed themselves to the annoyance of firearms, whilst they could not possibly succeed in any of their designs.

Captain Cook, Mr Banks, and Dr Solander landed upon the island. The gentlemen were now in a small cove, and were presently surrounded by near four hundred armed Indians; but the captain, not suspecting any hostile design on the part of the natives, remained peaceably disposed. The gentlemen marching towards them drew a line, intimating that they were not to pass it; they did not infringe upon this boundary for some time, but at length sung the song of defiance, and began to dance, whilst a party attempted to draw the *Endeavour*'s boats on shore. These signals for an attack being immediately followed by the Indians breaking in upon the line, the gentlemen judged it time to defend themselves, and accordingly the captain fired his musket, loaded with small shot (not with ball), which was seconded by Mr Banks discharging his piece, and two of the men followed his example. This threw the Indians into great confusion, and they retreated; but were rallied again by one of their chiefs, who shouted and waved his patoo patoo. The Doctor now pointed his musket at this hero, and hit him: this stopped his career, and he took to flight with the other Indians. They retired to an eminence in a collective body, and seemed dubious whether they should return to the charge. The

Indians had in this skirmish two of their people wounded, but none killed. Peace being again restored, the gentlemen began to gather celery and other herbs; but suspecting some of the natives were lurking about with evil designs, they repaired to a cave, which was at a small distance; here they found the chief, who had that day received a present from the captain; he came forth with his wife and brother, and solicited their clemency. It appeared that one of the wounded Indians was a brother of this chief, who was under great anxiety lest the wound should prove mortal; but his grief was in a great degree alleviated when he was made acquainted with the different effects of small shot and ball; he was at the same time assured, that upon any future hostilities being committed, ball would be used. This interview terminated very cordially, after some trifling presents were made to the chief and his companions.

The prudence of the gentlemen upon this occasion cannot be much commended. Had these four hundred Indians boldly rushed in upon them at once with their weapons, the musketry could have done very little execution; but supposing twenty or thirty of the Indians had been wounded, for it does not appear their pieces were loaded with ball, but only small shot, there would have remained a sufficient number to have massacred them, as it appears they do not give any quarter, and none could have been expected upon this occasion.

Being again in their boats, they rowed to another part of the same island, when, landing and gaining an eminence, they had an agreeable and romantic view of a great number of islands, well inhabited and cultivated. The inhabitants of an adjacent town approached unarmed, and testified great humility and submission. Some of the party on shore, who had been very violent for having the Indians punished for their fraudulent conduct, were now guilty of trespasses equally reprehensible, having forced into some of the plantations and dug up potatoes. Captain Cook upon this occasion showed, as he always did, strict justice, in punishing each of the offenders with twelve lashes. One of them being very refractory upon the occasion, and complaining of the hardship, thinking an Englishman had a right to plunder an Indian with impunity, was flogged out of his opinion with six additional lashes. Probably his adding, 'that in this he had only followed the example of his superiors', might have had no little weight in procuring him this last sentence.

On Tuesday the 5th, in the morning, they weighed anchor, but were soon becalmed, and a strong current setting towards the shore, they were driven in with such rapidity, that they expected every moment to run upon the breakers, which appeared above water not more than a cable's length distance; they were so near the land, that Tupia, who was totally ignorant of the danger, held a conversation with the Indians, who were standing on the beach. They were happily relieved, however, from this alarming situation by a fresh breeze suddenly springing up from the shore.

December 7th, several canoes put off and followed the *Endeavour*, but a breeze arising, Captain Cook did not wait for them. They beat to windward four days, and made but little way. On the 10th, the land appeared low and barren, but was not destitute of inhabitants; the next morning they stood in with the land, which forms a peninsula, and which the captain named Knuckle Point. On the 16th they came off the northern extremity of New Zealand, which Captain Cook called North Cape. Their situation varied but little till the 24th, when they discovered land, which they judged to be the islands of the Three Kings, though they did not resemble the description of them in Dalrymple's account.

January 1, 1770, they tacked and stood to eastward, and on the 3rd they saw land again; it was high and flat, and tended away to the south-east, beyond the reach of the naked eye. It is remarkable that the *Endeavour* was three weeks in making ten leagues to the westward.

On the 9th they saw a point remarkably high to the east-north-east; the captain named it Albatross Point. At about two leagues' distance from this point, to the north-east, they discovered a remarkable high mountain, equal in height to that of Tenerife, the summit of which was covered with snow, and it was named Mount Egmont.[1] The Captain proposed careening the ship here, and taking in wood and water; and accordingly, on the 15th, steered for an inlet. Four canoes came from shore to visit the ship, but none of the Indians would venture on board, except an old man, who

1 'At 5 a.m., on the 13th, saw for a few minutes the top of the peaked mountain above the clouds, bearing N.E. It is of a prodigious height, and its top is covered with everlasting snow. It is in the latitude of 39° 16' S., and longitude 185° 15' W.' – Extract Captain Cook's Journal, Records, Admiralty, Whitehall, p. 180.

seemed of elevated rank; he was received with the utmost hospitality. The Captain and the other gentlemen now went on shore, where they met with plenty of wood and water, and were very successful in fishing; catching some hundredweight in a short time.

On the 16th the *Endeavour*'s people were engaged in careening her, when three canoes came off with a great number of Indians, and brought several of their women with them. This circumstance was judged a favourable presage of their peaceable disposition, but they soon gave proofs of the contrary, by attempting to stop the longboat that was sent on shore for water, when Captain Cook had recourse to the old expedient of firing some shot, which intimidated them for the present.

Tupia in conversing with them, and making many inquiries concerning the curiosities of New Zealand, asked them if they had ever before seen a ship of the magnitude of the *Endeavour*; to which they replied they had never seen such a vessel, nor ever heard that one had been upon the coast. There is great plenty of fish in all the coves of this bay. The inhabitants catch their fish as follows: their net is cylindrical, extended by several hoops at the bottom, and contracted at the top; the fish, going in to feed upon what is put in the net, are caught in great abundance. There are also birds of various kinds, and in large numbers, particularly parrots, wood pigeons, water hens, hawks, and many different singing birds. An herb, a species of philadelphus, was used here instead of tea; and a plant, called *teegoomme*, resembling rug cloaks, served the natives for garments. The environs of the cove where the *Endeavour* lay are covered entirely with wood. The air of the country is very moist, and has some qualities that promote putrefaction; as birds that had been shot but a few hours were found with maggots in them.

Captain Cook, Mr Banks, and the Doctor visited a cove, about two miles from the ship. There was a family of Indians, who appeared greatly alarmed at their approach. They found by their provisions that they were cannibals, there being several human bones that had lately been dressed and picked. They made no secret of this fearful custom, but answered Tupia, who was desired to ascertain the fact, with much composure. His conjectures, they said, were just, that they were the bones of a man, and testified by signs that they thought human flesh delicious food; but that they never ate any save their enemies. There was a woman in this family whose arms and legs were cut in a shocking manner, and it appeared she had thus wounded herself, because her husband had lately been killed and eaten by the enemy.[1]

Some of the Indians brought four skulls to sell, which they rated at a high price. The gentlemen likewise saw the bail of a canoe, which was made of a human skull. In a word, their ideas were so horrid and brutal, that they seemed to pride themselves upon their cruelty and barbarity, and took a peculiar pleasure in showing the manner in which they killed their enemies, it being considered meritorious to be expert at this destruction. The method was to knock them down with their patoo patoos, and then rip up their bellies.

An amazing number of birds usually began their melody about two o'clock in the morning. This harmony was very agreeable, as the ship lay at a convenient distance from the shore to hear it. These feathered choristers never sing in the day time.

Some of the company in their excursion met with fortifications that had not the advantage of an elevated situation, but were surrounded by two or three wide ditches, with a drawbridge, which though simple in its structure, was capable of answering every purpose against the arms of the natives.

On the 24th they visited a hippah, which was situated on a high rock, hollow underneath, forming a fine natural arch, one side of which joined to the land, and the other rose out of the sea. This hippah was partly surrounded with a palisade. Here they met with a cross resembling a crucifix, which was ornamented with feathers, and which was erected as a monument for a deceased person; but they could not learn how his body was disposed of.

Some of the people who had been sent out to gather celery, met with several natives, among whom were some women, whose husbands had lately fallen into the hands of the enemy, and they were cutting many parts of their body in the most shocking manner with sharp stones, in testimony of their excessive grief. What made this ceremony appear ridiculous, as well as shocking, was that the male Indians, who were with them, paid not the least

---

1 'Mr Banks got from one of them a bone of the forearm. To show us that they had ate the flesh, they bit and gnawed the bone, and drew it through their mouth, and this in such a manner that plainly showed that the flesh to them was a dainty bit.' – Extract, Captain Cook's Journal, Records, Admiralty, Whitehall, p. 182.

attention to it, but, with the greatest unconcern imaginable, employed themselves in repairing some empty huts upon the spot.

On the 30th, two posts were erected, inscribed with the ship's name, etc., as usual; one was placed at the watering place, with the Union flag upon it, and the other, in the same manner, on the island of Motuara; and the inhabitants being informed that these posts were meant as memorials of the *Endeavour* having touched at this place, promised never to destroy them. The Captain then named this inlet Queen Charlotte's Sound, and took possession of it in the name, and for the use of his majesty, and a bottle of wine was drank to the queen's health.

On the 6th February, in the morning, the *Endeavour* sailed out of the bay, which the ship's company, from an abhorrence of the brutal custom that prevails here of eating men, called Cannibal Bay. The natives about this sound are not above four hundred in number; they are scattered along the coast, and live upon fern-root and fish; the latter of which was the only commodity they traded in.

The *Endeavour* having left the sound, steered eastward, and about six o'clock in the evening they were greatly alarmed at being carried, by the rapidity of the current, very close to one of the two islands which lie off Cape Koamaroo, at the entrance of the sound. The ship was in such imminent danger, that they expected, every minute, she would be dashed to pieces; but letting go an anchor, and veering one hundred and sixty fathoms of cable, she was brought up, when they were not above two cables length from the rocks; in this situation they were obliged to wait for the ebb of the tide, which was not till after midnight. At three o'clock in the morning they weighed anchor, and a fine breeze springing up soon after, they were carried through the strait with great velocity. At the entrance of the strait, on the north side, there is a small island, which was named Entry Island.

On the 8th, they were off Cape Palliser, when they discovered that the land trended to the north-east towards Cape Turnagain. Three canoes came off in the afternoon, with several people in them; they made a good appearance, and came on board with great alacrity. One old man was tattooed in a very remarkable manner; he was likewise marked with a streak of red paint across the nose, and over both cheeks; his hair was quite white, as well as his beard.

His garment was made of flax with a wrought border, under which was a kind of petticoat, made of cloth; his ears were decorated with teeth and pieces of green stone.

On the 14th of February, about sixty Indians, in four double canoes, came within a stone's cast of the ship, which they beheld with surprise. Tupia endeavoured to persuade them to approach nearer, but they refused, and made toward the shore. They had various winds and seas till the 4th of March, when they saw several whales and seals. On the 9th they saw a ledge of rocks, and soon afterwards another ledge, three leagues from the shore, which they passed to the north during the night, and discovered the others under their bow at daybreak. Thus they had a narrow escape from destruction.

In the morning they sailed northward, and on the day following, discovered a barren rock, about a mile in circumference, very high, and five leagues from the mainland. This was called Solander's Island. On the 13th they discovered a bay, which contains several islands, behind which, if there be depth of water, there must be shelter from all winds. Captain Cook called this Dusky Bay.

They had now almost passed the whole of the north-west coast of Tovy Poenammoo; the face of the country afforded nothing worth notice, but a ridge of rocks of a stupendous height, which Dr Hawkesworth describes as 'totally barren and naked, except where they are covered with snow, which is to be seen in large patches in many parts of them, and has probably lain there ever since the creation of the world; a prospect more rude, craggy, and desolate, than this country affords from the sea, cannot possibly be conceived; for as far inland as the eye can reach, nothing appears but the summits of rocks, which stand so near together, that, instead of valleys, there are only fissures between them.'

By the 27th they had sailed round the whole country, and determined to depart from the coast as soon as they had taken in a stock of water. For this purpose Captain Cook went ashore in the longboat, and found an excellent watering-place, and a proper berth for the ship. A council of the officers was now held, as to the passage they should take to England, when it was resolved to return by the East Indies; and, with that view, to steer for the east coast of New Holland, and then follow the direction of that coast to the northward.

This resolution being made, they sailed at daybreak, on March 31, 1770, and taking their departure from an eastern point, which they had seen on the 23rd, they called it Cape Farewell.

Abel Jansen Tasman, a Dutchman, was the first European that made a discovery of New Zealand, to which he gave the name of Staaten Land; that is, the land of the States General. Tasman never went on shore, as the Indians attacked him soon after he came to an anchor, in the bay to which he gave the name of Murderers Bay; this was in December 1642.

The situation of these islands, as observed by Captain Cook, is between 34° and 48° of south latitude, and 181° and 194° of west longitude. The natives call the northern island Eaheinomauwe, and the southernmost Tovy Poenammoo.

Eaheinomauwe, though hilly, and in some places mountainous, is well stored with wood, and there is a rivulet in every valley. The soil of the valleys is light, but is so fertile, as to be well adapted for the plentiful production of all sorts of the fruits, plants, and corn of Europe.

Dogs and rats are the only quadrupeds that were seen, and of the latter only a few. The inhabitants breed the dogs for the sole purpose of eating them. The birds are hawks, owls, quails; and there are song-birds, whose note is wonderfully melodious.

Tovy Poenammoo appears to be a barren country, very mountainous, and almost destitute of inhabitants.

The sea which washes these islands abounds with fish, which are equally delicate and wholesome food. They seldom came to anchor but caught enough, with hook and line only, to supply the whole ship's company.

This country abounds with forests, filled with large, straight, and clean timber. Upwards of four hundred species of plants were found, almost all of which are unknown in England. There is only one shrub or tree in this country which produces fruit, a kind of berry almost tasteless; but they have a plant which answers all the uses of hemp and flax. There are two kinds of this plant, the leaves of one of which are yellow, and the other a deep red. Of these leaves they make lines and cordage, much stronger than anything of the kind in Europe.

The men are as large as the largest Europeans. Their complexion is brown, but little more so than that of a Spaniard. They are full of flesh, but not lazy and luxurious; and are stout and well shaped. The women do not possess that delicacy which distinguishes European ladies; but their voice is singularly soft, which, as the dress of both sexes is similar, chiefly distinguishes them from the men.

The inhabitants of New Zealand are as modest and reserved in their behaviour and conversation as the most polite nations of Europe.

These Indians anoint their hair with oil, melted from the fat of fish or birds. Both sexes, but the men more than the women, mark their bodies with black stains, called *amoco*. Exclusive of the *amoco*, they mark themselves with furrows. These furrows make a hideous appearance, the edges being indented, and the whole quite black. The paintings on their bodies resemble filigree work, and the foliage in old chased ornaments; but no two are painted exactly after the same model.

Their dress is formed of leaves split into slips, which are interwoven, and made into a kind of matting. One piece of this matting being tied over the shoulders, reaches to the knees; the other piece being wrapped round the waist, falls almost to the ground.

The women never tie their hair on the top of their head, nor adorn it with feathers; and are less anxious about dress than the men. Their lower garment is bound tight round them, except when they go fishing, and then they are careful that the men shall not see them.

The ears of both sexes are bored, and the holes stretched so as to admit a man's finger. The ornaments of their ears are feathers, cloth, bones, and sometimes bits of wood. The men wear a piece of green talc, or whalebone, with the resemblance of a man carved on it, hanging to a string round the neck. One man had the gristle of his nose perforated, and a feather being passed through it, projected over each cheek.

These people show less ingenuity in the structure of their houses, than in anything else belonging to them; they are from sixteen to twenty-four feet long, ten or twelve wide, and six or eight in height. The frame is of slight sticks of wood, and the walls and roof are made of dry grass, pretty firmly compacted. Some of them are lined with the bark of trees, and the ridge of the house is formed by a pole, which runs from one end to the other. The door is only high enough to admit a person crawling on hands and knees, and the roof is sloping. There is a square hole near the door, serving both for window and chimney, near which is the fire-place.

The canoes of this country are not unlike the whale-boats of New England, being long and narrow. The larger sort seem to be built for war, and will hold from thirty to one hundred men. One of these at Tolaga was found to measure near seventy feet in length, six in width, and four in depth.

They are rowed with a kind of paddles, between five and six feet in length, the blade of which is a long oval, gradually decreasing till it reaches the handle; and the velocity with which they row is really surprising. The vessels are steered by two men, each having a paddle, and sitting in the stern; but they can only sail before the wind, in which direction, however, they move with considerable swiftness.

These Indians use axes, adzes, and chisels, with which last they likewise bore holes. The chisels are made of jasper, or of the bone of a man's arm; and their axes and adzes of a hard black stone.

Their warlike weapons are spears, darts, battle-axes, and the patoo patoo. The spear, which is pointed at each end, is about sixteen feet in length, and they hold it in the middle, which renders it difficult to parry a push from it. Whether they fight in boats or on shore, the battle is hand to hand, so that they must make bloody work of it.

When they came to attack the English, there was usually one or more thus distinguished in each canoe. It was their custom to stop at about fifty or sixty yards' distance from the ship, when the commanding officer, arising from his seat, and putting on a garment of dog's skin, used to direct them how to proceed.

In the war-dance their motions are numerous, their limbs distorted, and their faces are agitated. Their tongue hangs out of their mouths to a vast length, and their eyelids are drawn so as to form a circle round the eye; they shake their darts, brandish their spears, and wave their patoo patoos to and fro in the air. They accompany this dance with a song, which is sung in concert; every strain ending with a loud and deep sigh. There is an activity and vigour in their dancing, which is truly admirable; and their idea of keeping time in music is such, that sixty or eighty paddles will strike at once against the sides of their boats, and make only one report.

With regard to religion, they acknowledge one superior being, and several subordinate. Their mode of worship could not be learned, nor was any place proper for that purpose seen.

A great similitude was observed between the dress, furniture, boats, and nets of the New Zealanders, and those of the inhabitants of the South Sea islands, which furnished a strong proof, that the common ancestors of both were natives of the same country. Indeed, the inhabitants of these different places have a tradition, that their ancestors migrated from another country many ages since; and they both agree, that this country was called Heawige. But perhaps a yet stronger proof that their origin was the same, arises from the similitude of their language, which appears to be only different dialects.

They sailed from Cape Farewell on the 31st of March 1770, and had fine weather and a fair wind till the 9th of April, when they saw a tropic bird. On the 16th a small land-bird perched on the rigging, from which they concluded they were near land; but found no ground with one hundred and twenty fathoms. At six o'clock in the morning of the 19th, they discovered land four or five leagues distant; the southernmost part of which was called Point Hicks, in compliment to the first lieutenant. At noon they discovered another point of the same land, rising in a round hillock, extremely like the Ram Head at the entrance of Plymouth Sound, for which reason Captain Cook gave it the same name. What they had yet seen of the land was low and even; and the inland parts were green, and covered with wood. They now saw three waterspouts at the same time, one of which continued a quarter of an hour.

On the 27th they saw several of the inhabitants walking along the shore, four of them carrying a canoe on their shoulders; but as they did not attempt coming off to the ship, the Captain took Messrs Banks and Solander and Tupia in the yawl, to that part of the shore where the natives appeared, near which four small canoes laid close inland. The Indians sat on the rocks till the yawl was within a quarter of a mile of the shore, and then ran away into the woods. The surf beating violently on the beach, prevented the boat from landing.

At five in the evening they returned to the ship, and a light breeze springing up, they sailed to the northward, where they discovered several people on shore. They brandished their weapons, and threw themselves into threatening attitudes. They talked to each other with great emotion and each of them held a kind of scimitar in his hand.

They anchored opposite a village of about eight houses, and observed an old woman and three children come out of a wood, laden with fuel: all of them were quite naked. The old woman frequently looked at the ship with the utmost indifference, and, as soon as she had made a fire, they set about dressing their dinner with perfect composure.

Having formed a design of landing, the boats were manned; and they had no sooner come near the shore, than two men advanced, as if to dispute their setting foot on land. Captain Cook threw them beads, nails, and other trifles, which they took up and seemed to be delighted with. He then made signs that he wanted water, and used every possible means to convince them that no injury was intended. They now made signs to the boat's crew to land, on which they put the boat in; but they had no sooner done so, than the two Indians came again to oppose them. A musket was now fired between them, on the report of which one of them dropped a bundle of lances, which he instantly snatched up again. One of them then threw a stone at the boat, on which Captain Cook ordered a musket, loaded with small shot, to be fired, which wounded the eldest of them on the legs; he retired with speed. The people in the boats now landed, imagining that the wound which this man had received would put an end to the contest; in this, however, they were mistaken, for he immediately returned with a kind of shield, and advancing with great intrepidity, they both discharged their lances at the boat's crew, but did not wound any of them. Another musket was now fired at them; on which they threw another lance, and then took to their heels. The crew now went up to the huts, in one of which they found the children, who had secreted themselves behind some bark. Here they left some pieces of cloth, ribbons, beads, and other things; and taking several of the lances, re-embarked in the boat.

They now sailed to the north point of the bay, where they found plenty of fresh water. Some men having been sent to get wood and water, they no sooner came on board to dinner, than the natives came down to the place, and examined the casks with great attention, but did not offer to remove them.

On Tuesday, May the 1st, the south point of the bay was named

Sutherland Point, one of the seamen, of the name of Sutherland, having died that day, and been buried on shore. This day Captain Cook, Messrs Banks, Solander, and a few other gentlemen, went on shore, and left more presents in the huts, such as looking-glasses, combs, etc., but the former presents had not been taken away. The second lieutenant, Mr Gore, having been with a boat to dredge for oysters saw some Indians, who made signs for him to come on shore, which he declined. Having finished his business he sent the boat away, and went by land with a midshipman, to join the party that was getting water. In their way they met with more than twenty of the natives, who followed them so close as to come within a few yards of them. Mr Gore stopped and faced them; on which the Indians stopped also, and when he proceeded again they followed him; but they did not attack him, though they had each man his lance. The Indians coming in sight of the waterers, stood still at the distance of a quarter of a mile, while Mr Gore and his companion reached their shipmates in safety.

Tupia, having learnt to shoot, frequently strayed alone to shoot parrots, and the Indians constantly fled from him with as much precipitation as from the English.

They fished with great success here, and the second lieutenant struck what is called the sting-ray, which weighed near two hundred and fifty pounds. Soon after a fish of the same kind was caught, which weighed three hundred and fifty pounds.

While Captain Cook remained in the harbour, the English colours were displayed on shore daily, and the name of the ship, with the date of the year, was carved on a tree near the place where they took in their water.

They sailed from Botany Bay, as Captain Cook had named this place, on the 6th of May, 1770; at noon were off a harbour, which they called Port Jackson, and in the evening near a bay, to which they gave the name of Broken Bay. On the 13th, they saw the smoke of many fires on a point of land, which was therefore called Smoky Cape. As they proceeded northward from Botany Bay, the land appeared high and well covered with wood. Two days after, the captain discovered a high point of land, which he called Cape Byron.

They had, for some days past, seen the sea-birds, called boobies, which, from half an hour before sunrising, to half an hour after, were continually passing the ship in large flights; from which it was conjectured that there was a river or inlet of shallow water to the southward, where they went to feed in the day, returning in the evening to some islands to the northward. In honour of Captain Hervey, this bay was called Hervey's Bay.

The Captain and Tupia, with a party, went on shore the 23rd. They landed a little within the point of a bay, which led into a large lagoon, by the sides of which grows the true mangrove. There were many nests of a singular kind of ant, as green as grass, in the branches of these mangroves, which likewise afforded shelter for immense numbers of green caterpillars – their bodies were covered with hairs, which, on the touch, gave a pain similar to the sting of a nettle, but much more acute. They saw, among the sand-banks, many birds larger than swans, which they imagined were pelicans; and they shot a kind of bustard, which weighed seventeen pounds. This bird proved very delicate food, and gave name to the place, which was called Bustard Bay. They likewise shot a duck of a most beautiful plumage, with a white beak. They found vast numbers of oysters of various sorts, and, among the rest, some hammer oysters of a curious kind. While they were in the woods, several of the natives came down and took a survey of the ship, and then departed. They sailed the next morning, and on the day following were abreast of a point, which lying immediately under the tropic, the captain called Cape Capricorn, on the west side of which they saw an amazing number of birds resembling the pelican, some of which were near five feet high.

On the 27th, in the morning, they sailed to the northward, and to the northernmost point of land Captain Cook gave the name of Cape Manifold, from the number of high hills appearing above it. Between this cape and the shore is a bay called Keppel's Bay, and some islands bearing the same name. In this place the Captain intended to lay the ship ashore and clean her bottom; and accordingly landed, in search of a proper place for the purpose. They found walking extremely incommodious, the ground being covered with grass, the seeds of which were sharp and bearded. They were likewise tormented with the perpetual stinging of mosquitoes. In the interior parts of the country they found gum-trees, on the branches of which were white ants' nests formed of clay, as big as a bushel. On another tree they found black ants, which formed their lodging in the body of it, after they had eaten away the pith; yet the trees were in a flourishing condition. They found butterflies in such incredible numbers, that whichever way they looked, many thousands were to be seen in the air; while every bough and twig was covered with multitudes. They likewise discovered on dry ground, where it was supposed to have been left by the tide, a fish about the size of a minnow, having two strong breast fins, with which it leaped away as nimbly as a frog. There being no good water to be found here they did not lay the ship ashore, as they intended.

After passing Cape Cleveland, they ranged northward along the shore, towards a cluster of islands, on one of which about forty men, women, and children were standing together and looking at the ship with a curiosity never observed among these people before. Here Messrs Banks and Solander went on shore with Captain Cook, whose chief view was to procure water, which not being easily to be got, they soon returned on board, and the next day arrived near Trinity Bay, so called, because it was discovered on Trinity Sunday. As no accident of any moment had befallen our adventurers, during a navigation of more than 1300 miles, upon a coast everywhere abounding with the most dangerous rocks and shoals, no name expressive of distress had hitherto been given to any cape or point of land which they had seen. But they now gave the name of Cape Tribulation to a point which they had just discovered, as they here became acquainted with misfortune.[1] This cape is in 16° 6' south latitude, and 214° 39' west longitude.

To avoid the danger of some rocks, they shortened sail, and kept standing off from six o'clock in the evening till near nine, with a fine breeze, and bright moon. They had got from fourteen into twenty-one fathoms water, when suddenly they fell into twelve, ten, and eight fathoms, in a few minutes. Every man was instantly ordered to his station, and they were on the point of anchoring, when, on a sudden, they had again deep water, so that they thought all danger was at an end, concluding they had sailed over

1 'The shore between Cape Grafton and the northern point of land in sight forms a large but not very deep bay, which I named Trinity Bay, after the day on which it was discovered; the north point, Cape Tribulation, because here began all our troubles.' – Extract, Captain Cook's Journal, Records, Admiralty, Whitehall, p. 262.

the tail of some shoals which they had seen in the evening. In less than an hour, however, the water shallowed at once from twenty to seventeen fathoms; and, before soundings could be again taken, the ship struck against a rock, and remained fixed but from the motion given her from the beating of the surge. Everyone was instantly on deck, with countenances fully expressive of the agitation of their minds. As they knew they were not near the shore, they concluded they had struck against a rock of coral, the points of which being sharp, and the surface so rough, as to grind away whatever is rubbed against it, though with a gentle motion, they had reason to dread the horror of their situation.

The sails being taken in, and boats hoisted out to examine the depth of water, they found that the ship had been carried over a ledge of the rock, and lay in a hollow within it. She beat so violently that the crew could scarcely keep on their legs. The moon now shone bright, by the light of which they could see the sheathing boards float from the bottom of the vessel, till at length the false keel followed, so that they expected instant destruction. Their best chance of escaping seemed now to be by lightening her. They therefore instantly started the water in the hold, and pumped it up. The decayed stores, oil-jars, casks, ballast, six of their guns, and other things, were thrown overboard, in order to get at the heavier articles; and in this business they were employed till daybreak, during all which time it was observed that not an oath was sworn, so much were the minds of the sailors impressed with a sense of their danger.

At daylight they saw land at eight leagues' distance; but not a single island between them and the main; so that the destruction of the greater part of them would have been inevitable, had the ship gone to pieces. It happened, however, that the wind died away to a dead calm before noon. As they expected high water at eleven o'clock, everything was prepared to make another effort to free the ship; but the tide fell so much short of that in the night, that she did not float by eighteen inches, though they had thrown overboard near fifty tons weight; they now, therefore, renewed their toil, and threw overboard everything that could be possibly spared. As the tide fell, the water poured in so rapidly, that they could scarcely keep her free by the constant working of two pumps. Their only hope now depended on the midnight tide, and preparations were accordingly made for another effort to get the ship off. The tide began to rise at five o'clock, when the leak likewise increased to such a degree, that three pumps were kept going till nine o'clock, at which time the ship righted; but so much water had been admitted by the leak, that they expected she would sink as soon as the water should bear her off the rock.

Their situation was now deplorable beyond description, and the imagination must paint what would baffle the powers of language to describe. They knew that when the fatal moment should arrive, all authority would be at an end. The boats were incapable of conveying them all on shore, and they dreaded a contest for the preference, as more shocking than the shipwreck itself; yet, it was considered, that those who might be left on board, would eventually meet with a milder fate than those who, by gaining the shore, would have no chance but to linger the remains of life among the rudest savages in the universe, and in a country where firearms would barely enable them to support a wretched existence.

At twenty minutes after ten the ship floated, and was heaved into deep water; when they were happy to find she did not admit more water than she had done before; yet, as the leak had for a considerable time gained on the pumps, there was now three feet nine inches water in the hold. By this time the men were so worn by fatigue of mind and body, that none of them could pump more than five or six minutes at a time, and then threw themselves, quite spent, on the deck. The succeeding man being fatigued in his turn, threw himself down in the same manner, while the former jumped up and renewed his labour; thus mutually struggling for life, till the following accident had like to have given them up a prey to absolute despair.

Between the inside lining of the ship's bottom, and the outside planking, there is a space of about seventeen or eighteen inches. The man who had hitherto taken the depth of water at the well, had taken it no farther than the ceiling; but being now relieved by another person, who took the depth to the outside planking, it appeared by this mistake that the leak had suddenly gained upon the pumps, the whole difference between the two plankings. This circumstance deprived them of all hopes, and scarce anyone thought it worth while to labour for the longer preservation of a life which must so soon have a period. But the mistake was soon discovered; and the joy arising from such unexpected good news, inspired the men with so much vigour, that before eight o'clock in the morning, they had pumped out considerably more water than they had shipped. They now talked confidently of getting the ship into some harbour, and set heartily to work to get in their anchors; one of which, and the cable of another, they lost. Having a good breeze from the sea, they got under sail at eleven o'clock, and stood for the land.[1]

As they could not discover the exact situation of the leak, they had no prospect of stopping it within side of the vessel; but the following expedient, which one of the midshipmen had formerly seen tried with success, was adopted. They took an old studding-sail, and having mixed a large quantity of oakum and wool, chopped small, it was stitched down in handfuls on the sail, as light as possible; the dung of their sheep and other filth being spread over it. Thus prepared, the sail was hauled under the ship by ropes, which kept it extended till it came under the leak, when the suction carried in the oakum and wool from the surface of the sail. This experiment succeeded so well, that instead of three pumps, the water was easily kept under with one.

1 'Such are the vicissitudes attending this kind of service, and must always attend an unknown navigation, was it not for the pleasure which naturally results to a man from being the first discoverer; even was it nothing more than sand and shoals, this service would be insupportable, especially in far distant parts like this, short of provisions, and almost every other necessary. The world will hardly admit of an excuse for a man leaving a coast unexplored he has once discovered. If dangers are his excuse, he is then charged with timorousness and want of perseverance, and at once pronounced the unfittest man in the world to be employed as a discoverer. If, on the other hand, he boldly encounters all the dangers and obstacles he meets, and is unfortunate enough not to succeed, he is then charged with temerity and want of conduct. The former of these aspersions cannot with justice be laid to my charge; and if I am fortunate enough to surmount all the dangers we may meet, the latter will never be brought in question. I must own, I have engaged more among the islands and shoals upon this coast than may be thought with prudence I ought to have done, with a single ship, and everything considered; but if I had not, we should not have been able to give any better account of the one half of it, than if we had never seen it; that is, we should not have been able to say whether it consisted of main land or islands; and as to its produce, we must have been totally ignorant of, as being inseparable with the other.' – Extract, Captain Cook's Journal, Records, Admiralty, Whitehall, p. 291.

They hitherto had no further view than to run the ship into a harbour, and build a vessel from her materials in which they might reach the East Indies; but they now began to think of finding a proper place to repair her damage, and then to pursue their voyage on its original plan. At six in the evening they anchored seven leagues from the shore; and next morning they passed two islands, which were called Hope Islands. In the afternoon the master was sent out with two boats to sound, and search for a harbour where the ship might be repaired. They anchored at sunset in four fathoms, two miles from the shore. One of the mates being out in the pinnace, returned at nine o'clock, reporting that he had found just such a harbour as was wanted, at the distance of two leagues.

At six o'clock the next morning they sailed, and soon anchored about a mile from the shore, when the Captain went out and found the channel very narrow, but the harbour was better adapted to their present purpose than any place they had seen in the whole course of their voyage. As it blew very fresh this day and the following night, they could not venture to run into the harbour, but remained at anchor during the two succeeding days.

The men by this time began to be afflicted with the scurvy, and their Indian friend, Tupia, was so bad with it, that he had livid spots on both his legs. Mr Green, the astronomer, was likewise ill of the same disorder; so that their being detained from landing was every way disagreeable. The wind continued fresh till the 17th, but they then resolved to push in for the harbour, and, with some difficulty, moored the ship alongside of a beach.

Next morning they erected a tent for the sick, several of whom were brought on shore as soon as it was ready for their reception. They likewise built a tent to hold the provisions and stores, which were landed the same day. The boat was now despatched in search of fish for the refreshment of the sick, but she returned without getting any.

The Captain ordered the smith's forge to be set up, and directed the armourer to prepare the necessary iron work for the repair of the vessel. He likewise ordered out the officers' stores and water, in order to lighten the ship. Same day Mr Banks crossed the river to view the country, which was little else than sand-hills. He saw vast flocks of crows and pigeons, of the latter of which he shot several, which were most beautiful birds.

Early in the morning of the 22nd, the tide left the ship, and they proceeded to examine the leak, when they found that the rocks had cut through four planks into the timbers, and that three other planks were damaged. In these breaches, not a splinter was to be seen, the whole being smooth, as if cut away by an instrument: but the preservation of the vessel was owing to a very singular circumstance. One of the holes was large enough to have sunk her, even with eight pumps constantly at work; but this hole was, in a great measure, stopped up by the fragment of the rock being left sticking in it. They likewise found some pieces of oakum, wool, etc., which had got between the timbers, and stopped many parts of the leak, which had been left open by the stone. Exclusive of the leak, great damage was done to various parts of the ship's bottom.

While the smiths and carpenters were engaged, some of the crew were sent across the river to shoot pigeons for the sick. These people found a stream of fresh water, discovered many Indian houses, and had sight of a mouse-coloured animal, extremely swift, and about the size of a greyhound. Next day many of the crew saw the animal above-mentioned; and one of the seamen declared he had seen the devil, which he described in the following words: 'He was as large, says he, as a one gallon keg, and very like it; he had horns and wings, yet he crept so slowly through the grass, that if I had not been afeared, I might have touched him.' It appeared afterward that this poor fellow had seen a bat, which is almost black, and as large as a partridge; and his own apprehensions had furnished his devil with horns.

A midshipman saw a wolf exactly resembling those of America. Mr Gore also saw two straw-coloured animals, of the size of a hare, but shaped like a dog. So much fish was taken, that each man had two pounds and a half; and plenty of greens were gathered, which being boiled with the pease, their fare was deemed excellent.

Cockles were found by the master so large, that one of them was more than sufficient for two men; and likewise plenty of other shell fish, of which he brought a supply to the ship.

Mr Banks and a party made an excursion up a river, and saw several animals, one of which was judged to be a wolf. At night they made a fire, and took up their quarters on the banks of the river; but the night was rendered extremely disagreeable by the stings of the mosquitoes. At break of day they set out in search of game, and saw four animals, two of which were chased by Mr Banks's greyhound; but they greatly outstripped him in speed. It was observed of this animal, that he leaped or bounded forward on two legs, instead of running on four.

The tide favouring their return, they lost no time in getting back to the ship. The master, who had been seven leagues at sea, returned soon after, bringing with him three turtle, which he took with a boat-hook, and which, together, weighed near eight hundred pounds.

In the morning, four Indians, in a small canoe, were within sight. They soon came quite alongside the ship; and having received presents, landed where Tupia and a few sailors were on shore. They had each two lances, and a stick with which they throw them. Advancing towards the English, Tupia persuaded them to lay down their arms, and sit by him, which they readily did.

These men were of the common stature, with very small limbs; their complexion a deep chocolate; their hair black, either lank or curled, but not of the wool kind.

The visit of three of these Indians was renewed the next morning, and they brought with them a fourth, whom they called Yaparico, who appeared to be a person of some consequence. The bone of a bird, about six inches long, was thrust through the gristle of his nose; and, indeed, all the inhabitants of this place had their noses bored, for the reception of such an ornament. These people being quite naked, the Captain gave one of them an old shirt, which he bound round his head like a turban, instead of using it to cover any part of his body. The canoe was about ten feet long, and calculated to hold four persons; and when it was in shallow water, they moved it by means of poles.

On the 14th, Mr Gore shot one of the mouse-coloured animals above mentioned. The skin of this beast, which is called kangaroo, is covered with short fur; the head and ears are somewhat like those of a hare: this animal was dressed for dinner, and proved fine eating.

The natives being now become familiar with the ship's crew, one of them was desired to throw his lance, which he did with such dexterity and force, that though it was not above four feet from the ground, at the highest, it penetrated deeply into a tree at the distance of fifty yards. On the 19th, they saw several of the women, who, as well as the men, were quite naked. They were this day visited by ten of the natives, who seemed resolved to have one of the turtle that was on board, which being refused, they expressed the utmost rage and resentment. At length they laid hands on two of the turtles, and drew them to the side of the ship where the canoe lay; but the sailors took them away. They made several similar attempts, but being equally unsuccessful they leaped suddenly into their canoe, and rowed off. At this instant the Captain with Mr Banks and five or six seamen, went ashore, where they arrived before the Indians. As soon as the Indians landed, one of them snatched a firebrand from under a pitch-kettle, and running to the windward of what effects were on shore, set fire to the dry grass, which burnt rapidly, damaged the smith's forge, and endangered one of the tents. Appearing determined on farther mischief, a musket loaded with small shot was now fired, and one of them being wounded, they ran off.

The natives continuing still in sight, a musket charged with ball was fired near them: upon hearing which they soon got out of sight: but their voices being soon heard in the woods, the Captain, with a few of the men, went to meet them. When they were in sight of each other, both parties stopped, except an old Indian, who advanced before the rest a little way, and speaking a few words, retreated to his brethren. The English having seized some of their darts, followed them about a mile, and then sat down; the Indians sitting about a hundred yards from them. The old man again came forward, having in his hand a lance with a point. He stopped and spoke several times; on which the Captain made signs of friendship. The old Indian now turned to his companions, and having spoken to them, they placed their lances against a tree, and came forward as in friendship; whereupon their darts, which had been taken, were returned and the whole quarrel seemed to be at an end. When Captain Cook got on board, he saw the woods burning at the distance of two miles from the fire thus kindled by the natives.

The master having been sent to search for a passage to the northward, returned with an account that he could not find any. By the night of the 20th, the fire had extended many miles round them on the hills. The next day one of the seamen, who had strayed from his company, met with four Indians at dinner; he was alarmed at this unexpected meeting, but had prudence enough to conceal his apprehensions, and sitting down by them, gave them his knife, which having all looked at, they returned. He would then have left them; but they chose to detain him, till, by feeling his hands and face, they were convinced he was made of flesh and blood like themselves. They then dismissed him, directing him the nearest way to the ship.

On the 4th of August they put to sea, and at noon came to an anchor, when the Captain gave the name of Cape Bedford to the northernmost point of land in sight, and that of Endeavour River to the harbour which they had quitted. The provisions they obtained, while in this harbour, consisted of turtle, oysters of three different sorts, large cavalhe or scomber, large mullets, some flat fish, a great number of small scombri, and skate or ray-fish; purslain, wild beans, the tops of cocoas, and cabbage palms. Of quadrupeds there are goats, wolves, and polecats, and a spotted animal of the viverra kind. Dogs are the only tame animals.

During the six following days, they struggled incessantly to sail safely past the shoals and breakers, by which they were every way surrounded. After a conversation held among the officers, it was their concurrent opinion, that it would be best to leave the coast, and stand out to sea; and in consequence of these sentiments, they sailed on the 13th of August 1770, and got in an open sea, after having been surrounded by dreadful shoals and rocks for nearly three months. They had now sailed above a thousand miles, during all which run they had been obliged to keep sounding, without intermission; a circumstance which, it is supposed, never happened to any ship but the *Endeavour*. Captain Cook observes in his Journal that they were made 'quite easy at being freed from fears of shoals, etc., after having been entangled among them more or less ever since the 26th May, in which time they had sailed 360 leagues without ever having had a man out of the chains heaving the lead when the ship was under sail.'[1]

Having anchored on the 14th, they steered a westerly course on the following day, to get sight of the land, that a passage between that land and New Guinea might not be missed, if there was any

1 Captain Cook's Journal, p. 287 – Records, Admiralty, Whitehall.

such passage. They stood northward till midnight. When day-light came on, they saw a dreadful surf break at a vast height, within a mile of the ship, towards which the rolling waves carried her with great rapidity. Thus distressed, the boats were sent ahead to tow, and the head of the vessel was brought about, but not till she was within one hundred yards of the rock, between which and her there was nothing left but the chasm, made by the last wave which had washed her side. In the moment they expected instant destruction, a breeze, hardly discernible, aided the boats in getting the vessel in an oblique direction from the rock.

At this time a small opening was seen in the reef, and a young officer being sent to examine it, found that there was smooth water on the other side of the rocks. Animated by the hope of preserving life, they now attempted to pass the opening; but this was impossible; for it having become high water in the interim, the ebb tide rushed through it with amazing impetuosity, carrying the ship to a considerable distance from the reef. When the ebb tide was spent, the tide of flood again drove the vessel very near the rocks; so that their prospect of destruction was renewed, when they discovered another opening, and a light breeze springing up, they entered it, and were driven through it with a rapidity that prevented the ship from striking against either side of the channel.

The name Providential Channel was given to the opening through which the ship had thus escaped the most imminent dangers.[1] A high promontory on the main land, in sight, was denominated Cape Weymouth, and a bay near it Weymouth Bay. This day the boats went out to fish, and met with great success, particularly in catching cockles; some of which were of such an amazing size, as to require the strength of two men to move them.

On the 21st, several islands were discovered, which were called York Isles. In the afternoon they anchored between some islands, and observed that the channel now began to grow wider. They observed two distant points, between which no land could be seen; so that the hope of having at length explored a passage into the Indian Sea, began to animate every breast.

1 '. . . this truly terrible situation not one man ceased to do his utmost, and that with as much calmness as if no danger had been near.' – Extract, Captain Cook's Journal, Records, Admiralty, Whitehall, p. 289.

The Captain and his company now ascended a hill, upon one of these islands, from whence they had a view of near forty miles, in which space there was nothing that threatened to oppose their passage; so that the certainty of a channel seemed to be almost ascertained. Previous to their leaving the island, Captain Cook displayed the English colours, and took possession of all the eastern coast of the country, by the name of New South Wales, for his sovereign the King of Great Britain.

They were now advanced to the northern extremity of New Holland, and had the satisfaction of viewing the open sea to the westward. The north-east entrance of the passage is formed by the mainland of New Holland, and by a number of islands, which took the name of the Prince of Wales Islands, and which Captain Cook imagines may reach to New Guinea. To the passage which they had sailed through, Captain Cook gave the name of Endeavour Straits.

New South Wales was ascertained to be a much larger country than any hitherto known, not deemed a continent, being larger than all Europe; which was proved by the *Endeavour* having coasted more than two thousand miles, even if her track was reduced to a straight line. To the northward the grass is not so rich, nor the trees so high as in the southern parts; and almost everywhere, even the largest trees grow at a distance of not less than thirteen yards asunder.

The men were well made, of the middle size, and active in a high degree; but their voices were soft, even to effeminacy. Their colour is the chocolate; but they were so covered with dirt, as to look almost as black as negroes. The chief ornament of these people is the bone that is thrust through the nose, which the sailors whimsically termed their spirit-sail yard. Some few of them had an ornament of shells hanging across the breast. Besides these ornaments they painted their bodies and limbs white and red, in stripes of different dimensions; and they had a circle of white round each eye, and spots of it on the face.

Their huts were built with small rods, the two ends of which were fixed into the ground, so as to form the figure of an oven; they are covered with pieces of bark and palm leaves. The door of this building, which is only high enough to sit upright in, is opposite to the fire-place; they sleep with their heels turned up towards their heads, and even in this posture the hut will not hold more than four people.

They produce fire, and extend the flames in a very singular manner: they reduce one end of a stick into an obtuse point, they place this point upon a piece of dry wood, and turning the upright stick very fast backward and forward between their hands, the fire is soon produced. One of the natives was frequently observed to run along the sea coast, leaving fire in various places. These fires were supposed to be intended for the taking of the kangaroo, as that animal was so very shy of fire, that when forced by the dogs it would not cross places which had been newly burnt, even when the fire was extinguished. The same method of obtaining fire is common to the Esquimaux. It would be difficult to conjecture how each arrived at the same mode.

The points of their lances are sometimes made of fish bones, and sometimes of a hard, heavy wood; they are barbed with other pieces of wood or bone, so that when they have entered any depth into the body, they cannot be drawn out without tearing the flesh in a shocking manner, or leaving splinters behind them.

In the northern parts of this coast, the canoes are formed by hollowing out the trunk of a tree; and it was conjectured that this operation must have been performed by fire, as the natives did not appear to have any instrument proper for the purpose. The canoes are in length about fourteen feet, and so narrow that they would be frequently overset, but that they are provided with an outrigger. The natives row them with paddles, using both hands in that employment.

The short intercourse which the English gentlemen had with these people, prevented them from obtaining so perfect a know-ledge of the language of the natives as could have been wished. They articulated their words very distinctly; and frequently repeated the word 'tut', when in company with the English, several times together – which was supposed to be an expression of astonishment and admiration. Upon the whole, their language was neither harsh nor inharmonious.

The 24th of August 1770, the cable broke near the ring, in the attempt to weigh the anchor; on which another was dropped, which prevented the ship driving. The anchor was recovered the next morning.

Weighing on the 25th of August,[1] they steered north-west, and
in a few hours one of the boats, which was ahead, made the signal
for shoal water. The ship instantly brought to, with all her sails
standing. It was now found that she had met with another narrow
escape, as she was almost encompassed with shoals, and was
likewise so situated between them, that she must have struck
before the boat's crew had made the signal, if she had been half the
length of a cable on either side. In the afternoon she made sail with
the ebb tide, and got out of danger before sunset. The ship now
held a course due north, barely within sight of land, till the 3rd of
September; and as the water was but just deep enough to navigate
the vessel, many unsuccessful attempts were made to bring her near
enough to get on shore; it was therefore determined to land in one
of the boats, while the ship kept plying off and on. In consequence
of this resolution, the Captain, accompanied by Messrs Banks and
Solander, set out in the pinnace; but when they came within two
hundred yards of the shore, the water was so shallow, that they
were obliged to leave the boat to the care of two of the sailors, and
wade to land. They were no sooner clear of the water, than they
saw several prints of human feet on the sand.

Our adventurers were now near a quarter of a mile from the
pinnace, when three of the natives ran out of the woods, about one
hundred yards beyond them, shouting in the most violent manner.
They instantly ran towards our countrymen, the first of the three
throwing something out of his hand, which burnt like gunpowder,

1 Captain Cook makes the following observations on quitting New Holland:
'Having satisfied myself of the great probability of a passage, through which I
intend going with the ship, and therefore may land no more upon this eastern
coast of *New Holland*, and on the western side I can make no new discovery, the
honour of which belongs to the Dutch navigators, but the eastern coast, from the
latitude of 38°S., down to this place (Endeavour Straits), I am confident was
never seen or visited by any European before us; and notwithstanding I had, in
the name of His Majesty, taken possession of several places upon this coast, I now
once more hoisted English colours, and in the name of His Majesty King George
the Third, took possession of the whole eastern coast, from the above latitude
down to this place, by the name of New South Wales, together with all the bays,
harbours, rivers, and islands situate upon the said coast, upon which we fired
three volleys of small arms, which were answered by the like number from the
ship.' – Extract, Captain Cook's Journal, Records, Admiralty, Whitehall, p. 297.

but made no noise, while the other two threw their lances. The English now fired; when the natives stopped and cast another lance; on which the muskets were loaded with ball, and again fired. The poor Indians now ran off with expedition, having, most probably, been wounded in the unequal conflict.

Captain Cook and his companions, unwilling farther to injure those who could not originally have intended them any harm, retreated hastily to the boat, which they rowed abreast of the natives, who by this time were assembled to the number of about eighty. Their stature was nearly the same with that of the inhabitants of New South Wales, but their colour was not quite so dark.

The whole coast of this country is low land, but clothed with a richness of trees and herbage, which exceeds all description. On the 16th, they had sight of the little island called Rotte; and the same day saw the island Semau. At ten o'clock this night, a dull reddish light was seen in the air. This phenomenon, which reached about ten degrees above the horizon, bore a considerable resemblance to the Aurora Borealis, only that the rays of light which it emitted had no tremulous motion. It was surveyed for two hours, during which time its brightness continued undiminished.

As the ship was now clear of all the islands which had been laid down in such maps as were on board, they made sail during the night, and were surprised the next morning at the sight of an island to the west-south-west, which they flattered themselves was a new discovery. Before noon they had sight of houses, groves of coconut trees, and large flocks of sheep. This was a welcome sight to people whose health was declining for want of refreshments. The second lieutenant was immediately despatched in the pinnace, in search of a landing place; and he took with him such things as it was thought might be acceptable to the natives.

Two horsemen were seen from the ship, one of whom had a laced hat on, and was dressed in a coat and waistcoat of the fashion of Europe. These men rode about on shore, regarding the ship with the utmost attention. As soon as the boat reached the shore, some other persons on horseback, and many on foot, hastened to the spot, and it was observed that some coconuts were put into the boat. A signal being made from the boat, that the ship might anchor in a bay at some distance, which had been pointed out by the natives, she immediately bore away for it.

When the lieutenant came on board, he reported that he could not purchase any coconuts, as the owner of them was absent, and that what he had brought were given him: in return for which he had presented the natives with some linen.

He saw several of the principal inhabitants of the island, who wore chains of gold about their necks, and were dressed in fine linen.

In the evening, when the ship had entered the bay, to which they had been recommended, an Indian town was seen at a small distance, upon which a jack was hoisted on the fore-topmast-head. Presently afterwards three guns were fired, and Dutch colours were hoisted in the town. The ship, however, held on her way, and came to an anchor at seven in the evening.

The colours being seen hoisted on the beach the next morning, the captain concluded that the Dutch had a settlement on the island; he therefore despatched the second lieutenant to mention what necessaries they were in want of.

He was conducted to the raja, or king of the island, to whom, by means of a Portuguese interpreter, he made known his business. The raja said, he was ready to supply the ship with the necessary refreshments; but that he could not trade with any other people but the Dutch, without having first obtained their consent; but that he would make application to the Dutch agent, who was the only white man among them. This agent, whose name was Lange, behaved politely to the lieutenant, and told him, he might buy what he thought proper of the inhabitants of the island.

Immediately after, the raja and Mr Lange intimated their wishes to go on board the ship, and that two of the boat's crew might be left as hostages for their safe return; the lieutenant gratified both these requests, and took them on board just before dinner was served. The chief part of the dinner was mutton, which the raja having tasted, he begged an English sheep, and the only one which they had left was given him. He then asked for a dog, and Mr Banks gave him his greyhound; and a spying glass was presented to him, on Mr Lange's intimating that it would be acceptable.

The visitors now told Captain Cook, that there was great plenty of fowls, hogs, sheep, and buffaloes on the island, numbers of which should be conveyed to the seashore on the following day, that he might purchase what was necessary for the recovery of the sick, and for sea stores. This welcome news gave great spirits to the company; and the bottle went so briskly round, that Mr Lange and his companion became almost intoxicated. They had, however, the resolution to depart before they were quite drunk.

On the following day, the Captain attended by several gentlemen, went on shore, to return the raja's visit. When they landed, they were chagrined to find that the cattle had not been driven down to the beach. They, however, went on to the town.

They were invited to dine with the raja, but he did not partake of the entertainment, as it was not customary here to sit down with their guests. Their dinner consisted of pork and rice, very excellent of their kinds, served up in thirty-six dishes, and three earthen bowls, filled with a kind of broth, in which the pork had been boiled. The spoons were formed of leaves, but were so small, that the hunger of the guests would scarcely allow them patience to use them.

When dinner was ended, the Captain invited the raja to drink wine with him; but this he declined, saying, that the man who entertained company should never get drunk with his guests.

When the bottle had circulated some time, Captain Cook began to inquire after the cattle that were promised to be driven down to the beach; when Mr Lange informed him, that in a letter which he had received from the Governor of Concordia, in Timor, instructions were given, that if the ship should touch at the island, and be in want of provisions, she should be supplied; but that he was not to permit her to remain longer than was absolutely necessary. That no presents were to be made to the natives of low rank; but, he added, that any trifling civilities received from the Indians, might be acknowledged by a present of beads, or any other articles of small value. It is a very probable conjecture that the whole of this story was of Mr Lange's own manufacture, and solely calculated to draw all the presents of any value into his own pocket.

Soon after this the Captain was informed that some sheep had been driven down to the beach; but had been conveyed away before the men could get money from the ship to pay for them, and that not a single hog or buffalo had been produced. Heartily vexed to be thus disappointed of the chief articles which were wanted, the Captain remonstrated with Mr Lange, who told him, that if he and his officers had gone to the spot, they might have purchased anything they pleased; but that the Indians imagined the seamen would impose upon them with counterfeit money,

This story was no more credited than the former; but not to lose more time, in a case of such urgency, the Captain instantly repaired to the beach, but there were no cattle to be bought. During his absence, Lange informed Mr Banks that the Indians were offended that the seamen had not offered gold for what they had to sell, and that no other metal would purchase their commodities; but Mr Banks, disdaining to hold farther conversation with a man who had been guilty of such repeated subterfuges, left him abruptly.

On the 20th, Captain Cook and Dr Solander went again on shore, and while the latter proceeded to the town in search of Lange, the Captain stayed on the beach, with a view to buy cattle. At this place was an old man, who had been distinguished by the name of prime minister, because he appeared to be invested with considerable authority; and the Captain now presented him with a spying-glass, in order to make a friend of him. At present there was nothing brought for sale but a small buffalo, for which five guineas were demanded. Though the Captain knew that this was double its value, yet he bid three guineas, as he was willing to begin dealing at any rate. The person who had it to sell, said he could not take the money till the raja had been informed what was offered; on which a man was sent to him, who soon came back with a message, that five guineas would be the lowest price: this the Captain refused to give; on which a second messenger was despatched, who, staying a long time, Captain Cook was anxiously expecting his return, when he saw Dr Solander coming towards the beach, escorted by more than a hundred persons, some of whom had lances in their hands, and the rest were armed with muskets. When the Doctor arrived at the marketing place, he informed the Captain that Lange had interpreted to him a message from the raja, the substance of which was, that the natives were averse to all traffic with the English, because they would not give above half the real worth of the things which were offered for sale; and that all trading whatever should be prohibited after that day.

The English gentlemen had no doubt but that the supposed order of the raja was a contrivance of Lange and his confederates, in the way of extortion; and while they were debating how they should act in this critical conjuncture, one of Lange's adherents began to drive away such of the natives as had brought palm-syrup and fowls to sell, and others who were now bringing sheep and buffaloes to the market.

Just at this juncture Captain Cook happening to look at the old man, who had been distinguished by the name of prime minister, imagined that he saw in his features a disapprobation of the present proceedings; and willing to improve the advantage, he grasped the Indian's hand, and gave him an old broadsword. This well-timed present produced all the good effects that could be wished; the prime minister was enraptured at so honourable a mark of distinction, and exerted himself with such success, that the whole business was now speedily accomplished. The natives, eager to supply whatever was wanted, brought their cattle in for sale, and the market was soon stocked. For the first two buffaloes Captain Cook gave ten guineas; but he afterwards purchased them by way of exchange, giving a musket for each; and at this rate he might have bought any number he thought proper. There seems to be no doubt but that Lange had a profit out of the first two that were sold, and that his reason for having said that the natives would take nothing but gold for their cattle, was, that he might the more easily share in the produce.

Having at length obtained these necessary refreshments Captain Cook prepared for sailing from this place.

This island is called Savu; it is situated in 10° 35' south latitude, and 237° 30' west longitude, and has hitherto been very little known, or very imperfectly described. Its length is between twenty and thirty miles; but its breadth could not be ascertained. At the time the *Endeavour* lay there it was near the end of the dry season, when it had not rained for almost seven months, nor was there a running stream of fresh water to be seen, and the natives were supplied only by small springs, situated at a distance up the country.

Besides millet and maize, this island produces tobacco, cotton, betle, tamarinds, limes, oranges, mangoes, guinea-corn, rice, callevances, watermelons, and other tropical fruits. A trifling quantity of cinnamon was seen, and some European herbs.

Several buffaloes were seen on this island, which were almost as large as an ox, yet they did not weigh more than half as much, having lost the greater part of their flesh through the late dry weather; the meat, however, was juicy, and of a delicate flavour.

The horns of these animals bend backwards, they have no dewlaps, nor scarce any hair on their skins, and their ears are remarkably large. The other tame animals on the island are dogs, cats, pigeons, fowls, hogs, goat, sheep, asses, and horses.

Few of the horses are above twelve hands high, yet they are full of mettle, and pace naturally in an expeditious manner. The sheep are not unlike a goat, and are therefore called cabritos. The sea-coast furnishes the inhabitants with turtle, but not in any great abundance.

The natives of the island of Savu are rather below the middle stature; their hair is black and straight, and persons of all ranks, as well those that are exposed to the weather as those that are not, have one general complexion, which is dark brown. The men are well formed and sprightly, and their features differ much from each other; the women, on the contrary, have all one set of features, and are very short and broad built.

The dress of the men consists of two pieces of cotton cloth, one of which is bound round the middle, and the lower edge of it being drawn pretty tight between the legs, the upper edge is left loose, so as to form a kind of a pocket, in which they carry their knives and other things; the other piece being passed under the former, on the back of the wearer, the ends of it are carried over the shoulders, and tucked into the pocket before. The women draw the upper edge of the piece round the waist tight, while the lower edge, dropping to the knees, makes a kind of a petticoat; the other piece of cloth is fastened across the breast, and under the arms. This cloth, which is manufactured by the natives, is dyed blue while in the yarn; and, as it is of various shades, it looks very beautiful. They have a variety of ornaments.

The houses on the island of Savu are of different lengths, from twenty feet to four hundred, according to the rank of the inhabitant, and are fixed on posts about four or five feet from the ground. The houses are generally divided into three rooms of equal size, the centre room being set apart for the use of the women; and some-times smaller rooms are enclosed from the sides of the building, the whole of which is thatched with the leaves of the palm tree.

The natives eat of all the tame animals which the island produces, but they prefer the hog to all the rest; next to the hog's flesh they admire that of the horse, to which succeeds the buffalo, and then the poultry, and they like the flesh of cats and dogs much better than that of goats and sheep. They seldom eat fish.

The fan-palm is the most remarkable and most useful tree that grows on the island, its uses being equally great and various. Soon after the buds put forth, the natives cut them, and tying under them little baskets, formed of the leaves of the tree, a liquor drops into them, which has the taste of a light wine, and is the common liquor of all the inhabitants. The leaves of the tree are applied to the various uses of making tobacco-pipes, umbrellas, cups, baskets, and the thatching of houses. The fruit is nearly of the size of a full-grown turnip, but the natives are not fond of it.

The island consists of five divisions, each of which has a raja, or chief governor of its own. The inhabitants are also divided into five ranks; the rajas, the land-owners, manufacturers, labourers, and slaves. The land-owners are respected in proportion to the extent of their lands and the number of their slaves, which last are bought and sold with the estates to which they belong; but when a slave is bought separately, a fat hog is the price of the purchase. Though a man may sell his slave in this manner, or convey him with his lands, yet his power over him extends no farther, for he must not even strike him without the raja's permission.

The natives in general are robust and healthy, and had the appearance of being long-lived. The smallpox has found its way to this island, and is as much dreaded as the pestilence. When this disorder attacks any person, he is carried to some spot at a great distance from any house, where his food is conveyed to him by means of a long stick, for no one will venture very near the invalid, who is thus left to take his chance of life or death.

The island of Savu having being visited by the Portuguese almost at their first sailing into this part of the world, they established a settlement upon it; but in a little time they were succeeded by the Dutch, who, though they did not formally possess themselves of the island, sent a number of trading vessels to establish a treaty of commerce with the natives. The principal object of this treaty is, that the rajas should furnish the Dutch, for the consumption of their spice islands, with rice, maize, etc., annually; and they are to return the value in arrack, cutlery, wares, linen, and silk. In this agreement the rajas stipulated, that a Dutch resident should be constantly on the island, to observe that their part of the contract was fulfilled.

As soon as this was accomplished, they sent Mr Lange to act as their resident, who had now been on this island ten years.

The morality of these people is of the purest kind. A robbery is scarce ever committed, and a murder is never perpetrated. When any disputes arise between the natives they instantly submit the point in debate to the decision of the raja, and rest perfectly satisfied with his determination. No man is permitted to marry more than one wife, and their conduct is strictly virtuous.

The *Endeavour* sailed from the island of Savu on the 21st of September, and bent her course westward.

On the 28th they steered north-west the whole day, in order to get sight of the land of Java; and on the 30th the Captain received from most of the officers and seamen their respective journals of the voyage, respecting which he advised them to observe the most profound secrecy: and he likewise possessed himself of the log-book. In the night following there was a storm of thunder and lightning, when the land of Java was seen to the eastward by the brightness of the lightning.

Early in the morning of the 2nd of October, they were close in with the coast of Java, along which they now steered. As their faithful Indian friend, Tupia, was at this time extremely ill, the Captain despatched a boat to the shore to endeavour to bring him some refreshing fruits, and likewise to procure grass for the buffaloes. In a few hours they obtained what they were sent for, and returned to the ship, which proceeded at a slow rate during the night.

On the 3rd, in the morning, the Dutch packet-boat was observed sailing after the *Endeavour*. The master had brought with him two books, in one of which he wrote down the Captain's name, and that of the vessel, to be sent to the Governor and Council of the Indies; and in the other book he requested that some of the gentlemen on board would likewise write down the name of the vessel, with that of the Captain; whence she came, and to what port she was bound.

Soon after, the ship was obliged to come to an anchor, for want of wind. A breeze, however, springing up, she held on her way till the following morning, when she was again obliged to be brought to an anchor, owing to the rapidity of the current. This day and the next, they weighed anchor and brought to several times. On the

8th, they were once more obliged to anchor near a little island, which was not laid down in any of their charts. It is one of those that bear the name of the Milles Isles; and Messrs Solander and Banks having landed upon it, collected a few plants, and shot a bat which was a yard long, being measured from the extreme points of the wings.

In a little time after the gentlemen came back to the ship, some Malays came alongside, in a boat, bringing with them some pumpkins, dried fish, and turtle for sale; one of the turtles, which weighed near one hundred and fifty pounds, they sold for a dollar.

The ship now made but slow way till night, when the land breeze springing up, they sailed to the east-south-east, and on the following day they came to an anchor in the road of Batavia.

The *Endeavour* had no sooner anchored, than a ship was observed, with a broad pennant flying, from which a boat was despatched to demand the name of the vessel, with that of the commander. To these inquiries Captain Cook gave such answers as he thought proper, and the officer who commanded the boat departed. This gentleman and the crew that attended him were so worn down by the unhealthiness of the climate, that they appeared but as the shadows of men; which the Captain deemed a sad presage of the havoc which death would soon make among his crew; yet at present there was not one invalid on board, except the Indian Tupia. The English tars, whose want of foresight and defiance of danger is notorious, seemed not to entertain the least idea that even sickness would attack a set of men so hardened as they were by different climates; but, alas! they had very little idea of the fatal contagion which impregnates the air of Batavia.

The officers and seamen concurring in opinion that the ship could not safely put to sea again in her present condition, the Captain resolved to solicit permission to heave her down; but as he had learnt that this must be done in writing, he drew up a petition, and had it translated into Dutch.

On the 10th of October 1770, the Captain and the rest of the gentlemen went on shore, and applied to the only English gentleman then resident at Batavia. This gentleman, whose name was Leith, received his countrymen in the politest manner, and entertained them at dinner with great hospitality.

In the afternoon, Captain Cook attended the governor-general, who received him politely, and told him to wait on the council the next morning, when his petition should be laid before them, and everything he solicited would be readily granted.

Late in the evening of this day, there happened a most terrible storm of thunder and lightning, accompanied with very heavy rain, by which a Dutch East Indiaman was greatly damaged both in her masts and rigging. The *Endeavour*, though near this Dutch ship, escaped without damage, owing, in Captain Cook's opinion, to an electrical chain, which conducted the lightning over the side of the vessel.[1] A sentinel on board the *Endeavour*, who was charging his musket at the time of the storm, had it shaken out of his hand, and the ramrod was broken in pieces. The electrical chain looked like a stream of fire, and the ship sustained a very violent shock.

Next day Captain Cook waited on the gentlemen of the council, who informed him that all his requests should be complied with.

Their Indian friend, Tupia, had been till this time on board very dangerously ill, yet persisted in refusing every medicine that was offered him. Mr Banks now sent for him to his house, in the hope that he might recover his health. While he was in the ship, and even after he was put into the boat, he was indisposed, and low spirited in the utmost degree; but the moment he came into the town, his whole frame appeared as if reanimated. The houses, the carriages, the people, and many other objects, were totally new to him; and astonishment took possession of his features at sights so wonderful. But if Tupia was astonished at the scene, his boy, Tayota, was perfectly enraptured, dancing along the streets in an ecstasy of joy, and examining the several objects as they presented themselves, with the most earnest inquisitiveness and curiosity.

Of all these circumstances which engaged the attention of Tupia, nothing struck him so much as the variety of dresses worn by the inhabitants of Batavia: he inquired the reason of what appeared so extraordinary in his eyes, and being informed that the people were

1 'In all probability we should have shared the same fate as the Dutchman had it not been for the electrical chain which we had but just before got up. This carried the lightning, or electrical matter, over the side, clear of the ship. The shock was so great as to shake the whole of the ship very sensibly. This instance alone is sufficient to recommend these chains to all ships whatever.' – Extract, Captain Cook's Journal, Records, Admiralty, Whitehall.

of a variety of nations, and that all were dressed according to the mode of their own country, he requested permission to follow the fashion; this request being readily complied with, a person was despatched to the ship for some South Sea cloth, with which he soon clothed himself in the dress of Otaheite.

Captain Cook now applied to several persons to advance him money sufficient to defray the expense of repairing the ship; but not one could be found in the whole town who had the requisite sum in his possession, or if he had was willing to advance it; he therefore made application to the governor, who issued his orders that he should be supplied out of the treasury of the Dutch East India Company.

After little more than a week spent at Batavia, the ill effects of the climate began to be severely felt. Dr Solander and Mr Banks were indisposed with fevers; Mr Banks's two servants were exceedingly ill; the Indian boy, Tayota, had an inflammation on his lungs; and Tupia was so bad that his life was despaired of. Their indisposition was attributed, partly to the heat of the climate, and partly to the swampy situation of the town, and the stench of the dirty canals with which it abounds.[1]

---

1 The following interesting letter from Captain Cook, dated only three days previously, detailing his successful voyage, and that he 'had not lost a man by sickness', is sadly corroborative of the ill effects of the climate of Batavia, aided possibly by the excesses of the men, on the arrival of the ship at that place:

Endeavour Bark, near Batavia,
23rd October 1770

SIR – Please to acquaint my Lords Commissioners of the Admiralty that I left Rio de Janeiro the 28th of December 1768, and on the 16th of January following arrived in Success Bay, in Straits La Maire, where we recruited our wood and water, and on the 21st of the same month we quitted Straits La Maire, and arrived at George's on the 13th of April. In our passage to this island I made a far more westerly track than any ship had ever done before, yet it was attended with no discovery until we arrived within the tropic, where we discovered several islands. We met with as friendly a reception by the natives of George's island as I could wish, and I took care to secure ourselves in such a manner as to put it out of the power of the whole island to drive us off. Some days preceding the June 3rd, I sent Lieut. Hicks to the eastern part of this island, and Lieut. Gore to York island with others of the officers (Mr Green having furnished them with instruments), to observe the transit of Venus, that we may have the better chance of succeeding should the day prove unfavourable, but in this we were so fortunate that the observations were

By the 26th of the month, very few of the crew were well enough to do duty; and on this day a tent was erected for their reception. Tupia now requested to be conveyed to the ship, in the hope of breathing a purer air than in the town, but his request could not be granted, as she was unrigged, and preparations were making to lay her down, in order that she might undergo a thorough repair. On the 28th, however, Mr Banks attended Tupia to Cooper's island, and a tent was pitched for him, in such a situation, where he was alternately refreshed by the land and sea breezes; and the poor creature was extremely thankful that he was so agreeably lodged.

---

everywhere attended with every favourable circumstance. It was the 13th of July before I was ready to quit this island, after which I spent near a month exploring some other islands which lay to the westward before we steered to the southward. On the 14th of August we discovered a small island laying in the latitude of 22° 27' south, longitude 150° 47' west. After quitting this island I steered to the south, inclining a little to the east, until we arrived in the latitude of 40° 12' south, without seeing the least signs of land. After this I steered to the westward, between the latitude of 30° and 40°, until the 6th of October, on which day we discovered the east coast of New Zealand, which I found to consist of two large islands extending from 34° to 48° of south latitude, both of which I circumnavigated. On the 1st of April 1770, I quitted New Zealand and steered to the westward until I fell in with the east coast of New Holland, in the latitude of 38° south. I coasted the shore of this country to the north, putting in at such places as I saw convenient, until we arrived in the latitude of 15° 45' south, where on the night of the 10th of June we struck upon a reef of rocks, where we lay twenty-three hours and received some very considerable damage. This proved a fatal stroke to the remainder of the voyage, as we were obliged to take shelter in the first port we met with, where we were detained repairing the damage we had sustained, until the 4th of August, and after all put to sea with a leaky ship, and afterwards coasted the shore to the northward through the most dangerous navigation that ever perhaps ship was in, until the 22nd of same month, when being in the latitude of 10° 30' south, we found a passage into the Indian Sea, between the northern extremity of New Holland and New Guinea. After getting through this passage I stood over for the coast of New Guinea, which we made on the 29th; but as we found it absolutely necessary to heave the ship down to stop her leak before we proceeded home, I made no stay here, but quitted this coast on the 3rd of September, and made the best of my way to Batavia, where we arrived on the 10th instant, and soon after obtained leave of the governor and council to be hove down at Onrust, where we have but just got alongside of the wharf in order to take out our stores, etc.

I send herewith a copy of my journal containing the proceedings of the

On the 5th of November died Mr Monkhouse, the surgeon, whose loss was the more severely felt, as he was a man of skill in his profession, and fell a sacrifice to the pestiferous air of the country at a time when his abilities were most wanted.

Death now advanced with hasty strides among our adventurous countrymen, who were equally unable to resist his power, or shun his embraces. Several Malay servants were engaged to wait on those who were ill; but these people were so remiss in their duty

---

whole voyage, together with such charts as I have had time to copy, which I judge will be sufficient for the present to illustrate said journal. I have with undisguised truth and without gloss inserted the whole transactions of the voyage, and made such remarks and have given such description of things as I thought was necessary, in the best manner I was capable of. Although the discoveries made in this voyage are not great, I flatter myself they are such as may merit the attention of their Lordships. Although I have failed in discovering the so much talked of southern continent, which perhaps do not exist, and which I myself have much at heart, yet I am confident that no part of the failure of such discovery can be laid to my charge; had we been so fortunate not to have run ashore, much more would have been done in the latter part of the voyage than what was; but as it is, I presume this voyage will be found as complete as any before made to the South Seas on the same account. The plans I have drawn of the places where I have been at were made with all the care and accuracy that time and circumstances would admit of this; for I am certain that the latitude and longitude of few parts of the world are better settled than these. In this I was very much assisted by Mr Green, who let slip no opportunity for making observations for settling the longitude during the whole course of the voyage, and the many valuable discoveries made by Mr Banks and Dr Solander in natural history, and other things useful to the learned world, cannot fail of contributing very much to the success of the voyage.

In justice to the officers and the whole crew, I must say they have gone through the fatigues and dangers of the whole voyage with that cheerfulness and alertness that will always do honour to British seamen, and I have the satisfaction to say that I have not lost one man by sickness during the whole voyage.

I hope the repairs wanted to the ship will not be so great as to detain us any length of time. You may be assured that I shall make no unnecessary delay, either here or at any other place, but shall make the best of my way home.

I have the honour to be, with the greatest respect, Sir, your most obedient humble servant,

(Signed) JAMES COOK

(From the original letter of Captain Cook, Records of the Admiralty, Whitehall, Captain's Letters, C. vol. 22.)

that it was no uncommon thing for the sick man to leave his bed in search of his attendant. The Indian boy, Tayota, paid the debt of nature on the 9th of this month, and Tupia, whose tender affection for the youth can be equalled only by that of a parent for a favourite child, was so shocked at the loss, that it was evident he could not long survive him.

By this time the ship's bottom having been carefully surveyed, our countrymen had ample reason to be grateful to that Providence by which they had been preserved during a passage of several hundred miles, through the most dangerous seas on the face of the globe; for the sheathing in several places was torn from the vessel, the false keel was in a great measure gone, the main keel was damaged in many parts, several of the planks had received great injury, and a part of three of them was thinner than the sole of a shoe.

Messrs Solander and Banks were now so worn down by their disorders, that the physician, who attended them, recommended the country air, as the only thing that could possibly restore them to the wishes of their friends. In consequence of this advice, they hired a country house of the master of the hotel, who engaged to supply them with slaves, and to furnish their table; but as they had sufficiently experienced the worthlessness of these slaves, they bought two Malay women, who soon became excellent nurses, from that tenderness of nature which does so much honour to the sex. While these gentlemen were taking measures for the recovery of their health, poor Tupia fell a victim to the ravages of his disorder, and to his grief for the deceased Tayota: they were both buried in the island of Edam.

By this time not above ten men out of the whole ship's crew were able to do duty, and these were employed in getting the water and stores aboard, and in putting up the rigging.

Captain Cook was now taken ill, and Mr Sporing and a sailor, who attended Messrs Banks and Solander, at their country-house, were attacked with intermitting fevers; but those two gentlemen grew something better, though their recovery was very slow. Their house was situated on the borders of a rivulet, which, of course, assisted the circulation of the air, and it was likewise open to the sea breeze.

In the night of the 25th, there fell such a shower of rain, for the space of four hours, as even our voyagers had scarce ever remembered. The water poured through every part of Mr Banks's house; and the lower apartments admitted a stream sufficient to have turned a mill. As this gentleman was now greatly restored in health, he went to Batavia the following day, and was surprised to see that the inhabitants had hung out their bedding to dry. The westerly monsoon set in about the 26th of this month; it blows in the day time from the north, or north-west, and from the south-west during the night. Previous to this there had been violent thunder, and hard showers of rain for several nights.

The mosquitoes and gnats, whose company had been sufficiently disagreeable in the dry weather, now began to swarm in immense numbers, rising from the puddles of water like bees from a hive. They were extremely troublesome during the night, but the pain arising from their sting, though very severe, seldom lasted more than half an hour; and in the daytime they seldom made their attacks. The frogs kept a perpetual croaking in the ditches; a certain sign that the wet season was commenced, and that daily rain might be expected.

The ship being repaired, the sick people being received on board her, and the greater part of her water and stores taken in, she sailed from Onrust on the 8th of December, and anchored in the road of Batavia.

On the 24th Captain Cook took leave of the governor, and some other gentlemen, who had distinguished themselves by the civilities they showed him. Immediately after, he went on board, attended by Mr Banks and the other gentlemen who had hitherto lived in the town, and they got under sail the next morning. Since the arrival of the ship in Batavia road, every person belonging to her had been ill, except the sailmaker, who was more than seventy years old; yet this man got drunk every day while they remained there! The *Endeavour* buried seven of her people at Batavia, viz., Tupia and his boy, three of the sailors, the servant of Mr Green, the astronomer, and the surgeon; and at the time of the vessel's sailing, forty of the crew were sick, and the rest so enfeebled by their late illness, as to be scarcely able to do their duty.

The town of Batavia is situated in 60 10' S. lat., and 106° 50' E. long., from the meridian of Greenwich. It is built on the bank of a large bay, something more than twenty miles from the Strait of Sunda, on the north side of the island of Java, in low boggy ground.

Several small rivers, which rise forty miles up the country in the mountains of Blaeuwen Berg, discharge themselves into the sea at this place, having first intersected the town in different directions. There are wide canals of nearly stagnated water in almost every street, and as the banks of these canals are planted with rows of trees, the effect is very agreeable; but these trees and canals combine to render the air pestilential.

They were informed, that it was a very uncommon thing for fifty soldiers, out of a hundred brought from Europe, to be alive at the expiration of the first year, and that of the fifty who might happen to be alive, not ten of those would be in sound health, and probably not less than half of them in the hospital. One would imagine that no man of common sense would be tempted to reside at Batavia for any consideration of interest whatever; yet such is the insatiable thirst for gold, that men will voluntarily risk the loss of life to obtain it, and even insure the loss of that health, without which the most splendid fortune cannot be enjoyed.

Any number of ships may anchor in the harbour of Batavia, the ground of which is so excellent, that the anchor will never quit its hold. This harbour is sometimes dangerous for boats, when the sea breeze blows fresh; but, upon the whole, it is deemed the best and most commodious in all India.

The environs of Batavia have a very pleasing appearance, and would, in almost any other country, be an enviable situation. Gardens and houses occupy the country for several miles; but the gardens are so covered with trees, that the advantage of the land having been cleared of the wood that originally covered it, is almost wholly lost; while these gardens, and the fields adjacent to them, are surrounded by ditches which yield not the most fragrant smell, and the bogs and morasses in the adjacent fields are still more offensive.

At near forty miles from the town, the land rises into hills, and the air is purified in a great degree; to this distance the invalids are sent by their physicians, when every other prospect of their recovery has failed, and the experiment succeeds in almost every instance, for the sick are soon restored to health; but they no sooner return to the town than their former disorders visit them.

The choicest fruits are astonishingly plentiful and cheap; and it is wonderful to see what quantities of them are eaten at Batavia. Two large markets are held weekly, at distant places, for the accommodation of persons residing in different parts of the country. At these markets it is common to see 'fifty or sixty cart-loads of the finest pineapples carelessly tumbled together'.

The Batavians, and the natives of other parts of the island of Java, strew an immense number of flowers about their houses, and are almost always burning aromatic woods and gums, which, it is imagined, is done by way of purifying the air.

Formerly the island of Java produced no kind of spices but pepper, and the quantity which the Dutch bring annually from thence is very considerable; but the quantity that is made use of in the country is very small, as the people there give the preference to Cayenne pepper. The inhabitants are extremely fond of nutmegs and cloves; but they bear too high a price to be much in use, as the trees which produce them are all become Dutch property.

The island of Java produces goats, sheep, hogs, buffaloes, and horses. The horse, which is said to have been met with here when the country was originally discovered, is a small, but nimble animal, being seldom above thirteen hands high. The horned cattle of this country are different from those of Europe; the flesh is extremely lean, but of a very fine grain. Both the Chinese and the natives of the island feed on the buffalo; but the Dutch will neither taste the flesh nor the milk, from a ridiculous idea, that they are productive of fevers. The sheep are tough and ill-tasted; their skins are hairy, and they have pendulous ears.

The hogs, especially those of the Chinese breed, are exquisitely fine food, but so extravagantly fat, that the lean is always sold separately.

The quantity of fish taken here is astonishingly great, and all the kinds of them are fine food, except a few which are very scarce; yet such is the false pride of the inhabitants, that these few sorts are sold at very high rates, while those that are good are sold for a mere trifle, nor are they eaten but by the slaves. A gentleman with whom Captain Cook dined told him, he could have bought a finer dish of fish for a shilling, than what he had given ten for; but that he should have been the ridicule of all the politer people, if he had gone to so good a market.

Mr Banks shot a lizard five feet in length, which was extremely well tasted: our adventurers were informed that some of these animals had been seen which were full as thick as the thigh of a man.

Captain Cook was informed that, at the time he was there, the whole place could not furnish fifty women who were natives of Europe, yet the town abounded with white women who were descended from Europeans, who had settled there at different times, all the men having paid the debt of nature; for so it is, that the climate of Batavia destroys the men much faster than the women.

The Indian inhabitants of Batavia and the country in its neighbourhood are not native Javanese, but are either born on the several islands whence the Dutch bring their slaves, or the offspring of such as have been born on those islands; and these having been made free, either in their own persons or in the persons of their ancestors, enjoy all the privileges of freemen. They receive the general appellation of Oranslam, which implies, 'Believers of the true faith'.

The various other Indian inhabitants of this country attach themselves each to the original customs of that in which either themselves or their ancestors were born; keeping themselves apart from those of other nations, and practising both the virtues and vices peculiar to their own countries.

The hair of the people, which is black, without a single exception, grows in great abundance. The women fasten it to the crown of the head with a bodkin, having first twisted it into a circle, round which circle they place an elegant wreath of flowers; so that the whole headdress has the most beautiful appearance that imagination can form an idea of.

It is the universal custom, both with the men and women, to bathe in a river once a day, and sometimes oftener, which not only promotes health, but prevents that contraction of filth, which would be otherwise unavoidable in so hot a climate.

Almost every person has read or heard of the Mohawks; and these people are so denominated from a corruption of the word Amock, which will be well explained by the following story and observations. To run amuck is, to get drunk with opium, and then seizing some offensive weapon, to sally forth from the house, kill the person or persons supposed to have injured the Amock, and any other person that attempts to impede his passage, till he himself is taken prisoner, or killed on the spot. While Captain Cook was at Batavia, a person whose circumstances in life were independent, becoming jealous of his brother, intoxicated himself with opium, and then murdered his brother and two other men who endeavoured to seize him. This man, contrary to the usual custom, did not leave his own house, but made his resistance from within it; yet he had taken such a quantity of the opium that he was totally delirious.

During the time that Captain Cook was at Batavia, several instances of the like kind occurred; and he was informed by an officer, whose duty it was to take such offenders into custody, that hardly a week passed in the year in which he was not obliged to exercise his authority. When he takes one of them alive, he is amply rewarded; but this is not often the case, as they are so desperate as not to be easily apprehended. When they are killed in the attempt to take them, the officer has only the customary gratification. Those who are taken alive are broken on the wheel, as near as possible to the place where the first murder was perpetrated; and, as they are seldom apprehended without being previously wounded, the time of their execution is sooner or later, according to the opinions of the physicians, whether the wounds are or are not mortal.

These people have some singular superstitions in regard to dreams; but the following is the most extraordinary of any in the circle of human weaknesses. They are possessed with an idea, that when one of their wives is brought to bed, a crocodile is born, as a brother to the infant; and they imagine that the midwife conveys the young crocodile to an adjacent river, into which she puts it, with the utmost care and tenderness. Those who suppose themselves honoured by the birth of this new relation fail not to put food in the river for his subsistence; but this is the peculiar duty of the twin-brother, who performs this service regularly, at fixed periods, during the whole course of his life; firmly believing, at the same time, that sickness or death would be the consequence of an omission on his part.

In the islands of Boutou and Celebes the natives keep crocodiles in their families; and it is conjectured, that the strange idea of the twin crocodile was first conceived in one of those islands: it extends, however, to Java and Sumatra westward, and among the islands to the eastward as far as Ceram and Timor. It is a matter of perfect astonishment how even the most ignorant and credulous of the human race should firmly believe an utter impossibility to occur daily; yet it is certain, that not one of the Indians whom Captain Cook questioned on the subject entertained the least doubt about the matter. The crocodiles supposed to be thus born are distinguished by the name of Sudaras; and our readers cannot fail of being entertained with the following story respecting them, which Mr Banks heard from a young woman who was born at Bencoolen; and having lived among the English at that place, had learnt to speak as much of our language as was sufficient to make her story intelligible.

She said that, when her father was on his death-bed, he laid the strongest injunctions on her to feed a crocodile that was his Sudara; that he told her the name by which he might be called up, and the particular part of the river where she would find him. Soon after the death of her father, she hastened to the river, and calling Radja Pouti (which signifies white king), the Sudara crocodile made his appearance, and she fed him with her own hands. She described him as being more beautiful than crocodiles are in general, for he had a red nose, and spots on his body; his ears were adorned with rings, and his feet with ornaments of gold. This story will appear the more extravagantly ridiculous when it is recollected that crocodiles have not any ears.

A man whose mother was a native of the island of Java, and whose father was a Dutchman, was engaged in the service of Mr Banks during his residence at Batavia. The man told his master that several Dutchmen, and many Javanese, as well as himself, had seen such a crocodile as was described by the girl who told the preceding story, and that, like hers, its feet were adorned with gold. On Mr Banks remarking the absurdity of these tales, and saying that crocodiles had not ears, he replied, that the Sudaras differed considerably from other crocodiles; that they had ears, though he acknowledged they were small, that their tongues filled their mouths, and that on each foot they had five toes.

The Chinese inhabitants of Batavia are, like those of their own country, some of the most industrious people on the face of the earth. They act as embroiderers, dyers of cotton, tailors, carpenters, joiners, smiths, and makers of slippers; some of them are shop-keepers, and deal largely in the manufactures of Europe and China. Their knavery is proverbial.

The lawyers of Batavia are partial in their administration of justice to a very reprehensible degree. When an Indian has committed any crime deemed worthy of death, he is impaled, hanged, or broken on the wheel, without ceremony. On the contrary, if a Christian is capitally convicted, execution very seldom follows the sentence; and what is more extraordinary, no pains are taken to apprehend the offender, till time enough has been allowed him to run away, if he thinks proper.

We shall now proceed to a recital of the incidents which occurred during their passage from Batavia to the Cape of Good Hope.

Early in the morning of the 27th of December 1770, the *Endeavour* left the road of Batavia, and after several delays occasioned by the wind being contrary, she stood over for the shore of Java, on the 1st of January 1771. As many of the ship's crew, who had been very ill while at Batavia, had become much worse, the vessel was brought to an anchor on the afternoon of the 5th near Princes Island, with a view to get some necessary refreshments, and likewise to take in wood and water.

Messrs Solander and Banks now went ashore with the Captain, and they were no sooner landed than some of the natives conducted them to the king of the island, with whom they endeavoured to make a bargain for some turtle, but the price could not be agreed on. As our adventurers had no doubt but that they should purchase on their own terms the following day, they left the Indians, and proceeded in search of a proper place to fill water, which was found.

Next day they purchased, at very moderate prices, as many turtle as they had occasion for, and the whole ship's company fed on this delicious fish. The king was at this time at a house situated in a rice field, where Mr Banks waited on him, and found him cooking his own victuals.

On the 12th, while the Captain was on shore giving orders to the people who were cutting wood and filling water, he was told that one of the natives had stolen an axe. The thief was unknown; but Captain Cook, resolving not to pave the way for future depredations of this kind, by taking no notice of the first offence, immediately applied to the king; and in consequence of this application, the axe was brought down to the watering place next day. The Indian who brought it back, said it was left at his house in the night; but it was suspected that himself was the thief.

After a stay of ten days at Princes Island, during which they purchased vegetables of various kinds, fowls, deer, and turtle, the anchor was weighed, and the vessel once more put to sea.

The island, which lies in the western mouth of the Strait of Sunda, is small and woody, and has been cleared only in very few places. Our India ships used to touch at Princes Island to take in water, but they omitted this practice for some years, on account, as it was said, of the water being brackish; yet Captain Cook says it is exceedingly good, if filled towards the head of the brook.

The houses are constructed in the form of an oblong square; they are built on pillars four feet above the ground, and well thatched with palm leaves, as a defence from the sun and rain; the flooring is of bamboo canes, placed at a distance from each other, to admit the air; these houses consist of four rooms, one of which is destined for the reception of visitants, the children sleep in a second, and the two others are allotted, the one for the purpose of cookery, and the other for the bed-chamber of the owner and his wife. The residence of the king of the island, and that of another person of great authority, has boards on the sides, while the houses of all the inferior people have walls made of the bamboo cane, slit into small sticks, and wrought across the beams of the building, in the manner of a hurdle. The king of the island is subject to the Sultan of Bantam.

Captain Cook represents the natives as very honest in their dealings, with the single exception of demanding more than double the sum they intended to sell for.

At the time the *Endeavour* left Princes Island, her crew began to feel, in all its force, the ill effects of the putrid air of Batavia; and soon afterwards the ship was a mere hospital, filled with unhappy wretches, sinking under the rage of fevers and dysenteries.[1] In the space of six weeks twenty-three persons died, exclusive of the seven which had been buried at Batavia; these were nine seamen, the corporal of the marines, the ship's cook, two of the carpenter's crew,

---

1 '30th January 1771. In the course of this twenty-four hours, we have had four men died of the flux, a melancholy proof of the calamitous situation we are at present in, having hardly well men enough to tend the sails and look after the sick, many of whom are so ill that we have not the least hopes of their recovery.' – Extract, Captain Cook's Journal, Records, Admiralty, Whitehall.

the carpenter[1] and his mate, a midshipman, the old sail-maker, who was in perfect health when all the rest were ill in Batavia, and his mate, the boatswain, Mr Monkhouse, Mr Sporing, who accompanied Mr Banks, Mr Parkinson, draftsman to that gentleman, and Mr Green, the astronomer.[2]

After a passage in which nothing remarkable occurred, the ship was brought to an anchor off the Cape of Good Hope on the 15th of March 1771. Captain Cook repaired instantly to the governor, who said that such refreshments as the country supplied should be cheerfully granted him; on which a house was hired for the sick.

At the time the *Endeavour* lay at anchor here, an English East Indiaman sailed for the port of London, who had buried above thirty of her crew while she was in India, and at that time had many others severely afflicted with the scurvy; so that the sufferings of the crew of the *Endeavour*, considering her long absence from England, is a circumstance not at all to be wondered at.

Cape Town consisted at this time of about a thousand brick houses, the outsides of which were generally plastered and had a pleasing appearance; the streets, which cross each other at right angles, were spacious and handsome – the inhabitants, chiefly Dutch, or of Dutch extraction, the women beautiful in a high degree, and possessing those blooming countenances which denote the most perfect health; they were most of them mothers of many children, and Captain Cook says, they are the best wives in the world.

1 '12th February 1771. – Died of the flux, after a long and painful illness, Mr John Satterly, a man much esteemed by me and every gentleman on board.'

'27th February. Died of the flux, H. Jeffs, E. Parrey, and P. Morgan, seamen. The death of these three men in one day did not in the least alarm us. On the contrary, we are in hopes that they will be the last that will fall a sacrifice to this fatal disorder, for such as are now ill of it are in a fair way of recovery.' – Extract, Captain Cook's Journal, Records, Admiralty, Whitehall.

These were happily the last deaths recorded.

2 In a letter in the Records of the Admiralty, dated Endeavour Bark, 9th May 1771, Captain Cook makes mention of the deplorable sickness on board in the following terms: 'That uninterrupted state of health we had all along enjoyed was soon after our arrival at Batavia succeeded by a general sickness, which delayed us there so much, that it was the 26th of December, before we were able to leave this place. We were fortunate enough to lose but few men at Batavia, but in our passage from thence to the Cape of Good Hope we had twenty-four men died – all, or most of them, of the bloody flux. That fatal disorder reigned in the ship with such obstinacy that medicine, however skilfully administered, had not the least effect.'

The air of the Cape of Good Hope is pure and salubrious.

The Constantia wine which is made here is excellent, but the genuine sort is made only at one particular vineyard a few miles from the town. The gardens produce many sorts of European and Indian fruits, and almost all the common kinds of vegetables. The sheep of this country have tails of a very extraordinary size, many of which weigh upwards of a dozen pounds; the meat of this animal, as well as of the ox, is very fine food; the wool of the sheep is rather of the hairy kind, and the horns of the black cattle spread much wider than those of England, while the beast himself is handsomer and lighter made.

On the 14th of April 1771, the anchor of the *Endeavour* was weighed, and she once more put to sea. On Monday, May-day, they came to anchor off the island of St Helena; and as they proposed to remain three days, Mr Banks employed the interval in surveying every object that was thought worthy of notice.

The island of St Helena, which rises out of the Atlantic Ocean, is about eighteen hundred miles from the coast of America, and twelve hundred from that of Africa. It has the appearance of a huge mountain, the foundation of which is probably at the centre of the globe. It had formerly volcanoes in several parts, as is evident from the appearance of the earth and stones in many places; and it looks like a cluster of rocks, bounded by precipices of immense height, which overhang a vessel sailing along the coast.

On the 4th of May, the *Endeavour* sailed from St Helena, together with the *Portland* man-of-war, and several sail of Indiamen. They kept company till the 10th. But Captain Cook, observing that they were outsailed by the other ships, and consequently imagining that some would reach England before him, made signals to speak with the *Portland*. The captain of that vessel came on board, and received from Captain Cook a letter to the Admiralty, together with a box, in which were deposited the journals of many of the officers, and the ship's log-books.

On the 23rd, they lost sight of all the ships they sailed in company with from St Helena; and in the afternoon of the same day, Mr Hicks, the first lieutenant, died of a consumption, with which he had been afflicted during the whole voyage.

No single occurrence worth recording happened from this time till the ship came to an anchor in the Downs, which was on the

12th of July following, after an absence of two years, nine months, and fourteen days.

Whoever has carefully read, and duly considered, the wonderful protection of this ship, in cases of danger the most imminent and astonishing, particularly when encircled in the wide ocean with rocks of coral, her sheathing beaten off, her false keel floating by her side, and a hole in her bottom, will naturally turn his thoughts with adoration to that Divine Being, whose mercies are over all his works.

The grand object of Captain Cook's expedition will be found detailed in the sixty-first volume of the *Philosophical Transactions*. But independent of this, no navigator, since the time of Columbus, had made more important original discoveries. Exclusive of several islands, never visited before, he ascertained New Zealand to be composed of two islands, by sailing between them; and he explored an immense tract of the coast of New Holland, till then little known by Europeans.

These are the appropriate merits of Captain Cook's first and glorious voyage; and though the sequel will show that he improved on himself, he still remains unrivalled for what he had already accomplished.

The curiosities alluded to in the following letter from Captain Cook will be found in the Ethnographical Collection in the British Museum:

Mile End, 13th August 1771

SIR – Herewith you will receive the bulk of the curiosities I have collected in the course of the voyage as undermentioned, which you will please dispose of as you think proper.

I am, Sir, your most humble servant,   JAMES COOK

One chest of So. Sea Islands cloth, breast-plates, and New Zeland clothing, etc.
One long-box or So. Sea Island chest, sundry small articles.
One cask, a small carved box from New Zeland, full of several small articles from the same place, 1 drum, 1 wooden tray, 5 pillows, 2 scoops, 2 stone and 2 wooden axes, 2 cloth beaters, 1 fish hook, 3 carved images and 8 paste beaters, all from the So. Sea Islands; 5 wooden, 3 bone, and 4 stone patta pattows, and 5 buga bugaes from New Zeland.

One bundle of New Zeland weapons.
One   do   of South Sea Islands.
One   do   of New Holland fish gigs.
One   do   of a head ornament worn at the Heivas at Ulietea.

The following is Captain Cook's letter reporting his arrival:

Endeavour Bark, Downs, 12th July 1771

SIR – It is with pleasure I have to request that you will be pleased to acquaint my Lords Commissioners of the Admiralty with the arrival of H.M. bark under my command at this place, where I shall leave her to wait until further orders, and in obedience to their Lordships' orders immediately, and with this letter, repair to their office in order to lay before them a full account of the proceedings of the whole voyage.

I make no doubt but that you have received my letters and journal forwarded from Batavia in Dutch ships in October last, and likewise my letter of the 10th of May, together with some of the officers' journals, which I put on board his majesty's ship *Portland*, since which time nothing material hath happened, excepting the death of Lieut. Hicks. The vacancy made on this occasion I filled up by appointing Mr Charles Clerke, a young man well worthy of it, and as such, must beg leave to recommend him to their Lordships. This, as well as all other appointments made in the bark vacant by the death of former officers, agreeable to the enclosed list, will I hope meet their Lordships' approbation.

You will herewith receive my journals containing an account of the proceedings of the whole voyage, together with all the charts, plans, and drawings I have made of the respective places we touched at, which you will be pleased to lay before their Lordships. I flatter myself that the latter will be found sufficient to convey a tolerable knowledge of the places they are intended to illustrate, and that the discoveries we have made, though not great, will apologise for the length of the voyage.

I have the honour to be, Sir, your most obedient humble servant,

JAMES COOK

(*Captain's letters, C. vol. 22, Records of the Admiralty, Whitehall*)

List of Officers appointed to His Majesty's bark, the *Endeavour*, by Lieutenant James Cook, commander, in the room of others, deceased.

1770, Nov. 6, William Perry, surgeon, in the room of Wm. B. Munkhouse, dd. 5th Nov. 1770, at Batavia.

1771. Feb. 5, Samuel Evans, boatswain, in the room of John Gathrey, dd. 4th Feb. 1771.

1771, Feb. 13, George Nowell, carpenter, in the room of John Satterley, dd. 12th Feb.

1771, April 16, Richard Pickersgill, master, in the room of Robt. Molineux, dd. 15th April.

1771, May 26, John Gore, 2nd lieut., in the room of Zachariah Hicks, dd. 25th May.

1771, May 26, Charles Clerke, 3rd lieut., in the room of John Gore, appointed 2nd lieut.

JAMES COOK

SECOND VOYAGE

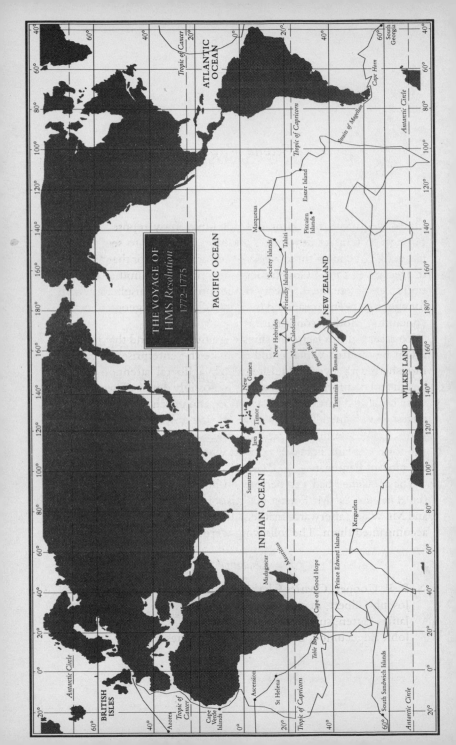

THE VOYAGE OF
HMS *Resolution*
1772–1775

ATLANTIC OCEAN

PACIFIC OCEAN

INDIAN OCEAN

BRITISH ISLES

NEW ZEALAND

WILKES LAND

Tropic of Cancer

Tropic of Capricorn

Tropic of Capricorn

Tropic of Cancer

Antarctic Circle

Antarctic Circle

Antarctic Circle

Cape Horn

Straits of Magellan

South Georgia

Easter Island

Marquesas

Society Islands

Tahiti

Pitcairn Islands

Friendly Islands

New Hebrides

New Caledonia

Botany Bay

Tasman Sea

Tasmania

New Guinea

Timor

Java

Sumatra

Madagascar

Mauritius

Cape of Good Hope

Table Bay

Prince Edward Island

Kerguelen

South Sandwich Islands

St Helena

Ascension

Cape Verde Islands

Azores

Second Voyage

Our adventurous navigator did not long enjoy repose. 'Having business to transact down in Yorkshire, as well as to see an aged father,' he obtained 'three weeks' leave of absence for that purpose' in December 1771.[1] Government soon projected another expedition to complete the discovery of the southern hemisphere, which for ages had been considered by some of the ablest geographers, as containing another continent.

To ascertain this fact, two ships were fitted out; and that nothing might be omitted which could facilitate the enterprise, they were furnished with every requisite which a liberal attention to the health and comfort of the crews could possibly devise. These vessels were built on a particular construction, and purchased at Hull. The largest was named the *Resolution*, of 462 tons burthen, Captain James Cook, commander; the other was named the *Adventure*, of 336 tons, Captain Tobias Furneaux, who had been promoted from the rank of lieutenant.

The *Resolution* had 112 persons on board, officers included, and the *Adventure* 81. Mr Forster and his son, both eminent naturalists, and Mr Wales, afterwards mathematical master of Christ's Hospital, accompanied them. The following were the principal officers:

Resolution

R. P. Cooper, Charles Clerke, Richard Pickersgill, lieutenants.
Joseph Gilbert, master.
James Patten, surgeon.
John Edgecumbe, lieutenant, royal marines.

1 Captain Cook's Letters, Admiralty Records, Whitehall.

Adventure

Joseph Shank, Arthur Kempe, lieutenants.
Peter Fannin, master.
Thomas Andrews, surgeon.
James Scott, lieutenant, royal marines.

On the 13th of July 1772, both ships sailed from Plymouth Sound, and, on the evening of the 29th, anchored in Funchal Road, in the island of Madeira. The Captain and Mr Forster having landed, were received by a gentleman from the vice-consul, who conducted them to the house of Mr Loughnans, the most considerable English merchant in the place. This gentleman not only obtained leave for Mr Forster to search the island for plants, but procured them every other thing they wanted, and insisted on their occupying his house.

During their stay the crews were supplied with fresh beef and onions; and a quantity of the latter was distributed amongst them for sea store.

Having taken on board a supply of water, wine, and other necessaries, they left Madeira on the 1st of August and steered southward.

Captain Cook now made three puncheons of beer, of the inspissated juice of malt. The proportion was about ten of water to one of juice. They stopped at St Jago for a supply of water on the 10th, which having completed, and got on board a supply of refreshments, such as hogs, goats, fowls, and fruit, they put to sea, and proceeded on their voyage.

Port Praya, where they anchored, is a small bay, situated about the middle of the south side of the island of St Jago. The water was found to be tolerable, but scarce; and difficult to be got off on account of a great surf on the beach.

On the 19th, one of the carpenter's mates fell overboard, and was drowned. He was over the side, sitting on one of the scuttles; whence it was supposed he had fallen; for he was not seen till the very instant he sunk under the ship's stern, when all endeavours to save him were too late. This loss was sensibly felt during the voyage, as he was a sober man and a good workman.

With variable winds they advanced but slowly, and without meeting with anything remarkable. On the 29th of October they made the land of the Cape of Good Hope. Table Mountain, which was over Cape Town, distant twelve or fourteen leagues, was a good deal obscured by clouds, otherwise it might, from its height, have been seen at a much greater distance. In the evening the whole sea, within the compass of their sight, became at once, as it were, illuminated, or, what the seamen call, all on fire. This appearance of the sea, in some degree, is very common; but the cause has been differently accounted for, though generally supposed to arise from the phosphorescence of marine insects.

They had no sooner anchored in Table Bay, than they were visited by the captain of the port and Mr Brandt. This last gentleman brought off such things as could not fail of being acceptable to persons coming from sea. The master attendant also visited them, according to custom, to take an account of the ships; to inquire into the health of the crews; and, in particular, if the smallpox was on board; a thing they dread above all others at the Cape.

Captain Cook waited upon the governor, accompanied by Captain Furneaux and the two Mr Forsters. He received them with great kindness, and promised every assistance the place could afford.

After having visited the governor and other principal persons of the place, they took up their abode at Mr Brandt's, then the usual residence of officers belonging to English ships.

It was the 18th of November before they were ready to put to sea. During this stay the crews of both ships were served every day with fresh beef or mutton, new-baked bread, and as much greens as they could eat. The ships were caulked and painted; and, in every respect, put in as good a condition as when they left England.

Mr Forster, whose whole time was taken up in the pursuit of natural history and botany, met with a Swedish gentleman, who had studied under Linnaeus. This gentleman, by Captain Cook's consent, embarked as an assistant to Mr Forster, who generously bore his expenses on board, and allowed him a yearly stipend in addition.

In the afternoon of the 22nd they weighed, and on the 25th had abundance of albatross about them, several of which were caught with hook and line; and were well relished by many of the crew, notwithstanding that they were at this time served with fresh mutton. Judging that they should soon come into cold weather, the Captain ordered the men to be supplied with the warm clothing which had been furnished gratis by the Admiralty.

A violent gale, attended with rain and hail, blew at times with such violence, that they could carry no sails; by which means they were driven far to the eastward of their intended course, and no hopes were left of reaching Cape Circumcision. But the greatest misfortune that attended them was the loss of great part of their livestock, which they had brought from the Cape. A sudden transition from warm, mild weather, to extreme cold and wet, made every man in the ship feel its effects; for, by this time, the mercury in the thermometer had fallen to 38°, whereas at the Cape it was generally at 67° and upwards. The night proved clear and serene, the only one that was so since they set sail; and the next morning the rising sun gave such flattering hopes of a fine day, that they were induced to let out all the reefs of the topsails. Their hopes, however, soon vanished; for by one o'clock the wind blew almost a hurricane.

On the 10th of December, the weather being hazy, they did not see an island of ice which they were steering directly for, till they were less than a mile from it. It appeared to be about fifty feet high, and half a mile in circuit. It was flat at the top, and its sides rose in a perpendicular direction, against which the sea broke exceedingly high.

As the weather continued hazy, with sleet and snow, they were obliged to proceed with great caution, on account of the ice islands. Six of these they passed in one day, some of them near two miles in circuit, and sixty feet high. And yet such was the force and height of these waves, that the sea broke quite over them. Captain Cook says, 'This exhibited a view which for a few moments was pleasing to the eye; but when we reflected on the danger, the mind was filled with horror; for, were a ship to get against the weather side of one of these islands when the sea runs high, she would be dashed to pieces in a moment.'

At eight o'clock on the 14th, they brought to under a point of the ice, where they had smooth water: the two captains now fixed on a rendezvous in case of separation, and some other matters for the better keeping company.

Next day they had a small gale, thick foggy weather, with much snow; their sails and rigging were hung with icicles. The fog was so thick at times, that they could not see the length of the ship; and they had much difficulty to avoid the many islands of ice that surrounded them.

On the 17th they saw many whales, one seal, some penguins, and white birds (probably the *Procellaria nivea* which was found by Sir James Ross in his Antarctic expedition, as far south as he proceeded). They found the skirts of the loose ice to be more broken than usual; and it extended some distance beyond the main field, insomuch that they sailed amongst it the most part of the day; and the high ice islands without were innumerable. The weather was sensibly colder than the thermometer seemed to indicate, insomuch that the whole crew complained. In order to enable them to support this the better, the sleeves of their jackets were lined with baize, and a cap was made for each man of the same stuff, together with canvas, which proved of great service.

After proceeding some days through fields and islands of ice, on the 29th they resolved to run as far west as the meridian of Cape Circumcision, provided that they met with no impediment, as the distance was not more than eighty leagues, the wind favourable, and the sea seemed to be pretty clear. At one o'clock they steered for an island of ice, thinking, if there were any loose ice round it, to take some on board, and convert it into fresh water. At four they brought to, close under the lee of the island, where they did not find what they wanted, but saw upon it eighty six penguins. This piece of ice was about half a mile in circuit, and one hundred feet high and upwards; for they lay for some minutes with every sail becalmed under it.

They continued to the westward, with a gentle gale, the weather being sometimes tolerably clear, and at other times thick and hazy, with snow. On the 30th they shot one of the white birds, upon which they lowered a boat into the water to take it up, and by that means killed a penguin, which weighed eleven pounds and a half. The white bird was of the petrel tribe; the bill, which is rather short, is of a colour between black and dark blue, and the legs and feet are blue.

On the 2nd of January 1773, the weather was so clear that they might have seen land at fourteen or fifteen leagues' distance.

On the 5th, however, they had much snow and sleet, which, as usual, froze on the rigging as it fell, so that every rope was covered with the finest transparent ice.

On the 9th they brought to, and took up as much ice as yielded fifteen tuns of good fresh water. The pieces taken up were hard, and solid as a rock; some of them so large, that they were obliged to break them with pickaxes before they could be taken into the boats.

The salt water which adhered to the ice was so trifling, as not to be tasted, and after it had lain on the deck a short time, entirely drained off; and the water which the ice yielded was perfectly sweet and well tasted. Captain Cook says, this is the most expeditious method of watering he ever met with.[1]

On the 17th they saw no less than thirty-eight ice islands, about which many whales were playing.

On the 1st of February, in the afternoon, Captain Furneaux informed Captain Cook that he had just seen a large float of sea or rock weed, and about it several birds. These were, certainly, signs of the vicinity of land; but whether it lay to the east or west, was not possible for them to know. 'Being nearly in the meridian of the island of Mauritius, where we were to expect to find the land, said to be discovered by the French, we saw not the least signs of it,' observes Captain Cook.[2]

On the 8th of February, having lost sight of the *Adventure*, they suspected a separation had taken place, though they were at a loss to tell how it had happened. Captain Furneaux had been ordered by Captain Cook, in case he was separated, to cruise three days in the place where he last saw him; he therefore continued making short boards, and firing half-hour guns, till the 9th in the afternoon, when the weather having cleared up, they could see several leagues round them, and found that the *Adventure* was not within the limits of their horizon. At this time they were about two or three leagues to the eastward of the situation they were in when they last saw her. Next

1 After meeting with this ice, Captain Cook did not think it prudent to persevere further south at present, as the summer was already half spent. He had reached the latitude of 67° 15' S., the ice being entirely closed to the whole extent from E. to W.S.W., without the least appearance of any opening.

2 'We've been for these six or seven days past cruizing for the land the Frenchman gave intelligence of at the Cape of Good Hope. If my friend Monsieur found any land, he has been confoundedly out in the latitude and longitude of it, for we have searched the spot he represented it in, and its environs too, pretty narrowly, and the devil an inch of land is there.' – Extract Lieutenant Clerke's Log, Records, Admiralty, Whitehall.

day they saw nothing of her, notwithstanding the weather was pretty clear, and Captain Cook had kept firing guns, and burning false fires all night. He therefore gave over looking for her, made sail, and steered S.E. with a fresh gale, accompanied with a high sea.

On the 17th, at nine in the morning, they bore down to an island of ice, which they reached by noon. It was full half a mile in circuit, and two hundred feet high at least, though very little loose ice about it. But while they were considering whether or no they should hoist out boats to take some up, a great quantity broke from the island. Of this detached part they made a shift to get on board about nine or ten tons before eight o'clock, when they hoisted in the boats and made sail to the east, inclining to the south.

On the 23rd, they tacked, and spent the night, which was exceedingly stormy, thick, and hazy, with sleet and snow, in making short boards. Surrounded on every side with danger, they wished for daylight. This, when it came, served only to increase their apprehensions, by exhibiting to view those huge mountains of ice which, in the night, they had passed without seeing.

These dangers were, however, now become so familiar, that the apprehensions they caused were never of long duration, and were, in some measure, compensated both by the seasonable supplies of fresh water the ice islands afforded, and also by their romantic appearance, greatly heightened by the foaming of the waves, which at once filled the mind with admiration and horror, and can only be described by the hand of an able painter.

On the 7th of March, the weather became fair, the sky cleared up, and the night was remarkably pleasant, as well as the morning of the next day; which, for the brightness of the sky, and serenity and mildness of the weather, gave place to none they had seen since they had left the Cape of Good Hope. It was such as is little known in this sea; and, to make it still more agreeable, they had not one island of ice in sight.

March 17th, Captain Cook now resolved to quit the high southern latitudes, and to proceed to New Zealand, to look for the *Adventure*, and to refresh his people. As the wind, which continued between the north and west, would not permit them to touch at Van Diemen's Land, they shaped their course to New Zealand; and being under no apprehensions of meeting with any danger, the captain was not backward in carrying sail.

For the three days past, the mercury in the thermometer had risen to forty-six, and the weather was quite mild. Seven or eight degrees of latitude had made a surprising difference in the temperature of the air, which they felt with an agreeable satisfaction.

On the 26th, they steered and entered Dusky Bay, about noon. In this bay they were all strangers; in Captain Cook's former voyage he only discovered and named it

After running about two leagues up the bay, and passing several of the isles which lay in it, they brought to, and hoisted out two boats, one of which was sent away with an officer, to look for anchorage. This he found, and signified the same by signal. They then followed with the ship, and anchored in fifty fathoms water, so near the shore as to reach it with a hawser. They had now been one hundred and seventeen days at sea, in which time they sailed 3660 leagues, without having once sight of land.

After such a long continuance at sea, in a high southern latitude, it is but reasonable to think that many of the people must be ill of the scurvy. The contrary, however, happened. Sweetwort had been given to such as were scorbutic. This had so far the desired effect, that they had only one man on board that could be called very ill of this disease, occasioned chiefly by a bad habit of body, and a complication of other disorders.

Their first care, after the ship was moored, was to send a boat and people fishing, in which they were very successful, returning with fish sufficient for all hands for supper; and in a few hours in the morning they caught as many as served for dinner. This gave them certain hopes of being plentifully supplied with this article. Nor did the shores and woods appear less destitute of wild fowl; so that they hoped to enjoy with ease what, in their situation, might be called the luxuries of life These circumstances determined them to stay some time in this bay, in order to examine it thoroughly, as no one had ever landed before on any of the southern parts of this country.

About one hundred yards from the stern was a fine stream of fresh water. Thus situated, they began to clear places in the woods, in order to set up the astronomer's observatory, the forge, and tents for the different artificers. They also began to brew beer from the branches or leaves of a tree, which much resembles the American black spruce.

The few sheep and goats they had left were not likely to fare well, there being no grass here, but what was coarse and harsh. It was expected, however, that they would devour it with great greediness, but they were surprised to find that they would not taste it. Upon examination, they found their teeth loose, and many of them had every other symptom of an inveterate sea scurvy. Out of four ewes and two rams, which Captain Cook brought from the Cape, with an intent to put ashore in this country, he had only been able to preserve one of each; and even these were in so bad a state that it was doubtful if they could recover, notwithstanding all the care possible had been taken of them.

On the 28th a canoe appeared, and in it seven or eight people. They remained looking at the ship for some time, and then returned, though signs of friendship were made. After dinner, the Captain took two boats, and went in search of them. They found a canoe hauled up on the shore, near to two small huts, where were several fire-places, some fishing nets, a few fish lying on the shore, and some in the canoe, but saw no people. After a short stay, and leaving in the canoe some medals, looking-glasses, beads, etc., they embarked and rowed to the head of the cove, where they found nothing remarkable.

On the 6th of April, Captain Cook discovered a fine capacious cove, in the bottom of which is a fresh water river, on the west side several beautiful small cascades, and the shores so steep that a ship might lie near enough to convey the water into her by a hose.

As they returned in the evening, they had a short interview with three of the natives, one man, and two women. They were the first that discovered themselves on the N.E. point of Indian Island, named so on this occasion. The man could not help betraying signs of fear, when they approached the rock with the boat. He however, stood firm; nor did he move to take up some things that were thrown to him. At length they landed, went up and embraced him; and presented him with such articles as they had, which at once dissipated his fears. Presently after they were joined by the two women, and some of the seamen. Night approaching, obliged them to return: when the youngest of the two women, whose volubility of tongue exceeded everything they ever met with, gave them a dance.

Next morning they made the natives another visit, accompanied by Mr Forster and Mr Hodges, carrying with them various articles which were received with a great deal of indifference, except hatchets and spike-nails. This interview was at the same place as last night, and now they saw the whole family. It consisted of the man, his two wives (as was supposed), the young woman before mentioned, a boy about fourteen years old, and three small children, the youngest of which was at the breast. They conducted them to their habitation, which was but a little way within the skirts of the wood, and consisted of two mean huts made of the bark of trees. Their canoe, which was a small double one just large enough to transport the whole family from place to place, lay in a small creek near the huts. When they took leave, the chief presented Captain Cook with a piece of cloth or garment of their own manufacturing, and some other trifles.

The 9th, they paid the natives another visit. They found them at their habitations all dressed and dressing in their very best, with their hair combed and oiled, tied upon the crowns of their heads, and stuck with white feathers. Some wore a fillet of feathers round their heads; and all of them had bunches of white feathers stuck in their ears. Captain Cook presented the chief with a cloak he had got made for him, with which he seemed so well pleased that he took his patoo from his girdle and gave it in return.

On the 12th, several of the natives came and sat down on the shore, abreast of the ship. The captain now caused the bagpipes and fife to play, and the drum to beat. The two first they did not regard, but the latter excited some little attention; nothing, however, could induce them to come on board. But they entered with great familiarity into conversation (little understood) with such of the officers and seamen as went to them, paying greater regard to some than to others.

After several days' rain, the weather again became clear, when the Captain set out with two boats to survey the north-west side of the bay, accompanied by the two Mr Forsters, and several of the officers, whom he detached in one boat to a cove, where they intended to lodge the night, while he proceeded in the other, examining the harbours and isles which lay in his way. In the doing of this he picked up about a score of wild fowl, and caught fish sufficient to serve the whole party; and reaching the place of rendezvous a little before dark, after a hearty repast on what the day had produced, they lay down to rest.

At daylight they prepared for duck shooting, in which they were very successful, from which circumstance this was called Duck Cove. About a mile from hence, across an isthmus, they found an immense number of wood-hens. After breakfast they set out to return to the ship, which they reached by seven o'clock in the evening, with about seven dozen of wild fowl, and two seals.

On the 17th, two of the natives, the chief and his daughter, ventured on board; Captain Cook took them both down into the cabin, where they were to breakfast; but they would not taste any of the victuals. The chief pried into every corner of the cabin, all parts of which he viewed with some surprise; but it was not possible to fix his attention to any one thing a single moment. The works of art appeared to him in the same light as those of nature, and were as far removed beyond his comprehension.

The chief before he came aboard presented the Captain with a piece of cloth, and a green talc hatchet; to Mr Forster he also gave a piece of cloth; and the girl gave another to Mr Hodges. This custom of making presents, before they receive any, is common with the natives of the South Sea Islands; but they never saw it practised in New Zealand before. Of all the various articles which were given to the chief, hatchets and spike-nails were the most valuable in his eyes.

On the 20th, they went ashore to examine the head of the bay, and in their way, firing at some ducks, the natives, who were not discovered before, set up a most hideous noise in two or three places close by them. The falling tide obliged them to retire out of the river to the place where they had spent the night. There they breakfasted, and just as the Captain was returning on board, he saw two men on the opposite shore, hallooing to them, which induced him to row over to them. He landed, with two others, unarmed; the two natives standing, with each a spear in his hand.

At last, one of them was prevailed on to lay down his spear, and met the Captain with a grass plant in his hand; one end of which he gave him to hold, while he held the other. Standing in this manner, he began a speech, and made some long pauses. As soon as this ceremony was over, they saluted each other. He then took his hahou, or coat, from off his own back, and put it upon the Captain; after which peace seemed firmly established.

When they took leave, the natives followed them to their boat, and seeing the muskets lying across the stern, they made signs for them to be taken away, which being done, they came alongside, and assisted to launch her. At this time it was necessary to look well after them, for they wanted to take away everything they could lay their hands upon, except the muskets. These they took care not to touch, being taught by the slaughter they had seen made among the wild fowl, to look upon them as instruments of death.

In the afternoon of the 21st, they went seal hunting. The surf ran so high that they could only land in one place, where they killed ten. These animals served three purposes; the skins were made use of for the rigging; the fat gave oil for their lamps; and the flesh they ate, finding it little inferior to beef-steaks.

In the morning of the 23rd, Mr Pickersgill, Mr Gilbert, and two others ascended one of the mountains. In the evening they returned on board, and reported that, inland, nothing was to be seen but barren mountains, with huge craggy precipices, disjoined by valleys, or rather chasms, frightful to behold.

Having five geese left out of those brought from the Cape of Good Hope, the Captain turned them out where there was the greatest appearance of food and security, having no doubt but that they would breed, and in time, spread over the whole country, and fully answer the intention of leaving them.

On the 27th, they had hazy weather. In the morning Captain Cook set out, accompanied by Mr Pickersgill and the two Mr Forsters, to explore an inlet seen the day before. After rowing about two leagues up, it was found to communicate with the sea, and to afford a better outlet for ships bound to the north, than the one they came in by. After making this discovery, and refreshing themselves on broiled fish and wild fowl, they set out for the ship, and got on board at eleven o'clock at night. In this expedition they shot no less than forty-four birds of different kinds.

Having got the tents and every other article on board, on the 28th, they weighed with a light breeze, and stood up the bay for the new passage.

In the morning of the 11th of May, they weighed and stood out to sea; and by noon they got clear of the land.

The country which they had visited was found to be exceedingly mountainous – a prospect more rude and craggy rarely to be met with; for inland appeared nothing but the summits of mountains of a stupendous height, consisting of rocks that were totally barren and naked, except where they were covered with snow. But the land bordering on the sea coast and all the islands were thickly clothed with wood, almost down to the water's edge. The trees were of various kinds, such as are common to other parts of the country, and useful for the shipwright, house-carpenter, cabinet-maker, and for other purposes.

Here were, as well as in all other parts of New Zealand, a great number of aromatic trees and shrubs, most of the myrtle kind; but amidst all this variety, there were none which bore fruit fit to eat. They saw supplejacks fifty fathoms long.

The soil was a deep black mould, evidently composed of decayed vegetables, and so loose that it sunk under them at every step. Except the flax or hemp plant, and a few other plants, there was very little herbage of any sort. What Dusky Bay most abounded with was fish. Of this article the variety was almost equal to the plenty, and of such kinds as are common to the more northern coasts; but some were superior, and in particular the cole-fish, as it was called, was, in the opinion of most on board, the highest luxury the sea afforded. The shellfish were mussels, cockles, scallops, crawfish, and many other sorts.

They found here five different kinds of ducks, some of which Captain Cook did not recollect to have anywhere seen before. The largest was as big as a Muscovy duck, with a very beautiful variegated plumage, on which account they called it the Painted Duck.

For three or four days after they arrived, and were clearing the woods to set up their tents, a four-footed animal was seen by three or four of the sailors, but as no two gave the same description of it, it is not easy to say of what kind it was. All, however, agreed that it was about the size of a cat, with short legs, and of a mouse colour. One of the seamen, and he who had the best view of it, said it had a bushy tail, and was the most like a jackal of any animal he knew.

The most mischievous animals here were the small black sand flies, which were very numerous, and exceedingly troublesome. Wherever they bite they are said to cause a swelling, and intolerable itching, which at last brings on ulcers like the smallpox.

The inhabitants of this bay were of the same race of people with those in the other parts of this country, speaking the same language, and observing nearly the same customs. What could induce three or four families (for there does not appear to have been more) to separate themselves so far from the society of the rest of their fellow-creatures, is not easy to guess. Few as they were, they did not seem to live in perfect amity one with another.

After leaving Dusky Bay,[1] they steered for Queen Charlotte's Sound, where they expected to find the *Adventure*. In this passage they met with nothing remarkable, or worthy of notice, till the afternoon of the 17th, when the sky became suddenly obscured by dark dense clouds, and seemed to forbode much wind. Presently after six water-spouts were seen. Four rose and spent themselves between them and the land; the fifth was without them; the sixth first appeared at the distance of two or three miles from them. Its progressive motion was not in a straight, but in a crooked line, and passed within fifty yards of the stern, without their feeling any of its effects. The diameter of the base of this spout was judged to be about fifty or sixty feet. From this a tube or round body was formed, by which the water, or air, or both, was carried in a spiral stream up to the clouds. Some of the sailors said, they saw a bird in the one near them, which was whirled round like the fly of a jack, as it was carried upwards. From the ascending motion of the bird, and several other circumstances, it is very plain, that these spouts are caused by whirlwinds; and that the water in them was violently hurried upwards, and did not descend from the clouds, as is generally supposed. The first appearance of them is by the violent agitation and rising up of the water; and, presently after, you see a round column or tube forming from the clouds above, which apparently descends till it joins the agitated water below. Captain Cook says, *apparently*, because he believes it not to be so in reality, but that the tube is already formed from the agitated water below, and ascends, though at first it is either too small or too thin to be

1 'The frequent and heavy rains here render it very disagreeable at times: however, this is my third trip round the world, and I cannot recollect any place I ever was at but had some disagreeable quality or other attending it; and I do think that Dusky Bay, for a set of hungry fellows, after a long passage at sea, is as good as any place I've ever met with. Our people are all in perfect health and spirits, owing, I believe, in a great measure, to the strict attention of Captain Cook to their cleanliness, and every other article that respects their welfare.' – Extract from Lieutenant Clerke's Log, Admiralty Records, Whitehall.

seen. When the tube is formed, or becomes visible, its apparent diameter increases until it is pretty large; after that, it decreases; and, at last, it breaks or becomes invisible towards the lower part. Soon after, the sea below resumes its natural state; and the tube is drawn, by little and little, up to the clouds, where it is dissipated.

At daylight, on the 18th of May, they arrived off Queen Charlotte's Sound, where they discovered the *Adventure*, by the signals she made; an event which everyone felt with an agreeable satisfaction. At noon, Lieutenant Kempe of the *Adventure* came on board; from whom they learnt that their ship had been there about six weeks. In the evening they came to an anchor in Ship Cove near the *Adventure*; when Captain Furneaux came on board, and gave Captain Cook the following account of his proceedings during their separation.

On the 7th of February 1773, in the morning, the *Resolution* being about two miles ahead, the wind shifting brought on a very thick fog, so that the *Adventure* lost sight of her. They soon after heard a gun; and steering in the supposed direction, they kept firing a four pounder every half hour; but had no answer. In the evening it began to blow hard, and was, at intervals, more clear, but could see nothing of the *Resolution*, which gave them much uneasiness. They then tacked and stood to cruise in the place where they last saw her, according to agreement in case of separation; but next day came on a very heavy gale of wind and thick weather, that obliged them to bring to, and thereby prevented their reaching the intended spot. They cruised as near the place as they could get for three days; when, giving over all hopes of joining company again, they bore away for winter quarters, distant fourteen hundred leagues, through a sea entirely unknown; and reduced the allowance of water to one quart per day. They were daily attended by great numbers of sea birds, and frequently saw porpoises.

On the 1st of March, they directed their course for the land laid down in their charts by the name of Van Diemen's Land, supposed at the time to be joined to New Holland.

On the 9th of March, they saw the land bearing N.N.E. about eight or nine leagues distant. It appeared moderately high, and uneven near the sea. Here the country was hilly and well clothed with trees; they saw no inhabitants.

The morning on the 10th of March being calm, the ship then about four miles from the land, they sent the great cutter on shore, with the second lieutenant, to find if there was any harbour or good bay. Soon after, it beginning to blow very hard, they made the signal for the boat to return several times, but they did not see or hear anything of it, which gave them much uneasiness, as there was a very great sea. To their great satisfaction, in the afternoon, the boat returned safe. They landed, but with much difficulty; and saw several places where the Indians had been, and one they lately had left, where they had made a fire. The weather obliged them to return without investigating the place properly, or finding any anchorage.

On the 16th they passed Maria's Islands, so named by Tasman; they appeared to be the same as the mainland. The land hereabouts was much pleasanter, low, and even; but no signs of a harbour or bay, where a ship might anchor with safety.

They stood to the eastward for Charlotte's Sound, with a light breeze at N.W. in the morning of the 5th of April, and on the 6th they had the sound open. As they sailed up it they saw the tops of high mountains covered with snow, which remains all the year. On the 7th they anchored in Ship Cove, in ten fathoms water.

The two following days were employed in clearing a place on Motuara Island, for erecting tents for the sick, the sail-makers, and coopers.

On the 9th, they were visited by three canoes with about sixteen of the natives; and to induce them to bring fish and other provisions, they gave them several things, with which they seemed highly pleased. One of the crew seeing something carefully wrapped up, had the curiosity to examine what it was; and, to his great surprise, found it to be the head of a man lately killed. The natives were very apprehensive of its being forced from them; and, as if sensible of their unnatural cannibalism, tried to conceal it, and to exculpate themselves from the charge. They frequently mentioned Tupia, and when they told them he was dead, some of them seemed to be much concerned, and, as well as they could understand them, wanted to know whether he was killed, or if he died a natural death. By these questions, they are the same tribe Captain Cook saw. In the afternoon, they returned again with fish and fern roots, which they sold for nails and other trifles.

Next morning the natives returned, to the number of nearly sixty, with their chief at their head (as was supposed) in five double canoes. They gave their implements of war, stone hatchets, and clothes, for nails and old bottles, on which they put a great value. A number of the men came on board, and it was with some difficulty they got them out of the ship by fair means; but on the appearance of a musket with a fixed bayonet, they all went into their canoes very quickly.

On the 11th of May, they felt two severe shocks of an earthquake, but received no kind of damage. On the 17th they had the pleasure of seeing the *Resolution* off the mouth of the Sound.

Such is a brief abstract of Captain Furneaux's transactions during an absence of fourteen weeks.

Captain Cook knowing that scurvy grass, celery, and other vegetables, were to be found in Queen Charlotte's Sound, gave orders that they should be boiled, with wheat and portable broth, every morning for breakfast; and with pease and broth for dinner; knowing from experience, that these vegetables, thus dressed, are extremely beneficial in removing all manner of scorbutic complaints.

In the morning of the 20th, he sent ashore the only ewe and ram remaining, of those which he had brought from the Cape of Good Hope, with an intent to leave in this country. Soon after he visited the several gardens Captain Furneaux had caused to be made and planted with various articles; all of which were in a flourishing state, and, if attended to by the natives, would prove of great utility to them.

On the 22nd, in the morning, the ewe and ram he had with so much care and trouble brought to this place, were both found dead; occasioned, as was supposed, by eating some poisonous plant. Thus his hopes of stocking this country with a breed of sheep were blasted in a moment. About noon they were visited, for the first time since they arrived, by some of the natives, who dined with them; and it was not a little they devoured.

In the morning of the 24th, they met a large canoe, in which were fourteen or fifteen people. One of the first questions they asked was for Tupia, the person brought from Otaheite on the former voyage; and they seemed to express some concern, when they told them he was dead.

One of these people, Captain Cook took and showed him some potatoes, planted there by Mr Fannin, master of the *Endeavour*. There seemed to be no doubt of their succeeding; and the man was so well pleased with them, that he, of his own accord, began to hoe the earth up about the plants. They next took him to the other gardens, and showed him the turnips, carrots, and parsnips; roots which, together with the potatoes, will be of more real use to them than any other articles they had planted. It was easy to give them an idea of these roots, by comparing them with such as they knew.

Two or three families of these people now took up their abode near the ships, employing themselves daily in fishing, and supplying them with the fruits of their labour, the good effects of which were soon felt, for they were far more expert fishermen than the English.

On the 2nd of June, the ships being nearly ready to put to sea, Captain Cook sent on shore two goats, male and female. Captain Furneaux also put on shore, in Cannibal Cove, a boar and two breeding sows; so that there was reason to hope this country would in time be stocked with these animals, if they were not destroyed by the natives before they become wild; for afterwards there would be no danger.

Early the next morning, some of the natives brought a large supply of fish. One of them desired Captain Cook to give his son a white shirt, which he accordingly did. The boy was so fond of his new dress, that he went all over the ship, presenting himself before everyone that came in his way. This freedom, used by him, offended 'Old Will' the ram goat, who gave him a butt with his horns and knocked him backward on the deck. Will would have repeated his blow, had not some of the people come to the boy's assistance. The misfortune, however, seemed to him irreparable. The shirt was dirtied, and he was afraid to appear in the cabin before his father, until brought in by Mr Forster; when he told a very lamentable story against Goury the great dog (for so they called all the quadrupeds that were on board), nor could he be reconciled, till the shirt was washed and dried.

About nine o'clock, a large double canoe, in which were twenty or thirty people, appeared in sight. The natives on board seemed much alarmed, saying that these were their enemies. Two of them, the one with a spear, and the other with a stone hatchet in his hand, mounted the arm-chests on the poop, and there, in a kind of bravado, bid those enemies defiance; while the others, who were on board, took to their canoe and went ashore, probably to secure the women and children.

However, they came on board, and were very peaceable. A trade soon commenced between the sailors and them. It was not possible to hinder the former from selling the clothes from off their backs for the merest trifles. This caused Captain Cook to dismiss the strangers sooner than he would have done.

June 4th, they spent their royal master's birthday in festivity; having the company of Captain Furneaux and all his officers. Double allowance enabled the seamen to share in the general joy.

During their stay in the Sound, Captain Cook observed that this second visit made to this country had not mended the morals of the natives of either sex. The men were become more mercenary; and the women less virtuous.

On the 7th of June at four in the morning, the wind being favourable, they unmoored, and at seven weighed and put to sea, with the *Adventure* in company.[1]

Nothing material occurred till the 29th, when Captain Cook was informed the crew of the *Adventure* was sickly; and this he found was but too true. Her cook was dead, and about twenty of her best men were down in the scurvy and flux.[2] At this time his ship had only three men on the sick list, and only one of them attacked with

1 The ships being ready for sea, Captain Cook determined upon pushing his discoveries as far as 46° south latitude, although now in the depth of winter. 'I was at least in hopes,' he says, 'of being able to point out to posterity, that these seas may be navigated, and that it is practicable to go on discovering, even in the very depth of winter.'

2 'At nine hoisted out the boat, and sent her on board the *Adventure*. She soon after returned, and brought on board Lieutenant Kempe, the captain being indisposed. Mr Kempe gave me the very disagreeable intelligence of that ship's crew being very sickly, having upwards of twenty men down with the scurvy, and having buried their cook, who fell a martyr to that confounded disorder a few days ago.' – Extract Lieutenant Clerke's Log, Admiralty Records, Whitehall.

the scurvy. Several more, however, began to show symptoms of it, and were put upon the wort, marmalade of carrots, rob of lemons, and oranges.

To introduce any new article of food among seamen, let it be ever so much for their good, requires both the example and authority of a commander, without both of which, it will be dropped before the crew are sensible of the benefits resulting from it. Many of the people, officers as well as seamen, at first disliked celery, scurvy-grass, etc., being boiled in the pease and wheat; and some refused to eat it. But as this had no effect on Captain Cook's conduct, this obstinate kind of prejudice by little and little wore off, and they began to like it as well as the others.

The sickly state of the *Adventure*'s crew made it necessary to make their best way to Otaheite, where they were sure of finding refreshments. Consequently they continued their course to the west; and at six o'clock in the evening land was seen from the mast-head, bearing W. by S. Captain Cook called it Doubtful Island; the getting to a place where they could procure refreshments was more an object at this time than discovery.

At daybreak on the 12th of August they discovered land right ahead, distant about two miles, so that daylight advised them of their danger but just in time. This proved another of these low or half-drowned islands, or rather a large coral shoal, of about twenty leagues in circuit, which was named after Captain Furneaux.

The next morning at four they made sail, and at daybreak saw another of these low islands, which obtained the name of Adventure Island. M. de Bougainville very properly called this cluster of low overflowed isles the Dangerous Archipelago. The smoothness of the sea sufficiently convinced them that they were surrounded by them, and how necessary it was to proceed with the utmost caution, especially in the night.

On the 15th, at five o'clock in the morning, they saw Osnaburg Island, or Maitea, discovered by Captain Wallis. Soon after they brought to, and waited for the *Adventure* to come up with them, to acquaint Captain Furneaux that it was his intention to put into Oaitipiha Bay in Otaheite, in order to get what refreshments they could from that part of the island, before they went down to Matavia. This done, they made sail, and at six in the evening saw the island bearing west.

As they approached the coast, a number of the inhabitants came off in canoes from different parts, bringing with them a little fish, a few coconuts, and other fruit, which they exchanged for nails and beads. Most of them knew Captain Cook again, and many inquired for Mr Banks and others who were with him before; but not one asked for Tupia.

As they were in the vicinity of a reef, the tide strong, and a perfect calm, they were in the most imminent danger of shipwreck. Every expedient was tried to haul off the ship, but in vain, till a light breeze springing up off the land, wafted the ship once more into the open sea, though not without considerable loss and damage.

Thus they were once more safe at sea, after narrowly escaping being wrecked on the very island they but a few days before had so ardently wished to be at. The calm, after bringing them into this dangerous situation, very fortunately continued; for had the sea-breeze, as is usual, set in, the *Resolution* must inevitably have been lost, and probably the *Adventure* too.

During the time they were in this critical situation, a number of the natives were on board about the ships. They seemed to be insensible of danger, showed not the least surprise, joy, or fear, when the ships were striking, and left them a little before sunset, quite unconcerned.

Next morning, being the 17th, they anchored in Oaitipiha Bay, about two cables' length from the shore, both ships being by this time crowded with a great number of the natives, who brought with them coconuts, plantains, bananas, apples, yams, and other roots, which they exchanged for nails and beads. To several, who called themselves chiefs, Captain Cook made presents of shirts, axes, and several other articles; and in return, they promised to bring hogs and fowls – a promise they never did, nor probably ever intended to perform.

Many who called themselves *earees*, or chiefs, came on board, partly with a view of getting presents, and partly to pilfer whatever came in their way. One of this sort of *earees* the Captain had most of the day in the cabin, and made presents to him and all his friends, which were not a few. At length he was caught taking things which did not belong to him, and handing them out at the quarter gallery. Many complaints of the like nature were made to him

against those on deck, which occasioned his turning them all out of
the ship. The cabin guest made good haste to be gone. The
Captain was so much exasperated at his behaviour, that after he had
got some distance from the ship, he fired two muskets over his
head, which made him quit the canoe and take to the water. He
then sent a boat to take up the canoe, and ordered a great gun,
loaded with ball, to be fired along the coast, which made all the
natives retire from the shore. A few hours after they were all good
friends again.

It was not till the evening of this day that anyone inquired after
Tupia, and then but two or three. As soon as they learned the cause
of his death they were quite satisfied; indeed, it did not appear that
it would have caused a moment's uneasiness in the breast of any
one, had his death been occasioned by any other means than by
sickness.

Nothing worthy of note happened on the 20th till the dusk of
the evening, when one of the natives made off with a musket
belonging to the guard on shore. Captain Cook was present when
this happened, and sent some of his people after him, which would
have been to little purpose had not some of the natives, of their
own accord, pursued the thief. They knocked him down, took
from him the musket, and brought it back. Fear on this occasion
certainly operated more with them than principle. They, however,
deserve to be applauded for this act of justice.

In the evening Captain Cook was informed that Waheatoua was
come into the neighbourhood, and wanted to see him. In consequence of this information, he determined to wait one day longer,
in order to have an interview with this prince. Accordingly, early
the next morning he set out, in company with Captain Furneaux,
Mr Forster, and several of the natives.

They found him seated on a stool, with a circle of people round
him. They knew each other at first sight, though they had not met
since 1769. At that time he was but a boy, and went by another
name; but upon the death of his father he took his present title.

After the first salutation was over, having seated the Captain on
the same stool with himself, and the other gentlemen on the
ground, he began to inquire after several by name, who were
engaged in the former voyage. He next inquired how long they
would stay; and when Captain Cook told him no longer than next

day, he seemed sorry, asked the Captain to stay some months, and at last came down to five days, promising in that time he should have hogs in plenty.

During the time they stayed, he never suffered Captain Cook to go from his side where he was seated. At length they took leave, in order to return on board to dinner. In consequence of this interview with the chief, they now got as much fresh pork as gave the crews of both ships a meal. The 24th, early in the morning, they put to sea with a light land breeze.

The fruits they got here greatly contributed towards the recovery of the *Adventure*'s sick people. Many of them who had been so ill as not to be able to move without assistance, were in this short time so far recovered that they could walk about of themselves. It was not till the evening of this day that they arrived in Matavia Bay.

Before they came to an anchor, their decks were crowded with the natives, many of whom Captain Cook knew, and almost all of them knew him. A great crowd was assembled together upon the shore, amongst whom was Otoo, their king. The Captain was just going to pay him a visit, when he was told he was gone to Oparree.

He set out on the 26th for Oparree, accompanied by Captain Furneaux, Mr Forster, and others. As soon as they landed, they were conducted to Otoo, whom they found seated on the ground, under the shade of a tree, with an immense crowd round him. After the first compliments were over, the Captain presented him with such articles as were supposed to be most valuable in his eyes, well knowing that it was his interest to gain the friendship of this man. He also made presents to several of his attendants; and, in return, they offered him cloth, which he refused to accept, telling them that what he had given was for friendship. The king inquired for Tupia, and all the gentlemen that were with the Captain in his former voyage, by name. He promised that they should have some hogs the next day, but he had some difficulty in obtaining a promise from him to visit him on board. He said he was afraid of the guns. Indeed, all his actions showed him to be timid. He was about thirty years of age, six feet high, and a fine, personable, well made man. All his subjects, his father not excepted, appeared uncovered before him, the head and shoulders being left bare, and no sort of clothing above the breast.

On the 27th, Otoo, attended by a numerous train, paid them a visit. He first sent into the ship a large quantity of cloth, fruits, a hog, and two large fish; and, after some persuasion, came aboard himself, with his sister, a younger brother, and several more attendants. Among other presents distributed on this occasion, Captain Furneaux presented the king with two fine goats, male and female, which it was hoped would multiply.

Early in the morning on the 28th they had another visit from Otoo, who brought more cloth, a pig, and some fruit. His sister, who was with him, and some of his attendants, came on board; but he and others went to the *Adventure*, with the like presents to Captain Furneaux. It was not long before he returned with Captain Furneaux on board the *Resolution*, when Captain Cook made him a handsome acknowledgment for the present he had brought him, and dressed his sister out in the best manner he could. When Otoo came into the cabin, Ereti and some of his friends were sitting there. The moment they saw the king enter, they stripped themselves in great haste, being covered before. This was all the respect they paid him, for they never rose from their seats, nor made any other obeisance. When the king thought proper to depart, he was carried to Oparree in a boat, where Captain Cook entertained him and his people with the bagpipes (of which music they are very fond), and dancing by the seamen. He, in return, ordered some of his people to dance also, which consisted chiefly of contortions.

Next morning they took a trip to Oparree, again to visit Otoo. They made him up a present of such things as he had not seen before. One article was a broad-sword; at the sight of which he was so frightened, that Captain Cook had difficulty to persuade him to accept of it, and to have it buckled upon him; where it remained but a short time before he desired leave to take it off and send it out of his sight.

Soon after they were conducted to the theatre, where they were entertained with a dramatic performance, in which were both dancing and comedy. The performers were five men and one woman who was no less a person than the king's sister. The music consisted of three drums only; it lasted about an hour and a half or two hours, and upon the whole was well conducted. It was not possible for them to find out the meaning of the play. Some part seemed adapted to the present time, as Captain Cook's name was frequently mentioned. Other parts were certainly wholly unconnected with them. The dancing dress of the lady was very handsome, being decorated with tassels, made of feathers, hanging from the waist downward. As soon as all was over, the king dismissed Captain Cook with presents of fruit and fish.

Nothing farther remarkable happened till ten o'clock in the evening, when they were alarmed with the cry of murder, and a great noise on shore, near the bottom of the bay, at some distance from the encampment. Captain Cook suspected that it was occasioned by some of his own people, and immediately armed a boat and sent on shore, which soon returned with three marines and a seaman. Some others belonging to the *Adventure* were also taken, and being all put under confinement, the next morning the Captain ordered them to be punished according to their deserts. He did not find that any mischief was done, and the people would confess nothing. The natives, however, were so alarmed that they fled from their habitations in the dead of the night, and the alarm spread many miles along the coast. When Captain Cook went to visit Otoo in the morning, by appointment, he found him removed, or rather fled, many miles from the place of his abode. Even there he was obliged to wait some hours before he could see him at all; and when he did, he complained of the last night's riot.

As this was intended to be the last visit, Captain Cook had taken with him a present suitable to the occasion. Among other things were three Cape sheep, which he had seen before and asked for. He was much pleased with them, though he could be but little benefited, as they were all wethers. The presents he got at this interview entirely removed his fears, and opened his heart so much, that he sent for three hogs, which he presented to them.

They now took leave, and informed him they should quit the island the next day, at which he seemed much moved, and embraced the Captain several times.

On the 1st of September the ships unmoored. Some hours before they got under sail, a young man came and desired the Captain would take him with him, to which he consented. Many more offered themselves, but Captain Cook refused to take them. This youth asked for an axe and a spike-nail for his father, who was then on board. He had them accordingly, and they parted just as they were getting under sail, more like two strangers than father and son. This raised a doubt as to the relationship, which was farther confirmed by a canoe coming alongside, as they were standing out of the bay, and demanding the young man in the name of Otoo. The artifice was now seen through; it was merely to extort something from the Captain that the youth had volunteered. However, he was given to understand that unless he returned the axe and nails he could not be dismissed. As these were on shore, he was carried away, pretty well satisfied, though a few tears fell when he viewed the land astern.

As soon as they were clear of the bay, they directed their course for the island of Huaheine, where they intended to touch; on the morning of the 3rd, they anchored in the harbour of Owharre. As soon as the ships were in safety, Captain Cook landed with Captain Furneaux, and was received by the natives with the utmost cordiality. Some presents were distributed among them; and presently after, they brought down hogs, fowls, dogs, and fruits, which they willingly exchanged for hatchets, nails, and beads. The like trade was soon opened on board the ship, so that they had a fair prospect of being plentifully supplied with fresh pork and fowls; and, to people in their situation, this was no unwelcome thing.

Early the next morning, Lieutenant Pickersgill sailed with the cutter on a trading party toward the south end of the isle. This gentleman had seen Oberea while they lay at Otaheite, who was now decrepit and poor. Captain Cook also sent another trading party on shore near the ships with which he went himself, to see that it was properly conducted at the first setting out, a very necessary point to be attended to.

On the 4th Captain Cook wanted to go to Oree, the king, but was told he would come to him; which he accordingly did, fell upon his neck, and embraced him. This was by no means ceremonious; the tears, which trickled plentifully down his venerable old cheeks, sufficiently bespoke the language of his heart. His friends were also introduced, to whom presents were made. In return he gave them a hog and a quantity of cloth, promising that all their wants should be supplied.

This good old chief paid them a visit early in the morning on the 5th, together with some of his friends, bringing a hog and some fruit. He carried his kindness so far, as not to fail to send every day, for Captain Cook's table, the very best of ready-dressed fruit and roots, and in great plenty. Lieutenant Pickersgill returned in the evening with twenty-eight hogs, and about four times that number were purchased on shore and alongside the ships.

Next day the people crowded in from every part with hogs, fowls, and fruit, so that they presently filled two boats. Oree himself presented a large hog and a quantity of fruit. Oree and Captain Cook were professed friends in all the forms customary among them; and he seemed to think that this could not be broken by the act of any other persons.

On the 7th, early in the morning, while the ships were unmooring, Captain Cook went to pay his farewell visit to Oree, accompanied by Captain Furneaux and Mr Forster. They took with them for a present, such things as were not only valuable but useful. He also left with him the inscription plate he had before in keeping, and another small copper plate, on which were engraved these words - 'Anchored here, His Britannic Majesty's ships *Resolution* and *Adventure*, September 1773', together with some medals, all put up in a bag of which the chief promised to take care, and to produce to the first ship or ships that should arrive at the island. He then gave a hog, and after loading the boat with fruit they took leave; when the good old chief embraced the Captain with tears in his eyes.

During their short stay at the small but fertile isle of Huaheine, they procured to both ships not less than three hundred hogs, besides fowls and fruits; and had they stayed longer, might have got many more; for none of these articles of refreshment were seemingly diminished, but appeared everywhere in as great abundance as ever.

Before they quitted this island, Captain Furneaux agreed to receive on board his ship a young man named Omai, a native of Ulietea, where he had some property, of which he had been dispossessed by the people of Bolabola. Captain Cook wondered that Captain Furneaux would encumber himself with this man, who, in his opinion, was not a proper sample of the inhabitants of these happy islands, not having any advantage of birth, or ac-quired rank, nor being eminent in shape, figure, or complexion. The Captain, however, on his arrival in England, was convinced of his error, and doubts whether any other of the natives would have given more general satisfaction by his behaviour among them. 'Omai,' observes Captain Cook, 'has certainly a very good understanding, quick parts, and honest principles; he is of good natural behaviour, which rendered him acceptable to the best company, and a proper degree of pride, which taught him to avoid the society of persons of inferior rank. He has passions of the same kind as other young men, but has judgment enough not to indulge them in any improper degree. I do not imagine that he has any dislike to liquor, and if he had fallen into company where the person who drank the most, met with the most approbation, I have no doubt but that he would have endeavoured to gain the applause of those with whom he associated; but fortunately for him, he perceived that drinking was very little in use but among inferior people, and as he was very watchful into the manners and conduct of the persons of rank who honoured him with their protection, he was sober and modest, and I never heard that, during the whole time of his stay in England, which was two years, he ever once was disguised with wine, or ever showed an inclination to go beyond the strictest rules of moderation.

'Soon after his arrival in London, the Earl of Sandwich, the First Lord of the Admiralty, introduced him to his Majesty at Kew, when he met with a most gracious reception, and imbibed the strongest impression of duty and gratitude to that great and amiable prince, which I am persuaded he will preserve to the latest moment of his life. During his stay among us, he was caressed by many of the principal nobility, and did nothing to forfeit the esteem of any one of them; but his principal patrons were the Earl of Sandwich, Mr Banks, and Dr Solander; the former probably thought it a duty of his office to protect and countenance an inhabitant of that hospitable country, where the wants and distresses of those in his department had been alleviated and supplied in the most ample manner; the others, as a testimony of their gratitude for the generous reception they had met with during their residence in his country. It is to be observed that, though Omai lived in the midst of amusements during his residence in England, his return to his native country was always in his thoughts, and though he was not impatient to go, he expressed a satisfaction as the time of his return approached. He embarked with me in the *Resolution*, when she was fitted out for another voyage, loaded with presents from his several friends, and full of gratitude for the kind reception and treatment he had experienced among us.'

On the 8th of September they anchored at Ulietea, and a trade soon commenced with the natives. Next morning they paid a formal visit to Oreo, the chief of this part of the isle, carrying with them the necessary presents. He was seated in his own house, which stood near the water side, where he and his friends received them with great cordiality. He expressed much satisfaction at seeing Captain Cook again, and desired that they might exchange names, which he accordingly agreed to. This is the strongest mark of friendship they can show to a stranger.

After breakfast, on the 10th, Captain Furneaux and Captain Cook paid the chief a visit, and they were entertained by him with a dramatic performance, such as is generally acted in these isles. The music consisted of three drums, the actors were seven men and one woman, the chief's daughter. The only entertaining part of the drama was a theft committed by a man and his accomplice, in such a masterly manner, as sufficiently displayed the genius of the people in this vice. Captain Cook says, 'I was very attentive to the whole of this part, being in full expectation that it would have ended very differently. For I had before been informed that Teto (that is, the thief) was to be acted, and had understood that the theft was to be punished with death, or a good tiparrahying (or beating), a punishment, we are told, they inflict on such as are guilty of this crime. Be this as it may, strangers are certainly excluded from the protection of this law; them they rob with impunity on every occasion that offers.'

On the 16th Captain Cook was told that his Otaheitean young man had taken a resolution to leave him, and was actually gone; having met with a young woman, for whom he had contracted a friendship, he went away with her, and he saw him no more.

Having now got on board a large supply of refreshments, the Captain determined to put to sea the next morning, and made the same known to the chief, who promised to see him again before he departed. As soon as it was light, Oreo, his son, and some of his friends, came on board. Many canoes also came off with fruit and hogs; the latter they even begged of them to take from them, calling out, 'I am your friend, take my hog, and give me an axe.' But the decks were already so full that they could hardly move, having on board both ships between three and four hundred. It is not easy to say how many they might have got, could they have found room for all that were offered them.

The chief and his friends did not leave them till they were under sail: and before he went away, pressed them much to know if they would not return, and when: questions which were daily put by many of these islanders. The Otaheitean youth's leaving Captain Cook proved of no consequence, as many young men of this island voluntarily offered to come away with them. He thought proper to take on board one who was about 17 or 18 years of age, named Oedidee, a native of Bolabola, and a near relation of the chief of that island.

The island of Otaheite which, in the year 1767 and 1768, swarmed, as it were, with hogs and fowls, was now so ill supplied, that hardly anything could induce the owners to part with them.

As Captain Cook had some reason to believe that, amongst the religious customs of these people, human sacrifices were sometimes considered as necessary, he went one day to a Marai in Matavia, in company with Captain Furneaux, having with them, as they had upon all other occasions, one of their own men who spoke their language tolerably well, and several of the natives, one of whom appeared to be an intelligent, sensible man. In the Marai was a tupapow, on which lay a dead corpse and some viands. He began with asking questions relating to the several objects before him; if the plantains, etc., were for the *eatua*? If they sacrificed to the *eatua*, hogs, dogs, fowls, etc. To all of which he answered in the affirmative; but they did not sufficiently understand the language to have a perfect comprehension of his meaning.

He has since learnt, from Omai, that they offer human sacrifices to the Supreme Being. According to his account, what men shall be so sacrificed depends on the caprice of the high priest, who, when they are assembled on any solemn occasion, retires alone into the house of God, and stays there some time. When he comes out, he informs them that he has seen and conversed with their great God, and that he has asked for a human sacrifice, and tells them that he has desired such a person, naming a man present, whom most probably the priest has an antipathy against. He is immediately killed, and so falls a victim to the priest's resentment, who, no doubt, if necessary, has address enough to persuade the people that he was a bad man.

After leaving Ulietea, on the 17th of September 1773, they steered to the west, and, on the 1st of October, they saw the island of Middleburg. As they approached the shore, two canoes came boldly alongside, and some of the natives entered the ship without hesitation. This mark of confidence gave Captain Cook a good opinion of these islanders, and determined him to visit them if possible. They found good anchorage, and came to in twenty-five fathoms water. They had scarcely got to an anchor, before they were surrounded by a great number of canoes full of people, who began a traffic. Among them was a chief, named Tioony, to whom the Captain made a present of a hatchet, spike-nails, and several other articles, with which he was highly pleased.

Soon after, a party of them embarked in two boats, in company with Tioony, who conducted them to a little creek formed by the rocks, right abreast of the ships, where landing was extremely easy, and the boats secure against the surf. Here they found an immense crowd of people, who welcomed them on shore with loud acclamations. Not one of them had so much as a stick, or any other weapon in his hand; an indubitable sign of their pacific intentions. They thronged so thick round the boats, with cloth and matting, to exchange for nails, that it was some time before they could get room to land. Many who could not get near the boats, threw into them, over the others' heads, whole bales of cloth, and then retired, without either asking or waiting to get anything in return. The chief conducted them to his house, about three hundred yards from the sea, at the head of a fine lawn, and under the shade of some shaddock trees. The situation was most delightful. In front was the sea, and the ships at anchor; behind, and on each side, were plantations, in which were some of the richest productions of nature. The floor was laid with mats, on which they were placed, and the people seated themselves in a circle round them on the outside. Having the bagpipes with them, Captain Cook ordered them to be played; and, in return, the chief directed three young women to sing a song, which they did with a very good grace; and having made each of them a present, this immediately set all the women in the circle singing. Their songs were musical and harmonious. Bananas and coconuts were set before them to eat, and a bowl of liquor prepared in their presence, of the juice of *eava*, for them to drink. But Captain Cook was the only one who tasted it; the manner of brewing it having quenched the thirst of everyone else. The bowl was, however, soon emptied of its contents by the natives.

They returned on board to dinner, with the chief in their company. He sat at table, but ate nothing; which, as they had fresh pork roasted, was a little extraordinary. Near some of the houses, and in the lanes that divided the plantations, were running about some hogs and very large fowls, which were the only domestic animals they saw; and these they did not seem willing to part with, which determined them to leave this place.

The evening brought everyone on board, highly delighted with the country, and the obliging behaviour of the inhabitants, who seemed to vie with each other in doing what they thought would give pleasure. After making the chief a present, consisting of various articles, and an assortment of garden seeds, Captain Cook gave him to understand that they were going away, at which he seemed not at all moved.

As soon as the Captain was on board, they made sail down to Amsterdam; opening the west side of the isle, they were met by several canoes, each conducted by three or four men. They came boldly alongside, presented them with some *eava* root, and then came on board, without farther ceremony, inviting them by all the friendly signs they could make to go to their island, and pointing to the place where they should anchor.

Having secured the ships, Captain Cook landed, accompanied by Captain Furneaux, Mr Forster, and several of the officers; having along with them a chief, or person of some note, whose name was Attago, who had attached himself to the Captain from the first moment of his coming on board, which was before they anchored.

After walking a little way into the country, they returned to the landing-place, and there found Mr Wales in a laughable, though distressed situation. The boats which brought them on shore not being able to get near the landing-place, for want of a sufficient depth of water, he pulled off his shoes and stockings to walk through, and as soon as he got on dry land, had put them down betwixt his legs to put on again, but they were instantly snatched away by a person behind him, who immediately mixed with the crowd. It was impossible for him to follow the man barefooted over the sharp coral rocks, which compose the shore, without having his feet cut to pieces. The boat was put back to the ship, his companions had each made his way through the crowd, and he left in this condition alone. The chief soon found out the thief, and recovered his shoes and stockings, and of his own accord conducted them to a plantation hard by, and showed them a pool of fresh water, though they had not made the least inquiry after any.

Mr Forster and his party spent the day in the country botanising, and several of the officers were out shooting. All of them were very civilly treated by the natives. A boat from each ship was employed trading on shore, and bringing off their cargoes as soon as they were laden, which was generally in a short time. By this method they got cheaper, and with less trouble, a good quantity of fruit, as well as other refreshments, from people who had no canoes to carry them off to the ships.

Though the natives began to show a propensity to pilfering, the different trading parties were so successful as to procure for both ships a tolerable good supply of refreshments. In consequence of which, Captain Cook, the next morning, gave everyone leave to purchase what curiosities they pleased. After this, it was astonishing to see with what eagerness everyone caught at everything he saw. It even went so far as to become the ridicule of the natives, who offered pieces of sticks and stones to exchange.

One of the natives having got into the master's cabin, took out some books and other things. He was discovered just as he was getting into his canoe, and pursued by one of the boats, which obliged him to quit the canoe and take to the water. The people in the boat made several attempts to lay hold on him; but he, as often, dived under the boat, and at last unshipping the rudder, he got clear off. Some other very daring thefts were committed at the landing-place. One fellow took a seaman's jacket out of the boat, and carried it off, in spite of all the people in her. The rest of the natives, who were very numerous, took very little notice of the whole transaction; nor were they the least alarmed when the man was fired at.

This day Captain Cook was told by the officers who were on shore, that a far greater man than any they had yet seen was come to pay them a visit. Mr Pickersgill informed them that he had seen him in the country, and found that he was a man of some consequence, by the extraordinary respect paid to him by the people. Some, when they approached him, fell on their faces, and put their head between their feet; and no one durst pass him without permission. The Captain found him seated near the landing-place with so much sullen and stupid gravity that notwithstanding what had been told him, he really took him for an idiot, whom the people, from some superstitious notions, were ready to worship. He saluted and spoke to him; but he neither answered, nor did he alter a single feature in his countenance. This confirmed him in his opinion, and he was just going to leave him, when one of the natives undertook to undeceive him; which he did in such a manner as left no room to doubt that he was the king, or principal man on the island. Accordingly he made him a present, which consisted of a shirt, an axe, a piece of red cloth, a looking-glass, some nails, medals, and beads. He received these things, or rather suffered them to be put upon him, and laid by him, without losing a bit of his gravity, speaking one word, or turning his head either to the right or left; sitting the whole time like a statue; in which situation he left him, to return on board, and he soon after retired. The Captain had not been long on board, before word was brought that a quantity of provisions had come from this chief. A boat was sent to bring it from the shore; and it consisted of about twenty baskets of roasted bananas, four bread and yams, and a roasted pig of about twenty pounds weight. The bearers said it was a present from the king of the island. After this they were no longer to doubt the dignity of this sullen chief.

The Captain again went on shore and made this great man a suitable return, and immediately prepared for quitting the place. At ten o'clock they got under sail. The supplies they got at this isle were about one hundred and fifty pigs, twice that number of fowls, as many bananas and coconuts as they could find room for, with a few yams; and had their stay been longer, they no doubt might have got a great deal more.

These islands were first discovered by Captain Tasman, in January 1642–3; and, by him, called Amsterdam and Middleburg. But the former is called by the natives Ton-ga-ta-bu, the latter Ea-oo-wee.

The produce and cultivation of Middleburg and Amsterdam are the same; with this difference, that a part only of the former, whereas the whole of the latter, is cultivated. The lanes or roads necessary for travelling are laid out in so judicious a manner, as to open a free and easy communication from one part of the island to the other. Here are no towns or villages; most of the houses are

built in the plantations, with no other order than what convenience requires. They have little areas before the most of them,
which are generally planted round with trees, or shrubs of ornament, whose fragrancy perfumes the very air in which they
breathe. Their household furniture consists of a few wooden
platters, coconut shells, and some wooden pillows, shaped like
four-footed stools or forms. Their common clothing, with the
addition of a mat, serves them for bedding.

They saw no other domestic animals amongst them but hogs and
fowls. The former are of the same sort as at the other isles in this
sea; but the latter are far superior, being as large as any we have in
Europe, and their flesh equally good, if not better. The land birds
are numerous. The produce of the sea they knew but little of; it is
reasonable to suppose that the same sorts of fish are found here as at
the other isles. Their fishing instruments are the same.

Nothing can be more demonstrative evidence of their ingenuity,
than the construction and make of their canoes, which, in point of
neatness and workmanship, exceed everything of the kind they
saw in this sea. They are built of several pieces sewed together with
bandage, in so neat a manner, that on the outside it is difficult to see
the joints. All the fastenings are on the inside, and pass through
kants or ridges, which are wrought on the edges and ends of the
several boards, which compose the vessel, for that purpose. At each
end is a kind of deck, one-third part of the whole length, and open
in the middle. These single canoes have all out-riggers, and are
sometimes navigated with sails, but more generally with paddles.
The two vessels which compose the double canoe are each about
sixty or seventy feet long, and four or five broad in the middle; and
each end terminates nearly in a point; so that the body or hull
differs a little in construction from the single canoe; but is put
together exactly in the same manner.

All the parts which compose the double canoe are made as strong
and light as the nature of the work will admit, and may be
immerged in water to the very platform, without being in danger of
filling. Nor is it possible, under any circumstances whatever, for
them to sink, so long as they hold together. Thus they are not only
made vessels of burthen, but fit for distant navigation. They are
rigged with one mast, and are sailed with a lateen-sail, or triangular
one, extended by a long yard, which is a little bent or crooked. The

sail is made of mats; the rope they made use of is laid exactly like those of Europe, and some of it is four or five inch. On the platform is built a little shed or hut, which screens the crew from the sun and weather, and serves for other purposes.

Their working tools are made of stone, bones, and shells, as at the other islands. When they viewed the work which is performed with these tools, they were struck with admiration at the ingenuity and patience of the workman. Their knowledge of the utility of iron was no more than sufficient to teach them to prefer nails to beads, and such trifles; some, but a very few, would exchange a pig for a large nail or a hatchet. Old jackets, shirts, cloth, and even rags, were in more esteem than the best edge-tool they could give them; consequently, they got but few axes but what were presents. The only piece of iron they saw among them was a small gimlet, which had been made of a nail.

Both men and women are of a common size with Europeans, and their colour is that of a lightish copper, and more uniformly so than amongst the inhabitants of Otaheite and the Society Isles. The women were found to be the merriest creatures they ever met with, and kept chattering by their side, without the least invitation, or considering whether they were understood, desiring only that they should be pleased with them. In general, they appeared to be modest, although there was no want of those of a different stamp.

They have fine eyes, and, in general, good teeth, even to an advanced age. The custom of tattooing, or puncturing the skin, prevails. The men are tattooed from the middle of the thigh to above the hips. The women have it only on their arms and fingers, and there but very slightly.

The dress of both sexes consists of a piece of cloth, or matting, wrapped round the waist, and hanging down below the knees. From the waist upwards they are generally naked, and it seemed to be a custom to anoint these parts every morning.

Their ornaments were amulets, necklaces, and bracelets of bones, shells, and beads of mother-of-pearl, and tortoise-shell, which were worn by both sexes. They make various sorts of matting – some of a very fine texture, which is generally used for clothing – and the thick and stronger sort serves to sleep on, and to make sails for their canoes. Among other useful utensils, they have various sorts of baskets – some made of the same materials as their mats, and others of the twisted fibres of coconuts. These are not only durable but beautiful, being generally composed of different colours, and studded with beads made of shells or bones. In short, they display abundance of ingenuity in their different manufactures.

The women frequently entertained them with songs, in a manner which was agreeable enough. They accompany the music by snapping their fingers, so as to keep time to it. Not only their voices, but their music was very harmonious, and they have a considerable compass in their notes. Their only instruments are a flute and a drum.

The common method of saluting one another is by touching or meeting noses, as is done in New Zealand, and by the Esquimaux; and their sign of peace to strangers is the displaying a white flag or flags; at least such were displayed to them when they first drew near the shore. From their unsuspicious manner of coming on board, and of receiving them at first on shore, it appears they are seldom disturbed by either foreign or domestic troubles. They are, however, not unprovided with very formidable weapons – such as clubs and spears, made of hard wood, also bows and arrows.

They have a singular custom of putting everything you give them to their heads, by way of thanks. Very often the women would take hold of Captain Cook's hand, kiss it, and lift it to their heads.

A peculiar barbarism prevails in these isles. They observed that the greater part of the people, both men and women, had lost one or both their little fingers. They endeavoured, but in vain, to find out the reason of this mutilation. It was neither peculiar to rank, age, nor sex; nor is it done at any certain age, as they saw those of all ages on whom the amputation had been just made; and except some young children, they found few who had both hands perfect. As it was more common among the aged than the young, some were of opinion that it was occasioned by the death of their parents, or some other near relation. They also burn or make incisions in their cheeks, near the cheek-bone. The reason of this was equally unknown. They all appeared healthy, strong, and vigorous – a proof of the goodness of the climate in which they live.

Leaving these islands, they made sail to the southward – it being Captain Cook's intention to proceed directly to Queen Charlotte's Sound in New Zealand, there to take in wood and water, and then to go on farther discoveries to the south and east. He was very desirous of having some intercourse with the natives of this country about Poverty or Tolaga Bays, where he apprehended they were more civilised than at Queen Charlotte's Sound, in order to give them some hogs, fowls, seeds, and roots, which he had provided for the purpose. They arrived on the 21st, and passing Cape Kidnapper, they saw some canoes put off from the shore. Upon this they brought to, in order to give them time to come on board.

Those in the first canoe which came alongside were fishers, and exchanged some fish for pieces of cloth and nails. In the next were two men, who, by their dress and behaviour, seemed to be chiefs. These two were easily prevailed on to come on board, when they were presented with nails and other articles. They were so fond of nails as to seize on all they could find, and with such eagerness as plainly showed they were the most valuable things they could give them. To the principal of these two men Captain Cook gave the pigs, fowls, seeds, and roots. At first he did not think it was meant to give them to him, for he took but little notice of them till he was satisfied they were for himself; nor was he then in such rapture as when he gave him a spike-nail half the length of his arm. However, at his going away, the Captain took notice that he took care to have them all collected together, and kept a watchful eye over them, lest any should be taken away. He made a promise not to kill any; and if he kept his word, and took proper care of them, there were enough to stock the whole island in due time. The seeds were wheat, French, and kidney beans, pease, cabbage, turnips, onions, carrots, parsnips, yams, etc. It was evident these people had not forgot the *Endeavour* being on their coast, for the first words they spoke were — 'We are afraid of the guns'. As they could be no strangers to the affair which happened off Cape Kidnapper, in the former voyage, experience had taught them to have some regard to these instruments of death.

They now stretched to the southward; presently after violent weather came on, and for two days they were beating up against a hard gale. When they arrived just in sight of port, they had the mortification to be driven off from the land by a furious storm.

They continued to combat tempestuous weather till the 30th, when they lost sight of the *Adventure*. In the afternoon the gale abated. Captain Cook now regretted the loss of her; for had she been with him, he should have given up all thoughts of going to Queen

Charlotte's Sound to wood and water, and have sought for a place to get these articles farther south, as the wind was now favourable for ranging along the coast. But their separation made it necessary for him to repair to the Sound, that being the place of rendezvous.

As they approached the land, they saw smoke in several places along the shore; a sure sign that the coast was inhabited. They continued to stand to the eastward all night, in hopes of meeting with the *Adventure* in the morning; but in this they were disappointed, and soon encountered another storm.

After a succession of calms and brisk gales, in tracing the coast, they discovered on the east side of Cape Teerawhitte, a new inlet they had never observed before, into which they entered and cast anchor.

Soon after they had anchored, several of the natives came off in their canoes; two from one shore, and one from the other. It required but little address to get three or four of them on board. These people were extravagantly fond of nails, above every other thing. To one man the Captain gave two cocks and two hens, which he received with so much indifference, as gave little hopes he would take proper care of them.

They had not been at anchor here above two hours, before the wind veered to N.E., with which they weighed, and steered for the Sound, where they arrived just at dark, with most of their sails split.

The next morning, the 3rd of November, the gale abated, and was succeeded by a few hours' calm; after that a breeze sprung up at N.W., with which they weighed and ran up into Ship Cove, where they did not find the *Adventure*, as was expected.

The first thing they did, after mooring the ship, was to unbend all the sails; there not being one but what wanted repair. In the afternoon, they gave orders for all the empty water casks to be landed, and tents to be set up for the sail-makers, coopers, and others, whose business made it necessary for them to be on shore. The next day, they began to caulk the ship's sides and decks, to overhaul her rigging, repair the sails, cut wood for fuel, and set up the smith's forge to repair the ironwork; all of which were absolutely necessary.

Here they saw the youngest of the two sows Captain Furneaux had put on shore in Cannibal Cove, when they were last here; it was lame of one of its hind legs, otherwise in good case, and very tame. If they understood these people right, the boar and other sow were also taken away and separated, but not killed. They were likewise told, that the two goats they had put on shore up the sound, had been killed. Thus, all their endeavours to stock this country with useful animals were likely to be frustrated, by the very people they meant to serve. The gardens had fared somewhat better. Everything in them, except the potatoes, they had left entirely to nature, who had acted her part so well, that they found most articles in a flourishing state; a proof that the winter must have been mild. The potatoes had most of them been dug up; some, however, still remained, and were growing; and, it is probable, they will never be out of the ground.

Next morning, the Captain sent over to the cove, where the natives resided, to haul the seine; and took with him a boar and a young sow, two cocks and two hens, which they had brought from the isles. These he gave to the natives. being persuaded they would take proper care of them, by their keeping Captain Furneaux's sow near five months. When they were purchasing fish of these people, they showed a great inclination to pick pockets, and to take away the fish with one hand, which they had just sold or bartered with the other. This evil one of the chiefs undertook to remove, and, with fury in his eyes, made a show of keeping the people at a proper distance. The Captain says, 'I applauded his conduct, but at the same time kept so good a look-out, as to detect him in picking my pocket of a handkerchief, which I suffered him to put in his bosom before I seemed to know anything of the matter, and then told him what I had lost. He seemed quite ignorant and innocent, till I took it from him; and then he put it off with a laugh, acting his part with so much address, that it was hardly possible for me to be angry with him; so that we remained good friends, and he accompanied me on board to dinner.' About that time they were visited by several strangers in four or five canoes. These newcomers took up their quarters in a cove near the tents; but very early the next morning moved off with six small water casks, and with them all the people they found here on their arrival. This precipitate retreat of these last, they supposed, was owing to the theft the others had committed. They left behind them some of their dogs, and the boar that had been given them the day before, which Captain Cook now took back again, as he had not another. The casks were the least loss felt by these people leaving them; while they remained, they were generally well supplied with fish, at a small expense.

In unpacking the bread, they found 4,292 pounds totally unfit to eat, and about 3,000 pounds more could only be eaten by people in their situation.

The 15th being a pleasant morning, a party went over to East Bay, and climbed one of the hills which overlooked the eastern part of the strait, in order to look for the *Adventure*. They had a fatiguing walk to little purpose; for when they came to the summit, they found the eastern horizon so foggy, that they could not see above two miles. Mr Forster, who was one of the party, profited by this excursion in collecting some new plants. They now began to despair of seeing the *Adventure* any more, and were totally at a loss to conceive what had befallen her.

Very early in the morning of the 22nd they were visited by a number of the natives, in four or five canoes, very few of whom they had seen before. They brought with them various articles, which they bartered. At first the exchanges were very much in the sailors' favour, till an old man, who was no stranger, came and assisted his countrymen with his advice, which in a moment turned the trade above 1,000 per cent against them.

After these people were gone the Captain took three sows and a boar, two cocks and two hens, which he landed in the bottom of the West Bay, carrying them a little way into the woods, where he left them with as much food as would serve them ten or twelve days. This was done with a view of keeping them in the woods, lest they should come down to the shore in search of food, and be discovered by the natives.

Having now put the ship in a condition for sea, and to encounter the southern latitudes, the tents were struck, and everything got on board.

The boatswain with a party of men being in the woods cutting broom, some of them found a private hut of the natives, in which were deposited most of the treasure they had received from them, as well as some other articles of their own. Complaint was soon made by the natives that some articles had been carried off, and they particularly charged one man with the theft. The Captain having ordered him to be punished before them, they went away seemingly satisfied, although they did not recover any of the things they had lost, nor could by any means find out what had become of them. It was ever a maxim with Captain Cook to punish the least crimes of any of his people, committed against these uncivilised nations. Their robbing with impunity is by no means a reason why Europeans should treat these uninformed people in the same manner.

Calm light airs from the north, all day on the 23rd, hindered them from putting to sea as intended. In the afternoon some of the officers went on shore to amuse themselves, where they saw the head and bowels of a youth, who had lately been killed, lying on the beach, and the heart stuck on a forked stick, which was fixed to the head of one of the largest canoes. One of the gentlemen bought the head and brought it on board, where a piece of the flesh was broiled and eaten by one of the natives, before all the officers and most of the men. Captain Cook was on shore at this time, but, soon after returning on board, was informed of the above circumstances, and found the quarter-deck crowded with the natives, and the mangled head, or rather part of it, lying on the taffrail. The skull had been broken on the left side, just above the temples, and the remains of the face had all the appearance of a youth under twenty.

The sight of the head, and the relation of the above circumstances, struck him with horror, and filled his mind with indignation against these cannibals. Curiosity, however, got the better of indignation, especially when Captain Cook considered that it would avail but little; and being desirous of becoming an eye-witness of a fact which many doubted, he ordered a piece of the flesh to be broiled and brought to the quarter-deck, where one of these cannibals ate it with surprising avidity. This had such an effect on some of the sailors as to make them sick. This youth was killed in a skirmish between two parties.

That the New Zealanders were cannibals could now no longer be doubted. The account given of this in Captain Cook's former voyage being partly founded on circumstances, was, as he afterwards understood, discredited by many persons. He was resolved that his statements should be no longer so, and took the right means. Few consider what a savage man is in his natural state, and even after he is in some degree civilised!

On the 25th they weighed with a light breeze. The morning before they sailed, Captain Cook wrote a memorandum, setting

forth the time he arrived, the day he sailed, the route he intended
to take, and such other information as he thought necessary for
Captain Furneaux, in case he should put into the Sound, and
buried it in a bottle under the root of a tree in the garden, in such
a manner as must have been found by him, or any European who
might put into the cove.

Everyone being unanimously of opinion that the *Adventure*
could neither be stranded on the coast, nor be in any of the
harbours thereof, they gave up looking for her, and all thoughts of
seeing her any more during the voyage, as no rendezvous was
absolutely fixed upon after leaving New Zealand.

On quitting the coast, and giving up all hopes of being joined by
their consort, not a man was dejected, or thought the dangers they
had yet to go through were the least increased by being alone.

On the 12th December, in lat. 62° 10' S., long. 172° W., they
saw the first ice island 11½° farther south than the first Ice they saw
in the preceding year.

On the 14th they fell in with several large islands, and about
noon, with a quantity of loose ice, through which they sailed. Grey
albatrosses, blue petrels, pintadoes, and fulmers were seen. As they
advanced, with a fresh gale at west, they found the number of ice
islands increase rapidly, also a considerable quantity of loose ice.
They tacked, stretched to the north, and soon got clear of it, but
not before they had received several hard knocks from the larger
pieces, which, with all their care, they could not avoid. After
clearing one danger they still had another to encounter; the
weather remained foggy, and many large islands lay in their way.
One they were very near falling aboard of; and if it had happened,
this circumstance would never have been related. These difficulties
determined them to get more to the north.

On the 21st, they very suddenly got in amongst a cluster of very
large ice islands, and a vast quantity of loose pieces; and as the fog
was exceedingly thick, it was with the utmost difficulty they wore
clear of them. They were now in lat. 67° 5' S.

On the 23rd, the wind being pretty moderate, and the sea
smooth, they brought to, at the outer edge of the ice, hoisted out
two boats, and sent to take some up. The snow froze to the rigging
as it fell, making the ropes like wires, and the sails like boards or
plates of metal.

While they were taking up ice, they got two of the antarctic petrels. They are about the size of a large pigeon; the feathers of the head, back, and part of the upper side of the wings, are of a light brown; the belly and under side of the wings white; the tail feathers are also white, but tipped with brown. These birds are fuller of feathers than any they had hitherto seen; such care has nature taken to clothe them, suitable to the climate in which they live.

On the 30th of January 1774, very early in the morning, they perceived the clouds, over the horizon to the south, to be of an unusual snow-white brightness, which they knew denoted their approach to field ice. Soon after they were close to its edge. It extended east and west, far beyond the reach of their sight. In the situation they were in, just the southern half of the horizon was illuminated by the rays of light reflected from the ice, to a considerable height. Ninety-seven ice-hills were distinctly seen within the field, besides those on the outside; many of them very large, and looking like a ridge of mountains, rising one above another, till they were lost in the clouds. The outer or northern edge of this immense field was composed of loose or broken ice closely packed together; so that it was not possible for anything to enter it. This was about a mile broad; within which was solid ice in one continued, compact body. It was rather low and flat, except the hills, but seemed to increase in height to the south; in which direction it extended beyond their sight.

Captain Cook says, 'I will not say it was impossible anywhere to get farther to the south; but the attempting it would have been a dangerous and rash enterprise, and what, I believe, no man in my situation would have thought of. I, who had ambition not only to go farther than anyone had been before, but as far as it was possible for man to go, was not sorry at meeting with this interruption; as it, in some measure, relieved us; at least, shortened the dangers and hardships inseparable from the navigation of the southern polar regions. Since, therefore, we could not proceed one inch further to the south, no other reason need be assigned for my tacking and standing to the north.'

He now resolved to proceed north, and to spend the ensuing winter within the tropic, if he met with no employment before he came there, as he was perfectly satisfied that no continent was to be found in this ocean, but what must lie so far to the south as to be

totally inaccessible on account of ice; and that if one should be
found in the southern Atlantic Ocean, it would be necessary to
have the whole summer before them to explore it.[1]

They now steered north, inclining to the east, and in the evening
they were overtaken by a furious storm attended with snow and
sleet. It came so suddenly upon them, that before they could take
in their sails, two of them were blown to pieces, and the others
much damaged.

On the 25th, Captain Cook was taken ill of the bilious cholic,
which was so violent as to confine him to his bed; so that the
management of the ship was left to Mr Cooper, the first officer,
who conducted her much to his satisfaction. It was several days
before the most dangerous symptoms of his disorder were removed; during which time Mr Patten, the surgeon, was to him
not only a skilful physician, but an affectionate nurse. When he
began to recover, a favourite dog, belonging to Mr Forster, fell a
sacrifice to his tender stomach. They had no other fresh meat
whatever on board; and the Captain could eat of this flesh, as well
as broth made of it, when he could taste nothing else. Thus he
received nourishment and strength from food which would have
made most people in Europe sick; so true it is, that necessity is
governed by no law.

At eight o'clock in the morning on the 11th of March, land was
seen from the mast-head, bearing west, about twelve leagues
distant. They now tacked and endeavoured to get into what
appeared to be a bay, on the west side of the point; but before this
could be accomplished, night came upon them, and they stood on
and off, under the land, till the next morning. This is called Easter
Island, or Davis's Land.

Here a canoe, conducted by two men, came off. They brought
with them a bunch of plantains, which they sent into the ship by a
rope, and then returned ashore. This gave Captain Cook a good
opinion of the islanders, and inspired them with hopes of getting
some refreshments, of which they were in great want.

1 Nothing could show a sounder judgment than this decision on the part of
Captain Cook, who, having now penetrated to 71° 10' S., long. 106° 54' W.,
wisely left it to a future navigator to discover a continent in the Southern Atlantic
Ocean, nearly a century afterwards: Admiral Sir James Clark Ross.

They continued to range along the coast, till they opened the northern point of the isle. While the ship was plying in, a native came on board. The first thing he did was to measure the length of the ship, by fathoming her from the taffrail to the stem; and as he counted the fathoms, they observed that he called the numbers by the same names that they do at Otaheite; nevertheless his language was nearly unintelligible to all of them.

Next morning the Captain went ashore, accompanied by some of the gentlemen, to see what the island was likely to afford. They landed at a sandy beach, where some hundreds of the natives were assembled, and who were so impatient to see them, that many of them swam off to meet the boats. Not one of them had so much as a stick or weapon of any sort in his hand. After distributing a few trinkets amongst them, they made signs for something to eat; on which they brought down a few potatoes, plantains, and sugar-canes, and exchanged them for nails, looking-glasses, and pieces of cloth.

They presently discovered that they were as expert thieves, and as tricking in their exchanges, as any people they had yet met with. It was with some difficulty that they could keep anything in their pockets, not even what the natives had themselves sold; for they would watch every opportunity to snatch it from them, so that they sometimes bought the same thing two or three times over, and after all did not get it.

The country appeared quite barren and without wood; there were, nevertheless, several plantations of potatoes, plantains, and sugar-canes; they also saw some fowls, and found a well of brackish water. The ship was now brought to an anchor about a mile from the nearest shore.

Captain Cook was obliged to content himself with remaining at the landing-place among the natives, as he was not yet quite recovered. They had a pretty brisk trade with them for potatoes, which they observed they dug out of an adjoining plantation; but this traffic, which was very advantageous to them, was soon put a stop to by the owner (as they supposed) of the plantation coming down, and driving all the people out of it. By this they concluded that he had been robbed of his property, and that they were not less scrupulous of stealing from one another than from those on whom they practised every little fraud they could think, and generally with success; for they had no sooner detected them in one than they found out another. A party who had been sent out in the morning to view the country now returned. They had not proceeded far before a middle-aged man, punctured from head to foot, and his face painted with a sort of white pigment, appeared with a spear in his hand, and walked alongside of them, making signs to his countrymen to keep at a distance, and not to molest them. When he had pretty well effected this, he hoisted a piece of white cloth on his spear, placed himself in the front, and led the way with this ensign of peace.

On the east side, near the sea, they met with three platforms of stonework, or rather the ruins of them. On each had stood four large statues, but they were all fallen down from two of them, and also one from the third; all except one were broken by the fall, or in some measure defaced. Mr Wales measured this one, and found it to be fifteen feet in length, and six feet broad over the shoulders. Each statue had on its head a large cylindric stone of a red colour, wrought perfectly round. The one they measured, which was not by far the largest, was fifty-two inches high, and fifty-six in diameter. In some the upper corner of the cylinder was taken off in a sort of concave quarter round, but in others the cylinder was entire.

Beyond this they came to the most fertile part of the island they saw, it being interspersed with plantations of potatoes, sugar-canes, and plantain-trees; but the could find no water, except what the natives twice or thrice brought them, which, though brackish and stinking, was rendered acceptable by the extremity of their thirst. They also passed some huts, the owners of which met them with roasted potatoes and sugar-canes; but at the very time some were relieving the thirsty and hungry, there were others who endeavoured to steal from them the very things which had been given them. At last, to prevent worse consequences, they were obliged to fire a load of small shot at one who was so audacious as to snatch the bag which contained everything they carried with them. The shot hit him in the back, on which he dropped the bag, ran a little way, and then fell; but he afterwards got up and walked, and what became of him they knew not, nor whether he was much wounded.

This affair occasioned some delay, and drew the natives together: they presently saw the man who had hitherto led the way, and one or two more, coming running towards them; but instead of stopping when they came up, they continued to run round them, repeating, in a kind manner, a few words until they set forwards again. Then their old guide hoisted his flag, leading the way as before, and none ever attempted to steal from them the whole day afterwards.

Towards the eastern end of the island, they met with a well whose water was perfectly fresh, being considerably above the level of the sea; but it was dirty, owing to the filthiness or cleanliness (call it which you will) of the natives, who never go to drink without washing themselves all over as soon as they have done; and if ever so many of them are together, the first leaps right into the middle of the whole, drinks, and washes himself without the least ceremony; after which another takes his place and does the same.

They observed that this side of the island was full of those gigantic statues before mentioned; some placed in groups on platforms of masonry; others single, fixed only in the earth, and that not deep; and these latter are, in general, much larger than the others. Having measured one, which had fallen down, they found it very near twenty-seven feet long, and upwards of eight feet over the breast or shoulders; and yet this appeared considerably short of the size of one they saw standing – its shade, a little past two o'clock, being sufficient to shelter all the party, consisting of nearly thirty persons, from the rays of the sun.

They saw not an animal of any sort, and but few birds; nor indeed anything which can induce ships that are not in the utmost distress to touch at this island. Captain Cook determined to sail the next morning, since nothing was to be obtained that could make it worth his while to stay longer.

The produce of the island is sweet potatoes, yams, terra, or eddy root, plantains, and sugar-canes, all pretty good, the potatoes especially, which are the best of the kind they ever tasted. They have a few tame fowls, such as cocks and hens, small, but well tasted. The coast seemed not to abound with fish; at least they could catch none with hook and line, and it was but very little they saw amongst the natives.

The inhabitants do not seem to exceed six or seven hundred souls, and above two-thirds of those they saw were males. They either have but few females among them, or else many were restrained from making their appearance.

In general the people of this island are a slender race. They did not see a man that would measure six feet; so far are they from being giants, as one of the authors of Roggewein's voyage asserts. They are brisk and active, have good features, and not disagreeable countenances, are friendly and hospitable to strangers, but as much addicted to pilfering as any of their neighbours.

The women's clothing is a piece or two of quilted cloth, about six feet by four, or a mat. One piece wrapped round their loins, and another over their shoulders, make a complete dress. But the men, for the most part, are in a manner naked, wearing nothing but a slip of cloth betwixt their legs, each end of which is fastened to a cord or belt they wear round the waist. The Otaheitean cloth, or indeed any sort, was much valued by them.

Harmless and friendly as these people seem to be, they are not without offensive weapons, such as short wooden clubs and spears.

Their houses are low miserable huts, constructed by setting sticks upright in the ground, at six or eight feet distance, then bending them towards each other, and tying them together at the top, forming thereby a kind of gothic arch. The whole is thatched over with leaves of sugar-cane. The doorway is in the middle of one side, formed like a porch and so low and narrow as just to admit a man to enter upon all fours.

The gigantic statues are not, in Captain Cook's opinion, looked upon as idols by the present inhabitants, whatever they might have been in the days of the Dutch; at least he saw nothing that could induce him to think so. On the contrary, he rather supposes that they are burying-places for certain tribes or families.

On the 16th of March they stood out to sea, and having now a steady settled trade-wind, and pleasant weather, the forge was ordered to be set up, to repair and make various necessary articles in the iron way.

On the 7th of April they saw an isle, which, as it was a new discovery, they named Hood's Island, after the young gentleman who first saw it; the second was that of St Pedro; the third, La Dominica; and the fourth, St Christina. They ranged the S.E. coast of La Dominica, without seeing the least signs of anchorage. Some canoes put off from these places, and followed them down the coast.

At length, having come before the port they were in search of, they cast anchor. This was no sooner done, than about thirty or forty of the natives came off in ten or twelve canoes; but it required some address to get them alongside. At last a hatchet and some spike-nails induced the people in one canoe to come under the quarter-gallery; after which all the others put alongside, and having exchanged some bread-fruit and fish for small nails, retired on shore.

Very early next morning, the natives visited them again in much greater numbers than before; bringing with them bread-fruit, plantains, and one pig, all of which they exchanged. But in this traffic they would frequently keep their goods and make no return, till at last the Captain was obliged to fire a musket ball over one man who had several times served them in this manner; after which they dealt more fairly, and soon after several of them came on board. As the Captain was going in a boat, to look for a more convenient place to moor the ship in, he observed too many of the natives on board, and advised the officers to be on their guard. He had hardly got into the boat, before he was told they had stolen one of the iron stanchions, and were making off with it. He ordered them to fire over the canoe, but not to kill anyone; but the natives made too much noise for him to be heard, and the unhappy thief was killed at the third shot.

At this sad accident, all the natives retired with precipitation. The Captain followed them into the bay, and prevailed upon the people in one canoe to come alongside the boat, and receive some nails, and other things which he gave them. One would have thought that the natives by this time would have been so sensible of the effect of firearms, as not to have provoked them to fire upon them any more; but the event proved otherwise. For the boat had no sooner left the kedge anchor, than two men in the canoe put off from the shore, took hold of the buoy rope, and attempted to drag it ashore, little considering what was fast to it. The Captain ordered a musket to be fired at them. The ball fell short, and they took not the least notice of it; but a second having passed over them, they let go the buoy and made for the shore. This was the last shot they had occasion to fire at any of them while they lay at this place. It probably had more effect than killing the man, by showing them that they were not safe at any distance.

On the 10th, early in the morning, some people from more distant parts came in canoes alongside, and sold them some pigs; so that they had now sufficient to give the crew a fresh meal. After dinner Captain Cook went on shore and collected eighteen pigs.

Next morning he went down to the same place where he had been the preceding evening; but instead of getting pigs, as he expected, found the scene quite changed. The nails and other things they were mad after but the evening before, they now despised. The reason was, several of the young gentlemen having landed the preceding day, had given away in exchange various articles which the people had not seen before, and which took with them more than nails or more useful iron tools. Trade being thus stopped, the Captain prepared to leave this place, and go where their wants might be effectually relieved; for after having been nineteen weeks at sea, and living all the time on salt diet, they could not but want some refreshments; yet they had not one sick man on board, owing to the many antiscorbutic articles they had, and to the great attention of the surgeon.

April the 11th, at three o'clock in the afternoon, they weighed. They had now but little wind, and that very variable, with showers of rain.

The Marquesas, which they had just left, were discovered by Mendana, a Spaniard, and from him obtained the general name they now bear. They are five in number, viz., La Magdalena, St Pedro, La Dominica, Santa Christina, and Hood's Island, which is the northernmost; La Dominica is the largest.

The inhabitants of these islands, collectively, are without exception the finest race of people in this sea. For fine shape and regular features, they perhaps surpass all other nations. Nevertheless the affinity of their language to that spoken in Otaheite and the Society Isles, shows that they are of the same nation. Oedidee could converse with them tolerably well, and it was easy to see that their language was nearly the same.

The men, for the most part, have nothing to cover their nakedness, except the *marra*, as it is called at Otaheite; which is a slip of cloth passed round the waist and betwixt the legs. This simple dress is quite sufficient for the climate, and answers every purpose modesty requires. The dress of the women is a piece of cloth, wrapped round the loins like a petticoat, which reaches down below the middle of the leg, and a loose mantle over their shoulders.

In the article of eating, these people are by no means so cleanly as the Otaheiteans. They are likewise dirty in their cookery. Captain

Cook says he saw them make a batter of fruit and roots, diluted with water, in a vessel that was loaded with dirt, and out of which the hogs had been but that moment eating, without giving it the least washing, or even washing their hands which were equally dirty; and when he expressed dislike, was laughed at.

Hogs are the only quadrupeds they saw; and cocks and hens were the only tame fowls. However, the woods seem to abound with small birds of a very beautiful plumage and fine notes.

With a fine easterly wind they steered till the 17th, when land was seen bearing W. half N., which, upon a nearer approach, they found to be a string of low islets connected together by a reef of coral rocks.

As they steered along the coast, the natives appeared in several places, armed with long spears and clubs, and some were got together on one side of the creek. Two boats well-armed were sent ashore, under the command of Lieutenant Cooper, with a view of having some intercourse with them. They saw them land without the least opposition. Some little time after, however, observing forty or fifty natives, all armed, coming towards the boats, they stood close in shore, in order to be ready to support their people in case of an attack. But nothing of this kind happened; and soon after the boats returned on board, when Mr Cooper informed the Captain that, on his landing, only a few of the natives met him on the beach, but there were many in the skirts of the woods with spears in their hands. The presents he made them were received with great coolness, which plainly showed they were unwelcome visitors. They brought on board five dogs, which seemed to be in plenty there. They saw no fruit but coconuts, of which they got by exchanges two dozen.

This island, which is called by the inhabitants Tiookea, was discovered and visited by Commodore Byron. It has something of an oval shape, and is about ten leagues in circuit.

On the 18th, at daybreak, they wore down to another isle which they had in sight to the westward, which they reached by eight o'clock, and ranged the S.E. side at one mile from shore. These must be the same islands to which Commodore Byron gave the name of George's Islands.

It cannot be determined with any degree of certainty whether this group of isles be any of those discovered by the Dutch navigators, or no; this part of the ocean is so strewed with those low isles that a navigator cannot proceed with too much caution.

They made the high land of Otaheite on the 21st of April, and at eight o'clock the next morning anchored in Matavai Bay. This was no sooner known to the natives than many of them came off to the ship, and expressed not a little joy at seeing them again.

On the 24th, Otoo the king, and several other chiefs, with a train of attendants, paid them a visit, and brought them as presents ten or a dozen large hogs, besides fruits. Captain Cook, knowing how much it was his interest to make this man his friend, met him at the tents, and conducted him and his companion on board, where they remained to dinner, after which they were dismissed with suitable presents, and highly pleased with the reception they had met with.

They now found these people were building a great number of large canoes and houses of every kind; people living in spacious habitations who had not a place to shelter themselves in eight months before; several large hogs about every house, and every other sign of a rising state.

Judging from these favourable circumstances that they should not mend themselves by removing to another island, Captain Cook resolved to make some stay

In the morning of the 26th, the Captain went down to Oparree, accompanied by some of the officers and gentlemen, to pay Otoo a visit. As they drew near they observed a number of large canoes in motion; but were surprised, when they arrived, to see upwards of three hundred ranged in order for some distance along the shore, all completely equipped and manned, besides a vast number of armed men upon the shore. So unexpected an armament collected together in their neighbourhood in the space of one night gave rise to various conjectures.

The vessels of war consisted of one hundred and sixty large double canoes, very well equipped, manned, and armed. The chiefs, and all those on the fighting stages, were dressed in their war habits – that is, in a vast quantity of cloth, turbans, breast-plates, and helmets. The vessels were decorated with flags and streamers, so that the whole made a grand and noble appearance, such as they had never before seen in this sea, and what no one would have expected. Their instruments of war were clubs, spears, and stones. Besides the vessels of war, there were one hundred and seventy sail of smaller double canoes, all with a little house upon them, and rigged with a mast and sail, which the war canoes had not. These were designed for transports and victuallers; for in the war canoes was no sort of provisions whatever. In these three hundred and thirty vessels there were no less than seven thousand seven hundred and sixty men.

Tupia informed them when they were first here that the whole island raised only between six and seven thousand men, but they now saw two districts only raise that number.

They had not been long gone from Oparree, where at that time they missed Otoo, before the whole fleet was in motion to the westward, whence it came. When they got to Matavai, they were told that this fleet was part of the armament intended to go against Eimea, whose chief had thrown off the yoke of Otaheite, and assumed an independency.

In the morning of the 27th of April, the Captain received a present from the chief named Towha, consisting of two large hogs and some fruit, sent by two of his servants, who had orders not to receive anything in return; nor would they when offered them. Soon after, he went down to Oparree in his boat, where having found both this chief and the king, after a short stay, he brought them both on board to dinner, together with the king's younger brother and Tee. As soon as they drew near the ship the admiral, who had never seen one before, began to express much surprise at so new a sight. He was conducted all over the ship, every part of which he viewed with great attention. On this occasion Otoo was the principal show-man; for by this time he was well acquainted with the different parts of the ship. Soon after the king and his attendants went away also. Captain Cook had been urged to assist them against Tiarabou, but to their solicitations he gave no encouragement.

On the 28th, one of the natives attempting to steal a water-cask from the watering-place, was caught in the act, sent on board, and put in irons; in which situation Otoo and the other chief saw him. Having made known his crime to them, Otoo begged he might be set at liberty. This the Captain refused, telling him, that since he punished his people, when they committed the least offence against the natives, it was but just this man should be punished also. Accordingly, he ordered the man to be carried on shore to the tents; and having expostulated with Otoo on the conduct of his people in general, telling him, that neither he nor any of his people took anything from them without first paying for it, he added, that the punishing this offender would be the means of saving the lives of others of his people, by deterring them from committing crimes of this nature. With these and other arguments, which he pretty well understood, he seemed satisfied, and only desired the man might not be killed. The Captain then ordered the crowd, which was very great, to be kept at a proper distance, and in the presence of them all ordered the fellow two dozen of lashes with a cat-of-nine-tails, which he bore with great firmness, and was then set at liberty. After this the natives were going away; but Towha stepped forth, called them back, and harangued them for near half an hour. His speech consisted of short sentences, which were not well understood; but from what they could gather, he condemned their present conduct, and recommended a different one for the future. The gracefulness of his action, and the attention with which he was heard, bespoke him a great orator.

Otoo said not one word. As soon as Towha had ended his speech, the Captain ordered the marines to go through their exercise, and to load and fire in volleys with ball; and as they were very quick in their manoeuvres, it is easier to conceive than to describe the amazement the natives were under the whole time.

This being over, the chiefs took leave and retired with all their attendants, scarcely more pleased than frightened at what they had seen.

On going ashore in the morning of the 7th of May, they found Otoo at the tents, and took the opportunity to ask his leave to cut down some trees for fuel, which he readily granted. The Captain told him he should cut down no trees that bore any fruit. He was pleased with this declaration, and told it aloud several times to the people about them.

The following night all their friendly connections received an interruption, through the negligence of one of the sentinels on shore. He having either slept or quitted his post, gave one of the natives an opportunity to carry off his musket. The first news the Captain heard of it was from Tee, whom Otoo had sent on board for that purpose. They were not well enough acquainted with their language to understand all Tee's story; but they understood enough to know that something had happened which had alarmed the king. In order, therefore, to be fully informed, the Captain went ashore with Tee. As soon as they landed, he was informed of the whole by the sergeant who commanded the party. The natives were all alarmed, and the most of them fled. Tee and the Captain went to look for Otoo; and as they advanced, he endeavoured to allay the fears of the people, but at the same time insisted on the musket being restored. After travelling some distance into the country, Tee stopped all at once, and advised the Captain to return, saying, that Otoo was gone to the mountains, and he would proceed and tell him that he (the Captain) was still his friend. Tee also promised that he would use his endeavours to recover the musket.

Captain Cook returned to the ship, and soon after he observed six large canoes coming round Point Venus. There being room for suspecting that some person belonging to these canoes had committed the theft, he came to a resolution to intercept them; and having put off in a boat for that purpose, gave orders for another to follow. One of the canoes, which was some distance ahead of the rest, came directly for the ship. He went alongside this, and was told that Otoo was then at the tents. Pleased with this news, he contradicted the orders he had given for intercepting the other canoes, thinking they might be coming on board also. But when he landed he was told that Otoo had not been there, nor knew they anything of him. On looking behind him, he saw all the canoes making off in the greatest haste; even the one he had left alongside the ship had evaded going on board, and was making her escape. Vexed at being thus outwitted, he resolved to pursue them, and as he passed the ship, gave orders to send another boat for the same purpose. Five out of six they took, and brought alongside; but the first, which acted the finesse so well, got clear off.

In one of the canoes they had taken was a chief, a friend of Mr Forster's, who had hitherto called himself an *earee*, and would have been much offended if anyone had called his title in question; also three women, his wife and daughter, and the mother of the late Toutaha. These, together with the canoes, the Captain resolved to detain, and to send the chief to Otoo; thinking he would have weight enough with him to obtain the return of the musket, as his own property was at stake.

In the dusk of the evening it was brought to the tents, together with some other things they had lost, which they knew nothing of, by three men who had pursued the thief, and taken them from him. The Captain knew not if they took this trouble of their own accord, or by order of Otoo. He rewarded them, and made no farther inquiry about it.

When the musket and other things were brought in, everyone then present, or who came after, pretended to have had some hand in recovering them, and claimed a reward accordingly. But there was no one acted this farce so well as Nuno, a man of some note, and well known to Captain Cook when he was here in 1769. This man came, with all the savage fury imaginable in his countenance, and a large club in his hand, with which he beat about him, in order to show how he alone had killed the thief; when, at the same time, they all knew he had not been out of his house the whole time.

Things were now once more restored to their former state; and Otoo promised, on his part, that the next day they should be supplied as usual.

They then returned with him to his proper residence at Oparree, and there took a view of some of his dockyards (for such they will deserved to be called) and large canoes; some lately built and others building; two of which were the largest they had ever seen under that name. They now returned to the ship.

Otoo desiring to see some of the great guns fire from the ship, Captain Cook ordered twelve to be shotted and fired toward the sea. As he had never seen a cannon fired before, the sight gave him as much pain as pleasure. In the evening, they entertained him with fireworks, which gave him great satisfaction. Thus ended all their differences.

As the most essential repairs of the ship were nearly finished, it was resolved to leave Otaheite in a few days, Captain Cook accordingly ordered everything to be got off from the shore, that the natives might see they were about to depart.

On the 12th, old Oberea, the woman who, when the *Dolphin* was here in 1767, was thought to be queen of the island, and whom they had not seen since 1769, paid them a visit, and brought a present of hogs and fruit. Soon after, came Otoo with great retinue, and a large quantity of provisions The Captain was pretty liberal in his returns, thinking it might be the last time he should see these good people, who had so liberally relieved their wants;

and, in the evening, entertained them with fireworks.

On the 14th they saw a number of war canoes coming round the point of Oparree. Being desirous of having a nearer view of them, accompanied by many officers and gentlemen, they hastened down to Oparree, which they reached before all the canoes were landed, and had an opportunity of seeing in what manner they approached the shore. When they got before the place where they intended to land, they formed themselves into divisions, and then each division, one after the other, paddled in for the shore with all their might, in the most exact and regular manner. All their motions were observed with such quickness as clearly showed them to be expert in their business. Otoo, who was present, caused some of their troops to go through their exercise on shore. Two parties first began with clubs, but this was over almost as soon as begun; so that they had no time to make observations. They then went to single combat, and exhibited the various methods of fighting with great alertness; parrying off the blows and pushes, which each combatant aimed at the other, with great dexterity. Their arms were clubs and spears; the latter they also use as darts. In fighting with the club, all blows intended to be given the legs, were evaded by leaping over it; and those intended for the head, by couching a little, and leaping on one side; thus the blow would fall to the ground.

Their treatment at this isle was such as had induced one of the gunner's mates to form a plan to remain at it; but he was discovered before he could effect his purpose. He was an Irishman by birth, and had sailed in the Dutch service. The Captain picked him up at Batavia on his return from his former voyage, and he had been with him ever since. He never learnt that he had either friends or connections, to confine him to any particular part of the world. All nations were alike to him. Where then could such a man be more happy than at one of these isles? Where, in one of the finest climates in the world, he could enjoy not only the necessaries, but the luxuries of life, in ease and plenty.

The two goats which Captain Furneaux gave to Otoo when they were last here, seemed to promise fair for answering the end for which they were put on shore. The ewe soon after had two female kids, which were now so far grown as to be nearly ready to propagate; and the old ewe was again with kid. The people seemed to be very fond of them, and they to like their situation as well; for they were in excellent condition. From this circumstance it was hoped that, in a few years, they would have some to spare to their neighbours; and, by that means, in time spread over all the isles in this ocean. The sheep which they left, died soon after, excepting one, which they understood was yet alive. They also furnished them with a stock of cats; no less than twenty having been given away at this isle.

In the afternoon, on the 15th of May, they anchored in O'Wharre Harbour, in the island of Huaheine, when Oree, the chief, brought a hog and other articles to the Captain, who in return invited him and his friends to dinner. In the evening of the 17th, some of the gentlemen went to a dramatic entertainment given by Oree. The piece represented a girl as running away with them from Otaheite; which was in some degree true; as a young woman had taken a passage with them down to Ulietea, and happened now to be present at the representation of her own adventures; which had such an effect upon her, that it was with great difficulty the gentlemen could prevail upon her to see the play out, or to refrain from tears while it was acting.

Some of the petty officers, who had leave to go into the country for their amusement, took two of the natives with them to be their guides, and to carry their bags, containing nails, hatchets, etc., the current cash they traded with here; which the fellows made off with in the following artful manner. The gentlemen had with them two muskets for shooting birds. After a shower of rain, their guides pointed out some for them to shoot. One of the muskets having missed fire several times, and the other having gone off, the instant the fellows saw themselves secure from both, they ran away, leaving the gentlemen gazing after them with so much surprise, that no one had presence of mind to pursue them.

Early in the morning of the 23rd they unmoored and put to sea. Oree, the chief, was the last man who went out of the ship. At parting, the Captain told him they should see each other no more, at which he wept, and said, 'Let your sons come, we will treat them well.' Oree was a good man in the utmost sense of the word; but many of the people were far from being of that disposition, and seemed to take advantage of his old age. During their stay here they got breadfruit and coconuts in abundance, but not hogs enough; and yet it did not appear that they were scarce in the isle. It must, however, be allowed, that the number they took away, when last here, must have thinned them greatly, and at the same time, stocked the isle with our articles.

As soon as they were clear of the harbour they made sail, and stood over for the south end of Ulietea, where they dropped anchor the next day.

On the 25th a party went ashore to pay the chief a visit, and make the customary present. At their first entering his house, they were met by four or five old women, weeping and lamenting, as it were, most bitterly, and at the same time cutting their heads with instruments made of sharks' teeth, till the blood ran plentifully down their faces and on their shoulders. What was still worse, they were obliged to submit to the embraces of these old hags, and by that means were all besmeared with blood. This ceremony being over, they went out, washed themselves, and immediately after appeared as cheerful as any of the company. The Captain made his presents, and after some little stay returned on board.

On the 27th they were entertained with a play called *Mididij Harramy*, which signifies the Child is Coming. It concluded with the representation of a woman in labour, acted by a set of great brawny fellows, one of whom at last brought forth a strapping boy, about six feet high, who ran about the stage, dragging after him a large wisp of straw which hung by a string from his middle. They had an opportunity of seeing this acted another time, when it was observed, that the moment they had got hold of the fellow who represented the child, they flattened or pressed his nose. From this they judged that they do so by their children when born, which may be the reason why all in general have flat noses. This part of the play, from its newness, and the ludicrous manner in which it was performed, gave them, the first time they saw it, some entertainment, and caused a loud laugh, which might be the reason why they acted it afterwards. But this, like all their other pieces, could entertain them no more than once.

On the 30th one of the chiefs made the Captain a present of two pigs; he invited the donor to dinner, and ordered one of the pigs to be killed and dressed, and attended himself to the first part of the operation, which was as follows: they strangled the hog, which was done by three men; the hog being placed on his back, two of them laid a pretty strong stick across his throat, and pressed with all their weight on each end; the third man held his hind legs, and kept him on his back. In this manner they held him for about ten minutes before he was quite dead. The hog weighed about fifty pounds. It was baked in their usual manner. It ate well, and had an excellent flavour.

Captain Cook having fixed on the 4th of June, George the Third's birthday, for sailing, Oreo, the chief, and his whole family, came on board to take their last farewell, accompanied by Oo-oo-rou and several of their friends. None came empty; but Oo-oo-rou brought a pretty large present, this being his first and only visit. The Captain distributed amongst them almost everything he had left. The very hospitable manner in which he had ever been received by these people had endeared them to him, and given them a just title to everything in his power to grant.

Oreo pressed him to return; when the Captain declined making any promises on that head, he asked the name of his *morai* (burying-place). As strange a question as this was, he hesitated not a moment to tell him Stepney, the parish in which he lived when in London. He was requested to repeat it several times over till they could pronounce it; then, 'Stepney *morai no toote*' was echoed through a hundred mouths at once. What greater proof could they have of these people esteeming them as friends, than their wishing to remember them even beyond the grave? They had been repeatedly told that they should see them no more; they then wanted to know where they were to mingle with their parent dust.

As they could not promise, or even suppose, that more English ships would be sent to those isles, their faithful companion Oedidee chose to remain in his native country. But he left the ship with a regret fully demonstrative of the esteem he had for them. Just as Oedidee was going out of the ship, he asked the Captain to *tatou parou* for him, in order to show the commanders of other ships which might stop here. He complied with his request, gave him a certificate of the time he had been with them, and recommended him to the notice of those who might touch at the island after them.

Nature is exceedingly kind to these islands; and the natives, copying her bounty, are equally liberal, contributing plentifully and cheerfully to the wants of navigators. On leaving the harbour they fired a salute in honour of the day.

Nothing particular happened for more than a week.

On the 16th, just after sunrise, land was seen from the masthead. They immediately steered for it, and found it to be an island, composed of five or six woody islets, connected together by sand-banks and breakers, enclosing a lake, into which they could see no entrance. The Captain looked upon this as a new discovery, and named it Palmerston Island, in honour of Lord Palmerston, one of the lords of the Admiralty.

On the 20th they saw land; and as they drew nearer, found it to be an island of considerable extent. Perceiving some people on the shore, and landing seeming to be easy, they hoisted out two boats, with which they put off to the land, accompanied by some of the officers and gentlemen.

Friendly signs were made to the natives, which were answered by menaces. All endeavours to bring them to a parley were to no purpose; for they advanced with the ferocity of wild boars, and threw their darts. Two or three muskets, discharged in the air, did not hinder one of them from advancing still farther, and throwing another dart, which passed close over the Captain's shoulder. His temerity would have cost him his life, had not the Captain's musket missed fire.

The conduct and aspect of these islanders occasioned the Captain's naming it Savage Island. They seemed to be stout well made men, were naked, except round the waists, and some of them had their faces, breast, and thighs, painted black.

On the 26th of June they arrived off the coast of Rotterdam. Before they had well got to an anchor, the natives came off from all parts in canoes, bringing with them yams and shaddocks, which they exchanged for small nails and old rags. Early in the morning the captain went ashore with Mr Gilbert, to look for fresh water, and were received with great courtesy by the natives. After they had distributed some presents amongst them, he asked for water, and was conducted to a brackish pond of it, about three-fourths of a mile from the landing-place; which he supposed to be the same that Tasman watered at. In the meantime, the people in the boat had laden her with fruit and roots which the natives had brought down, and exchanged for nails and beads. In the afternoon the surgeon was robbed of his gun, by a fellow who ran off with it, and would have stripped him, as he imagined, had he not presented a tooth-pick case, which the natives probably thought was a little gun. As soon as the Captain heard of this he went to the place where the robbery was committed, but took no steps to recover it; in this he acknow—ledges he was wrong, as it encouraged farther aggressions.

Early in the morning of the 28th, Lieutenant Clerke, with the master and fourteen or fifteen men, went on shore in the launch for water. She was no sooner landed than the natives gathered about her, behaving in so rude a manner that the officers were in some doubt if they should land the casks; however, they ventured, and with difficulty got them filled, and into the boat again. While thus employed, Mr Clerke's gun was snatched from him and carried off; as were also some of the cooper's tools and other articles. All this was done, as it were, by stealth; for they laid hold of nothing by main force. Captain Cook landed just as the launch was ready to put off, and the natives, who were pretty numerous on the beach, as soon as they saw him, fled; so that he suspected something had happened. However, he prevailed on many to stay; being informed of all the preceding circumstances, he quickly resolved to force them to make restitution; and for this purpose ordered all the marines to be armed and sent on shore. He then sent all the boats off but one, with which he stayed, having a good many of the natives about him, who behaved with their usual courtesy; but he made them so sensible of his intention, that long before the mariners came, Mr Clerke's musket was brought; but they used many excuses to divert him from insisting on the surgeon's. At length Mr Edgecumbe arriving with the marines, this alarmed them so much that some fled. Only one person was wounded before the other musket was brought and laid down at his feet. That moment he ordered the same canoes he had seized to be restored, to show them on what account they were detained.

On returning to go on board, he found a good many people collected together, from whom they understood that the man he had fired at was dead. This story the Captain treated as improbable, and addressed a man, who seemed of some consequence, for the restitution of a cooper's adze they had lost in the morning. He immediately sent away two men, as he thought, for it; but he soon found they had greatly mistaken each other; for instead of the adze, they brought the wounded man, stretched out on a board, and laid him down by him, to all appearance dead. Captain Cook was much moved at the sight; but soon discovered that he was only wounded in the hand and thigh. He therefore sent for the surgeon to dress his wounds, which were not dangerous. In the meantime, he addressed several people for the adze; particularly an elderly woman, who had always a great deal to say to him from his first landing; but on this occasion she gave her tongue full scope. The Captain understood but little of her eloquence; but when she found he was determined, she and three or four more women went away, and soon after the adze was brought him, but he saw her no more. This he was sorry for, as he wished to make her a present, in return for the part she had taken in all their transactions.

After leaving Rotterdam, or Anamocka, on the 30th they saw the summit of Amattafoa, but not clear enough to determine, with certainty, whether there was a volcano or no; but everything they could see concurred to make them believe there was.

As the Captain intended to get to the south, in order to explore the land which might lie there, they continued to ply between the isle of Lepers and Aurora; and on the 19th of July, the last-mentioned isle bore south, distant twenty miles.

At daybreak, on the 21st, they found themselves before the channel that divides Whitsuntide Island from the South Land, which is above two leagues over. Having sent two armed boats to sound, and look for anchorage, they soon followed.

Next morning early, a good many of the natives came round them, some in canoes, and others swimming. The Captain soon prevailed on one to come on board; which he no sooner did, than he was followed by more than he desired; so that not only the deck, but rigging, was presently filled with them. He took four into the cabin, and gave them various articles, which they showed to those in the canoes, and seemed much pleased with their reception. While he was thus making friends with those in the cabin, an accident happened that threw all into confusion, but in the end proved advantageous. A fellow in a canoe having been refused admittance into one of the boats that lay alongside, bent his bow to shoot a poisoned arrow at the boat-keeper. Some of his countrymen prevented his doing it that instant, and gave time to acquaint the Captain with it. The fellow, however, seemed resolved, and directed his bow again to the boat-keeper; but, on the Captain calling to him, pointed it at him. Having a musket in his hand loaded with small shot, he gave him the contents. This staggered him for a moment, but did not prevent him from holding his bow still in the attitude of shooting. Another discharge of the same nature made him drop it. At this time, some began to shoot arrows on the other side. A musket discharged in the air had no effect; but a four pound shot fired over their heads, sent them off in the utmost confusion.

These people set no value on nails, or any sort of iron tools; nor indeed on anything they had. They would, now and then, exchange an arrow for a piece of cloth; but very seldom would part with a bow.

Being unwilling to lose the benefit of the moonlight nights, which now happened, they weighed on the 23rd, and proceeded out of the harbour.

When the natives saw them under sail, they came off in their canoes, making exchanges with more confidence than before, and giving such extraordinary proofs of their honesty as surprised them. As the ship, at first, had fresh way through the water, several of them dropped astern after they had received goods, and before they had time to deliver theirs in return. Instead of taking advantage of this, they used their utmost efforts to get up with them, and to deliver what they had already been paid for. Pieces of cloth and marble paper were in most esteem with them; but edge-tools, nails, and beads, they seemed to disregard.

Had they made a longer stay, they might soon have been upon good terms with this ape like nation. For, in general, they were the most ugly, ill-proportioned people they ever saw, and in every respect different from any they had met with in this sea. They are a very dark-coloured and rather diminutive race, with long heads, flat faces, and monkey countenances. Their hair, mostly black or brown, is short and curly; but not quite so soft and woolly as that of a negro. Their beards are very strong, crisp, and bushy, and generally black and short. The men go quite naked, except a piece of cloth or leaf used as a wrapper.

They saw but few women, and they were not less ugly than the men; their heads, faces, and shoulders are painted red; they wear a kind of petticoat; and some of them had something over their shoulders like a bag, in which they carry their children. None of them came off to the ship, and they generally kept at a distance when the ship's people were on shore. Their ornaments are ear-rings made of tortoise-shell, and bracelets. Round the right wrist they wear hogs' tusks, bent circular, and rings made of shells; and round their left, a round piece of wood, which they judged was to ward off the bow-string. The bridge of the nose is pierced, in which they wear a piece of white stone about an inch and a half long, formed like a bow. As signs of friendship they present a green branch, and sprinkle water with the hand over the head.

Their weapons are clubs, spears, and bows and arrows. The two former are made of hard or iron-wood. Their bows are about four feet long, made of a stick split down the middle, and are not circular, but bent more at one end than the other. The arrows, which are a sort of reeds, are sometimes armed with a long sharp point, made of hard wood, and sometimes with a very hard point made of bone; and these points are all covered with a substance which they took for poison. Indeed, the people themselves confirmed their suspicions, by making signs to them not to touch the point, and giving them to understand, that if they were pricked by them they would die.

The people of Mallicollo seemed to be a quite different nation from any they had yet met with, and speak a different language. Of about eighty words, which Mr Forster collected, hardly one bears any affinity to the language spoken in any other island or place they had ever been at. The letter 'r' is used in many of their words; and frequently two or three being joined together, such words were found difficult to pronounce. The Captain observed that they could pronounce most of the English words with great ease. They express their admiration by hissing like a goose.

To judge of the country by the little they saw of it, it must be fertile; but their fruits were not so good as those of the Society or Friendly Isles. They left them a couple of dogs, of which they soon became very fond.

The harbour, which is situated on the N.E. side of Mallicollo, the Captain named Port Sandwich; and it is so sheltered, that no winds can disturb a ship at anchor there. Another great advantage is, that the vessel can be brought so near the shore as to cover the people who may be at work upon it.

Soon after they got to sea they stood over for Ambrym. On the 24th they reached an island near Apee, about four leagues in circuit;

it is remarkable by having three high peaked hills upon it, by which it has obtained that name. They now steered to the east; and having weathered Threehills, stood for a group of small isles which lie off the S.E. point of Apee. These were called Shepherd's Isles, in honour of Dr Shepherd, professor of astronomy at Cambridge.

It should have been remarked, that the night before they came out of Port Sandwich, two reddish fish, about the size of large bream, and not unlike them, were caught with hook and line. On these fish most of the officers, and some of the petty officers, dined the next day. The night following, everyone who had eaten of them was seized with violent pains in the head and bones, attended with a scorching heat all over the skin, and numbness in the joints. There remained no doubt that this was occasioned by the fish being of a poisonous nature, and having communicated its bad effects to all who partook of them; even to the hogs and dogs. One of the former died about sixteen hours after; it was not long before one of the latter shared the same fate; and it was a week or ten days before all the gentlemen recovered. These must have been the same sort of fish mentioned by Quiros, under the name of pargos, which poisoned the crews of his ships, so that it was some time before they recovered; and they would doubtless have been in the same situation had more of them been eaten.

Continuing their course to the south, they drew near the southern lands, which they found to consist of one large island, whose southern and western extremities extended beyond their sight, and three or four smaller ones, lying off its north side. The two northernmost are much the largest, have a good height, and lie in the direction of E. by S. and W. by N. from each other, distant two leagues. They named the one Montagu, and the other Hinchinbrook, and the large island Sandwich, in honour of the Earl of Sandwich.

As they passed Hinchinbrook Isle, several people came down to the sea-side, and by signs seemed to invite them ashore. Some were also seen on Sandwich Island, which exhibited a most delightful prospect, being spotted with woods and lawns, agreeably diversified over the whole surface, with a gentle slope from the hills, which were of a moderate height, down to the sea-coast. This was low, and guarded by a chain of breakers, so that there was no approaching it at this part.

On the 3rd of August, they found themselves abreast a lofty promontory; and early next morning Captain Cook went, with two boats, to examine the coast, to look for a proper landing-place, wood, and water. At this time the natives began to assemble on the shore, and by signs invited them to land. The Captain went first to a small beach, where he found no good landing. Some of the natives who were there offered to haul the boats over the breakers, to the sandy beach, which was thought a friendly offer, but they had reason afterwards to alter their opinion. They put in to the shore in two or three places, but, not liking the situation, did not land. By this time the natives conceived what they wanted, as they directed the boat round a rocky point, where, on a fine sandy beach, the Captain stepped out of the boat without wetting a foot, in the face of a vast multitude, with only a green branch in his hand. They received him with great courtesy and politeness; and would retire back from the boat on his making the least motion with his hand. A man, whom he took to be a chief, seeing this, made them form a semicircle round the boat's bow, and beat such as attempted to break through this order. This man he loaded with presents, giving likewise to others, and asked by signs for fresh water, in hopes of seeing where they got it. The chief immediately sent a man for some, who ran to a house, and presently returned with a little in a bamboo; so that he gained but little information by this. He next asked, by the same means, for something to eat; and they as readily brought him a yam and some coconuts.

In short, he was charmed with their behaviour; and the only thing which could give the least suspicion was, that most of them were armed with clubs, spears, darts, bows and arrows. For this reason the Captain kept his eye continually upon the chief, and watched his looks as well as his actions. He made many signs to haul the boat upon the shore, and at last slipped into the crowd, where he observed him speak to several people, and then return repeating signs to haul the boat up, and hesitating a good deal before he would receive some spike-nails which were then offered him. This made him suspect something was intended, and immediately he stepped into the boat, telling them by signs that he should soon return. But they were not for parting so soon, and now attempted by force, what they could not obtain by gentler means.

As they were putting off the boat, the natives laid hold of the gang-board and unhooked it off the boat's stern. But as they did not take it away, it was thought this had been done by accident, and Captain Cook ordered the boat in again to take it up. Then the natives hooked it over the boat's stem, and attempted to haul her ashore; others at the same time snatched the oars out of the seamen's hands. On pointing a musket at them, they in some measure desisted, but returned in an instant seemingly determined to effect their purpose. At the head of this party was the chief. Signs and threats having no effect, the safety of the boats' crew became the only consideration; and yet the Captain was unwilling to fire on the multitude, and resolved to make the chief alone fall a victim to his own treachery; but his musket at this critical moment missed fire. Whatever idea they might have formed of their arms, the natives must now have looked upon them as childish weapons, and began to let them see how much better theirs were, by throwing stones and darts, and by shooting arrows. This made it absolutely necessary to give orders to fire. The first discharge threw them into confusion; but a second was hardly sufficient to drive them off the beach. Four lay, to all appearance, dead on the shore; but two of them afterwards crawled into the bushes. Happy it was for these people that not half the muskets would go off, otherwise many more must have fallen. One sailor was wounded in the cheek with a dart, the point of which was as thick as a little finger, and yet it entered above two inches, which shows that it must have come with great force. An arrow struck Mr Gilbert's naked breast from some distance; for it hardly penetrated the skin. These arrows were pointed with hard wood.

As soon as they got on board, the Captain ordered the anchor to be weighed. While this was doing, several people appeared on the low rocky point, displaying two oars which had been lost in the scuffle. This was supposed a sign of submission, and of their wanting to give them the oars. He, nevertheless, fired a four pound shot at them, to let them see the effect of their great guns. The ball fell short, but frightened them so much that none were seen afterwards and they left the oars standing up against the bushes.

These islanders seemed to be a different race from those of Mallicollo, and spoke a different language. They are of the middle size, have a good shape and tolerable features. Their colour is very dark, and they paint their faces, some with black, and others with red pigment. They saw a few women, who were very ordinary; they wore a kind of petticoat made of palm leaves, or some plant like it. But the men, like those of Mallicollo, were in a manner naked; having only the belt about the waist, and the piece of cloth or leaf used as a wrapper.

In the night of the 5th of August they saw a volcano, which they observed to throw up vast quantities of fire and smoke, with a rumbling noise heard at a great distance. They now made sail for the island whence it appeared, and presently after discovered a small inlet, which had the appearance of being a good harbour. The wind left them as soon as they were within the entrance, and obliged them to drop an anchor in four fathoms water. After this the boats were sent to sound.

Many of the natives now got together in parties on several parts of the shore, all armed. Some swam off to them, others came in canoes. At first they were shy, and kept at the distance of a stone's throw; they grew insensibly bolder, and at last came under their stern, and made some exchanges. The people in one of the first canoes, after coming as near as they durst, threw towards them some coconuts. The Captain went into a boat and picked them up, giving them in return some cloth and other articles. This induced others to come under the stern and alongside, where their behaviour was insolent and daring. They wanted to carry off everything within their reach; they got hold of the fly of the ensign, and would have torn it from the staff. A few muskets fired in the air had no effect; but a four pounder frightened them so much that they quitted their canoes that instant and took to the water. But as soon as they found themselves unhurt, they got again into their canoes, gave them some halloos, flourished their weapons, and returned once more to the buoys. This put them to the expense of a few musketoon balls, which had the desired effect, without killing any of them.

Towards the evening, Captain Cook landed at the head of the harbour with a strong party of men, without any opposition being made by a great number of the natives, who were assembled in two parties, the one on the right, the other on the left, all armed. After distributing to the old people (for they could distinguish no chief) and some others presents of cloth, medals, etc., he ordered two casks to be filled with water out of a pond, about twenty paces behind the landing-place, giving the natives to understand that this was one of the articles they wanted. Besides water, they got from them a few coconuts, which seemed to be in plenty on the trees; but they could not be prevailed upon to part with any of their weapons. These they held in constant readiness, and in the proper attitudes of offence and defence, so that little was wanting to make them attack them. Their early re-embarking probably disconcerted their scheme, and after that they all retired.

While they were bringing the ship nearer the shore, to wood and water, they observed the natives assembling from all parts, and forming themselves into two parties, as they did the preceding evening, one on each side the landing-place, to the amount of some thousands, armed as before. A canoe now and then came off, bringing a few coconuts or plantains. Captain Cook made an old man, who seemed well-disposed, understand, by signs, that they were to lay aside their weapons, and throwing those which were in the canoe overboard, made him a present of a large piece of cloth. There was no doubt that he understood him, and made this request known to his countrymen; for as soon as he landed, they observed him go first to the one party, and then to the other; nor was he ever after seen with anything like a weapon in his hand. After this, three fellows came in a canoe under the stern, one of them brandishing a club, with which he struck the ship's side, and committed other acts of defiance, but at last offered to exchange it for a string of beads, and some other trifles. These were sent down to him by a line; but the moment they were in his possession, he and his companions paddled off in all haste, without giving the club in return. This was what Captain Cook expected, and, indeed, what he was not sorry for, as he wanted an opportunity to show the multitude on shore the effect of their firearms without materially hurting any of them. Having a fowling-piece loaded with small shot, he gave the fellow the contents; and when they were above musket-shot off, he ordered some of the musketoons to be fired, which alarmed them much. This transaction, however, seemed to make little or no impression on the people there; on the contrary, they began to halloo, and to make sport of it.

After mooring the ship, and placing the guns in such a manner as to command the whole harbour, he embarked with the marines, and a party of seamen, in three boats, and rowed in for the shore. It has been already mentioned, that the two divisions of the natives were drawn up on each side the landing-place. They had left a space between then of about thirty or forty yards, in which were laid, to the most advantage, a few small bunches of plantains, a yam, and two or three roots. The old man before mentioned, and two more, invited them, by signs, to land; but the former trap was still in their memory, which they were so near being caught in at the last island; and this looked something like it. In short, everything conspired to make them believe they meant to attack them as soon as they should be on shore. To prevent this, Captain Cook ordered a musket to be fired over the party on the right, which was by far the stronger body; but the alarm it gave them was momentary. In an instant they recovered themselves, and began to display their weapons. The ship now fired a few great guns, which presently dispersed them; when the party landed, and marked out the limits, on the right and left by a line. The natives came gradually to them, seemingly in a more friendly manner; some even without their weapons, but by far the greatest part brought them; and when they made signs to lay them down, they gave the English to understand, that they must lay down theirs first. Thus all parties stood armed. Many were afraid to touch what belonged to the visitors, and they seemed to have no notion of exchanging one thing for another. The Captain took the old man (whose name was now found to be Paowang) to the woods, and made him understand he wanted to cut down some trees to take on board the ship. Paowang very readily gave his consent to cut wood; nor was there anyone who made the least objection. Having landed again, they loaded the launch with water, and after making three hauls with the seine, caught upwards of three hundred pounds of mullet and other fish. It was some time before any of the natives appeared, and not above twenty or thirty at last, amongst whom was their trusty friend Paowang, who made them a present of a small pig, which was the only one they got at this isle.

During the night, the volcano, which was about four miles to the west, vomited up vast quantities of fire and smoke, as it had also done the night before; and the flames were seen to rise above the hill which lay between. At every eruption it made a long rumbling noise, like that of thunder, or the blowing up of large mines. A heavy shower of rain, which fell at this time, seemed to increase it; and the wind blowing from the same quarter, the air was loaded with its ashes. It was a kind of fine sand or stone, ground or burnt to powder, and was exceedingly troublesome to the eyes.

Early in the morning of the 7th, the natives began again to assemble near the watering-place, armed as usual, but not in such numbers as at first. On landing, they found many of the islanders much inclined to be friends, especially the old people; on the other hand, most of the younger were daring and insolent, and obliged them to keep to their arms. The Captain stayed till he saw no disturbance was likely to happen, and then returned to the ship, leaving the party under the command of Lieutenants Clerke and Edgecumbe.

On the 9th, Mr Forster learnt from the people the proper name of the island, which they call Tanna. They gave them to understand, in a manner which they thought admitted of no doubt, that they eat human flesh, and that circumcision was practised among them. One of the men employed in taking in ballast, scalded his fingers in removing a stone out of some water. This circumstance produced the discovery of several hot springs at the foot of the cliff, and rather below high-water mark.

During the night of the 10th and 11th, the volcano was rather troublesome, and made a terrible noise, throwing up prodigious columns of fire and smoke at each explosion, which happened every three or four minutes; and at one time, great stones were seen high in the air. Mr Forster and his party went up the hill, on the west side of the harbour, where he found three places whence smoke of a sulphureous smell issued, through cracks or fissures in the earth. The ground about these was exceedingly hot, and parched or burnt, and they seemed to keep pace with the volcano; for, at every explosion of the latter, the quantity of smoke or steam in these was greatly increased, and forced out so as to rise in small columns, which they saw from the ship, and had taken for common fires made by the natives. At the foot of this hill are the hot springs before mentioned.

Several other parts of the hill emitted smoke or steam all the day, and the volcano was usually furious, insomuch that the air was loaded with its ashes. The rain which fell at this time was a compound of water, sand, and earth, so that it properly might be called showers of mud. Whichever way the wind was, they were annoyed by the ashes, unless it blew very strong indeed from the opposite direction.

In the morning of the 14th, a party set out for the country, to try if they could not get a nearer and better view of the volcano. The place affected by the heat was not above eight or ten yards square; and near it were some fig-trees, which spread their branches over a part of it, and seemed to like their situation. It was thought that this extraordinary heat was caused by the steam of boiling water, strongly impregnated with sulphur. They proceeded up the hill through a country so covered with trees, shrubs, and plants, that the bread-fruit and coconut trees, which seemed to have been planted here by nature, were in a manner choked up. Here and there they met with a house, some few people, and plantations. These latter they found in different states; some of long standing; others lately cleared; and some only clearing. Happening to turn out of the common path, they came into a plantation where they found a man at work, who, either out of good nature, or to get them the sooner out of his territories, undertook to be their guide. They followed him accordingly; but had not gone far before they came to the junction of two roads, in one of which stood another man with a sling and a stone, which he thought proper to lay down when a musket was pointed at him. The attitude in which they found him, the ferocity appearing in his looks, and his behaviour after, convinced them that he meant to defend the path he stood in. He, in some measure, gained his point; for the guide took the other road, and they followed, but not without suspecting he was leading them out of the common way. The other man went with them likewise, counting them several times over, and hallooing, as they judged, for assistance; for they were presently joined by two or three more, among whom was a young woman with a club in her hand. By these people they were conducted to the brow of a hill, and shown a road leading down to the harbour, which they wanted them to take. Not choosing to comply, they returned to that they had left, which they pursued alone, their guide refusing to go with them. After ascending another ridge as thickly covered with wood as those they had come over, they saw yet other hills between them and the volcano, which seemed as far off as at their first setting out. This discouraged them from proceeding farther, especially as they could get no one to be their guide. They therefore resolved to return, and had but just put this in execution, when they met between twenty and thirty people, whom the fellow before mentioned had collected together, with a design, no doubt, to oppose their advancing into the country.

In the evening, Captain Cook took a walk with some of the gentlemen into the country, on the other side of the harbour, where they had very different treatment from what they had met with in the morning. The people they now visited, among whom was their friend Paowang, being better acquainted with them, showed a readiness to oblige them in everything in their power. They came to a village; it consisted of about twenty houses, the most of which need no other description than comparing them to the roof of a thatched house in England taken off the walls and placed on the ground. Some were open at both ends; others partly closed with reeds; and all were covered with palm thatch. A few of them were thirty or forty feet long and fourteen or sixteen broad. This part of the island was well cultivated, open, and airy; the plantations were laid out by line, abounding with plantains, sugar-canes, yams, and other roots, and stocked with fruit-trees.

On the 15th, having finished wooding and watering, a few hands only were on shore making brooms, the rest being employed on board, setting up the rigging, and putting the ship in a condition for sea. Mr Forster in his botanical excursions, shot a pigeon, in the craw of which was a wild nutmeg. He took some pains to find the tree, but his endeavours were without success.

On the 17th, Captain Cook went ashore to pay a visit to an old chief, who was said to be king of the island. Paowang took little or no notice of him; the Captain made him a present, after which he immediately went away, as if he had got all he came for. His name was Geogy, and they gave him the title of Areeke. He was very old, but had a merry, open countenance. He wore round his waist a broad red and white chequered belt; but this was hardly a mark of distinction.

Next day, the Captain went again ashore, and found in the crowd old Geogy, and a son of his, who soon made him understand that they wanted to dine with him; and accordingly he brought them, and two more, on board. When he got them on board, he went with them all over the ship, which they viewed with uncommon surprise and attention. They happened to have for their entertainment, a kind of pie or pudding made of plantains, and some sort of greens which they had got from one of the natives. On this, and on yams, they made a hearty dinner. In the afternoon, having made each of them a present of a hatchet, a spikenail, and some medals, they were conducted on shore.

On the 19th, the Captain finding a good number of the natives collected about the landing-place as usual, he distributed among them all the articles he had with him, and then went on board for more. In less than an hour he returned, just as the people were getting some large logs into the boat. At the same time four or five of the natives stepped forward to see what they were about, and as they did not allow them to come within certain limits, unless to pass along the beach, the sentry ordered them back, which they readily complied with. At this time, Captain Cook having his eyes fixed on them, he observed the sentry present his piece, and was just going to reprove him for it, but he was astonished beyond measure when the sentry fired, for he saw not the least cause.

At this outrage most of the people fled. As they ran off he observed one man to fall, and he was immediately lifted up by two others, who took him into the water, washed his wound, and then led him off. Presently after, some came and described to the Captain the nature of his wound, and he sent for the surgeon. As soon as he arrived, the Captain went with him to the man, whom they found expiring. The ball had struck his left arm, which was much shattered, and then entered his body by the short ribs, one of which was broken. The rascal who fired, pretended that a man had laid an arrow across his bow, and was going to shoot at him; but this was no more than they had always done, and with no other view than to show they were armed also, at least there was reason to think so, as they never went farther. This affair threw the natives into the utmost consternation; and the few that were prevailed on to stay, ran to the plantations and brought coconuts and other fruits, which they laid down at their feet. So soon were these daring people humbled! When the Captain went on board to dinner, they all retired, and only a few appeared in the afternoon, among whom was Paowang. He promised to bring fruit the next morning, but their early departure put it out of his power.

On the 20th of August they put to sea. These people had not the least knowledge of iron, and cloth could be of no use to people who go naked.

In this island hogs did not seem to be scarce; but they saw not many fowls. These are the only domestic animals they have. Land birds are not more numerous than at Otaheite, and the other islands; but they met with some small birds with a very beautiful plumage, which they had never seen before. There was as great a variety of trees and plants here as at any island they had touched at, where their botanists had time to examine. No sort of fishing tackle was seen amongst them, nor anyone out fishing, except on the shoals, or along the shores of the harbour, where they would watch to strike with a dart such fish as came within their reach; and in this way they were expert. They seemed much to admire the European manner of catching fish with the seine.

These people were of the middle size, rather slender than otherwise; most of them had good features, and agreeable coun-tenances. They never would put a hand to any work they were carrying on, which the people of the other islands used to delight in. They make the females do the most laborious work, as if they were pack-horses. A woman has been seen in this island carrying a large bundle on her back, or a child on her back and a bundle under her arm, and a fellow strutting before her with nothing but a club or spear, or some such thing.

The women were not beauties; but were thought handsome enough for the men, and too handsome for the use that is made of them. Both sexes were of a very dark colour, but not black; nor had they the least characteristic of the negro about them. They used pigments of black, red, and brown, which they lay on with a liberal hand, not only on the face, but on the neck, shoulders, and breast. The men wore nothing but a belt, and a wrapping leaf. The women had a kind of petticoat made of the filaments of the plantain tree, flags, or some such thing, which reaches below the knee. Both sexes wore ornaments, such as bracelets, earrings, necklaces, and amulets.

With darts they kill both birds and fish, and are excellent marksmen. They always throw with all their might, let the distance be what it will. Mr Wales, speaking of their dexterity, says, 'I must confess I have been often led to think the feats which Homer represents his heroes as performing with their spears a little too much of the marvellous to be admitted into an heroic poem; I mean when confined within the strait stays of Aristotle. Nay, even so great an advocate for him as Mr Pope acknowledges them to be surprising. But since I have seen what these people can do with their wooden spears, and them badly pointed, and not of a very hard nature, I have not the least exception to any one passage in that great poet on this account. But If I see fewer exceptions, I can find infinitely more beauties in him; as he has, I think, scarce an action, circumstance or description of any kind whatever, relating to a spear, which I have not seen and recognised among these people; as their whirling motion, and whistling noise, as they fly; their quivering motion, as they stick in the ground when they fall; their meditating their aim, when they are going to throw; and their shaking them in their hand as they go along.'

As soon as the boats were hoisted in, they made sail, and stretched to the eastward. Nothing material occurred till September 4th, when looking S.E. the coast seemed to terminate in a high promontory, which the Captain named Cape Colnet, after one of his midshipmen, who first discovered this land.

Some gaps or openings were seen on the 5th to lie all along the coast, whither they plied up. After running two leagues down the outside of the reef (for such it proved) they came before an opening that had the appearance of a good channel. They wanted to get on shore, to have an opportunity to observe an eclipse of the sun, which was soon to happen. With this view they hoisted out two armed boats, and sent them to sound the channel; ten or twelve large sailing canoes being then near them. They had observed them coming off from the shore all the morning, from different parts.

The boats having made a signal for a channel, they stood in. They had hardly got to an anchor before they were surrounded by a great number of the natives, in sixteen or eighteen canoes, the most of whom were without any sort of weapons. At first they were shy of coming near the ship: but in a short time they prevailed on the people in one boat to get close enough to receive some presents. These they lowered down to them by a rope, to which, in return, they tied two fish that stunk intolerably. These mutual exchanges bringing on a kind of confidence, two ventured on board the ship; and presently after she was filled with them, and they had the company of several at dinner in the cabin. Like all the nations they had lately seen, the men were almost naked. They were curious in examining every part of the ship, which they

viewed with uncommon attention. They had not the least knowledge of goats, hogs, dogs, or cats, and had not even a name for one
of them. They seemed fond of large spike-nails and pieces of red
cloth, or indeed any other colour; but red was their favourite.

After dinner, Captain Cook went on shore with two armed
boats, having with them one of the natives who had attached
himself to him. They landed on a sandy beach before a vast number
of people, who had got together with no other intent than to see
them; for many of them had not a stick in their hands; consequently they were received with great courtesy, and with the
surprise natural for people to express at seeing men and things so
new to them as they must be. The Captain made presents to all
those his new friend pointed out, who were either old men, or
such as seemed to be of some note; but he took not the least notice
of a few women who stood behind the crowd, keeping back the
Captain's hand when he was going to give them some beads and
medals. Here they found a chief, whose name was Teabooma; and
they had not been on shore above ten minutes before he called for
silence. Being instantly obeyed by every individual present, he
made a short speech; and soon after another chief having called for
silence, made a speech also. It was pleasing to see with what
attention they were heard. Their speeches were composed of short
sentences; to each of which two or three old men answered, by
nodding their heads, and giving a kind of grunt, significant of
approbation. It was impossible for them to know the purport of
these speeches; but they had reason to think they were favourable
to them, on whose account they doubtless were made.

The natives conducted them, upon inquiring for water, about
two miles round the coast, to a little straggling village near some
mangroves; there they landed, and were shown fresh water. The
ground near this village was finely cultivated, being laid out in
plantations of sugar-canes, plantains, yams, and other roots. They
heard the crowing of cocks, but saw none. As they proceeded up
the creek, Mr Forster having shot a duck flying over their heads,
which was the first use these people saw made of firearms, the
native, whom Captain Cook distinguished by the name of his
friend, begged to have it; and when he landed, told his countryman
in what manner it was killed. The day being far spent they took
leave of the people, and got on board a little after sunset.

Next morning they were visited by some hundreds of the natives; so that before ten o'clock, their decks, and all other parts of the ship were quite full. The Captain's friend, who was of the number, brought him a few roots, but all the others came empty in respect to eatables. Some few had with them their arms, such as clubs and darts, which they exchanged for nails, pieces of cloth, etc. Next day Mr Wales, accompanied by Lieutenant Clerke, went to make preparations for observing the eclipse of the sun which was to happen in the afternoon.

This afternoon a fish being struck by one of the natives near the watering-place, the Captain's clerk purchased it, and sent it to him after his return on board. It was of a new species, something like a sun-fish, with a large, long, ugly head. Having no suspicion of its being of a poisonous nature, they ordered it to be dressed for supper; but, very luckily, the operation of drawing and describing took up so much time that it was too late, so that only the liver and roe were dressed, of which the two Mr Forsters and the Captain did but taste. About three o'clock in the morning they all found themselves seized with an extraordinary weakness and numbness all over their limbs. The Captain had almost lost the sense of feeling; nor could he distinguish between light and heavy bodies, of such as he had strength to move; a quart pot full of water and a feather being the same in his hand. They each of them took an emetic, and after that a sweat, which gave them much relief. In the morning, one of the pigs which had eaten the entrails was found dead. When the natives came on board and saw the fish hung up, they immediately gave them to understand it was not wholesome food, and expressed the utmost abhorrence of it, though no one was observed to do this when the fish was to be sold, or even immediately after it was purchased.

In the afternoon of the 8th, the Captain received a message acquainting him that Teabooma, the chief, was come with a present consisting of a few yams and sugar-canes. In return, he sent him, among other articles, a dog and a bitch, both young, but nearly full-grown. The dog was red and white, but the bitch was all red, or the colour of an English fox. The Captain says, he mentions this, because they may prove the Adam and Eve of their species in that country.

In the evening of the 11th the boats returned, when the Captain was informed the cutter was near being lost, by suddenly filling with water, which obliged them to throw several things overboard before they could free her and stop the leak she had sprung. From a fishing canoe, which they met coming in from the reefs, they got as much fish as they could eat; and they were received by Teabi, the chief of the isle of Balabea, with great courtesy. In order not to be too much crowded, they drew a line on the ground, and gave the natives to understand they were not to come within it. This restriction they observed, and one of them soon after turned it to his own advantage; for happening to have a few coconuts, which one of the sailors wanted to buy, and he was unwilling to part with, he walked off, and was followed by the man who wanted them. On seeing this he sat down on the sand, made a circle round him as he had seen them do, and signified that the other was not to come within it, which was accordingly observed.

In the afternoon of the 12th, Captain Cook went on shore, and on a large tree, which stood close to the shore, near the watering-place, had an inscription cut, setting forth the ship's name, date, etc., as a testimony of their being the first discoverers of this country. This being done, they took leave of the natives, and returned on board; when he ordered all the boats to be hoisted in, in order to be ready to put to sea in the morning.

The people of this island are strong, robust, active, and well-made; they are also courteous and friendly, and not in the least addicted to pilfering, which is more than can be said of any other nation in this sea. They are nearly of the same colour as the natives of Tanna, but have better features, more agreeable countenances, and are a much stouter race; a few being seen who measured six feet four inches. Their hair and beards are in general black. The former is very much frizzled; so that, at first sight, it appears like that of a negro. These rough heads most probably want frequent scratching; for which purpose they have a kind of comb made of sticks of hard wood, from seven to nine or ten inches long, and about the thickness of knitting needles. A number of these, seldom exceeding twenty, but generally fewer, are fastened together at one end, parallel to, and near one-tenth of an inch from each other. The other ends, which are a little pointed, will spread out or open like the sticks of a fan. These combs or scratchers, for they serve both purposes, they always wear in their hair on one side of their head. Swelled and ulcerated legs and feet are common among the men, as also a swelling of the scrotum. It is not known whether this is occasioned by disease, or by the mode of applying the wrapper, which they use as at Tanna and Mallicollo. This is their only covering, and is made generally of the bark of a tree, but sometimes of leaves. The small pieces of cloth, paper, etc., which they got from them, were commonly applied to this use. Some had a kind of concave, cylindrical, stiff black cap, which appeared to be a great ornament among them, and they supposed was only worn by men of note, or warriors. A large sheet of strong paper, when they got one in exchange for anything, was generally applied to this use.

Their houses, or at least most of them, are circular; something like a bee-hive and full as close and warm. The entrance is by a small door, or long square hole, just big enough to admit a man bent double. In most of them they found two fire-places, and commonly a fire burning; and as there was no vent for the smoke but by the door, the whole house was both smoky and hot, insomuch that they, who were not used to such an atmosphere, could hardly endure it a moment.

They have no great variety of household utensils, earthen jars being the only article worth notice. Each family has at least one of them, in which they bake their roots, and perhaps their fish.

They subsist chiefly on roots and fish and the bark of a tree, which also grows in the West Indies. This they roast, and are almost continually chewing. Water is their only liquor, at least they never saw any other made use of. It seems to be a country unable to support many inhabitants. Nature has been less bountiful to it than to any other tropical island known in this sea. The greatest part of its surface consists of barren rocky mountains.

Nevertheless, here are several plants common to the eastern and northern islands, and even a species of the passion-flower, which has never before been known to grow wild anywhere but in America. The botanists did not complain for want of employment at this place; every day bringing to light something new in botany or other branches of natural history.

Their fishing implements are turtle nets, made of the filaments of the plantain tree twisted, and small hand-nets with very minute meshes, made of fine twine, and fish-gigs.

The women of this country, and likewise those of Tanna, are far more chaste than those of the most eastern islands. The Captain says he never heard that one of his people obtained the least favour from any one of them.

Everything being in readiness to put to sea at sunrise on the 13th of September, they weighed, and stood out for sea.

Nothing remarkable occurred till the 28th in the evening, when two low islets were seen bearing W. by S., and as they were connected by breakers which seemed to join those on their starboard, it became necessary to haul off in order to get clear of them. Soon after more breakers appeared extending from the low isles to a great distance.

They spent the night in making short boards, under the terrible apprehension every moment of falling on some of the many dangers which surrounded them.

Daylight showed that their fears were not ill-founded, and that they had been in the most imminent danger, having had breakers continually under their lee, and at a very little distance from them. They owed their safety to the interposition of Providence, a good look-out, and the very brisk manner in which the ship was managed.

They were now almost tired of a coast which they could no longer explore but at the risk of losing the ship, and ruining the whole voyage.

The ship was at this time conducted by an officer placed at the mast-head; soon after, with great difficulty, they arrived within a mile of land, and were obliged to anchor in thirty-nine fathoms water; they then hoisted out a boat, in which the Captain went ashore, accompanied by the botanists. Here they found several tall trees, which had been observed before at a considerable distance; they appeared to be a kind of spruce pine, very proper for spars, of which they were in want; after making this discovery, they hastened on board in order to have more time after dinner, when they landed again with two boats to cut down such trees as were wanting.

The little isle upon which they landed was a mere sand-bank, not exceeding three-fourths of a mile in circuit, and on it, besides these pines, grew the *etos* tree of Otaheite, and a variety of other trees, shrubs, and plants. These gave sufficient employment to the botanists all the time they stayed upon it, and occasioned the

Captain's calling it Botany Isle. Several fire-places, branches and leaves very little decayed, showed that people had lately been on the isle. The hull of a canoe lay wrecked in the sand.

Having got ten or twelve small spars to make studding-sail booms, boats' masts, etc., and night approaching, they returned with them on board.

The purpose for which they anchored under this isle being answered, it was necessary to consider what was next to be done. They had, from the top-mast head, taken a view of the sea around, and observed the whole to the west to be strewed with small islets, sand-banks, and breakers to the utmost extent of their horizon. This induced the Captain to try to get without the shoals.

Next morning at daybreak, the 30th of September, they got under sail, and met with no occurrences worthy of remark for some days.

In the evening of the 8th of October, Mr Cooper having struck a porpoise with a harpoon, it was necessary to bring to, and have two boats out before they could kill it and get it on board. It was six feet long, a female of that kind which naturalists call dolphins of the ancients, and which differs from the other kind of porpoise in the head and jaw, having them long and pointed. This had eighty-eight teeth in each jaw. The haslet and lean flesh were to them a feast. It was eaten roasted, broiled, and fried, first soaking it in warm water. Indeed little art was wanting to make anything fresh palatable to those who had been living so long on salt meat.

On the 10th, at daybreak, they discovered land, bearing S.W., which on a nearer approach they found to be an island of good height, and five leagues in circuit. It was named Norfolk Isle, in honour of the noble family of Howard. After dinner a party embarked in two boats, and landed on the island without any difficulty, behind some large rocks, which lined part of the coast.

They found it uninhabited, and were undoubtedly the first that ever set foot on it. They observed many trees and plants common at New Zealand; and, in particular, the flax plant, which is rather more luxuriant here than in any part of that country; but the chief produce is a sort of spruce pine, which grows in abundance, and to a large size, many of the trees being as thick, breast high, as two men could fathom, and exceedingly straight and tall. It resembles the Quebec pine. For about two hundred yards from the shore, the ground is covered so thick with shrubs and plants as hardly to be penetrated farther inland. The woods were perfectly clear and free from underwood, and the soil seemed rich and deep. They found the same kind of pigeons, parrots, and parakeets, as in New Zealand, rails, and some small birds. The sea-fowl breed undisturbed on the shores, and in the cliffs of the rocks. On the isle is fresh water; and cabbage-palm, wood-sorrel, sow-thistle, and samphire, abounding in some places on the shore; they brought on board as much of each sort as the time they had to gather them would admit.

After leaving Norfolk Isle they steered for New Zealand, intending to touch at Queen Charlotte's Sound, to refresh the crew and put the ship in a condition to encounter the southern latitudes.

On the 17th, at daybreak, they saw Mount Egmont, which was covered with everlasting snow. Their distance from the shore was about eight leagues.

On the 18th, they anchored before Ship Cove; and in the afternoon, the Captain went into the cove, with the seine, to try to catch some fish. The first thing he did after landing was to look for the bottle he left when last here, in which was the memorandum. It was taken away, but by whom it did not appear. Two hauls with the seine producing only four small fish, they in some measure made up for this deficiency by shooting several birds.

Being little wind this morning, they weighed and warped the ship into the cove, and there moored. Here the forge was erected, and the ship and rigging repaired. The Captain gave orders that vegetables should be boiled every morning with oatmeal and portable broth for breakfast, and with peas and broth every day for dinner for the whole crew, over and above their usual allowance of salt meat.

In the afternoon, as Mr Wales was setting up his observatory, he discovered that several trees, which were standing when they last sailed from this place, had been cut down with saws and axes. It was therefore now no longer to be doubted that the *Adventure* had been in this cove after they had left it.

Nothing remarkable happened till the 24th, when, in the morning, two canoes were seen coming down the sound; but as soon as they perceived the ship, they retired. After breakfast they went in a boat to look for them; and as they proceeded along the shore, they shot several birds. The report of the muskets gave notice of their approach; and the natives discovered themselves in

Shag Cove, by hallooing to them. The moment they landed, they knew them. Joy then took place of fear; and the rest of the natives hurried out of the woods, and embraced them over and over again, leaping and skipping about like madmen; but it was observed that they would not suffer some women, whom they saw at a distance, to come near them. After they had made them presents of hatchets, knives, and what else they had with them, they gave in return a large quantity of fish, which they had just caught.

Next morning early, the inhabitants paid them a visit on board, and brought with them a quantity of fine fish, which they exchanged for Otaheitean cloth.

On the 28th, a party went a shooting to West Bay, and came to the place where they left the hogs and fowls; but saw no vestiges of them, nor of anybody having been there since. In the evening, they got on board with about a dozen and a half of wild fowls, shags, and sea-pies. The sportsmen who had been out in the woods near the ship, were more successful among the small birds.

On the 6th November, their old friends having taken up their abode near them, one whose name was Pedro (a man of some note) made the Captain a present of a staff of honour, such as the chiefs generally carry. In return, he dressed him in a suit of old clothes, of which he was not a little proud. Having got this person, and another, in a communicative mood, he began to inquire of them if the *Adventure* had been there during his absence; and they gave them to understand, in a manner which admitted of no doubt, that, soon after they were gone, she arrived; that she stayed between ten and twenty days, and had been gone ten months.

The 8th, they put two pigs, a boar, and a sow, on shore, in the cove next without Cannibal Cove; so that it is hardly possible all the methods the Captain has taken to stock this country with these animals should fail.

On the 9th, the natives having brought a very large and season-able supply of fish, the Captain bestowed on Pedro a present of an empty oil-jar, which made him as happy as a prince.

In the afternoon a party went on shore into one of the coves, where were two families of the natives variously employed; some sleeping, some making mats, others roasting fish and fire-roots, and one girl was heating of stones. As soon as the stones were hot, she took them out of the fire, and gave them to an old woman, who was sitting in the hut. She placed them in a heap, laid over them a handful of green celery, and over that a coarse mat, and then squatted herself down, on her heels, on the top of all; thus making a kind of Dutch warming-pan, on which she sat as close as a hare on her seat. The Captain supposes it was intended to cure some disorder she might have on her, which the steams arising from the green celery might be a specific for.

On the 10th of November, they took their farewell of New Zealand, and steered for Cape Campbell.

The Captain's intention now was to cross this vast ocean, so as to pass over those parts which were left unexplored the preceding summer.

On Saturday, the 17th of December, they made the land, about six leagues distant. On this discovery, they wore and brought to, with the ship's head to the south; and having sounded, found seventy-five fathoms water, the bottom stone and shells. The land now before them could be no other than the west coast of Terra del Fuego, and near the west entrance of the Straits of Magalhaens.

This was the first run that had been made directly across this ocean, in a high southern latitude. The Captain says he never made a passage, anywhere, of such length, where so few interesting circumstances occurred. For, the variation of the compass excepted, he met with nothing else worth notice. Here they took their leave of the South Pacific Ocean. 'I have now done with the Southern Pacific Ocean,' says Captain Cook in the quarto edition of his *Voyages*, 'and flatter myself that no one will think that I have left it unexplored, or that more could have been done in one voyage, towards obtaining that end, than has been done in this.'

On the 18th of December, as they continued to range the coast, about two leagues distance, they passed a projecting point, which was called Cape Gloucester. It shows a round surface of considerable height, and has much the appearance of being an island, distant seventeen leagues from the Isle of Landfall.

On the 20th, at noon, they observed York Minster, then distant five leagues. At ten o'clock, a breeze springing up at E. by S., they took this opportunity to stand in for the land, to recruit their stock of wood and water, and take a view of the country.

Here was found plenty of wood and water, and they set about doing what was necessary to the ship, the outside of which was become very foul. The Captain was now told of a melancholy accident which had befallen one of the marines. He had not been seen since eleven or twelve o'clock the preceding night. It was supposed that he had fallen overboard, out of the head, where he had been last seen, and was drowned.

On the 23rd, Mr Pickersgill was sent in the cutter to explore the east side of the sound, with an intent to survey the island, under which they were at anchor, and which the Captain called Shag Island. About seven in the evening he returned, and reported that the land opposite to their station was an island which he had been round; that between it and the east head lay a cove in which were many geese.

This information induced them to make up two shooting parties next day; Mr Pickersgill and his associates going in the cutter, and the Captain and the botanists in the pinnace. Mr Pickersgill went in one direction, and the Captain in another, and they had sport enough among the geese, whence this was denominated Goose Island. There being a high surf, they found great difficulty in landing, and very bad climbing over the rocks when they were landed, so that hundreds of the geese escaped, some into the sea, and others up into the land. They, however, by one means or other, got sixty-two, with which they returned on board all heartily tired; but the acquisition they had made overbalanced every other consideration, and they sat down with a good appetite to supper, on part of what the preceding day had produced. Mr Pickersgill and his associates had got on board some time before with fourteen geese, so that they were able to make distribution to the whole crew, which was the more acceptable on account of the approaching festival; for had not Providence thus singularly provided for them, their Christmas cheer must have been salt beef and pork.

The next morning, the 25th, some of the natives paid them a visit. They are a little ugly, half-starved, beardless race; not a tall person appeared amongst them. They were almost naked; their only clothing was a seal-skin. The women cover their nakedness with the flap of a seal-skin, but in other respects are clothed like the men. Two young children were seen at the breast entirely naked; thus they are inured from their infancy to cold and hardships. They had with them bows and arrows; and darts, or rather harpoons, made of bone, and fitted to a staff. They, and everything they had, smelt most intolerably of train-oil.

The women and children remained in their canoes. These were made of bark; and in each was a fire, over which the poor creatures huddled themselves. They likewise carry in their canoes large seal-hides to shelter them when at sea, and to serve as coverings to their huts on shore; and occasionally to be used for sails.

The natives all retired before dinner; indeed no one invited them to stay. Their dirty persons, and the stench they carried about them, were enough to spoil the appetite of any European, and that would have been a real disappointment, as the ship's company had not experienced such fare for some time. Roast and boiled geese, and goose-pie, was a treat little known to them, and they had yet some Madeira wine left, which was the only article of provision that was mended by keeping; so that their friends in England did not, perhaps, celebrate Christmas more cheerfully than they did. This was named Christmas Sound.

Next day the natives made another visit, and it being distressing to see them stand trembling and naked on the deck, Captain Cook humanely gave them some baize and old canvas to cover themselves.

The refreshments to be got here are precarious, as they are chiefly wild fowl, and may probably never be found in such plenty as to supply the crew of a ship. They consist of geese, ducks, sea-pies, shags, and that kind of gull called Port Egmont hen. Here is a kind of duck, called by the sailors race-horses, on account of the great swiftness with which they run on the water; for they cannot fly, the wings being too short to support the body in the air. The geese, too, are much smaller than English tame geese, but eat as well. They have short black bills and yellow feet. The gander is all white; the female is spotted black and white, or grey, with a large white spot on each wing. The Captain says, of all the nations he had seen, these people seem to be the most wretched. They are doomed to live in one of the most inhospitable climates in the world, without having sagacity enough to provide themselves with such conveniences as may render life, in some measure, more comfortable.

Barren as this country is, it abounds with a variety of unknown plants, and gave sufficient employment to Mr Forster and his party.

On the 28th they weighed and stood out to sea, resuming their course to the east; and the next day, they passed Cape Horn, and entered the Southern Atlantic Ocean. It is the most southern extremity on a group of islands of unequal extent, lying before Nassau Bay, known by the name of Hermit Islands.

From Cape Horn, they stood over for Success Bay, assisted by the currents, which set to the north. Before this they had hoisted their colours, and fired two guns; and soon after, they saw a smoke rise out of the woods, above the south point of the bay, which was supposed to be made by the natives. As soon as they got off the bay, Lieutenant Pickersgill went to see if any traces remained of the *Adventure*; but he saw not the least signs of any ship having been there lately. The Captain had inscribed his ship's name on a card, which he nailed to a tree, at the place where the *Endeavour* watered.

In the morning, at three o'clock, they bore up for the east end of Staten Land, where they arrived next day in the afternoon.

After dinner they hoisted out three boats, and landed with a large party of men; some to kill seals; others to catch or kill birds, fish, or what came in their way. To find the former, it mattered not where they landed, for the whole shore was covered with them; and, by the noise they made, one would have thought the island was stocked with cows and calves. On landing they found they were a different animal from seals, but in shape and motion exactly resembling them. The sailors called them lions, on account of the great resemblance the male has to that beast. Here were also the same kind of seals which they found in New Zealand, generally known by the name of sea-bears; at least they gave them that name. They were in general so tame, or rather stupid, as to suffer them to come near enough to knock them down with sticks; but the large ones were shot, not thinking it safe to approach them. They also found on the island abundance of penguins and shags. Here were geese and ducks, but not many; birds of prey, and a few small birds. In the evening they returned on board with plenty of spoil.

Next day, being January the 1st, 1775, finding that nothing was wanting but a good harbour to make this a tolerable place for ships to refresh at, which chance or design might bring hither, Mr Gilbert went over to Staten Land in the cutter, to look for a good harbour. The Captain also sent two other boats, which returned laden with sea-lions, sea-bears, etc. The old lions and bears were killed chiefly for the sake of their blubber, or fat, to make oil of; for, except their haslets, which were tolerable, the flesh was too rank to be eaten with any degree of relish. But the young cubs were very palatable; and even the flesh of some of the old lionesses was not much amiss.

About ten o'clock, Mr Gilbert returned from Staten Land, where he found a good port, situated three leagues to the westward of Cape St John. It is almost two miles in length; in some places near a mile broad. On the island were sea-lions and seals, and such an innumerable quantity of gulls, as to darken the air when disturbed, and almost to suffocate the people with their dung. This they seemed to void in a way of defence, and it stunk worse than asafoetida. The day on which this port was discovered, occasioned the Captain's calling it New-Year's Harbour.

The sea-lions found here, says Captain Cook, are not of that kind described, under the same name, by Lord Anson; but these would more properly deserve that appellation; the long hair with which the back of the head, the neck, and shoulders are covered, giving them greatly the air and appearance of a lion. The female is not half so big as the male, and is covered with a short hair, of an ash, or light dun colour. They live, as it were, in herds, on the rocks and near the sea-shore. As this was the time for engendering as well as bringing forth their young, they saw a male, with twenty or thirty females about him, and always very attentive to keep them all to himself, and beating off every other male who attempted to come into his flock. Others again had a less number; some no more than one or two.

The sea-bears are not so large, by far, as the lions, but rather larger than a common seal. They have none of that long hair which distinguishes the lion. Theirs is all of an equal length, and finer than that of the lion, something like an otter's, and the general colour is that of iron grey. This is the kind which the French call sea-wolves, and the English seals; they are, however, different from the seals in Europe and North America. The lions may, too, without any great impropriety, be called overgrown seals; for they are all of the same species. It was not at all dangerous to go among them; for they either fled or lay still. The only danger was in going between them and the sea; for if they took fright at anything, they would come down in such numbers, that, if you could not get out of their way, you would be run over.

The oceanic birds were gulls, tern, Port Egmont hens, and a large brown bird of the size of an albatross. The sailors called them Mother Cary's geese, and found them pretty good eating. The land birds were eagles or hawks, bald-headed vultures, or what the seamen called turkey-buzzards, thrushes, and a few other small birds.

It is amazing to see how the different animals which inhabit this place are mutually reconciled. They seem to have entered into a league not to disturb each other's tranquillity. The sea-lions occupy most of the coast; the sea-bears take up their abode in the isle; the shags have post in the highest cliffs; the penguins fix their quarters where there is the most easy communication to and from the sea; and the other birds choose more retired places. Captain Cook says he has seen all these animals mix together like domestic cattle and poultry in a farm-yard, without one attempting to molest the other.

Having left the land in the evening of the 3rd, they saw it again next morning, bearing west.

On the 14th, at nine o'clock in the morning, they descried an island of ice, as they then thought; but at noon were doubtful whether it was ice or land; it turned out to be the latter, and was in a manner wholly covered with snow.

On the 16th, they began to explore the northern coast, and next morning they made sail in for the land. As soon as they drew near the shore, having hoisted out a boat, the Captain embarked in it, accompanied by Mr Forster and his party, with a view of reconnoitring before they ventured in with the ship, which they afterwards declined, as the inner parts of the country were savage and horrible. The wild rocks raised their lofty summits, till they were lost in the clouds, and the valleys lay covered with everlasting snow. Not a tree was to be seen, or a shrub even big enough to make a tooth-pick. They found here nearly the same animals as in New-Year's Harbour.

Since their arrival on this coast, the Captain ordered, in addition to the common allowance, wheat to be boiled every morning for breakfast; but any kind of fresh meat was preferred by most on board to salt. For his part, he says, he was heartily tired of salt meat of every kind; and though the flesh of the penguins could scarcely vie with bullock's liver, its being fresh was sufficient to make it go down. They called the bay they had been in Possession Bay.

As soon as the boat was hoisted in, they made sail along the coast to the east, for the space of eleven or twelve leagues, to a projecting point, which obtained the name of Cape Saunders. Beyond this cape is a pretty large bay, which was named Cumberland Bay.

On the 20th they fell in with an island, which they named the Isle of Georgia, in honour of His Majesty. It extends thirty-one leagues in length, and its greatest breadth is about ten leagues. It seems to abound with bays and harbours, the N.E. coast especially; but the vast quantity of ice coast renders them inaccessible the greatest part of the year.

From the 20th to the 27th they had a continuation of foggy weather. They, now growing almost tired of high southern lati-tudes, where nothing was to be found but ice and thick fogs, stood to the east, when they soon fell in, all at once, with a vast number of large ice islands, and a sea strewed with loose ice. For this reason they tacked and stood to the west, with the wind at N. The ice islands, which at this time surrounded them, were nearly all of equal height, and showed a flat even surface.

On the 1st of February they got sight of a new coast. It proved a high promontory, which was named Cape Montagu, but prudence would not permit them to venture near the shore, where there was no anchorage, and where every port was blocked or filled up with ice, and the whole country, from the summits of the mountains down to the very brink of the cliffs which terminate the coast, covered many fathoms thick with everlasting snow.

It was now necessary to take a view of the land to the north, before they proceeded any farther to the east.

On the 3rd they saw two isles. The day on which they were discovered was the occasion of calling them Candlemas Isles. They were of no great extent, but of considerable height, and were covered with snow. On the 4th they resumed their course to the east. About noon they met with several ice islands and some loose ice, the weather continuing hazy, with snow and rain.

The risk run in exploring a coast, in these unknown and icy seas, is so very great, that no man, Captain Cook says, will ever venture farther than he has done: and therefore the lands which may lie to the south will never be explored. 'Thick fogs, snowstorms, intense cold, and every other thing,' as Captain Cook says, 'that can render navigation dangerous, must be encountered; and these difficulties are greatly heightened by the inexpressibly horrid aspect of the country; a country doomed by nature never once to feel the warmth of the sun's rays, but to lie buried in everlasting snow and ice. The ports which may be on the coast are, in a manner, wholly filled up with frozen snow of vast thickness; but if any should be so far open as to invite a ship into it, she would run a risk of being fixed there for ever, or of coming out in an ice island.'

After such an explanation as this, the reader will not expect to find them much farther to the south. It was, however, not for want of inclination, but for other reasons. It would have been rashness to have risked all that had been done during the voyage, in discovering a coast which, when discovered, would have answered no end whatever, or have been of the least use either to navigation or geography, or indeed to any other science, save magnetic; and besides all this, they were not now in a condition to undertake great things, nor indeed was there time, had they been ever so well provided.

These reasons induced Captain Cook to alter his course to the east, with a very strong gale at north, attended with an exceedingly heavy fall of snow. The quantity which lodged in their sails was so great, that they were frequently obliged to throw the ship up in the wind to shake it out of them, otherwise neither they nor the ship could have supported the weight.

On the 10th the weather became fair, but piercing cold, so that the water on deck was frozen, and at noon the mercury in the thermometer was no higher than 34½°.

On the 22nd of February, as they were within two degrees of longitude from their route to the south, when they left the Cape of Good Hope, it was to no purpose to proceed any farther to the east under this parallel, knowing that no land could be there.

They had now made the circuit of the Southern ocean in a high latitude, and traversed it in such a manner as to leave not the least room for the possibility of there being a continent, unless near the pole, and, as it was then thought, out of the reach of navigation. By twice visiting the tropical sea, they had not only settled the situation of some old discoveries, but made there many new ones, and left very little more to be done in that part. Thus the intention of the voyage had in every respect been fully answered, the southern hemisphere sufficiently explored, and a final end put to the searching after a southern continent.

Their sails and rigging were so much worn, that something was giving way every hour, and they had nothing left either to repair or replace them. Their provisions were in a state of decay, and yielded little nourishment, and they had been a long time without refreshments. The sailors indeed were yet healthy, and, like true British seamen, would have cheerfully gone, as they ever have and ever will, wherever they are led, but they dreaded the scurvy laying hold of them, at a time when they had nothing left to remove it. It would, however, have been cruel to have continued the fatigues and hardships they were continually exposed to, longer than was absolutely necessary. Their behaviour throughout the whole voyage merited every indulgence which it was possible to give them. Animated by the conduct of the officers, they showed themselves capable of surmounting every difficulty and danger which came in their way, and never once looked either upon one or the other as being at all heightened by their separation from their consort the *Adventure*.

On the 8th of March the mercury in the thermometer rose to 61°, and they found it necessary to put on lighter clothes.

On the 12th they put a boat in the water and shot some albatrosses and petrels, which at this time were highly acceptable. Everyone was impatient to get into port; which induced the Captain to yield to the general wish, and to steer for the Cape of Good Hope. Captain Cook now demanded of the officers and petty officers the log-books and journals they had kept, which were delivered accordingly, and sealed up for the inspection of the Admiralty. He also enjoined them and the whole crew not to divulge where they had been, till they had their Lordships' permission to do so.[1]

---

1 Notwithstanding this injunction, so great was the sensation caused by the voyage, that the publishers of the day were anxious to obtain the account of it. The following correspondence is somewhat amusing.

Mile End, 18th September 1775

Sir – Last Saturday morning I examined Mr Anderson, the gunner, about the publication of my late voyage, said to be in the press, and told him that he was suspected of being the author, He affirmed that he had no knowledge or hand in it, and would use his endeavours to find out the author, and yesterday made me the enclosed report.

In the evening of the 17th they saw land about six leagues distant. Next day, having little or no wind, they hoisted out a boat and sent on board a ship which was about two leagues from them; but they were too impatient after news to regard the distance. Soon after three sail more appeared in sight to windward, one of which showed English colours.

Today Marra called upon me, and confirmed what is therein set forth; and farther added, that Bordel, my coxswain, and Reardon, the boatswain's mate, each kept a journal, which they had offered to the booksellers, but they were so badly written that no one could read them. I have no reason to suspect this story, but will, however, call upon the printer, and endeavour to get a sight of the manuscript, as I know most of their writings. This Marra was one of the gunner's mates, the same as wanted to remain at Otaheite. If this is the only account of the voyage that is printing, I do not think it worth regarding. I have taken some measures to find out if there are any more, and such information as I may get shall be communicated to you by, Sir, your most obedient humble servant,

(Signed) JAMES COOK

Philip Stephens, Esq., Admiralty (Enclosure)

SIR – According to your direction I overhauled every bookseller's shop in St Paul's, till at last I came to Mr Francis Newbury's. I fairly caught his shopman, who answered me (when I demanded the *Resolution*'s Voyage), that they had not time to print it yet; I then asked him if it was the Captain's Journal they had; on which he looked at me, and said they had no journal at all yet, but stood as fair a chance to publish the voyage as others. By this time he understood I was pumping of him, so went and brought me one of the shop bills, and bid me good day; telling me that before the voyage was published it would be advertised. I then drove to Marra and Peckover's lodging; found the former at home. I told him I had a message from you, Sir, to deliver to Peckover, on which he, Marra, went and found him. I told him that there would be nothing ever done for him or me, unless we could find out who it was that was publishing the voyage. This made all present very sorry; there was some of your late crew. Some told me Reading wrote a journal, which Enell produced. I deposited five guineas if he would let me show you the account. He consented. Others told me Rollet kept a journal, interlined in his Bible. I wrote down all this information for your satisfaction. At last, Marra pulled the paper from before me (wrote at the Angel, Angel Court, in the borough of Southwark). 'Send that to Captain Cook; if he pleases to send a line for or to me, I'll clear every man that is suspected;' adding, 'I'm the man that is publishing the voyage; I want no preferment, and God forbid I should hinder those whose bread depends on the navy; and, Mr Anderson, as you have always been my friend, come with me, I'll convince you further that the name of Anderson was never intended to be prefixed to the voyage.' He ordered the

The boat returning, reported that they had visited a Dutch East Indiaman, whose captain very obligingly offered them sugar, arrack, and whatever he had to spare. They were told by some English seamen on board this ship, that the *Adventure* had arrived at the Cape of Good Hope twelve months ago, and that the crew of one of her boats had been murdered and eaten by the people of New Zealand.

On the 19th the *True Briton*, Captain Broadly, from China, bore down to them. As this ship did not intend to touch at the Cape, the Captain put a letter on board for the Secretary of the Admiralty.

The melancholy account which they had heard of the *Adventure* was now confirmed. From this ship they procured a parcel of old newspapers, which were new to them, and gave them some amusement; but these were the least favours they received from Captain Broadly. With a generosity peculiar to the commanders of the India Company's ships, he sent them fresh provisions, tea, and other articles, which were very acceptable; and deserve public acknowledgment. In the afternoon they parted company. The *True Briton* stood out to sea, and they in for the land.

The next morning, being with them Wednesday the 22nd, but with the people here Tuesday the 21st, they anchored in Table Bay, where they found several Dutch ships, some French, and the *Ceres*, Captain Newte, an English East India Company's ship from

---

coach to drive to Newbury's; carried me into a back parlour; informed Mr Newbury his friend was kept out of bread, therefore he had discovered all. 'Now,' says he, 'what name is my journal of the voyage to come out in?' 'In no name at all,' says the bookseller. 'Then,' says the other, 'let it come out in the name of John Marra!' At length adding, 'If Captain Cook pleases to call here, Mr Newbury, give him all the satisfaction in your power.' Mr Newbury said he would; after which Mr Newbury invited us both to dinner.

I should, Sir, have waited on you last night, but I'm so lame I could not come up. If you will be pleased to let me know when you will send for Marra, I'll wait on you at the same time to confront him; but there is too many witnesses for him to retract.

Honoured Sir, you'll please to observe that this is twice I innocently fell under your displeasure, which God has been pleased to clear me of. – I am, Sir, with the greatest respect, your most obedient and most humble servant,

(Signed) Rt. Anderson

Records of the Admiralty, Whitehall, Captain's Letters, C vol. 23.

China, bound directly to England, by whom they sent a copy of the preceding part of this journal, some charts, and other drawings, to the Admiralty. Before they had well got to an anchor, the Captain dispatched an officer to acquaint the governor with their arrival, and to request the necessary stores and refreshments, which were readily granted.

The Captain now learned that the *Adventure* had called here on her return; and he found a letter here from Captain Furneaux, acquainting him with the loss of his boat and of ten of his best men in Queen Charlotte's Sound. He afterwards, on his arrival in England, put into Captain Cook's hands a complete narrative of his proceedings from the time of their second and final separation, which we now detail, to complete the history of this voyage.

In October 1773, they were blown off the coast of New Zealand, when they parted company with the *Resolution*, and never saw her afterwards. They combated violent storms till the 6th of November, when, being to the north of Cape Palliser, they bore away for some bay to complete their water and wood, being in great want of both, having been at the allowance of one quart of water for some days past; and even that pittance could not be come at above six or seven days longer. They anchored in Tolaga Bay. Wood and water are easily to be had. The natives here are the same as those at Charlotte Sound, but more numerous. In one of their canoes they observed the head of a woman lying in state, adorned with feathers and other ornaments. It had the appearance of being alive; but, on examination, they found it dry, being preserved with every feature perfect, and kept as the relic of some deceased relation.

Having got about ten tuns of water and some wood, they sailed for Charlotte Sound on the 12th; but violent weather prevented them from reaching it till the 30th. They saw nothing of the *Resolution*, and began to doubt her safety; but on going ashore they discerned the place where she had erected her tents; and on an old stump of a tree in the garden, observed these words cut out, 'Look underneath.' There they dug, and soon found a bottle, corked and waxed down, with a letter in it from Captain Cook, signifying their arrival on the 3rd instant, and departure on the 24th, and that they intended spending a few days in the entrance of the Straits to look for them.

They immediately set about the necessary repairs of the ship, which employed them till the 16th of December.

Next day they sent their large cutter, with Mr Rowe, a midshipman, and the boat's crew, to gather wild greens for the ship's company, with orders to return that evening, as they intended to sail the next morning. But, on the boat's not returning the same evening, nor the next morning, the second lieutenant, Mr Burney, in the launch, manned with the boat's crew and ten marines, went in search of her. Mr Burney returned about eleven o'clock the same night, and informed them of a horrible scene indeed, which cannot be better described than in his own words.

'On the 18th we left the ship; and having a light breeze in our favour, we soon got round Long Island. I examined every cove on the larboard hand as we went along, looking well all around with a telescope. At half-past one we stopped at a beach on the left-hand side, going up East Bay to boil some victuals. Whilst we were cooking, I saw an Indian on the opposite shore running along a beach to the head of the bay. Our meat being dressed, we got into the boat and put off, and in a short time arrived at the head of this reach, where we saw an Indian settlement.

'As we drew near, some of the Indians came down on the rocks, and waved for us to be gone; but seeing we disregarded them, they altered their notes. Here we found six large canoes hauled up on the beach, most of them double ones, and a great many people. Leaving the boat's crew to guard the boat, I stepped ashore with the marines (the corporal and five men) and searched a good many of their houses; but found nothing to give me any suspicion. Coming down to the beach, one of the Indians had brought a bundle of hepatoes (long spears), but seeing I looked very earnestly at him, he put them on the ground, and walked about with seeming unconcern. Some of the people appearing to be frightened, I gave a looking-glass to one, and a large nail to another. From this place the bay ran, as nearly as I could guess, a good mile. I looked all around with the glass, but saw no boat, canoe, or any sign of inhabitant. I therefore contented myself with firing some guns, which I had done in every cove as I went along.

'I now kept close to the east shore, and came to another settlement, where the Indians invited us ashore. I inquired of them about the boat, but they pretended ignorance. They appeared very friendly here, and sold us some fish. Within an hour after we left this place, in a small beach adjoining to Grass Cove, we saw a very large double canoe just hauled up, with two men and a dog. The men, on seeing us, left their canoe, and ran up into the woods. This gave me reason to suspect I should here get tidings of the cutter. We went ashore, and searched the canoe, where we found one of the rullock-ports of the cutter, and some shoes, one of which was known to belong to Mr Woodhouse, one of our midshipmen. One of the people, at the same time, brought me a piece of meat, which he took to be some of the salt meat belonging to the cutter's crew. On examining this, and smelling it, I found it was fresh. Mr Fannin (the master), who was with me, supposed it was dog's flesh, and I was of the same opinion; for I still doubted their being cannibals. But we were soon convinced by the most horrid and undeniable proof.

'A great many baskets (about twenty) lying on the beach, tied up, we cut them open. Some were full of roasted flesh, and some of fern-root, which serves them for bread On farther search, we found more shoes, and a hand, which we immediately knew to have belonged to Thomas Hill, one of our forecastlemen, it being marked T. H. with an Otaheite tattoo-instrument. I went with some of the people a little way up the woods, but saw nothing else. Coming down again, there was a round spot, covered with fresh earth about four feet diameter, where something had been buried. Having no spade, we began to dig with a cutlass; and in the meantime I launched the canoe with intent to destroy her; but seeing a great smoke ascending over the nearest hill, I got all the people into the boat, and made what haste I could to be with them before sunset.

'On opening the next bay, which was Grass Cove, we saw four canoes, and a great many people on the beach, who, on our approach, retreated to a small hill, within a ship's length of the water side, where they stood talking to us. A large fire was on the top of the high land, beyond the woods, whence, all the way down the hill, the place was thronged like a fair. The savages on the little hill still kept hallooing and making signs for us to land; however, as soon as we got close in, we all fired. The first volley did not seem to affect them much; but on the second, they began to scramble away as fast as they could, some of them howling. We continued firing as long as we could see the glimpse of any of them through the bushes. Amongst the Indians were two very stout men, who never offered to move till they found themselves forsaken by their companions; and then they marched away with great composure and deliberation, their pride not suffering them to run. One of them, however, got a fall, and either lay there, or crawled off on all fours. The other got clear, without any apparent hurt. I then landed with the marines, and Mr Fannin remained to guard the boat.

'On the beach were two bundles of celery, which had been gathered for loading the cutter. A broken oar was stuck upright in the ground, to which the natives had tied their canoes; a proof that the attack had been made here. I then searched all along at the back of the beach, to see if the cutter was there. We found no boat, but instead of her, such a shocking scene of carnage and barbarity, as can never be mentioned or thought of but with horror; for the heads, hearts, and lungs of several of our people were seen lying on the beach; and at a little distance, the dogs gnawing their entrails.

'Whilst we remained almost stupefied on the spot, Mr Fannin called to us that he heard the savages gathering together in the woods; on which I returned to the boat, and hauling alongside the canoes, we demolished three of them. Whilst this was transacting, the fire on the top of the hill disappeared, and we could hear the Indians in the woods at high words; I suppose quarrelling whether or no they should attack us, and try to save their canoes. It now grew dark; I therefore just stepped out, and looked once more behind the beach, to see if the cutter had been hauled up in the bushes; but seeing nothing of her, returned and put off. Our whole force would have been barely sufficient to have gone up the hill; and to have ventured with half (for half must have been left to guard the boat) would have been foolhardiness.

'As we opened the upper part of the sound, we saw a very large fire about three or four miles higher up, which formed a complete oval, reaching from the top of a hill down almost to the water side, the middle space being enclosed all round by the fire, like a hedge. I consulted with Mr Fannin, and we were both of opinion, that we could expect to reap no other advantage than the poor satisfaction of killing some more of the savages.

'Coming between two round islands, situated to the southward of East Bay, we imagined we heard somebody calling; we lay on our oars and listened, but heard no more of it; we hallooed several times, but to little purpose; the poor souls were far enough out of hearing; and, indeed, I think it some comfort to reflect, that, in all probability, every man of them must have been killed on the spot.'

Thus far Mr Burney's report; and, to complete the account of this tragical transaction, it may not be unnecessary to mention, that the people in the cutter were Mr Rowe: Mr Woodhouse; Francis Murphy, quarter-master; William Facey, Thomas Hill, Michael Bell, and Edward Jones, forecastle-men; John Cavenaugh and Thomas Milton, belonging to the after-guard; and James Sevilley, the Captain's man, being ten in all. Most of these were their very best seamen, the stoutest and most healthy people in the ship. Mr Burney's party brought on board two hands, one belonging to Mr Rowe, known by a hurt he had received on it; the other to Thomas Hill, as before mentioned; and the head of the Captain's servant. These, with more of the remains, were tied in a hammock, and thrown overboard, with ballast and shot sufficient to sink it.

In all probability this unhappy business originated in some quarrel, which was decided on the spot; or incautiousness on the part of the boat's crew might have tempted the natives to seize the opportunity of satisfying their inhuman appetites.

They were detained in the Sound, by contrary winds, four days after this melancholy affair happened, during which time they saw none of the inhabitants.

On the 23rd they weighed and made sail out of the Sound and stood to the eastward, but were baffled for two or three days with light winds, before they could clear the coast.

January the 10th, 1774, they arrived abreast of Cape Horn. They were very little more than a month from Cape Palliser, in New Zealand, to Cape Horn, which is 121° of longitude.

On opening some casks of peas and flour that had been stowed on the coals, they found them very much damaged, and not eatable; so thought it most prudent to make for the Cape of Good Hope. On the 17th of February they made the land of the Cape of Good Hope, and on the 19th anchored at Table Bay, where they found Commodore Sir Edward Hughes, with His Majesty's ships *Salisbury* and *Seahorse*. On the 16th of April, Captain Furneaux sailed for England, and on the 14th of July anchored at Spithead.

We now return to Captain Cook and give to our readers, in his own words, the following brief but masterly summary of the latter part of his interesting voyage:

H.M. Sloop Resolution, Table Bay, Cape Good Hope,
22nd March 1775

SIR – As Captain Furneaux must have informed you of my proceedings prior to our final separation, I shall confine this letter to my transactions afterwards. The *Adventure* not arriving in Queen Charlotte's Sound before the 26th of November, I put to sea, and after spending two days looking for her on the coast, I stood away to the south, including to the east. I met with little interruption from ice till we got into the latitude of 66°, where the sea was so covered with it that we could proceed no farther; we then steered to the east, inclining to the south, over a sea strewed with mountains of ice, and crossed the Antarctic Circle in the meridian of 14° 6' west. After this I found it necessary to haul to north, not only to get clear of the ice islands which were very numerous, but to explore a space of sea we had left nearly in the middle of the ocean in that direction. After getting to the latitude of 48°, I edged away to the east, and then again to the south, till we arrived in the latitude of 71° 10', longitude 106½° west. Farther it was not possible to go, all the sea to the south being wholly covered with a solid sheet of ice, in which were ice mountains whose lofty summits were lost in the clouds. Hitherto we had not seen the least signs of land, or any one thing to encourage our researches, nevertheless I did not think the Pacific Ocean sufficiently explored, and as I found we were in a condition to remain in it another year, I resolved to do it, and accordingly stood away to the north, and searched in vain for Juan Fernandez Land. I was more successful with Easter Island, where I made a short stay, and next visited the Marquesas; from the Marquesas I proceeded to Otaheite and the Society Isles, where we were received with an hospitality altogether unknown among more civilised nations. These good people supplied all our wants with a liberal and full hand, and I found it necessary to spend six weeks with them. I left these isles on the 4th of June, proceeded to the west, touched at Rotterdam, stayed two or three days, and then continued our route for Terra del Espirette Santo of Quiros, which we made the 16th of July. I found this land to be composed of a large group of isles (many of them never seen by any European before) lying between the latitude of 14° and 20°, and nearly under the meridian of 168° east. The exploring these isles finished all I had intended to do within the tropic, accordingly I hauled to the south, intending to touch at New Zealand, but on the 4th of September, in the latitude of 20°, I fell in with a large country, which I called New Caledonia. I coasted the N.E. coast of this country, and partly determined the extent of the S.W. I found the whole so encompassed with the shoals, that the risk we ran in exploring it was very great. We were at last blown off the coast, and it was now time for us to return to the south. I was obliged to leave it unfinished, and to continue our route to Queen Charlotte's Sound, where we arrived on the 6th of October. I remained here refitting the sloop and refreshing my people till the 9th of November, when I put to sea and proceeded directly for Terra del Fuego, but over such parts of the sea as I had not visited before. I chose to make the west entrance of the Straits of Magellan, that I might have it in my power to explore the S.W. and south coast of Terra del Fuego, which was accordingly done as well as that of Staten Land. This last coast I left on the 3rd of January last (1775), and on the 14th, in the latitude of 54°, longitude 38° west, we discovered a coast which, from the immense quantity of snow upon it, and the vast height of the mountains, we judged to belong to a great continent, but we found it to be an isle of no more than 70 or 80 leagues in circuit. After leaving this land, I steered to S.E., and in 59° discovered another, exceeding high and mountainous, and so buried in everlasting snow, that it was necessary to be pretty near the shore to be satisfied that the foundation was not of the same composition. I coasted this land to the north, and found it to terminate in isles in that direction. These isles carried us insensibly from the coast which we could not afterwards regain, so that I was obliged to leave it without being able to determine whether it belonged to a continent extending to the south, or was only a group of isles. Our thus meeting with land gave me reason to believe there was such a land as Cape Circumcision, so that I quitted this horrid southern coast with less regret. But our second search for Cape Circumcision was attended with no better success than the first, and served only to assure us that no such land existed. At length, after having made the circuit of the globe, and nothing more remained to be done, the season of the

year, and other circumstances, unnecessary I presume to mention, determined me to steer for the Cape of Good Hope, where
I arrived on the date hereof (22nd March 1775), and found
Ceres, Captain Newte, bound directly for England, by whom I
transmit this, together with an account of the proceedings of the
whole voyage, and such surveys, views, and other drawings as
have been made in it. The charts are partly constructed from my
own observations, and partly from Mr Gilbert's, my master,
whose judgment and assiduity in this, as well as every other
branch of his profession, is exceeded by none. The views are all
by Mr Hodges, and are so judiciously chosen and executed in so
masterly a manner, as will not only show the judgment and skill
of the artist, but will of themselves express their various designs;
but these are not all the works of that indefatigable gentleman;
there are several other views, portraits, and some valuable
designs in oil colours, which, for want of proper colours, time,
and conveniences, cannot be finished till after our arrival in
England. The other gentlemen whom Government thought
proper to send out, have each contributed his share to the
success of the voyage. I have received every assistance I could
require from Mr Walls, the astronomer. Mr Kendal's watch
exceeded the expectations of its most zealous advocates, and by
being now and then corrected by lunar observations, has been
our faithful guide through all the vicissitudes of climates. In
justice to my officers and crew, I must say they have gone
through the dangers and fatigues of the voyage with the utmost
constancy and cheerfulness: this, together with the great skill,
care, and attention of Mr Patten, the surgeon, has not a little
contributed to that uninterrupted good state of health we have
all along enjoyed; for it cannot be said that we have lost one man
by sickness since we left England. If I have failed in discovering
a continent, it is because it does not exist in a navigable sea, and
not for want of looking after; – insurmountable difficulties were
the bounds to my researches to the south. Whoever has resolution and perseverance to find one beyond where I have been, I
shall not envy him the honour of the discovery; but I will be
bold to say that the world will not be benefited by it. My
researches have not been confined to a continent alone, but to
the isles and every other object that could contribute to finish

the exploring the Southern Hemisphere; how far I may have succeeded I submit to their Lordships' better judgment.[1]

The day after Captain Cook's arrival at the Cape of Good Hope, he waited on the governor, Baron Plettenberg, and other principal officers, who received and treated him with the greatest politeness.

They had only three men on board, whom it was thought necessary to send on shore for the recovery of their health; and for these the Captain procured quarters at the rate of thirty stivers, or half a crown per day, for which they were provided with victuals, drink, and lodging.

On examining the rudder, it was found necessary to unhang it, and take it on shore to repair. They were also delayed for want of caulkers. At length they obtained two workmen from one of the Dutch ships; and the *Dutton* English East Indiaman coming in from Bengal, Captain Rice obliged Captain Cook with two more, so that by the 26th of April this work was finished; and having got on board all necessary stores, and a fresh supply of provisions and water, they took leave of the governor and other principal officers, and the next morning repaired on board.

As soon as they were under sail they saluted the garrison with thirteen guns, which compliment was immediately returned with the same number. A Spanish frigate and Danish Indiaman both saluted them as they passed, and Captain Cook returned each salute with an equal number of guns.

While at the Cape, Captain Cook wrote the following preface to his Voyage, which we give verbatim from the original documents:

EXPLANATIONS

I had begun this journal from the time the voyage was first resolved upon, and the sloops put in commission. I had given some account of the various alterations the *Resolution* underwent, and of the final equipment of the two sloops, and in what manner, etc., etc. I had also mentioned the gentlemen who were to embark in the voyage, and those who did actually embark and for what purpose. I had likewise mentioned the watches, and various other articles being put on board for trial

1 Records of the Admiralty, Whitehall, Captain Cook's Letters, C vol. 23.

and experiments; but when I considered that all these things were well-known to the Admiralty, for whose information only I was to keep an account of my proceedings, I thought it would be quite unnecessary to prefix them to this journal, and that it would be sufficient to let it commence at the time of my sailing from Plymouth.

The natural day is made use of throughout the journal, and not the nautical: so that whenever the terms 'a.m.' and 'p.m.' are used, the former signifies the forenoon, or first half of the day; and the latter, the afternoon, or latter half.

In all the courses, bearings, etc., the variation of the compass is allowed, unless the contrary is expressed.

Greenwich is supposed to be the first, or fixed meridian; all to the east of this meridian is called east longitude, and all to the west, west longitude, as far as to the opposite meridian, or 180° each way.

The charts are constructed agreeable to this rule, and with all the accuracy that circumstances would admit, partly from my own observations, and partly from Mr Gilbert's, my master, whose judgment and assiduity in this, as well as every other branch of his profession, is exceeded by none.

The views, etc., are all by Mr Hodges, and are so judiciously chosen, and executed in so masterly a manner, as not only to elucidate what I may have said, but will of themselves fully express the different subjects they represent.

It will be found that some days have been passed over unnoticed; on such days no interesting circumstance accrued.

On reading over the journal, I find I have omitted some things, and others were not sufficiently explained; these defects are attempted to be made up by notes. In short, I have given the most candid and best account of things I was able. I have not natural, nor acquired abilities for writing. I have been, I may say, constantly at sea from my youth; and have dragged myself (with the assistance of a few good friends) through all the stations belonging to a seaman, from apprentice boy to a commander. After such a candid confession, I shall hope to be excused from all the blunders that will appear in this journal.

(Signed) JAMES COOK
Cape of Good Hope, March 22, 1774.[1]

At daybreak in the morning of the 15th of May they saw the island of St Helena, at the distance of fourteen leagues; and at midnight anchored in the road before the town.

Governor Skettowe, and the principal gentlemen of the island, received and treated the Captain, during his stay, with the greatest politeness, by showing him every kind of civility in their power.

During their stay here, they finished some necessary repairs of the ship, which they had not time to do at the Cape. They also filled their empty water-casks; and the crew were served with fresh beef, purchased at five pence per pound. Their beef was found to be exceedingly good, and the only refreshment they had worth mentioning.

On the 21st of May the Captain took leave of the governor and repaired on board. Upon leaving the shore, he was saluted with thirteen guns, which he returned.

In the morning of the 28th, they made the island of Ascension; and the same evening anchored in Cross Bay. They remained here till the evening of the 31st, and notwithstanding they had several parties out every night, they got but twenty-four turtles, it being rather too late in the season. However, as they weighed between four and five hundred pounds each, they were pretty well off.

The island of Ascension is about nine miles in length, in the direction of N.W. and S.E., and six in breadth. It presents a surface composed of barren hills and valleys, on the most of which not a shrub or plant was then to be seen for several miles, but stones and ashes in plenty, an indubitable sign that the isle, at some remote time, had been destroyed by a volcano, which has thrown up vast heaps of stones, and even hills. A high mountain at the S.E. end of the isle seemed to be left in its original state, and to have escaped the general destruction. Its soil was described as a kind of white marl, which yet retained its vegetative qualities, and produced a kind of purslain, spurge, and one or two grasses. On these the goats subsisted; and it was at this part of the isle only where they were to be obtained.

While they lay in the road, a sloop belonging to Bermuda had

---

1 Records of the Admiralty, Whitehall, Captain Cook's Journal, H.M. Discovery Sloop *Resolution*.

sailed but a few days before with 105 turtle on board, which was as many as she could take in; but having turned several more on the different sandy beaches, they had ripped open their bellies, taken out the eggs, and left the carcases to putrefy – an act as inhuman as injurious to those who came after them.

Turtle are to be found at this isle from January to June. The method of catching them is to have people upon the several sandy bays to watch their coming on shore to lay their eggs, which is always in the night, and then to turn them on their backs till there be an opportunity to take them on the next day. Nothing is more certain than that all the turtle which are found about this island, come here for the sole purpose of laying their eggs; for they met with none but females; and of all those which they caught, not one had any food worth mentioning in its stomach; a sure sign that they must have been a long time without any; and this may be the reason why the flesh of them is not so good as those caught on the coast of New South Wales, where they feed.

On the 31st of May they left Ascension, and steered to the northward. They had a great desire to visit the island of St Matthew, to settle its situation; but as they found the wind would not let them fetch it, they steered for the island of Fernando de Noronha, on the coast of Brazil, in order to determine its longitude.

On the 9th of June, at noon, they made that place, distant six or seven leagues. It appeared in detached and peaked hills, the largest of which looked like a church-tower or steeple. When they arrived in the road, a gun being fired from one of the forts, the Portuguese colours were displayed, and the example was followed by all the other forts. Having speedily ascertained the longitude, they stood away without landing.

By the 18th they made no doubt that they had now got the N.E. trade-wind, as it was attended with fair weather, except now and then some light showers of rain; and as they advanced to the north, the wind increased and blew a fresh top-gallant gale.

On the 21st, Captain Cook ordered the still to be fitted to the largest copper, which held about 64 gallons. The fire was lighted at four o'clock in the morning, and at six the still began to run. It was continued till six in the evening, in which time they obtained 32 gallons of fresh water, at the expense of one bushel and a half of coals, which was about three-fourths of a bushel more than was necessary to have boiled the ship's company's victuals only; but the expense of fuel was no object with them. Upon the whole, this was a useful invention; but the Captain said he would advise no man to trust wholly to it; for although you may, provided you have plenty of fuel and good coppers, obtain as much water as will support life, you cannot, with all your efforts, obtain sufficient to support health, in hot climates especially, where it is the most wanting.

Nothing worth mentioning happened till the 13th of July, when they made the Island of Fayal, one of the Azores, and soon after that of Pico. At daybreak the next morning they bore away for the Bay of Fayal, or de Horta, where at eight o'clock they anchored.

The sole design in stopping here was to give Mr Wales an opportunity to find the rate of the watch, the better to enable them to fix, with some degree of certainty, the longitude of these islands. The moment they anchored, the Captain sent an officer to wait on the English Consul, and to notify his arrival, requesting permission for Mr Wales to make observations on shore. Mr Dent, who acted as consul, not only procured this permission of the governor, but accommodated Mr Wales with a convenient place in his garden to set up his instruments; and, indeed, entertained all the gentlemen on board in the most liberal and hospitable manner.

During their stay, the ship's company was served with fresh beef, and they took on board about fifteen tuns of water.

Fayal, although the most noted for wines, does not raise sufficient for its own consumption. This article is raised on Pico, where there is no road for shipping; but being brought to De Horta, and from thence shipped abroad, chiefly to America, it has acquired the name of Fayal wine.

Having left the bay in the morning of the 19th, they steered for the island of Tercera, in order to ascertain its length; but the weather coming on very thick and hazy, and night approaching, they gave up the design, and proceeded with all expedition for England.

On the 29th of July, they made the land near Plymouth. The next morning they anchored at Spithead, and the same day Captain Cook landed at Portsmouth, and set out for London, in company with Messrs Wales, Forster, and Hodges.

On the 9th of August, Captain Cook was promoted to the rank of Post Captain, in acknowledgment of his eminent services and brilliant discoveries.

Having been absent from England three years and eighteen days, in which time, and under all changes of climate, he lost but four men, and only one of them by sickness, it may not be amiss, at the conclusion of this journal, to enumerate the several causes, to which, under the care of Divine Providence, Captain Cook says he conceives this uncommon good state of health experienced by his people was owing.

They were furnished with a quantity of malt, of which was made sweet-wort. To such of the men as showed the least symptoms of scurvy, this was given, from one to two or three pints a day each man, or in such proportion as the surgeon found necessary. This was, without doubt, one of the best antiscorbutic sea medicines then discovered, when used in time.

Sauerkraut, of which they had a large quantity, is a wholesome vegetable food, highly antiscorbutic, and does not spoil by keeping. A pound of this was served to each man, when at sea, twice a week, or oftener, as was thought necessary.

Portable broth was another great article of which they had a large supply. An ounce of this to each man, or such other proportion as circumstances pointed out, was boiled in their peas three days a week; and when they were in places where vegetables were to be got, it was boiled with them, and wheat or oatmeal, every morning for breakfast, and also with peas and vegetables for dinner. Rob of lemon and orange, also, the surgeon made use of in many cases with great success.

But the introduction of the most salutary articles, either as provisions or medicines, will generally prove unsuccessful, unless supported by certain regulations. On this principle, many years' experience, together with some hints Captain Cook had from other intelligent officers, enabled him to lay a plan whereby all were to be governed.

The crew were at three watches, except upon some extraordinary occasions. By this means they were not so much exposed to the weather as if they had been at watch and watch, and had generally dry clothes to shift themselves, when they happened to get wet. Proper methods were used to keep their persons, hammocks, bedding, and clothes constantly clean and dry. Equal care was taken to keep the ship clean and dry betwixt decks. Once or twice a week she was aired with fires; and when this could not be done, she was smoked with gunpowder mixed with vinegar or water. They had, also, frequently a fire made in an iron pot at the bottom of the well, which was of great use in purifying the air in the lower parts of the ship. To this, and to cleanliness, as well in the ship as amongst the people, too great attention cannot be paid; the least neglect occasions a putrid and disagreeable smell below, which nothing but fires will remove.

Captain Cook concludes his account of this his second voyage round the world as follows:

'It doth not become me to say how far the principal objects of our voyage have been obtained. Had we found out a continent there, we might have been better enabled to gratify curiosity; but we hope our not having found it, after all our persevering re-searches, will leave less room for future speculation about unknown worlds remaining to be explored.

'But whatever may be the public judgment about other matters, it is with real satisfaction, and without claiming any merit but of attention to my duty, that I can conclude this account with an observation which facts enable me to make, that our having discov-ered the possibility of preserving health amongst a numerous ship's company, for such a length of time, in such varieties of climate, and amidst such continued hardships and fatigues, will make this voyage remarkable in the opinion of every benevolent person, when the disputes about a southern continent shall have ceased to engage the attention, and to divide the judgment of philosophers.'

We shall only add, that during this voyage, Captain Cook was considered to have resolved the great problem of a southern continent, having traversed that hemisphere in such a manner as not to leave a possibility, as was thought, of its existence within the reach of navigation.[1] In his progress, however, he discovered New Caledonia, the largest island in the Southern Pacific, except New Zealand; the island of Georgia, and an unknown coast, which he named Sandwich Land, the thule of the southern hemisphere; and having twice visited the tropical seas, he settled the situations of the old, and made several new discoveries.

1 It was reserved for Sir James Clark Ross, some seventy years after, to navigate further south, and to prove not only its existence, but the possibility of reaching it.

THIRD VOYAGE

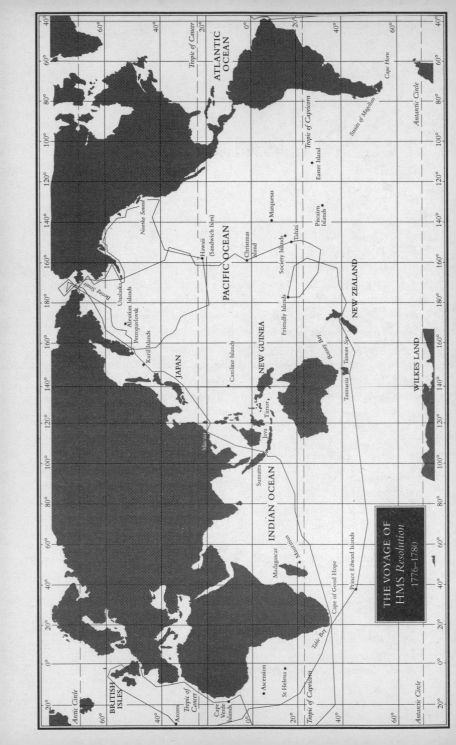

Third Voyage

In the preceding voyage, the question respecting the existence of a southern continent was for the time set at rest, but the practicability of a northern passage to the Pacific Ocean was still an object of so vast importance to England as to excite an earnest desire for the most diligent investigation.

It had long been a favourite scheme with the most celebrated navigators, and with the learned men of the day, to discover a shorter and more commodious course to the Oriental regions than by the Cape of Good Hope. This had been attempted in various directions for two centuries and upwards, but the completion of this favourite object was as distant as ever, and the problem of a junction of the two great oceans, the Atlantic and Pacific, by the northern shores of America, was left to be solved in our own time by the several voyages and discoveries of Sir Edward Parry, Ross, Sir John Franklin, Collinson, McClure, Sir Leopold McClintock, Dease, Simpson, Back, Richardson, and Rae Franklin being now proved, beyond all doubt, to be the first discoverer of a north-west passage.

For the conduct of such an enterprise, it was evident that great skill, perseverance, and abilities, were required; and though, by the universal voice of mankind, Captain Cook was the best qualified, no one could venture to solicit him on the subject. The services he had already rendered to his country, the labours he had sustained, and the dangers he had encountered, were so many and so various, that it was deemed unreasonable to urge him to engage in fresh perils.

As an honourable testimony, however, to his merit and knowledge, it was resolved to ask his advice respecting the most proper person to be entrusted with the conduct of this voyage; and to determine this point, some of the most distinguished naval characters were invited to meet Captain Cook at the house of Lord Sandwich, who then presided over the Board of Admiralty.

While the conversation became animated on the subject, Cook's mind was fired with the magnitude of the design, and the consequences likely to result from it. He suddenly started up, under the impression of a noble enthusiasm, and offered his best services to direct the important objects in view. No proposal could have been more grateful. Captain Cook was immediately invested with the command.[1]

This preliminary step settled, the exact plan of the undertaking was next taken into serious consideration. All former navigators round the globe had returned by the Cape of Good Hope; but to Captain Cook was assigned the arduous task of attempting the same thing by reaching the high northern latitudes between Asia and America; and it appears that this plan was adopted in consequence of his own suggestions. His instructions were, to proceed to the Pacific Ocean, and through that cluster of islands he had before visited within the southern tropic, and thence, if practicable, to make his way into the Atlantic, along the northern coast of America, in whatever latitude it might be found to lie; for nothing whatever was known at that time respecting it.

To give every stimulus to the prosecution of this great design, motives of interest were superadded to the obligations of duty. An Act of Parliament, which passed in 1745, offering a reward of £20,000 to such as should discover a passage through Hudson's Bay, was enlarged and explained; and it was now enacted, that if any ship belonging to his Majesty, or his subjects, should find and sail through any passage by sea, between the Atlantic and Pacific Oceans, in any direction or parallel of the northern

---

1 The following letter formally offers his services:

Admiralty Office, 10th February 1776
Sir – Having understood that their Lordships have ordered two ships to be fitted out for the purpose of making further discoveries in the Pacific Ocean, I take the liberty, as their Lordships, when they were pleased to appoint me a captain in Greenwich Hospital, were at the same time pleased also to say, it should not be in prejudice to any further offer which I might make of my service, to submit myself to their directions, if they think fit to appoint me to the command on the said intended voyage; relying, if they condescend to accept this offer, they will on my return, either restore me to my appointment in the Hospital, or procure for me such other mark of the royal favour as their Lordships, upon the review of my past services, shall think me deserving of. I am, Sir, your most humble servant,

JAMES COOK

To George Jackson, Esq.

Admiralty Records.

hemisphere, to the northward of the 52nd degree of northern latitude, the sum of £20,000 was to reward such discovery.

The vessels destined for this service were the Resolution *and the* Discovery. *The command of the former was given to Captain Cook, and that of the latter to Captain Clerke, who had been second lieutenant on the former voyage. Nearly the same complement of men and officers was assigned to each as before. The following is the list of the principal officers appointed to the two ships:*

Resolution

John Gore, James King, John Williamson, lieutenants.
William Bligh, master.
William Anderson, surgeon.
Molesworth Philips, lieutenant, royal marines.

Discovery

James Burney, John Rickman, lieutenants.
Thomas Edgar, master.
John Law, surgeon.

Several months were spent in the equipment and preparation of the ships, that the health of the seamen and the success of the expedition might have every advantage which a liberal and enlightened attention could bestow. In order that the inhabitants of Otaheite, and other islands in the South Seas where the English had been treated with so much hospitality, might be benefited by the voyage, his Majesty was graciously pleased to order some of the most useful European animals to be put on board for those countries.

Besides these, Captain Cook was furnished with a quantity of garden seeds, and the Board of Admiralty added such articles of commerce as were most likely to promote a friendly intercourse with the natives and to induce them to open a traffic with the English.

Omai, who has been mentioned in the preceding voyage, was likewise to be carried back to his native country. He left his friends in London with a mixture of regret and satisfaction. When he reflected on the kindnesses he had received, he could not refrain from tears; but the pleasing idea of revisiting his original connections, soon made his eyes sparkle with joy.

As the original voyage, from which this historical account is abstracted, is written in the words of Captain Cook, till his lamented death, and afterwards in those of Captain King, who published the whole, we have preferred giving the narrative in the same person, with occasional remarks; the propriety and advantage of which will be obvious to our readers. Some of the general descriptions were furnished by Mr Anderson, the surgeon of the Resolution; *a man of distinguished abilities, and to whose talents Captain Cook acknowledged himself much indebted for many interesting parts of his voyage.*

Contrary winds and other circumstances prevented the ships from clearing the Channel till the 14th of July 1776. On board both vessels were one hundred and ninety-two persons, officers included. 'Nothing material happened,' says Captain Cook, 'till the 1st of August, when we arrived off Tenerife, one of the Canaries, where several of the gentlemen landed. It is said, that none of the aboriginal inhabitants remain here as a distinct people; but that the produce of their intermarriages with the Spaniards may still be traced in a strong and muscular race, dispersed over the islands.'

On the 4th, we weighed anchor and proceeded on our voyage. At nine o'clock in the evening of the 10th, we saw the island of Bonavista, bearing south, distant little more than a league, though, at this time, we thought ourselves much farther off; but this proved a mistake. For, after hauling to the eastward till twelve o'clock, to clear the sunken rocks that lie about a league from the south east point of the island, we found ourselves at that time close upon them, and did but just weather the breakers. Our situation, for a few minutes, was very alarming. I did not choose to sound, as that might have heightened the danger, without any possibility of lessening it.

We had, for some days preceding the 6th of October, seen albatrosses, pintadoes, and other petrels; and now we saw three penguins, which occasioned us to sound; but we found no ground with a line of one hundred and fifty fathoms.

On the 8th, in the evening, one of those birds which sailors call noddies, settled on our rigging, and was caught.

On the 18th of October, we arrived at the Cape of Good Hope, and found in the bay two French East India ships; the one outward, and the other homeward bound. And two or three days before our arrival, another homeward-bound ship of the same nation had parted from her cable and was driven on shore at the head of the bay, where she was lost. The crew were saved; but the greatest part of the cargo shared the fate of the ship.

As soon as we had saluted, I went on shore, accompanied by some

of my officers, and waited on the governor, the lieutenant governor, the fiscal, and the commander of the troops. These gentlemen
received me with the greatest civility; and the governor, in particular, promised me every assistance that the place afforded. At the
same time, I obtained his leave to set up our observatory, to pitch
tents for the sailmakers and coopers, and to bring the cattle on
shore, to graze near our encampment. Before I returned on board,
I ordered soft bread, fresh meat, and greens, to be provided every
day for the ship's company.

Nothing remarkable happened till the evening of the 31st, when
it began to blow excessively hard at south-east, and continued for
three days; during which time there was no communication
between the ship and the shore. The *Resolution* was the only ship in
the bay that rode out the gale without dragging her anchors. We
felt its effects as sensibly on shore. Our tents and observatory were
torn to pieces, and our astronomical quadrant narrowly escaped
irreparable damage. On the 3rd of November the storm ceased.

The *Discovery*, having been detained some days at Plymouth, did
not arrive here till the 10th. Captain Clerke informed me that he
had sailed from Plymouth on the 1st of August, and should have
been with us here a week sooner, if the late gale of wind had not
blown him off the coast. Upon the whole, he was seven days
longer in his passage from England than we had been. He had the
misfortune to lose one of his marines, by falling overboard; but
there had been no other mortality amongst his people, and they
now arrived well and healthy.

While the ships were getting ready, some of our officers made an
excursion into the neighbouring country. Mr Anderson, my surgeon, who was one of the party, gave me the following relation of
their proceedings.

On the 16th, in the forenoon, I set out in a waggon, with five
more, to take a view of some part of the country. We crossed
the large plain that lies to the eastward of the town, which is
entirely a white sand, like that commonly found on beaches,
and produces only heath, and other small plants of various sorts.
At five in the afternoon we passed a large farmhouse, with some
cornfields and vineyards, situated beyond the plain, near the
foot of some low hills, where the soil becomes worth cultivating.

Between six and seven we arrived at Stellenbosch, the colony next to that of the Cape for its importance.

The village does not consist of more than thirty houses, and stands at the foot of the range of lofty mountains, above twenty miles to the eastward of the Cape Town. The houses are neat; and, with the advantage of a rivulet which runs near, and the shelter of some large oaks, planted at its first settling, forms a rural prospect in this desert country. There are some vineyards and orchards, which, from their thriving appearance, indicate an excellent soil; though, perhaps, they owe much to climate, as the air has an uncommon serenity.

I employed the next day in searching for plants and insects, but had little success. Few plants are in flower here at this season, and insects scarce. I examined the soil in several places, and found it to consist of yellowish clay, mixed with a good deal of sand.

We left Stellenbosch next morning, and arrived at the house we had passed on Saturday; the owner, Mr Cloeder, had sent us an invitation to visit him. This gentleman entertained us with the greatest hospitality. He received us with music, and a band also played while we were at dinner; which, considering the situation of the place, might be reckoned elegant. He showed us his wine-cellars, orchards, and vineyards; all which inspired me with a wish to know how these industrious people could create such plenty, where, I believe, no other European nation would have attempted to settle.

In the afternoon we crossed the country, and passed a few plantations, one of which seemed very considerable, and was laid out in a taste somewhat different from any other we saw. In the evening we arrived at a farmhouse, which is the first in the cultivated tract, called the Pearl. We had, at the same time, a view of Drakenstein, the third colony, which lies by the foot of the lofty hills already mentioned, and contains several farms or plantations, not very extensive.

On the morning of the 20th, we set out from the Pearl; and going a different road from that by which we came, passed through a country wholly uncultivated, till we got to the Tyger Hills, when some tolerable cornfields appeared. At noon, we stopped in a hollow for refreshment; but, in walking about here, were plagued with a vast number of mosquitoes or sand-flies, which were the first I saw in the country.

Here Captain Cook added to his original stock of live animals, by purchasing two young bulls, two heifers, two young stone horses, two mares, two rams, several ewes and goats, and some rabbits and poultry. All of them were intended for New Zealand, Otaheite, and the neighbouring islands, or any other places, in the course of their voyage where there might be a prospect that leaving any of them would be useful to posterity.

The following is an extract from Captain Cook's letter on this subject:

Cape of Good Hope, 28th November 1776

I am now ready to put to sea with the first wind, having filled the sloops with provisions, and made some considerable addition to the live stock on board the *Resolution* intended to be sent to Otaheite. As I have taken the liberty to do this with a view of serving posterity, by having some to spare to leave on the lands I may touch at before I arrive at that island, I hope it will meet their Lordships' approbation, and that they will order the bill to be honoured, which I have taken the liberty to draw on you of this date in favour of Mr Christoffel Brand, or order, for the sum of two hundred and fourteen pounds ten shillings and sixpence sterling, in a set of bills of exchange of the same time and date, and payable at thirty days' sight, it being for the purchase and keeping the live stock, supporting Omai, and for defraying Mr Webber's expenses, all of which will appear by the enclosed vouchers. A painting which he made of St Cruz, in the island of Tenerife, I have left with Mr Brand, of this place, to be forwarded to their Lordships by the first safe opportunity.[1]

Having given Captain Clerke a copy of his instructions, and an order directing him how to proceed in case of separation, in the morning of the 30th they repaired on board, and at five in the afternoon weighed, and stood out of the bay.

We steered a south-east course, with a very strong gale from the westward, followed by a mountainous sea, which made the ship roll and tumble exceedingly, and gave us much trouble to preserve the cattle we had on board. Notwithstanding our care, several

1 Records, Admiralty, Whitehall.

goats, especially the males, died, and some sheep. This misfortune was, in a great measure, owing to the cold, which we now began most sensibly to feel.

Nothing of interest happened from the 5th of December till the 26th of January, when they arrived at Van Diemen's Land; where, as soon as they had anchored in Adventure Bay, Captain Cook ordered the boats to be hoisted out. In one of them he went himself, to look for the most commodious place for furnishing themselves with the necessary supplies; and Captain Clerke went in his own boat upon the same service.

Next morning early, I sent Lieutenant King to the east side of the bay, with two parties, one to cut wood and the other grass, under the protection of the marines. For although, as yet, none of the natives had appeared, there could be no doubt that some were in our neighbourhood. I also sent the launch for water; and afterwards visited all the parties myself. In the evening, we drew the seine at the head of the bay, and, at one haul, caught a great quantity of fish. Most of them were of that sort known to seamen by the name of elephant fish.

In the afternoon, next day, we were agreeably surprised, at the place where we were cutting wood, with a visit from some of the natives – eight men and a boy. They approached us from the woods, without betraying any marks of fear, for none of them had any weapons except one, who held in his hand a stick about two feet long, and pointed at one end.

They were of common stature, but rather slender. Their skin was black, and also their hair, which was as woolly as that of any native of Guinea; but they were not distinguished by remarkably thick lips, nor flat noses. On the contrary, their features were far from being disagreeable. Most of them had their hair and beards smeared with a red ointment; and some had their faces also painted with the same composition.

They received every present we made to them without the least appearance of satisfaction. When some bread was given, as soon as they understood that it was to be eaten, they either returned it or threw it away, without even tasting it. They also refused some elephant fish, both raw and dressed, which we offered to them. But upon giving them some birds, they did not return these, and easily made us comprehend that they were fond of such food. I had brought two pigs ashore, with a view to leave them in the woods. The instant these came within their reach, they seized them as a dog would have done, by the ears, and were for carrying them off immediately, with no other intention, as we could perceive, but to kill them.

Being desirous of knowing the use of the stick which one of our visitors carried in his hand, I made signs to them to show me; and so far succeeded, that one of them set up a piece of wood as a mark, and threw at it, at the distance of about twenty yards. But we had little reason to commend his dexterity; for, after repeated trials, he was still very wide from the object. Omai, to show them how much superior our weapons were to theirs, then fired his musket at it, which alarmed them so much, that, notwithstanding all we could do or say, they ran instantly into the woods.

Thus ended our first interview with the natives. Immediately after their final retreat, I ordered the two pigs, being a boar and a sow, to be carried about a mile within the woods, at the head of the bay. I saw them left there, by the side of a fresh water brook. A young bull and a cow, and some sheep and goats, were also, at first, intended to have been left by me as an additional present to Van Diemen's Land. But I soon laid aside all thought of this, from a persuasion that the natives, incapable of entering into my views of improving their country, would destroy them.

The morning of the 29th we had a dead calm, which continued all day, and effectually prevented our sailing. I therefore sent a party over to the east point of the bay to cut grass, and another to cut wood. I accompanied the latter. We had observed several of the natives this morning sauntering along the shore, which assured us that though their consternation had made them leave us so abruptly the day before, they were convinced that we intended them no mischief, and were desirous of renewing the intercourse. It was natural that I should wish to be present on the occasion.

We had not been long landed before about twenty of them, men and boys, joined us, without expressing the least sign of fear or distrust. There was one of this company conspicuously deformed; and who was not more distinguishable by the hump on his back, than by the drollery of his gestures, and the seeming humour of his speeches; which he was very fond of exhibiting, as we supposed, for our entertainment. His language appeared to me to be different from that spoken by the inhabitants of the more northern parts of this country, whom I met with in my first voyage, which is not extraordinary, since those we now saw, and those we then visited, differ in many other respects.

Some of our present group wore, loose, round their necks, three or four folds of small cord, made of the fur of some animal; and others of them had a narrow slip of the kangaroo skin tied round their ankles. I gave to each of them a string of beads and a medal, which I thought they received with some satisfaction. They seemed to set no value on iron or on iron tools. They were even ignorant of the use of fish-hooks, if we might judge from their manner of looking at some of ours which we showed to them – though it is certain they derive no inconsiderable part of their subsistence from the sea. We saw, however, no vessel in which they could go on the water. Their habitations were little sheds or hovels built of sticks, and covered with bark.

After staying about an hour with the wooding party and the natives, I went over to the grass-cutters. Having seen the boats loaded, I returned on board to dinner, where, some time after, Lieutenant King arrived.

From him I learnt that I had but just left the shore when several women and children made their appearance. These females wore a kangaroo skin tied over the shoulders, and round the waist. But its only use seemed to be to support their children when carried on their backs, for it did not cover their persons, being in all other respects as naked as the men, and as black, and their bodies tattooed in the same manner. But in this they differed from the men, that though their hair was of the same colour, some of them had their heads completely shorn, in others this operation had been performed only on one side, while the rest of them had all the upper part of the head shorn close, leaving a circle of hair all round, somewhat like the tonsure of the Romish ecclesiastics. Many of the children had fine features, and were thought pretty; but of the persons of the women, especially those advanced in years, a less favourable report was made.

The only animal of the quadruped kind we got, was a sort of opossum, about twice the size of a large rat. It is of a dusky colour above, tinged with a brown or rusty cast, and whitish below. About a third of the tail towards its tip is white, and bare underneath, by which it probably hangs on the branches of trees, as it climbs these, and lives on berries. The kangaroo, another animal found farther northward in New Holland, without doubt also inhabits here, as the natives we met with had some pieces of their skins; and we several times saw an animal, though indistinctly, run from the thickets when we walked in the woods, which, from the size, could be no other.

There are several sorts of birds, but all so scarce and shy, that they are evidently harassed by the natives, who perhaps draw much of their subsistence from them. In the woods the principal sorts are large brown hawks or eagles, crows nearly the same as ours in England, yellowish parakeets, and large pigeons. There are also three or four small birds, one of which is of the thrush kind. On the shore were several common and sea-gulls, a few black oyster-catchers or sea-pies, and a pretty plover of a stone colour, with a black hood. About the lake behind the beach, a few wild ducks were seen; and some shags used to perch upon the high leafless trees near the shore.

The sea affords a much greater plenty, and at least as great a variety, as the land. Of these the elephant fish, or pejegallo, mentioned in Frezier's Voyage, are the most numerous; and though inferior to many other fish, were very palatable food. Next in number, and superior in goodness, to the elephant fish, was a sort none of us recollected to have seen before. It partakes of the nature both of a round and of a flat fish, having the eyes placed very near each other, the forepart of the body very much flattened or depressed, and the rest rounded. It is of a brownish sandy colour, with rusty spots on the upper part and below. From the quantity of slime it was always covered with, it seems to live after the manner of flat fish, at the bottom. Upon the rocks are plenty of mussels, and some other small shellfish. There are also great numbers of sea-stars, some small limpets, and large quantities of sponge – one sort of which, that is thrown on shore by the sea, but not very common, has a most delicate texture.

Insects, though not numerous, are here in considerable variety. Among them are grasshoppers, butterflies, and several sorts of small moths, finely variegated. There are two sorts of dragonflies, gad-flies, camel-flies, several sorts of spiders; and some scorpions; but the last are rather rare. The most troublesome, though not very numerous tribe of insects, are the mosquitoes; and a large black ant, the pain of whose bite is almost intolerable, during the short time it lasts.

The inhabitants, whom we met here, had little of that fierce or wild appearance common to people in their situation; but, on the contrary, seemed mild and cheerful, without reserve or jealousy of strangers. This, however, may arise from their having little to lose or care for. With respect to personal activity or genius, we can say but little of either. They do not seem to possess the first in any remarkable degree; and as for the last, they have, to appearance, less than even the half-animated inhabitants of Terra del Fuego, who have not invention sufficient to make clothing for defending themselves from the rigour of their climate, though furnished with the materials. Their colour is a dull black, and not quite so deep as that of the African negroes. Their hair, however, is perfectly woolly, and it is clotted or divided into small parcels, like that of the Hottentots, with the use of some sort of grease, mixed with a red paint or ochre, which they smear in great abundance over their heads; and they wear their beards long, and clotted with paint, in the same manner as the hair on their heads. At eight o'clock in the morning of the 30th of January, a light breeze springing up at west, we weighed anchor and put to sea from Adventure Bay. We pursued our course to the eastward, without meeting with anything worthy of note, till the night between the 6th and 7th of February, when a marine belonging to the *Discovery* fell overboard, and was never seen afterward.

On the 12th of February, at four in the afternoon, we discovered the land of New Zealand; and soon after came to an anchor in Queen Charlotte Sound. Here several canoes, filled with natives, came alongside of the ships; but very few of them would venture on board; which appeared the more extraordinary, as I was well known by them all. There was one man in particular amongst them, whom I had treated with remarkable kindness during the whole of my stay when I was last here. Yet now, neither professions of friendship nor presents could prevail upon him to come into the ship. This shyness was to be accounted for only on this supposition, that they were apprehensive we had revisited their country in order to revenge the death of Captain Furneaux's people.

On the 13th we set up two tents, one from each ship, on the

same spot where we had pitched them formerly. The observatories were at the same time erected; and Messrs King and Bayly began their operations immediately.

During the course of this day a great number of families came from different parts of the coast, and took up their residence close to us, so that there was not a spot in the cove where a hut could be put up that was not occupied by them, except the place where we had fixed our little encampment.

It is curious to observe with what facility they build their huts. I have seen about twenty of them erected on a spot of ground, that, not an hour before, was covered with shrubs and plants. They generally bring some part of the materials with them, the rest they find upon the premises. I was present when a number of people landed and built one of these villages.

Besides the natives who took up their abode close to us, we were occasionally visited by others whose residence was not afar off; and by some who lived more remote. Their articles of commerce were, curiosities, fish, and women. The two first always came to a good market, which the latter did not. The seamen had taken a kind of dislike to these people, and were either unwilling, or afraid to associate with them; which produced this good effect, that I knew no instance of a man's quitting his station to go to their habitations.

Amongst our occasional visitors was a chief named Kahoora, who, as I was informed, headed the party that cut off Captain Furneaux's people, and himself killed Mr Rowe, the officer who commanded. To judge of the character of Kahoora, by what I had heard from many of his countrymen, he seemed to be more feared than beloved amongst them. Not satisfied with telling me that he was a very bad man, some of them even importuned me to kill him: and I believe they were not a little surprised that I did not listen to them; for according to their ideas of equity, this ought to have been done. But if I had followed the advice of all our pretended friends, I might have extirpated the whole race; for the people of each hamlet or village, by turns, applied to me to destroy the other.

On the 16th, at daybreak, I set out with a party of men, in five boats, to collect food for our cattle. Captain Clerke, and several of the officers, Omai, and two of the natives accompanied me. We proceeded about three leagues up the sound, and then landed on the east side at a place where I had formerly been. Here we cut as much grass as loaded the two launches.

As we returned down the sound, we visited Grass Cove, the memorable scene of the massacre of Captain Furneaux's people. Whilst we were at this place, our curiosity prompted us to inquire into the circumstances attending the melancholy fate of our countrymen, and Ōmai was made use of as our interpreter for this purpose. The natives present answered all the questions that were put to them on the subject without reserve, and like men who are under no dread of punishment for a crime of which they are not guilty. For we already knew that none of them had been concerned in the unhappy transaction. They told us, that while our people were sitting at dinner, surrounded by several of the natives, some of the latter stole, or snatched from them, some bread and fish, for which they were beat. This being resented, a quarrel ensued, and two New Zealanders were shot dead by the only two muskets that were fired. For before our people had time to discharge a third, or to load again those that had been fired, the natives rushed in upon them, overpowered them with their numbers, and put them all to death.

We stayed here till the evening, when, having filled the rest of the boats with grass, celery, and scurvy-grass, we embarked to return to the ships, where some of the boats did not arrive till one o'clock the next morning; and it was fortunate that they got on board then, for it afterwards blew a perfect storm. In the evening the gale ceased, and the wind having veered to the east, brought with it fair weather.

By this time more than two-thirds of the inhabitants of the Sound had settled themselves about us. Great numbers of them daily frequented the ships, while our people were there melting some seal blubber. No Greenlander was ever fonder of train-oil than our friends here seemed to be. They relished the very skimmings of the kettle; but a little of the pure stinking oil was a delicious feast.

Having got on board as much hay and grass as we judged sufficient to serve the cattle till our arrival at Otaheite, and having completed the wood and water of both ships, on the 24th we weighed anchor and stood out of the cove.

While we were unmooring and getting under sail, many of the

natives came to take their leave of us, or rather to obtain, if they could, some additional presents from us before we left them. Accordingly, I gave to two of their chiefs two pigs, a boar, and a sow. They made me a promise not to kill them, though I must own I put no great faith in this. The animals which Captain Furneaux sent on shore here, and which soon after fell into the hands of the natives, I was now told were all dead; but I was afterwards informed that Tiratou, a chief, had a great many cocks and hens in his possession, and one of the sows.

We had not been long at anchor near Mortuara, before three or four canoes, filled with natives, came off to us from the south-east side of the Sound, and a brisk trade was carried on with them for the curiosities of this place. In one of these canoes was Kahoora, leader of the party who cut off the crew of the *Adventure*'s boat. This was the third time he had visited us, without betraying the smallest appearance of fear.

Next morning he returned again with his whole family, men, women, and children, to the number of twenty and upwards. Omai was the first who acquainted me with his being alongside the ship, and desired to know if he should ask him to come on board. I told him he might; and accordingly he introduced the chief into the cabin; saying, 'There is Kahoora; kill him!' He afterwards expostulated with me very earnestly, saying, 'Why do you not kill him? You tell me if a man kills another in England, that he is hanged for it. This man has killed ten, and yet you will not kill him, though many of his countrymen desire it, and it would be very good.' Omai's arguments, though specious enough, having no weight with me, I desired him to ask the chief why he had killed Captain Furneaux's people. At this question Kahoora folded his arms, hung down his head, and looked like one caught in a trap; and I firmly believe he expected instant death. But no sooner was he assured of his safety, than he became cheerful. He did not, however, seem willing to give me an answer to the question that had been put to him, till I had, again and again, repeated my promise that he should not be hurt. Then he ventured to tell us, that one of his countrymen having brought a stone hatchet to barter, the man to whom it was offered took it, and would neither return it, nor give anything for it; on which the owner of it snatched up the bread as an equivalent and then the quarrel began.

For some time before we arrived at New Zealand, Omai had expressed a desire to take one of the natives with him to his own country. We had not been there many days, before he had an opportunity of being gratified in this; for a youth, about seventeen or eighteen years of age, named Taweiharooa, offered to accompany him. Finding that he was fixed in his resolution to go with us, and having learnt that he was the only son of a deceased chief, I told his mother that, in all probability, he would never return; but this made no impression on either; for when she returned the next morning, to take her last farewell of him, all the time she was on board she remained quite cheerful, and went away wholly unconcerned. Another youth about ten years of age, accompanied him as a servant, named Kokoa; he was presented to me by his own father, who stripped him, and left him naked as he was born; indeed, he seemed to part with him with perfect indifference.

From my own observations, and from the information of Taweiharooa and others, it appears to me that the New Zealanders must live under perpetual apprehensions of being destroyed by each other; there being few of their tribes that have not, as they think, sustained wrongs from some ether tribe, which they are continually upon the watch to revenge. And, perhaps, the desire of a good meal may be no small incitement. One hardly ever finds a New Zealander off his guard, either by night or by day; indeed, no other man can have such powerful motives to be vigilant, as the preservation of both body and of soul depends upon it. For, according to their system of belief, the soul of the man whose flesh is devoured by the enemy, is doomed to a perpetual fire: whilst the soul of the man whose body has been rescued from those who killed him, as well as the souls of all who die a natural death, ascend to the habitations of the gods.

Polygamy is allowed amongst these people; and it is not uncommon for a man to have two or three wives. The women are marriageable at a very early age; and it should seem, that one who is unmarried, is but in a forlorn state.

Their public contentions are frequent, or rather perpetual; for it appears, from their number of weapons, and dexterity in using them, that war is their principal profession. Before they begin the onset, they join in a war-song, to which they all keep the exactest time, and soon raise their passions to a degree of frantic fury, attended with the most horrid distortion of their eyes, mouths, and tongues, to strike terror into their enemies; which, to those who have not been accustomed to such a practice, makes them appear more like demons than men, and would almost chill the boldest with fear. To this succeeds a circumstance, almost foretold in their fierce demeanour, horrid, cruel, and disgraceful to human nature, which is, cutting in pieces, even before being perfectly dead, the bodies of their enemies, and, after dressing them on a fire, devouring the flesh, not only without reluctance, but with peculiar satisfaction.

On the 25th of February we sailed from New Zealand, and had no sooner lost sight of the land than our two young adventurers repented heartily of the step they had taken. All the soothing encouragement we could think of availed but little. They wept both in public and private, and made their lamentations in a kind of song, which was expressive of their praises of their country. Thus they continued for many days, but at length their native country and their friends were forgot, and they appeared to be as firmly attached to us as if they had been born amongst us.

On the 29th of March, as we were standing to the north-east, the *Discovery* made the signal of seeing land, which we soon discovered to be an island of no great extent.

On approaching the shore, we could perceive with our glasses that several of the natives were armed with long spears and clubs, which they brandished in the air with signs of threatening, or, as some on board interpreted their attitudes, with invitations to land. Most of them appeared naked, except having a sort of girdle, which, being brought up between the thighs, covered that part of the body. But some of them had pieces of cloth of different colours, white, striped, or chequered, which they wore as a garment thrown about their shoulders; and almost all of them had a white wrapper about their heads, not much unlike a turban. They were of a tawny colour, and of a middling stature.

At this time a small canoe was launched in a great hurry from the further end of the beach, and putting off with two men, paddled towards us, when I brought to. They stopped short, however, as if afraid to approach, until Omai, who addressed them in the Otaheitean language, in some measure quieted their apprehensions. They then came near enough to take some beads and nails, which were tied to a piece of wood, and thrown into the canoe. Omai, perhaps improperly, put the question to them, whether they ever eat human flesh, which they answered in the negative, with a mixture of indignation and abhorrence. One of them, whose name was Mourooa, being asked how he came by a scar on his forehead, told us that it was the consequence of a wound he had got in fighting with the people of an island which lies to the north-eastward, who sometimes came to invade them. They afterward took hold of a rope. Still, however, they would not venture on board.

Mourooa was lusty and well made, but not very tall. His features were agreeable, and his disposition seemingly no less so; for he made several droll gesticulations, which indicated both good nature and a share of humour. His colour was nearly of the same cast with that common to the most southern Europeans. The other man was not so handsome. Both of them had strong straight hair, of a jet colour, tied together on the crown of the head with a bit of cloth. They wore girdles of a substance made from the *Morus papyrifera*, in the same manner as at the other islands of this ocean. They had on a kind of sandals, made of a grassy substance interwoven; and, as we supposed, intended to defend their feet against the rough coral rock. Their beards were long, and the inside of their arms, from the shoulder to the elbow, and some other parts, were punctured or tattooed after the manner of the inhabitants of almost all the other islands in the South Sea. The lobe of their ears was slit to such a length, that one of them stuck there a knife and some beads, which he had received from us; and the same person had two polished pearl shells, and a bunch of human hair, loosely twisted, hanging about his neck, which was the only ornament we observed. The canoe they came in was not above ten feet long, and very narrow, but both strong and neatly made. They paddled either end of it forward indifferently.

We now stood off and on; and as soon as the ships were in a proper station, I ordered two boats to sound the coast, and to endeavour to find a landing-place. With this view, I went in one of them myself, taking with me such articles to give the natives as I thought might serve to gain their good-will. I had no sooner put off from the ship than the canoe with the two men, which had not left us long before, paddled towards my boat, and, having come alongside, Mourooa stepped into her, without being asked, and without a moment's hesitation.

Omai, who was with me, was ordered to inquire of him where we could land, and he directed us to two different places. But I saw, with regret, that the attempt could not be made at either place, unless at the risk of having our boats filled with water, or even staved to pieces. Nor were we more fortunate in our search for anchorage, for we could find no bottom till within a cable's length of the breakers.

While we were thus employed in reconnoitring the shore, great numbers of the natives thronged down upon the reef, all armed. Mourooa, who was now in my boat, probably thinking that this warlike appearance hindered us from landing, ordered them to retire back. As many of them complied, I judged he must be a person of some consequence among them. Indeed, if we understood him right, he was the king's brother. So great was the curiosity of several of them, that they took to the water, and swimming off to the boats, came on board them without reserve. Nay, we found it difficult to keep them out, and still more difficult to prevent them carrying off everything they could lay their hands upon. At length, when they perceived that we were returning to the ships, they all left us, except our original visitor Mourooa. He, though not without evident signs of fear, kept his place in my boat, and accompanied me on board the ship.

The cattle, and other new objects that presented themselves to him there, did not strike him with so much surprise as one might have expected. Perhaps his mind was too much taken up about his own safety, to allow him to attend to other things. I could get but little new information from him; and therefore, after he had made a short stay, I ordered a boat to carry him in toward the land. As soon as he got out of the cabin, he happened to stumble over one of the goats. His curiosity now overcoming his fear, he stopped, looked at it, and asked Omai what bird this was; and not receiving an immediate answer from him, he repeated the question to some of the people upon deck. The boat having conveyed him pretty near to the surf, he leapt into the sea, and swam ashore. He had no sooner landed than the multitude of his countrymen gathered round him, as if with an eager curiosity to learn from him what he had seen; and in this situation they remained when we lost sight of them.

After leaving Mangeea, as this island was called, on the afternoon of the 30th, we continued our course northward all that night, and till noon on the 31st, when we again saw land in the direction of north-east by north, distant eight or ten leagues, and next morning we got abreast of its north end. I sent three armed boats to look for anchoring-ground and a landing-place. In the meantime, we plied up under the island with the ships.

Just as the boats were putting off, we observed several single canoes coming from the shore. They went first to the *Discovery*, she being the nearest ship. It was not long after when three of the canoes came alongside of the *Resolution*, each conducted by one man. They are long and narrow, and supported by out-riggers. Some knives, beads, and other trifles, were conveyed to our visitors, and they gave us a few coconuts, upon our asking for them. But they did not part with them by way of exchange for what they had received from us. For they seemed to have no idea of bartering, nor did they appear to estimate any of our presents at a high rate.

With a little persuasion, one of them came on board; and the other two, encouraged by his example, soon followed him. Their whole behaviour marked that they were quite at their ease.

After their departure, another canoe arrived, conducted by a man who brought a bunch of plantains as a present to me, asking for me by name, having learnt it from Omai, who was sent before us in a boat with Mr Gore. In return for this civility, I gave him an axe and a piece of red cloth, and he paddled back to the shore well satisfied. I afterward understood from Omai, that this present had been sent from the king, or principal chief of the island.

Not long after a double canoe, in which were twelve men, came towards us. As they drew near the ship, they recited some words in concert, by way of chorus, one of their number first standing up, and giving the word before each repetition. When they had finished their solemn chant, they came alongside, and asked for the chief. As soon as I showed myself, a pig and a few coconuts were conveyed up into the ship, and the principal person in the canoe made me an additional present of a piece of matting.

Our visitors were conducted into the cabin, and to other parts of the ship. Some objects seemed to strike them with a degree of surprise; but nothing fixed their attention for a moment. They were afraid to come near the cows and horses; nor did they form the least conception of their nature. But the sheep and goats did not surpass the limits of their ideas; for they gave us to understand, that they knew them to be birds. I made a present to my new friend, of what I thought might be most acceptable to him; but, on his going away, he seemed rather disappointed than pleased. I afterwards understood that he was very desirous of obtaining a dog, of which animal this island could not boast.

The people in these canoes were in general of a middling size, and not unlike those of Mangeea; though several were of a blacker cast than any we saw there. Their features were various, and some of the young men rather handsome. Like those of Mangeea, they had girdles of glazed cloth, or fine matting, the ends of which, being brought betwixt their thighs, covered the adjoining parts. Ornaments, composed of a sort of broad brass stained with red, and strung with berries of the nightshade, were worn about their necks. Their ears were bored, but not slit; and they were punctured upon their legs, from the knee to the heel, which made them appear as if they wore a kind of boots. Their behaviour was frank and cheerful, with a great deal of good nature.

Soon after daybreak, we observed some canoes coming off to the ships, and one of them directed its course to the *Resolution*. In it was a hog with some plantains and coconuts, for which the people who brought them demanded a dog from us, and refused every other thing that we offered in exchange. To gratify these people, Omai parted with a favourite dog he had brought from England; and with this acquisition they departed highly satisfied.

I despatched Lieutenant Gore with three boats, two from the *Resolution*, and one from the *Discovery*. Two of the natives, who had been on board, accompanied him, and Omai went with him in his boat as an interpreter. The ships being a full league from the island when the boats put off, it was noon before we could work up to it. We then observed a prodigious number of the natives abreast of the boats. In order to observe their motions, and to be ready to give such assistance as our people might want, I kept as near the shore as was prudent. Some of the islanders now and then came off to the ships in their canoes, with a few coconuts, which they exchanged for whatever was offered to them.

These occasional visits served to lessen my solicitude about the people who had landed. Though we could get no information from our visitors, yet their venturing on board seemed to imply, at least, that their countrymen on shore had not made an improper use of the confidence put in them. At length, a little before sunset, we had the satisfaction of seeing the boats put off. When they got on board, I found that Mr Gore himself, Omai, Mr Anderson, and Mr Burney, were the only persons who had landed. The transactions of the day were now fully reported to me by Mr Anderson; I shall give them nearly in his words.

'We rowed towards a small sandy beach, upon which a great number of the natives had assembled. Several of the natives swam off, bringing coconuts; and Omai, with their countrymen whom we had with us in the boats, made them sensible of our wish to land.

'Mr Burney, the first lieutenant of the *Discovery*, and I, went in one canoe, a little time before the other; and our conductors, watching attentively the motions of the surf, landed us safely upon the reef. An islander took hold of each of us, obviously with an intention to support us in walking over the rugged rocks to the beach, where several of the others met us, holding the green boughs of a species of mimosa in their hands, and saluted us by applying their noses to ours.

'We were conducted from the beach amidst a crowd of people, who flocked with very eager curiosity to look at us. We were then led up an avenue of cocoa-palms; and soon came to a number of men, arranged in two rows, armed with clubs. After walking a little way amongst these, we found a person who seemed a chief, sitting on the ground cross-legged, cooling himself with a sort of triangular fan made from a leaf of the cocoa-palm. In his ears were large bunches of beautiful red feathers; but he had no other mark to distinguish him from the rest of the people, though they all obeyed him.

'We proceeded still amongst the men armed with clubs, and came to a second chief, who sat fanning himself, and ornamented as the first. In the same manner we were conducted to a third chief, who seemed older than the two former. He also was sitting, and adorned with red feathers; and after saluting him as we had done the others, he desired us both to sit down.

'In a few minutes, we saw, at a small distance, about twenty young women, ornamented as the chiefs with red feathers, engaged in a dance, which they performed to a slow and serious air, sung by them all. We got up and went forward to see them; and though we must have been strange objects to them, they continued their dance without paying the least attention to us. Their motions and song were performed in exact concert. In general, they were rather stout than slender, with black hair flowing in ringlets down the neck, and of an olive complexion. Their eyes were of a deep black, and each countenance expressed a degree of complacency and modesty, peculiar to the sex in every part of the world; but perhaps more conspicuous here, where Nature presented us with her productions in the fullest perfection, unbiased in sentiment by custom, or unrestrained in manner by art.

'The natives now seemed to take some pains to separate us from each other; every one of us having his circle, to surround and gaze at him; and when I told the chief with whom I sat, that I wanted to speak to Omai, he peremptorily refused my request. At the same time, I found the people began to steal several trifling things which I had in my pocket; and when I took the liberty of complaining to the chief of this treatment, he justified it. From these circumstances, I now entertained apprehensions that they might have formed the design of detaining us amongst them.

'Mr Burney happening to come to the place where I was, I mentioned my suspicions to him; and, to put it to the test, whether they were well founded, we attempted to get to the beach. But we were stopped, when about halfway, by some men who told us that we must go back to the place where we had left. On coming up, we found Omai entertaining the same apprehensions. But he had, as he fancied, an additional reason for being afraid; for he had observed, that they had dug a hole in the ground for an oven, which they were now heating; and he could assign no other reason for this, than that they meant to roast and eat us, as is practised by the inhabitants of New Zealand.

'In this manner we were detained the greatest part of the day, being sometimes together and sometimes separated, but always in a crowd; who, not satisfied with gazing at us, frequently desired us to uncover parts of our skin; the sight of which commonly produced a general murmur of admiration.

'Upon our urging the business we came upon, they gave us to understand, that we must stay and eat with them; and a pig which we saw soon after lying near the oven, which they had prepared and heated, removed Omai's apprehensions of being put into it himself; and made us think it might be intended for our repast. A piece of the young hog that had been dressed was set before us, of which we were desired to eat. Our appetites, however, had failed, from the fatigue of the day; and though we did eat a little to please them, it was without satisfaction to ourselves.

'It being now near sunset, we told them it was time to go on board. This they allowed; and sent down to the beach the remainder of the victuals that had been dressed, to be carried with us to the ships. They put us on board our boats, with the coconuts, plantains, and other provisions, which they had brought; and we rowed to the ships, very well pleased that we had at last got out of the hands of our troublesome masters.

'We regretted much that our restrained situation gave us so little opportunity of making observations on the country. For, during the whole day, we were seldom a hundred yards from the place where we were introduced to the chiefs on landing; and, consequently, were confined to the surrounding objects. The first thing that presented itself, worthy of our notice, was the number of people, which must have been, at least, two thousand. In general, they had their hair tied on the crown of the head, long, black and of a most luxuriant growth. Many of the young men were perfect models in shape, of a complexion as delicate as that of the women, and, to appearance, of a disposition as amiable.

'The wife of one of the chiefs appeared with her child, laid in a piece of red cloth, which had been presented to her husband; and seemed to carry it with great tenderness, suckling it much after the manner of our women. Another chief introduced his daughter, who was young and beautiful; but appeared with all the timidity natural to the sex, though she gazed on us with a kind of anxious concern, that seemed to struggle with her fear, and to express her astonishment at so unusual a sight.

'About a third part of the men were armed with clubs and spears. The clubs were generally about six feet long, made of hard black wood, lance-shaped at the end, but much broader, with the edge nicely scalloped, and the whole neatly polished.

'What the soil of the island may be, farther inland, we could not tell. But, toward the sea, it is nothing more than a bank of coral, ten or twelve feet high, steep and rugged; except where there are small sandy beaches, at some clefts where the ascent is gradual. The reef or rock, that lines the shore entirely, runs to different breadths into the sea, where it ends all at once, and becomes like a high, steep wall.'

Though the landing of our gentlemen proved the means of enriching my journal with the foregoing particulars, the principal object I had in view was, in a great measure, unattained; for the day was spent without getting any one thing from the island worth mentioning. The natives, however, were gratified with a sight they never before had; and, probably, will never have again. And mere curiosity seems to have been the chief motive for keeping the gentlemen under such restraint, and for using every art to prolong their continuance amongst them.

Omai was Mr Gore's interpreter; but that was not the only service he performed this day. He was asked, by the natives, a great many questions concerning us; and according to the account he gave me, his answers were not a little upon the marvellous. As, for instance, he told them that our country had ships as large as their island, on board which were instruments of war, of such dimensions, that several people might sit within them; and that one of them was sufficient to crush the whole island at one shot. This led them to inquire of him what sort of guns we actually had in our two ships. He said, that though they were but small, in comparison with those he had just described, yet, with such as they were, we could, with the greatest ease, and at the distance the ships were from the shore, destroy the island, and kill every soul in it. They persevered in their inquiries to know by what means this could be done; and Omai explained the matter as well as he could. He happened luckily to have a few cartridges in his pocket. These he produced; the balls, and the gunpowder which was to set them in motion, were submitted to inspection; and, to supply the defects of his description, an appeal was made to the senses of the spectators. In the centre of a circle formed by the natives, the inconsiderable quantity of gunpowder, collected from his cartridges, was properly disposed upon the ground, and, by means of a bit of burning wood from the oven, where dinner was dressing, set on fire. The sudden blast and loud report, the mingled flame and smoke, that instantly succeeded, now filled the whole assembly with astonishment; they no longer doubted the tremendous power of our weapons, and gave full credit to all that Omai had said. This probably induced them to liberate the gentlemen.

Omai found three of his countrymen here; their story is an affecting one, as related by him. About twenty persons had embarked on board a canoe at Otaheite, to cross over to the neighbouring island, Ulietea. A violent contrary wind arising, they could neither reach the latter, nor get back to the former. Their intended passage being a very short one, their stock of provisions was scanty, and soon exhausted. The hardships they suffered, while driven along by the storm, are not to be conceived. They passed many days without sustenance. Their numbers gradually diminished, worn out by famine and fatigue. Four only survived, when the canoe overset. However, they kept hanging by the side of the vessel, till Providence brought them in sight of the people of this island, who immediately sent out canoes and brought them ashore. Of the four, one was since dead. The other three, still living, spoke highly of the kind treatment they here met with. And so well satisfied were they with their situation, that they refused the offer made to them by our gentlemen, at Omai's request, of giving them a passage on board our ships, to restore them to their native islands.

The landing of our gentlemen on this island, though they failed in the object of it, cannot but be considered as a very fortunate circumstance. It has proved, as we have seen, the means of bringing to our knowledge a matter of fact, not only very curious, but very instructive. The application of the above narrative is obvious. It will serve to explain, better than a thousand conjectures of speculative reasoners, how the detached parts of the earth, and in particular how the islands of the South Seas may have been first peopled; especially those that lie remote from any inhabited continent, or from each other.

With a gentle breeze at east, we got up with Wateeoo on the 3rd of April, and I immediately despatched Mr Gore, with two boats, to endeavour to procure some food for our cattle. As there seemed to be no inhabitants here to obstruct our taking away whatever we might think proper, our boats no sooner reached the west side of the island, but they ventured in, and Mr Gore and his party got safe on shore.

The supply obtained here, consisted of about a hundred coconuts for each ship; we also got for our cattle some grass, and a quantity of the leaves and branches of young cocoa-trees, and of the wharra tree, as it is called at Otaheite.

The only birds seen here were a beautiful cuckoo, of a chestnut brown, variegated with black, which was shot; and upon the shore, some egg-birds, a small sort of curlew, blue and white herons, and great numbers of noddies.

One of our people caught a lizard of a most forbidding aspect, though small, running up a tree; and many of another sort were seen.

Though there were, at this time, no fixed inhabitants upon the island, indubitable marks remained of its being, at least, occasionally frequented. In particular, a few empty huts were found. In one of them Mr Gore left a hatchet and some nails, to the full value of what we took away.

As soon as the boats were hoisted in, I made sail again to the northward. Although Hervey's Island, discovered in 1773, was not above fifteen leagues distant, yet we did not get sight of it till daybreak in the morning. As we drew near it, we observed several canoes put off towards the ships. There were from three to six men in each of them. They stopped at the distance of about a stone's throw from the ship, and it was some time before Omai could prevail upon them to come alongside; but no entreaties could induce any of them to venture on board. Indeed, their disorderly and clamorous behaviour by no means indicated a disposition to trust us, or treat us well. We afterwards learnt that they had attempted to take some oars out of the *Discovery*'s boat that lay alongside, and struck a man who endeavoured to prevent them. They also cut away, with a shell, a net with meat, which hung over that ship's stern, and absolutely refused to restore it; though we afterwards purchased it of them. Those who were about our ship behaved in the same daring manner. At the same time, they immediately showed a knowledge of bartering, and sold some fish they had for small nails, of which they were immoderately fond, and called them *goore*. But they caught, with the greatest avidity, bits of paper, or anything else that was thrown to them.

These people seemed to differ as much in person as in disposition from the natives of Wateeoo, though the distance between the two islands is not very great. Their colour was of a deeper cast; and several had a fierce, rugged aspect, resembling the natives of New Zealand. The shell of a pearl oyster, polished, hung about the neck, was the only personal decoration that we observed amongst them;

for not one of them had adopted that mode of ornament, so generally prevalent amongst the natives of this ocean, of puncturing, or tattooing their bodies.

Though singular in this, we had the most unequivocal proofs of their being of the same common race. Their language approached still nearer to the dialect of Otaheite than that of Wateeoo or Mangeea.

Having but very little wind, it was one o'clock before we drew near the north-west part of the island; when I sent Lieutenant King, with two armed boats, to sound and reconnoitre the coast, while we stood off and on with the ships.

At three o'clock the boats returned; and Mr King informed me that there was no anchorage for the ships, and that the boats could only land on the outer edge of the reef, which lay about a quarter of a mile from the dry land. He said that a number of the natives came down upon the reef, armed with long pikes and clubs. But, as he had no motive to land, he did not give them an opportunity to use them.

If I had been so fortunate as to have procured a supply of water and of grass, at any of the islands we had lately visited, it was my purpose to have stood back to the south till I had met with a westerly wind. But the certain consequences of doing this, without such a supply, would have been the loss of all the cattle, before we could possibly reach Otaheite, without gaining one advantage, with regard to the great object of our voyage. I therefore determined to bear away for the Friendly Islands, where I was sure of meeting with abundance of everything I wanted.

April the 7th, I steered west by south, with a fine breeze easterly. I proposed to proceed first to Middleburg, or Eooa; thinking, if the wind continued favourable, that we had food enough on board for the cattle, to last till we should reach that island. But, about noon next day, those faint breezes, that had attended and retarded us so long, again returned; and I found it necessary to haul more to the north, to get into the latitude of Palmerston's and Savage Islands, discovered in 1774, during my last voyage; that if necessity required it, we might have recourse to them.

At length, at daybreak on the 13th, we saw Palmerston Island, distant about five leagues. However, we did not get up with it till eight o'clock the next morning. I then sent four boats, with an officer in each, to search the coast for the most convenient landing-place.

The boats first examined the south-easternmost part, and failing there, ran down to the east, where we had the satisfaction to see them land. This place is not inhabited.

About one o'clock, one of the boats came on board, laden with scurvy-grass and young coconut trees; which at this time was a feast for the cattle. Before evening, I went ashore in a small boat, accompanied by Captain Clerke.

We found everybody hard at work, and the landing-place to be in a small creek. Upon the bushes that front the sea, or even farther in, we found a great number of men-of-war birds, tropic birds, and two sorts of boobies, which, at this time, were laying their eggs, and so tame, that they suffered us to take them off with our hands.

At one part of the reef, which looks into, or bounds, the lake that is within, there was a large bed of coral, almost even with the surface, which afforded, perhaps, one of the most enchanting prospects that nature has anywhere produced. Its base was fixed to the shore, but reached so far in, that it could not be seen; so that it seemed to be suspended in the water, which deepened so suddenly, that, at the distance of a few yards, there might be seven or eight fathoms. The sea was at this time quite unruffled; and the sun shining bright, exposed the various sorts of coral in the most beautiful order. This scene was enlivened by numerous species of fishes gliding along in apparent security.

There were no traces of inhabitants having ever been here, if we except a small piece of a canoe that was found upon the beach, which probably may have drifted from some other island.

After the boats were laden I returned on board, leaving Mr Gore, with a party, to pass the night on shore, in order to be ready to go to work early next morning.

That day was accordingly spent as the preceding one had been, in collecting food for the cattle. Having got a sufficient supply by sunset, I ordered everybody on board. But having little or no wind, I determined to wait, and to employ the next day in trying to get some coconuts from the next island, where we could observe that those trees were in much greater abundance than where we had already landed.

With this view I went with the boats to the west side of the island, and landed with little difficulty, and immediately set the people to gather coconuts, which we found in great abundance. Omai, who was with me, caught, with a scoop net, in a very short time, as much fish as served the whole party on shore for dinner, besides sending some to both ships. Here were also great abundance of birds, particularly men-of-war and tropic birds; so that we fared sumptuously. And it is but doing justice to Omai to say, that in these excursions he was of the greatest use. For he not only caught the fish, but dressed these, and the birds we killed, in an oven with heated stones, after the fashion of his country, with a dexterity and good humour that did him great credit.

We found this islet near a half larger than the other, and almost entirely covered with cocoa palms. A young turtle had been lately thrown ashore here, as it was still full of maggots. We found some scorpions, a few other insects, and a greater number of fish upon the reefs.

Upon the whole, we did not spend our time unprofitably at this last islet; for we got there about twelve hundred coconuts, which were equally divided amongst the whole crew.

The nine or ten low islets, comprehended under the name of Palmerston's Island, may be reckoned the heads or summits of the reef of coral rock that connects them together, covered only with a thin coat of sand, yet clothed, as already observed, with trees and plants.

The heat, which had been great for about a month, became now much more disagreeable, from the close rainy weather; and, from the moisture attending it, threatened soon to be noxious. However, it is remarkable enough, that though the only refreshment we had received since leaving the Cape of Good Hope, was that at New Zealand, there was not yet a single person on board sick, from the constant use of salt food, or vicissitude of climate.

In the night between the 24th and 25th we passed Savage Island, which I had discovered in 1774. I steered for the south, and then hauled up for Annamooka.

It was no sooner daylight, than we were visited by six or seven canoes from different islands, bringing with them, besides fruits and roots, two pigs, several fowls, some large wood-pigeons, small rails, and large violet-coloured coots. All these they ex-

changed with us for beads, nails, hatchets, etc. They had also
other articles of commerce; but I ordered that no curiosities
should be purchased till the ships should be supplied with provisions, and leave given for that purpose. Knowing, also, from
experience, that if all our people might trade with the natives,
according to their own caprice, perpetual quarrels would ensue, I
ordered that particular persons should manage the traffic both on
board and on shore, prohibiting all others to interfere. Before
midday, Mr King, who had been sent to Komango, returned with
seven hogs, some fowls, a quantity of fruit and roots, and some
grass for the cattle. His party was very civilly treated at Komango.
The inhabitants did not seem to be numerous; and their huts,
which stood close to each other, within a plantain walk, were but
indifferent. Not far from them was a pretty large pond of fresh
water, tolerably good; but there was no appearance of any stream.
With Mr King came on board the chief of the island, named
Tooboulangee; and another, whose name was Taipa. They
brought with them a hog as a present to me, promising more the
next day; and they kept their word.

I now resumed the very same station which I had occupied when
I visited Annamooka three years before; and probably, almost in
the same place where Tasman, the first discoverer of this and some
of the neighbouring islands, anchored in 1643.

The following day I went ashore, accompanied by Captain
Clerke. Toobou, the chief of the island, conducted me and Omai to
his house. We found it situated on a pleasant spot, in the centre of
his plantation. While we were on shore, we procured a few hogs and
some fruit by bartering; and, before we got on board again, the ships
were crowded with the natives. Few of them coming empty-
handed, every necessary refreshment was now in the greatest plenty.

I landed again in the afternoon with a party of marines and, at
the same time, the horses, and such of the cattle as were in a
weakly state, were sent on shore. Everything being settled to my
satisfaction, I returned to the ship at sunset, leaving the command
upon the island to Mr King.

Next day, May 3rd, our various operations on shore began. In
the evening, before the natives retired from our post, Taipa
harangued them for some time. We could only guess at the subject;
and judged that he was instructing them how to behave towards us,

and encouraging them to bring the produce of the island to market. We experienced the good effects of his eloquence in the plentiful supply of provisions which next day we received.

On the 6th we were visited by a great chief from Tongataboo, whose name was Feenou, and whom Taipa was pleased to introduce to us as king of all the Friendly Isles. All the natives paid their obeisance to him, by bowing their heads as low as his feet, the soles of which they also touched with each hand, first with the palm and then with the back part. There could be little room to suspect that a person, received with so much respect, could be anything less than the king.

In the afternoon I went to pay this great man a visit, having first received a present of two fish from him, brought on board by one of his servants. As soon as I landed, he came up to me. He appeared to be about thirty years of age, tall, but thin, and had more of the European features than any I had yet seen here. After a short stay our new visitor and five or six of his attendants accompanied me on board. I gave suitable presents to them all, and entertained them in such a manner as I thought would be most agreeable.

In the evening I attended them on shore in my boat, into which the chief ordered three hogs to be put, as a return for the presents he had received from me.

The first day of our arrival at Annamooka, one of the natives had stolen, out of the ship, a large junk axe. I now applied to Feenou, who was my guest on the 8th, to exert his authority to get it restored to me; and so implicitly was he obeyed, that it was brought on board while we were at dinner. These people gave us very frequent opportunities of remarking what expert thieves they were. Even some of the chiefs did not think this profession beneath them. On the lower class a flogging seemed to make no greater impression than it would have done upon the mainmast. When any of them happened to be caught in the act, their superiors, far from interceding for them, would often advise us to kill them. As this was a punishment we did not choose to inflict, they generally escaped without any punishment at all Captain Clerke at last hit upon a mode of treatment, which we thought had some effect. He put them under the hands of the barber, and completely shaved their heads, thus pointing them out as objects of ridicule to their countrymen, and enabling our people to deprive them of future opportunities for a repetition of their rogueries, by keeping them at a distance.

Feenou, understanding that I meant to proceed directly to Tongataboo, importuned me strongly to alter this plan, to which he expressed as much aversion as if he had some particular interest to promote by diverting me from it. In preference to it, he warmly recommended an island, or rather a group of islands, called Hapaee, lying to the north-east. There, he assured us, we could be supplied plentifully with every refreshment in the easiest manner; and, to add weight to his advice, he engaged to attend us thither in person. He carried his point with me, and Hapaee was made choice of for our next station. As it had never been visited by any European ships, the examination of it became an object with me.

After some unimportant transactions, at daybreak in the morning of the 16th, we steered north-east for Hapaee, which was now in sight. Next day we came to anchor. By this time the ships were filled with the natives. They brought from the shore hogs, fowls, fruit, and roots, which they exchanged for hatchets, knives, nails, beads, and cloth. I went on shore, accompanied by Omai and Feenou, landing at the north part of Lesooga, a little to the right of the ship's station.

The chief conducted me to a hut, situated close to the sea-beach, which I had seen brought thither, but a few minutes before, for our reception. In this Feenou, Omai, and myself were seated. The other chiefs and the multitude composed a circle on the outside fronting us, and they also sat down. I was then asked how long I intended to stay. On my saying five days, Taipa was ordered to come and sit by me, and proclaim this to the people. He then harangued them, in a speech mostly dictated by Feenou. The purport of it, as I learned from Omai, was, that they were all, both old and young, to look upon me as a friend, who intended to remain with them a few days; that during my stay they must not steal anything, nor molest me in any other way; and that it was expected they should bring hogs, fowls, fruit, etc., to the ships, where they would receive, in exchange for them, such and such things, which he enumerated. Taipa then took occasion to signify to me that it was necessary I should make a present to the chief of the island, whose name was Earoupa. I was not unprepared for this, and gave him such articles as far exceeded his expectation. My liberality to him brought upon me demands of the same kind from two chiefs of other isles who were present, and from Taipa himself.

After viewing the watering-place, we returned to our former station, where I found a baked hog and some yams, smoking hot, ready to be carried on board for my dinner. I invited Feenou and his friends to partake of it, and we embarked for the ship; but none but himself sat down with us at the table. After dinner I conducted them on shore; and before I returned on board, the chief gave me a fine large turtle, and a quantity of yams. Our supply of provisions was copious, for in the course of the day we got, by barter, alongside the ship, about twenty small hogs, besides fruit and roots.

Next morning early, Feenou and Omai, who scarcely ever quitted the chief, and now slept on shore, came on board. The object of the visit was to require my presence upon the island, where I saw a large concourse of people already assembled. I guessed that something more than ordinary was in agitation, but could not tell what, nor could Omai inform me.

I had not long been landed before near a hundred of the natives appeared in sight, and advanced, laden with yams, breadfruit, plantains, coconuts, and sugar-canes. They deposited their burthens in two heaps or piles upon our left. Soon after arrived a number of others, bearing the same kind of articles, which were collected into two piles upon the right. To these were tied two pigs and six fowls; and to those upon the left, six pigs and two turtles.

As soon as this munificent collection of provisions was laid down in order, and disposed to the best advantage, the bearers of it joined the multitude, who formed a large circle round the whole. Presently after a number of men entered this circle, or area, before us, armed with clubs, made of the green branches of the coconut tree. These paraded about for a few minutes, and then retired – the one half to one side, and the other half to the other side, seating themselves before the spectators. Soon after they successively entered the lists, and entertained us with single combats. One champion, rising up and stepping forward from one side, challenged those of the other side by expressive gestures, more than by words, to send one of their body to oppose him. If the challenge was accepted, which was generally the case, the two combatants put themselves in proper attitudes, and then began the engagement, which continued till one or other owned himself conquered, or till their weapons were broken. As soon as each combat was over, the victor squatted himself down facing the chief, then rose up and retired. At the same time some old men, who seemed to sit as judges, gave their plaudit in a few words; and the multitude, especially those on the side to which the victor belonged, celebrated the glory he had acquired in two or three huzzas.

This entertainment was now and then suspended for a few minutes. During these intervals there were both wrestling and boxing matches. The first were performed in the same manner as at Otaheite, and the second differed very little from the method practised in England. But what struck us with the most surprise was to see a couple of lusty wenches step forth, and begin boxing without the least ceremony, and with as much art as the men. This contest, however, did not last above half a minute, before one of them gave it up. The conquering heroine received the same applause from the spectators, which they bestowed upon the successful combatants of the other sex. We expressed some dislike at this part of the entertainment, which, however, did not prevent two other females from entering the lists. They seemed to be girls of spirit, and would certainly have given each other a good drubbing if two old women had not interposed to part them. All these combats were exhibited in the midst of at least three thousand people, and were conducted with the greatest good humour on all sides.

As soon as these diversions were ended, the chief told me that the heaps of provisions on our right hand were a present to Omai, and that those on our left hand, being about two-thirds of the whole quantity, were given to me. He added that I might take them on board whenever it was convenient, but that there would be no occasion to set any of our people as guards over them, as I might be assured that not a single coconut would be taken away by the natives. So it proved; for I left everything behind, and returned to the ship to dinner, carrying the chief with me, and when the provisions were removed on board in the afternoon, not a single article was missing. There was as much as loaded four boats, and I could not but be struck with the munificence of Feenou, for this present far exceeded any I had ever received from any of the sovereigns of the various islands I had visited in the Pacific Ocean.

I lost no time in convincing our friend that I was not insensible of his liberality, for, before he quitted my ship, I bestowed upon him such of my commodities as, I guessed, were most valuable in his estimation.

Feenou had expressed a desire to see the marines go through the military exercise. As I was desirous to gratify his curiosity, I ordered them all ashore, from both ships, in the morning. After they had performed various evolutions, and fired several volleys, with which the numerous body of spectators seemed well pleased, the chief entertained us, in his turn, with an exhibition, which, as was acknowledged by us all, was performed with a dexterity and exactness far surpassing the specimen we had given of our military manoeuvres. It was a kind of a dance, so entirely different from anything I had ever seen, that I fear I can give no description that will convey any tolerable idea of it to my readers. It was performed by men; and one hundred and five persons bore their parts in it. Each of them had in his hand an instrument neatly made, shaped somewhat like a paddle, of two feet and a half in length, with a small handle and a thin blade, so that they were very light. With these instruments they made many and various flourishes, each of which was accompanied with a different movement. At first the performers ranged themselves in three lines, and, by various evolutions, each man changed his station in such a manner that those who had been in the rear came into the front. Nor did they remain long in the same position. At one time they extended themselves in one line, they then formed into a semicircle, and lastly into two square columns. While this last movement was executing, one of them advanced and performed an antic dance before me, with which the whole ended.

The musical instruments consisted of two drums, or rather two hollow logs of wood, from which some varied notes were produced by beating on them with two sticks. It did not, however, appear to me that the dancers were much assisted by these sounds, but by a chorus of vocal music, in which all the performers joined at the same time. Their song was not destitute of pleasing melody, and all their corresponding motions were executed with so much skill, that the numerous body of dancers seemed to act as if they were one great machine. It was the opinion of every one of us that such a performance would have met with universal applause on an

European theatre; and it so far exceeded any attempt we had made to entertain them, that they seemed to picque themselves upon the superiority they had over us. As to our musical instruments, they held none of them in the least esteem, except the drum, and even that they did not think equal to their own.

In order to give them a more favourable opinion of English amusements, and to leave their minds fully impressed with the deepest sense of our superior attainments, I directed some fire-works to be got ready, and, after it was dark, played them off in the presence of Feenou, the other chiefs, and a vast concourse of their people. Our water and sky-rockets, in particular, pleased and astonished them beyond all conception; and the scale was now turned in our favour.

This, however, seemed only to furnish them with an additional motive to proceed to fresh exertions of their very singular dexterity; and our fireworks were no sooner ended than a succession of dances began. As a prelude to them, a band of music, or chorus of eighteen men, seated themselves before us in the centre of the circle. Four or five of this band had pieces of large bamboo, from three to five or six feet long; the upper end open, but the other end closed by one of the joints. With this closed end the performers kept constantly striking the ground, though slowly, thus producing different notes, according to the different lengths of the instruments, but all of them of the hollow or bass sort; to counteract which, a person kept striking quickly, and with two sticks, a piece of the same substance, split, and laid along the ground, and by that means furnishing a tone as acute as those produced by the others were grave. The rest of the band, as well as those who performed upon the bamboos, sung a slow and soft air, which so tempered the harsher notes of the above instruments, that no bystander, however accustomed to hear the most perfect and varied modulation of sweet sounds, could avoid confessing the vast power and pleasing effect of this simple harmony.

Soon after they had finished, nine women exhibited themselves, and sat down fronting the hut where the chief was. A man then rose, and struck the first of these women on the back with both fists joined. He proceeded in the same manner to the second and third, but when he came to the fourth, whether from accident or design I cannot tell, instead of the back, he struck her on the breast. Upon this, a person rose instantly from the crowd, who brought him to the ground with a blow on the head, and he was carried off without the least noise or disorder. But this did not save the other five women from so odd a discipline, or perhaps necessary ceremony; for a person succeeded him who treated them in the same manner. Their disgrace did not end here; for when they danced, they had the mortification to find their performance twice disapproved of, and were obliged to repeat it.

Curiosity on both sides being now sufficiently gratified, by the exhibition of the various entertainments I have described, I began to have time to look about me. Accordingly, next day, I took a walk into the island of Leefooga, of which I was desirous to obtain some knowledge. I found it to be, in several respects, superior to Annamooka. The plantations were more numerous, and more extensive. We observed large spots covered with the paper mulberry-trees; and the plantations in general were well stocked with such roots and fruits as are the natural produce of the island. To these I made some addition, by sowing the seeds of Indian corn, melons, pumpkins, and the like.

The island is not above seven miles long, and in some places not above two or three broad. The east side of it, which is exposed to the trade wind, has a reef, running to a considerable breadth from it, on which the sea breaks with great violence.

When I returned from my excursion into the country, I found a large sailing canoe fast to the ship's stern. In this canoe was Latooliboula, whom I had seen at Tongataboo, during my last voyage, and who was then supposed by us to be the king of that island. He sat in the canoe with all that gravity by which he was so remarkably distinguished at that time; nor could I, by any entreaties, prevail upon him now to come into the ship. Many of the islanders were present, and they all called him Arekee, which signifies king. I had never heard any one of them give this title to Feenou, however extensive his authority over them, both here and at Annamooka, had appeared to be, which had all along inclined me to suspect that he was not the king; though his friend Taipa had taken pains to make me believe he was. Feenou was on board my ship at the same time, but neither of these great men took the least notice of each other.

In the morning of the 23rd, as we were going to unmoor, in

order to leave the island, Feenou, and his prime minister Taipa, came alongside in a sailing canoe, and informed me that they were setting out for Vavaoo, an island which, they said, lies about two days' sail to the northward of Hapaee. The object of their voyage, they would have me believe, was to get for me an additional supply of hogs, and some red-feathered caps for Omai to carry to Otaheite, where they are in high esteem. Feenou assured me that he should be back in four or five days; and desired me not to sail till his return, when he promised me he would accompany me to Tongataboo. I thought this a good opportunity to get some knowledge of Vavaoo, and proposed to him to go thither with the ships, but he seemed not to approve of the plan; and by way of diverting me from it, told me that there was neither harbour nor anchorage about it. I therefore consented to wait in my present station for his return, and he immediately set out.

In my walk, on the 25th, I happened to step into a house, where I found a woman shaving a child's head with a shark's tooth stuck into the end of a piece of stick. I observed that she first wetted the hair with a rag dipped in water, applying her instrument to that part which she had previously soaked. The operation seemed to give no pain to the child, although the hair was taken off as close as if one of our razors had been employed. Encouraged by what I now saw, I soon after tried one of those singular instruments upon myself, and found it to be an excellent succedaneum. However, the men of these islands have recourse to another contrivance when they shave their beards. The operation is performed with two shells; one of which they place under a small part of the beard, and with the other, applied above, they scrape that part off. In this manner they are able to shave very close. The process is, indeed, rather tedious, but not painful; and there are men amongst them who seem to profess this trade. It was as common, while we were here, to see our sailors go ashore to have their beards scraped off, after the fashion of Hapaee, as it was to see their chiefs come on board to be shaved by our barbers.

Finding that little or nothing of the produce of the island was now brought to the ships, I resolved to change our station, and in the afternoon of the 26th of May, I hauled into a bay that lies between the south end of Lefooga, and the north end of Hoolaiva, and there anchored.

Near the south end of the island of Lefooga we met with an artificial mount. From the size of some trees that were growing upon it, and from other appearances, I guessed that it had been raised in remote times. I judged it to be about forty feet high, and the diameter of its summit measured fifty feet. At the bottom of this mount stood a stone, which must have been hewn off coral rock. It was four feet broad, two and a half thick, and fourteen high; and we were told by the natives present, that not above half its length appeared above ground. They called it *tangata arekee*,[1] and said that it had been set up, and the mount raised by some of their forefathers, in memory of one of their kings, but how long since they could not tell.

About noon, a large sailing canoe came under our stern, in which was a person named Futtafaihe or Poulaho, or both, who, as the natives then on board told us, was king of Tongataboo, and of all the neighbouring islands. It being my interest, as well as my inclination, to pay court to all the great men, without making inquiry into the validity of their assumed titles, I invited Poulaho on board; he brought with him, as a present, two fat hogs, though not so fat as himself. If weight of body could give weight in rank or power, he was certainly the most eminent man in that respect we had seen. I found him to be a sedate, sensible man. He viewed the ship and the several new objects with uncommon attention, and asked many pertinent questions, one of which was, What could induce us to visit these islands? After he had satisfied his curiosity in looking at the cattle, and other novelties which he met with upon deck, I desired him to walk down into the cabin. To this his attendants objected, saying, that if he were to accept of that invitation, it must happen that people would walk over his head; but the chief himself, less scrupulous in this respect than his attendants, waived all ceremony and walked down.

Poulaho sat down with us to dinner, but he ate little and drank less. When we rose from the table, he desired me to accompany him ashore. I attended the chief in my own boat, having first made presents to him of such articles as I could observe he valued much, and were even beyond his expectation to receive. I was not disappointed in my view of thus securing his friendship, for the

1 *tangata*, in their language, is man: *arekee*, king.

moment the boat reached the beach he ordered two more hogs to be brought and delivered to my people. He was then carried out of the boat by some of his own people, upon a board resembling a hand-barrow, and went and seated himself in a small house near the shore, which seemed to have been erected there for his accommodation. He placed me at his side, and his attendants seated themselves in a semicircle before us on the outside of the house. Behind the chief, or rather on one side, sat an old woman with a sort of fan in her hand, whose office it was to prevent his being pestered with the flies.

I stayed till several of his attendants left him, first paying him obeisance by bowing the hand down to the sole of his foot, and touching or tapping the same with the upper and under side of the fingers of both hands. Others, who were not in the circle, came, as it seemed, on purpose, and paid him this mark of respect, and then retired without speaking a word. I was quite charmed with the decorum that was observed. I had nowhere seen the like, not even amongst more civilised nations.

Poulaho, the king, as I shall now call him, came on board betimes next morning, and brought as a present to me one of their caps, made or at least covered with red feathers. These caps, or rather bonnets, are composed of the tail feathers of the tropic bird, with the red feathers of the parakeets wrought upon them, or jointly with them. They are made so as to tie upon the forehead without any crown, and have the form of a semicircle, whose radius is eighteen or twenty inches.

At daybreak the next morning I weighed with a fine breeze, and stood to the westward with a view to return to Annamooka. We were followed by several sailing canoes, in one of which was the king. He quitted us in a short time, but left his brother and five of his attendants on board. We had also the company of a chief just then arrived from Tongataboo, whose name was Tooboueitoa. The moment he arrived he sent his canoe away, and declared that he, and five more who came with him, would sleep on board; so that I had now my cabin filled with visitors. They brought plenty of provisions with them, for which they always had suitable returns.

In our course the ship was very near running full upon a low, sandy isle, called Pootoo. It happened very fortunately that the people had just before been ordered upon deck to put the ship about, so that the necessary movements were executed with judgment and alertness; and this alone saved us from destruction. The *Discovery*, being astern, was out of danger. Such hazardous situations are the unavoidable companions of the man who goes upon a voyage of discovery.

This circumstance frightened our passengers so much that they expressed a strong desire to get ashore. Accordingly, as soon as daylight returned, I hoisted out a boat, and ordered the officer who commanded her, after landing them at Kotoo, to sound along the reef for anchorage.

Having met with a convenient station, we lay here until the 4th, when we weighed and stood away for Annamooka, where we anchored next morning.

I went on shore soon after, and found the inhabitants very busy in digging up yams to bring to market. These were now in the greatest perfection; and we procured a good quantity in exchange for pieces of iron.

About noon next day, Feenou arrived from Vavaoo. He told us that several canoes laden with hogs and other provisions, which had sailed with him from that island, had been lost, owing to the late blowing weather, and that everybody on board them had perished. This melancholy tale did not seem to affect any of his countrymen who heard it; and as to ourselves, we were by this time too well acquainted with his character to give much credit to such a story. The following morning Poulaho, and the other chiefs who had been wind-bound with him, arrived. I happened at this time to be ashore in company with Feenou, who now seemed to be sensible of the impropriety of his conduct, in assuming a character that did not belong to him. For he not only acknowledged Poulaho to be king of Tongataboo and the other isles, but affected to insist much on it, which no doubt was with a view to make amends for his former presumption. I left him to visit this greater man, whom I found sitting with a few people before him. But everyone hastening to pay court to him, the circle increased pretty fast. I was very desirous of observing Feenou's behaviour on this occasion, and had the most convincing proof of his inferiority; for he placed himself amongst the rest that sat before Poulaho as attendants on his majesty. Both he and Poulaho went on board with me to dinner; but only the latter sat at table. Feenou having made his obeisance in the usual way, saluting his sovereign's foot with his head and hands, retired out of the cabin. The king had before told us that this would happen; and it now appeared that Feenou could not even eat or drink in his royal presence.

At eight o'clock next morning we steered for Tongataboo, having a gentle breeze at north-east. About fourteen or fifteen sailing vessels belonging to the natives set out with us; but every one of them outran the ships considerably. In the afternoon of next day we came to an anchor off that island in a safe station.

Soon after I landed, accompanied by Omai and some of the officers. We found the king waiting for us upon the beach. He immediately conducted us to a small neat house, situated a little within the skirts of the woods, with a fine large area before it. This house, he told me, was at my service during our stay at the island; and a better situation we could not wish for.

We had not been long in the house before a pretty large circle of the natives were assembled before us, and seated upon the area. A root of the kava plant being brought and laid down before the king, he ordered it to be split into pieces, and distributed to several people of both sexes, who began the operation of chewing it; and a bowl of their favourite liquor was soon prepared. In the meantime a baked hog and two baskets of baked yams were produced, and afterwards divided into ten portions. These portions were then given to certain people present; but how many were to share in each I could not tell. The liquor was next served out, but I observed that not a fourth part of the company had tasted either the victuals or the drink.

As I intended to make some stay at Tongataboo we pitched a tent in the forenoon, just by the house which Poulaho had assigned for our use. The horses, cattle, and sheep, were afterwards landed, and a party of marines, with their officer, stationed there as a guard. The observatory was then set up, at a small distance from the other tent, and Mr King resided on shore, to attend the observations. The gunners were ordered to conduct the traffic with the natives, who thronged from every part of the island with hogs, yams, coconuts, and other articles of their produce. In a short time our land post was like a fair, and the ships were so crowded with visitors that we had hardly room to stir upon the decks.

Feenou had taken up his residence in our neighbourhood, but he was no longer the leading man. However, we still found him to be a person of consequence, and we had daily proofs of his opulence and liberality, by the continuance of his valuable presents. But the king was equally attentive in this respect; for scarcely a day passed without receiving from him some considerable donation. We now heard that there were other great men of the island whom we had not as yet seen. Otago and Toobou, in particular, mentioned a person named Mareewagee, who, they said, was of the first consequence in the place. Some of the natives even hinted that he was too great a man to confer the honour of a visit upon us. This account exciting my curiosity, I mentioned to Poulaho that I was very desirous of waiting upon Mareewagee, and he readily agreed to accompany me to the place of his residence; but we did not find him at home.

About noon the next day, this chief actually came to the neighbourhood of our post on shore, and with him a very considerable number of people of all ranks. I was informed that he had taken this trouble on purpose to give me an opportunity of waiting upon him. In the afternoon a party of us, therefore, accompanied by Feenou, landed to pay him a visit. We found a person sitting under a large tree, near the shore, a little to the right of the tent. A piece of cloth, at least forty yards long, was spread before him, round which a great number of persons of both sexes were seated. It was natural to suppose that this was the great man; but we were undeceived by Feenou, who informed us, that another, who sat on a piece of mat, a little way from this chief, to the right hand, was Mareewagee, who received us very kindly, and desired us to sit down by him. The person who sat under the tree, fronting us, was called Toobou. Both he and Mareewagee had a venerable appearance. The latter is a slender man, and from his appearance seems to be considerably above three-score years of age. The former is rather corpulent, and almost blind with a disorder in his eyes, though not so old.

We entertained them for about an hour with the performance of two French horns and a drum. But they seemed most pleased with the firing of a pistol which Captain Clerke had in his pocket. Before I took my leave the large piece of cloth was rolled up, and with a few coconuts presented to me.

Toward noon, Poulaho returned from the place where we had left him two days before, and brought with him his son, a youth about twelve years of age. I had his company at dinner; but the son, though present, was not allowed to sit down with him. It was very convenient to have him for my guest. For, when he was present, which was generally the case while we stayed here, every other native was excluded from the table; and but few of them would remain in the cabin. The king was very soon reconciled to our manner of cookery. But still, I believe he dined thus frequently with me, more for the sake of what we gave him to drink, than for what we set before him to eat; for he had taken a liking to our wine, could empty his bottle as well as most men, and was as cheerful over it.

Having visited Toobou, and interchanged presents with him, soon after Feenou came and acquainted me that young Fattafaihe, Poulaho's son, desired to see me. I obeyed the summons, and found the prince and Omai sitting under a large canopy of the finer sort of cloth, with a piece of the coarser sort spread under them and before them, that was seventy-six yards long and seven and a half broad. On one side was a large old hoar, and on the other side a heap of coconuts. A number of people were seated round the cloth; and amongst them I observed Mareewagee and others of the first rank. I was desired to sit down by the prince, and then Omai informed me that he had been instructed by the king to tell me, that as he and I were friends, he hoped that his son might be joined in this friendship; and that, as a token of my consent, I would accept of his present. I very readily agreed to the proposal; and it being now dinner-time, I invited them all on board.

Accordingly, the young prince, Mareewagee, Toobou, three or four inferior chiefs, and two respectable old ladies of the first rank, accompanied me. Mareewagee was dressed in a new piece of cloth, on the skirts of which were fixed six pretty large patches of red feathers. This dress seemed to have been made on purpose for this visit, for as soon as he got on board he put it off and presented it to me. Every one of my visitors received from me such presents as, I had reason to believe, they were highly satisfied with. When dinner came upon table, not one of them would sit down, or eat a bit of anything that was served up. On expressing my surprise at this, they were all *taboo*, as they said; which word has a very comprehensive meaning, but in general signifies that a thing is forbidden. Dinner being over, and having gratified their curiosity by showing to them every part of the ship, I then conducted them ashore.

As soon as the boat reached the beach, Feenou and some others instantly stepped out. Young Fattafaihe following them, was called back by Mareewagee, who now paid the heir-apparent the same obeisance, and in the same manner that I had seen it paid to the king.

By this time I had acquired some certain information about the relative situations of the several great men whose names have been so often mentioned. I now knew that Mareewagee and Toobou were brothers. Feenou was one of Mareewagee's sons; and Tooboueitoa was another.

On the 16th, in the morning, Mr Gore and I took a walk into the country; in the course of which nothing remarkable appeared, but our having opportunities of seeing the whole process of making cloth, which is the principal manufacture of these islands, as well as of many others in this ocean.

This is performed in the following manner. The manufacturers, who are females, take the slender stalks or trunks of the paper-mulberry, which they cultivate for that purpose, and which seldom grows more than six or seven feet in height, and about four fingers in thickness. From these they strip the bark, and scrape off the outer rind with a mussel-shell. The bark is then rolled up to destroy the convexity which it had round the stalk, and macerated in water for some time. After this it is laid across the trunk of a small tree, squared, and beaten with a squared wooden instrument about a foot long, full of coarse grooves on all sides, but sometimes with one that is plain. According to the size of the bark a piece is soon produced, but the operation is often repeated by another hand, or it is folded several times and beat longer, which seems rather intended to close than to divide its texture. When this is sufficiently effected it is spread out to dry, the pieces being from four to six or more feet in length, and half as broad. They are then given to another person, who joins the pieces, by smearing part of them over with the viscous juice of a berry, called *tooo*, which serves as a glue. Having been thus lengthened, they are laid over a large piece of wood with a kind of stamp, made of a fibrous substance, pretty closely interwoven, placed beneath. They then take a bit of cloth and dip it in a juice expressed from the bark of a tree called *kokka*, which they rub briskly upon the piece that is making. This at once leaves a dull brown colour and a dry gloss upon its surface. In this manner they proceed, joining and staining by degrees, till they produce a piece of cloth of such length and breadth as they want; generally leaving a border of a foot broad at the sides, and longer at the ends unstained. Throughout the whole, if any parts of the original pieces are too thin, or have holes, which is often the case, they glue square bits upon them till they become of an equal thickness. When they want to produce a black colour they mix the soot procured from an oily nut, called *dooedooe*, with the juice of the *kokka*, in different quantities, according to the proposed depth of the tinge.

Next day was fixed upon by Mareewagee for giving a grand *haiva* or entertainment, to which we were all invited. For this purpose a large space had been cleared before the temporary hut of this chief, near our post, as an area where the performances were to be exhibited. In the morning great multitudes of the natives came in from the country, every one carrying a pole about six feet long upon his shoulder, and at each end of every pole a yam was suspended. These yams and poles were deposited on each side of the area, so as to form two large heaps, decorated with different sorts of small fish, and piled up to the greatest advantage. They were Mareewagee's present to Captain Clerke and me.

Everything being thus prepared, about eleven o'clock they began to exhibit various dances, which they call *mai*. The music consisted at first of seventy men as a chorus, who sat down; and amidst them were placed three instruments, which we called drums, from their effect. The natives call them *naffa*. These instruments produce a rude, though loud and powerful sound.

The first dance consisted of four ranks of twenty-four men each, holding in their hands a little thin, light, wooden instrument, about two feet long, and in shape not unlike a small oblong paddle. With these, which are called *pagge*, they made a great many different motions, all which were accompanied by corresponding attitudes of the body. Their motions were at first slow, but quickened as the drums beat faster; and they recited sentences in a musical tone the whole time, which were answered by the chorus; but at the end of a short space they all joined, and finished with a shout; then the rear rank dividing, shifted themselves very slowly round each end, and meeting in the front, formed the first rank; the whole number continuing to recite the sentences as before. The other ranks did the same successively, till that which at first was the front became the rear; and their evolution continued in the same manner till the last rank regained its first situation. They then began a much quicker dance, though slow at first, and sung about ten minutes, when the whole body divided into two parts, retreated a little, and then approached, forming a sort of circular figure, which finished the dance.

In a short time seventy men sat down as a chorus to another dance. This consisted of two ranks of sixteen persons each, with young Toobou at their head. These danced, sung, and twirled the *pagge* as before, but, in general, much quicker. A motion that met with particular approbation was one in which they held the face aside as if ashamed. The back rank closed before the front one, and that again resumed its place, as in the two former dances. At that instant two men entered very hastily, and exercised the clubs which they use in battle. They did this, by first twirling them in their hands, and making circular strokes before them with great force and quickness, but so skilfully managed that, though standing quite close, they never interfered. To them succeeded a person with a spear, in the same hasty manner; looking about eagerly as if in search of somebody to throw it at. He then ran hastily to one side of the crowd in the front, and put himself in a threatening attitude, as if he meant to strike with his spear at one of them, bending the knee a little, and trembling, as it were with rage. He continued in this manner only a few seconds when he moved to the other side, and having stood in the same posture there for the same short time, retreated from the ground as fast as when he made his appearance; and various other evolutions were performed with much adroitness.

These dances lasted from eleven till near three o'clock; and though they were doubtless intended to show us a specimen of their dexterity, vast numbers of their own people attended as spectators. Some of us computed that there were not less than ten or twelve thousand within the compass of a quarter of a mile, drawn together for the most part by mere curiosity.

No pen can describe the numerous actions and motions, the singularity of which was not greater than was the ease and graceful-ness with which they were performed; and the whole was conducted with far better order than could have been expected in so large an assembly.

Early in the morning of the 18th an accident happened, that strongly marked one of their customs. A man got out of a canoe into the quarter gallery of the *Resolution*, and stole from thence a pewter basin. He was discovered, pursued, and brought alongside the ship. On this occasion, three old women who were in the canoe made loud lamentations over the prisoner, beating their breasts and faces in a most violent manner; and all this was done without shedding a tear.

This day I bestowed on Mareewagee some presents in return for those we had received from him the day before; and as the entertainments which he had then exhibited for our amusement called upon us to make some exhibition in our way, I ordered a party of marines to go through their exercise on the spot where his dances had been performed; and in the evening played off some fireworks at the same place. Poulaho, with all the principal chiefs, and a great number of people of all denominations were present. The platoon firing, which was executed tolerably well, seemed to give them pleasure; but they were lost in astonishment when they beheld our water rockets.

In expectation of this evening show, the circle of natives about our tent being pretty large, they engaged the greatest part of the afternoon in boxing and wrestling. When any of them chooses to wrestle, he gets up from one side of the ring, and crosses the ground in a sort of measured pace, clapping smartly on the elbow joint of one arm, which is bent, and produces a hollow sound; that is reckoned the challenge. If no person comes out from the opposite side to engage him, he returns in the same manner and sits down, but sometimes stands clapping in the midst of the ground to provoke some one to come out. If an opponent appears, they come together with marks of the greatest good nature, generally smiling, and taking time to adjust the piece of cloth which is fastened round the waist. Their combats seldom last long before one gives in. Some of our people ventured to contend with the natives in both these exercises, but were always worsted.

The animals which we had brought were all on shore. Knowing their thievish disposition, I thought it prudent to declare my intention of leaving some of them behind, and even to make a distribution of them previously to my departure.

With this view, in the evening of the 19th, I assembled all the chiefs before our house, and my intended presents to them were marked out. To Poulaho, the king, I gave a young English bull and cow; to Mareewagee, a Cape ram and two ewes; and to Feenou, a horse and a mare. As my design to make such a distribution had been known the day before, most of the people in the neighbourhood were then present. I instructed Omai to tell them that there were no such animals within many months' sail of their island; that we had brought them for their use, from that immense distance, at a vast trouble and expense; that therefore they must be careful not to kill any of them till they had multiplied to a numerous race; and lastly, that they and their children ought to remember that they had received them from the men of Britain. He also explained to them their several uses, and what else was necessary for them to know, or rather as far as he knew; for Omai was not very well versed in such things himself.

Next day I dined ashore. The king sat down with us, but he neither ate nor drank. I found that this was owing to the presence of a female, whom, as we afterwards understood, had superior rank to himself. As soon as this great personage had dined, she stepped up to the king, who put his hands to her feet, and then she retired. He immediately dipped his fingers into a glass of wine, and then received the obeisance of all her followers. This was the single instance we ever observed of his paying this mark of reverence to any person. At the king's desire, I ordered some fireworks to be played off in the evening, but unfortunately being damaged, this exhibition did not answer expectation.

As no more entertainments were to be expected on either side, and the curiosity of the populace was by this time pretty well satisfied, most of them left us. We still, however, had thieves about us; and encouraged by the negligence of our own people, we had continual instances of their depredations.

Some of the officers belonging to both ships, who had made an excursion into the interior parts of the island without my leave, and, indeed, without my knowledge, returned this evening after an absence of two days. They had taken with them their muskets, with the necessary ammunition, and several small articles of the favourite commodities, all which the natives had the dexterity to steal from them in the course of their expedition. Feenou and Poulaho, upon this occasion, very justly observed, that if any of my people at any time wanted to go into the country, they ought to be acquainted with it, in which case they would send proper persons along with them, and then they would be answerable for their safety. Though I gave myself no trouble about the recovery of the things stolen upon this occasion, most of them, through Feenou's interposition, were recovered, except one musket and a few other articles of inferior value.

We had now recruited the ships with wood and water, and had finished the repairs of our sails. However, as an eclipse of the sun was to happen upon the 5th of July, and it was now the 25th of June, I resolved to defer sailing till that time had elapsed, in order to have a chance of observing it.

Having, therefore, some days of leisure before me, a party of us, accompanied by Poulaho, set out early next morning in a boat for Mooa, the village where he and the other great men usually reside. As we rowed up the inlet, we met fourteen canoes fishing in company, in one of which was Poulaho's son. In each canoe was a triangular net, extended between two poles, at the lower end of which was a cod to receive and secure the fish. They had already caught some fine mullets, and they put about a dozen into our boat. I desired to see their method of fishing, which they readily complied with. A shoal of fish was supposed to be upon one of the banks, which they instantly enclosed in a long net like a seine or set-net. This the fishers, one getting into the water out of each boat, surrounded with the triangular nets in their hands, with which they scooped the fish out of the seine, or caught them as they attempted to leap over it.

Leaving the prince and his fishing party, we proceeded to the bottom of the bay. Here we observed a *fiataoka*, or burying place, which was much more extensive, and seemingly of more consequence than any we had seen at the other islands. We were told that it belonged to the king. It consisted of three pretty large houses, situated upon a rising ground, with a small one at a distance, all ranged longitudinally. They were covered and paved with fine pebbles, and the whole was enclosed by large flat stones of hard coral rock, properly hewn, placed on their edges; one of which stones measured twelve feet in length, two in breadth, and above one in thickness. Within one of these houses were two rude wooden busts of men. On inquiring what these images were intended for, we were told they were merely memorials of some chiefs who had been buried there, and not the representations of any deity. In one of them was the carved head of an Otaheitean canoe, which had been driven ashore on their coast, and deposited here.

After we had refreshed ourselves, we made an excursion into the country, attended by one of the king's ministers. Our train was not great, as he would not suffer the rabble to follow us. He also obliged all those whom we met upon our progress to sit down till we had passed, which is a mark of respect due only to their sovereigns. By far the greatest part of the country was cultivated, and planted with various sorts of productions. There were many public and well-beaten roads, and abundance of footpaths leading to every part of the island. It is remarkable that when we were on the most elevated parts, at least a hundred feet above the level of the sea, we often met with the same coral rock which is found at the shore; and yet these very spots, with hardly any soil upon them, were covered with luxuriant vegetation. We saw some springs, but the water was either stinking or brackish.

When we returned from our walk, which was not till the dusk of the evening, our supper was ready. It consisted of a baked hog, some fish, and yams, all excellently well cooked, after the method of these islands. As there was nothing to amuse us after supper, we followed the custom of the country, and lay down to sleep, our beds being mats spread upon the floor, and cloth to cover us. The king, who had made himself very happy with some wine and brandy which we had brought, slept in the same house, as well as several others of the natives.

Early next morning they began to prepare a bowl of kava. We had seen the drinking of this liquor sometimes at the other islands, but by no means so frequently as here, where it seems to be the only forenoon employment of the principal people. The kava is a species of pepper, which they cultivate for this purpose, and esteem it a valuable article. It seldom grows to more than a man's height; it branches considerably, with large heart-shaped leaves and jointed stalks. The root is the only part that is used. They break it in pieces, scrape the dirt off with a shell, and then each begins and chews his portion, which he spits into a plantain leaf. The person who is to prepare the liquor collects all these mouthfuls and puts them into a large wooden dish or bowl, adding as much water as will make it of a proper strength. It is then well mixed up with hands; and some loose stuff, of which mats are made, is thrown upon the surface. The immediate effect of this beverage is not perceptible on these people, who use it so frequently; but on some of ours, who ventured to try it, though so nastily prepared, it had the same power as spirits have in intoxicating them; or rather, it produced that kind of stupefaction, which is the consequence of using opium, or other substances of that kind. I have seen them drink it seven times before noon, yet it is so disagreeable, or at least seems so, that the greatest part of them cannot swallow it without making wry faces and shuddering afterward.

When we got on board the ship, I found that everything had been quiet during my absence, not a theft having been committed, of which Feenou and Futtafaihe, the king's brother, who had undertaken the management of his countrymen, boasted not a little. This shows what power the chiefs have when they have the will to execute it; which we were seldom to expect, since whatever was stolen from us generally, if not always, was conveyed to them.

The good conduct of the natives was of short duration, for the next day six or eight of them assaulted some of our people who were sawing planks. They were fired upon by the sentry; and one was supposed to be wounded, and three others taken. These I kept confined all night, and did not dismiss them without punishment. After this they behaved with a little more circumspection, and gave us much less trouble. This change of behaviour was certainly occasioned by the man being wounded, for before they had only been told the effect of firearms, but now they had felt it.

On the 30th I visited Futtafaihe, where we spent the night, but we were a good deal disturbed by a singular instance of luxury, in which their principal men indulge themselves; that of being beat while they are asleep. Two women sat by Futtafaihe and performed this operation, which is called *tooge tooge*, by beating briskly on his body and legs with both fists, as on a drum, till he fell asleep, and continuing it the whole night with some short intervals. When once the person is asleep, they abate a little in the strength and quickness of beating, but resume it if they observe any appearance of his awaking. In the morning we found that Futtafaihe's women relieved each other, and went to sleep by turns. In any other country it would be supposed that such a practice would put an end to all rest, but here it certainly acts as an opiate; and is a strong proof of what habit may effect. The noise of this, however, was not the only thing that kept us awake; for the people, who passed the night in the house, not only conversed amongst each other frequently, as in the day, but all got up before it was light, and made a hearty meal on fish and yams, which were brought to them by a person who seemed to know very well the appointed time for this nocturnal refreshment.

I had prolonged my stay at this island on account of the approaching eclipse; but on the 2nd of July, on looking at the micrometer belonging to the Board of Longitude, I found some of the rack-work broken, and the instrument useless till repaired; which there was not time to do before it was intended to be used. Preparing now for our departure, I got on board this day all the cattle, poultry, and other animals, except such as were destined to remain.

The next day we unmoored, that we might be ready to take the advantage of the first favourable wind. The king, who was one of our company this day at dinner, I observed took particular notice of the plates. This occasioned me to make him an offer of one, either of pewter or of earthenware. He chose the first, and then began to tell us the several uses to which he intended to apply it. Two of them are so extraordinary, that I cannot omit mentioning them. He said, that whenever he should have occasion to visit any of the other islands, he would leave this plate behind him at Tongataboo as a sort of representative in his absence, that the people might pay it the same obeisance they do to himself in person. He was asked what had been usually employed for this purpose before he got this plate; and we had the satisfaction of learning from him, that this singular honour had hitherto been conferred on a wooden bowl in which he washed his hands. The other extraordinary use to which he meant to apply it, in the room of his wooden bowl, was to discover a thief. He said, that when anything was stolen, and the thief could not be found, the people were all assembled together before him, when he washed his hands in water in this vessel, after which it was cleaned, and then the whole multitude advanced, one after another, and touched it in the same manner that they touch his foot when they pay him obeisance. If the guilty person touched it, he died immediately upon the spot, not by violence, but by the hand of Providence; and if anyone refused to touch it, his refusal was a clear proof that he was the man.

In the morning of the 5th, the day of the eclipse, the weather was dark and cloudy, with showers of rain, so that we had little hopes of an observation. About nine o'clock the sun broke out at intervals for about half an hour; after which it was totally obscured till within a minute or two of the beginning of the eclipse. We were all at our telescopes, viz., Mr Bayly, Mr King, Captain Clerke, Mr Bligh, and myself. I lost the observation by not having a dark glass at hand suitable to the clouds that were continually passing over the sun; and Mr Bligh had not got the sun into the field of his telescope; so that the commencement of the eclipse was only observed by the other three gentlemen.

The general appearance of the country conveys to the spectator an idea of the most exuberant fertility, whether we respect the places improved by art, or those still in a natural state. At a distance the surface seems entirely clothed with trees of various sizes; the tall cocoa-palms are far from being the smallest ornament to any country that produces them.

Of cultivated fruits the principal are the plantains and breadfruit. There is plenty of excellent sugar-cane.

The only quadrupeds, besides hogs, are a few rats and some dogs. Fowls, which are of a large breed, are domesticated here.

On July 6th we were ready to sail; but the wind being unfavourable, we were under the necessity of waiting two or three days. We took our final leave of Tongataboo on the 10th, and early in the morning of the second day after, reached Middleburgh, or Eooa.

We had no sooner anchored, than Taoofa, the chief, and several other natives, visited us on board, and seemed to rejoice much at our arrival. This Taoofa knew me when I was here during my last voyage, consequently we were not strangers to each other. In a little time I went ashore with him in search of fresh water, the procuring of which was the chief object that brought me to Eooa. I was first conducted to a brackish spring, between low and high-water mark, in the cove where we landed. Finding that we did not like this, our friends took us a little way into the island, where, in a deep chasm, we found very good water. But rather than undertake the tedious task of bringing it down to the shore, I resolved to rest contented with the supply the ships had got at Tongataboo.

I put ashore at this island the ram and two ewes of the Cape of Good Hope breed, entrusting them to the care of Taoofa, who seemed proud of his charge.

As we lay at anchor, this island bore a very different aspect from any we had lately seen, and formed a most beautiful landscape.

The 13th in the afternoon, a party of us made an excursion to the highest part of the island, in order to have a full view of the country. From the elevation to which we had ascended, we had a full view of the whole island, except a part of the south point. The plains and meadows, of which there are here some of great extent, lie all on the north-west side; and, as they are adorned with tufts of trees, intermixed with plantations, they form a very beautiful landscape in every point of view. While I was surveying this delightful prospect, I could not help flattering myself with the pleasing idea that some future navigators may, from the same station, behold these meadows stocked with cattle brought to these islands by the ships of England, and that the completion of this single benevolent purpose, independently of all other considerations, would sufficiently mark to posterity that our voyages had not been useless to the general interests of humanity.

The next morning I planted a pineapple, and sowed the seeds of melons and other vegetables, in the chief's plantation. I had some encouragement, indeed, to flatter myself that my endeavours of this kind would not be fruitless, for this day there was served up at my dinner a dish of turnips, being the produce of the seeds I had left during my last voyage.

I had fixed on the 15th for sailing, till Taoofa pressed me to stay a day or two longer, to receive a present he had prepared for me, consisting of two small heaps of yams and some fruit, which seemed to be collected by a kind of contribution, as at the other isles. For this liberality I made an adequate return, and soon after weighed.

We now took leave of the Friendly Islands after a stay of near three months, during which time we lived together in the most cordial friendship. Some accidental differences, it is true, now and then happened, owing to their great propensity to thieving, but too often encouraged by the negligence of our own people. The time employed amongst them was not thrown away. We expended very little of our sea provisions; subsisting in general upon the produce of the islands while we stayed, and carrying away with us a quantity of refreshments sufficient to last till our arrival at another station, where we could depend upon a fresh supply. I was not sorry, besides, to have had an opportunity of bettering the condition of these good people by leaving the useful animals before mentioned among them; and, at the same time, those designed for Otaheite received fresh strength in the pastures of Tongataboo. But besides the immediate advantages which both the natives of the Friendly Islands and ourselves received by this visit, future navigators from Europe, if any such ever tread in our steps, will profit by the knowledge I acquired of the geography of this part of the Pacific Ocean; and the more philosophical reader, who loves to view human nature in new situations, will perhaps find matter of amusement, if not of instruction, in the information which I have been enabled to convey to him concerning the inhabitants of this archipelago. According to the information that we received there, this archipelago is very extensive. Above one hundred and fifty islands were reckoned up to us by the natives, who made use of bits of leaves to ascertain their number.

The natives of the Friendly Islands seldom exceed the common stature (though we have measured some who were above six feet), but are very strong and well made, especially as to their limbs. They are generally broad about the shoulders; and though the muscular disposition of the men, which seems a consequence of much action, rather conveys the appearance of strength than of beauty, there are several to be seen who are really handsome. We met with hundreds of truly European faces, and many genuine Roman noses amongst them. Their eyes and teeth are good, but the last neither so remarkably white, nor so well set, as are often found amongst Indian nations.

The women are not so much distinguished from the men by their features as by their general form, which is, for the most part, destitute of that strong fleshy firmness that appears in the latter. Though the features of some are so delicate as not only to be a true index of their sex, but to lay claim to a considerable share of beauty and expression, for the bodies and limbs of most of the females are well proportioned, and some absolutely perfect models of a beautiful figure. But the most remarkable distinction in the women is the uncommon smallness and delicacy of their fingers, which may be put in competition with the finest in Europe.

The general colour is a cast deeper than the copper brown, but several of the men and women have a true olive complexion, and some of the last are even a great deal fairer. We saw a man and a boy at Hapaee, and a child at Annamooka, perfectly white. Such have been found amongst all black nations, but I apprehend that their colour is rather a disease than a natural phenomenon.

Their countenances very remarkably express the abundant mildness, or good nature, which they possess, and are entirely free from that savage keenness which marks nations in a barbarous state. They are frank, cheerful, and good-humoured, though sometimes, in the presence of their chiefs, they put on a degree of gravity, and such a serious air, as becomes stiff and awkward, and has an appearance of reserve.

Their peaceable disposition is sufficiently evinced from the friendly reception all strangers have met with who have visited them. Instead of offering to attack them openly or clandestinely, as has been the case with most of the inhabitants of these seas, they have never appeared in the smallest degree hostile, but, on the contrary, like the most civilised people, have courted an intercourse with their visitors by bartering, which is the only medium that unites all nations in a sort of friendship. Upon the whole, they seem possessed of many of the most excellent qualities that adorn the human mind – such as industry, ingenuity, perseverance, affability, and perhaps other virtues which our short stay with them might prevent our observing.

The only defect sullying their character that we know of, is a propensity to thieving, to which we found those of all ages, and both sexes, addicted; and to an uncommon degree. Great allowances should be made for the foibles of these poor natives of the Pacific Ocean, whose minds we overpowered with the glare of objects equally new to them as they were captivating. The thefts so frequently committed by the natives, of what we had brought along with us, may be said to arise solely from an intense curiosity or desire to possess something which they had not been accustomed to before, and belonged to a sort of people so different from themselves.

Their hair is in general straight, thick, and strong, though a few have it bushy or frizzled. The natural colour, I believe, almost without exception, is black; but the greatest part of the men, and some of the women, have it stained of a brown or purple colour, and a few of an orange cast.

The dress of both men and women is the same, and consists of a piece of cloth or matting (but mostly the former) about two yards wide and two and a half long – at least so long as to go once and a half round the waist, to which it is confined by a girdle or cord. It is double before, and hangs down like a petticoat, as low as the middle of the leg. The upper part of the garment, above the girdle, is plaited into several folds, so that, when unfolded, there is cloth sufficient to draw up and wrap round the shoulders, which is very seldom done. The inferior sort are satisfied with small pieces, and very often wear nothing but a covering made of leaves of plants, or the *maro*, which is a narrow piece of cloth or matting like a sash. This they pass between the thighs and wrap round the waist, but the use of it is chiefly confined to the men.

'The ornaments worn by both sexes are necklaces made of the fruit of the pandanus, and various sweet-smelling flowers which go under the general name of *kahulla*. Others are composed of small shells, the wing and leg-bones of birds, sharks' teeth, and other things, all which hang loose upon the breast, rings of tortoiseshell on the fingers, and a number of these joined together as bracelets on the wrists.

The employment of the women is of the easy kind, and for the most part such as may be executed in the house. The manufacturing their cloth is wholly consigned to their care.

The manufacture next in consequence, and also within the department of the women, is that of their mats, which excel everything I have seen at any other place, both as to their texture and their beauty.

The province allotted to the men, as might be expected, is far more laborious and extensive than that of the women. Agriculture, architecture, boat-building, fishing, and other things that relate to navigation, are the objects of their care. Cultivated roots and fruits being their principal support, this requires their constant attention to agriculture, which they pursue very diligently, and seem to have brought almost to as great perfection as circumstances will permit.

In planting the plantains and yams, they observe so much exactness that, whichever way you look, the rows present themselves regular and complete.

It is remarkable that these people, who in many things display much taste and ingenuity, should show little of either in building their houses. Those of the lower people are poor huts, and very small; those of the better sort are larger and more comfortable. The dimensions of one of a middling size are about thirty feet long, twenty broad, and twelve high. Their house is, properly speaking, a thatched roof or shed, supported by posts and rafters, disposed in a very judicious manner. The floor is raised with earth, smoothed, and covered with strong thick matting, and kept very clean. Their whole furniture consists of a bowl or two, in which they make kava, a few gourds, coconut shells, and some small wooden stools, which serve them for pillows.

Their weapons are clubs of different sorts (in the ornamenting of which they spend much time), spears, and darts. They have also bows and arrows, but these seemed to be designed only for amusement, such as shooting at birds, and not for military purposes.

They seem to have no set time for meals. They go to bed as soon as it is dark, and rise with the dawn in the morning.

Their private diversions are chiefly singing, dancing, and music, performed by the women. The dancing of the men has a thousand different motions with the hands, to which we are entire strangers; and they are performed with an ease and grace which are not to be described but by those who have seen them.

Whether their marriages be made lasting by any kind of solemn contract, we could not determine with precision, but it is certain that the bulk of the people satisfied themselves with one wife. The chiefs, however, have commonly several women, though some of us were of opinion that there was only one that was looked upon as the mistress of the family.

Nothing can be a greater proof of the humanity of these people than the concern they show for the dead. They beat their teeth with stones, strike a shark's tooth into the head till the blood flows in streams, and thrust spears into the inner part of the thigh, into their sides, below the armpits, and through the cheeks into the mouth. All these operations convey an idea of such rigorous discipline as must require an uncommon degree of affection, or the grossest superstition to exact. It should be observed, however, that the more painful operations are only practised on account of the death of those most nearly connected. The common people are interred in no particular spot.

Their long and general mourning proves that they consider death as a very great evil. And this is confirmed by a very odd custom which they practise to avert it. They suppose that the Deity will accept of the little finger as a sort of sacrifice efficacious enough to procure the recovery of their health. There was scarcely one in ten of them whom we did not find thus mutilated in one or both hands.

They seem to have little conception of future punishment. They believe, however, that they are justly punished upon earth, and consequently use every method to render their divinities propitious. The Supreme Author of most things they call Kallafootonga, who, they say, is a female residing in the sky, and directing the thunder, wind, rain, and in general all the changes of weather. They believe that when she is angry with them, the productions of the earth are blasted, that many things are destroyed by lightning, and that they themselves are afflicted with sickness and death, as well as their hogs and other animals. When this anger abates, they suppose that everything is restored to its natural order. They also admit a plurality of deities, though all inferior to Kallafootonga. But their notions of the power and other attributes of these beings are so very absurd, that they suppose they have no farther concern with them after death.

They have, however, very proper sentiments about the immateriality and the immortality of the soul. They call it life, the living principle; or, what is more agreeable to their notions of it, an *otooa*, that is, a divinity or invisible being.

Of the nature of their government, we know no more than the general outline. Some of them told us that the power of the king is unlimited, and that the life and property of the subject are at his disposal; and we saw instances enough to prove that the lower order of people have no property, nor safety for their persons, but at the will of the chief to whom they respectively belong.

The language of the Friendly Islands has the greatest affinity imaginable to that of New Zealand, of Wateeoo, and Mangeea; and, consequently, to that of Otaheite and the Society Islands.

Nothing material occurred for some time after we left the Friendly Islands. In the morning of the 8th of August, land was seen nine or ten leagues distant. As we approached, we saw it everywhere guarded by a reef of coral rock, extended in some places a full mile from the land, and a high surf breaking upon it. We also observed people on several parts of the coast; and in a little time after we had reached the lee-side of the island, we saw them launch two canoes, into which about a dozen men got, and paddled towards us.

I now shortened sail, as well to give these canoes time to come up with us, as to sound for anchorage. The canoes having advanced to about the distance of a pistol-shot from the ship, they stopped. Omai was employed, as he usually had been on such occasions, to use all his eloquence to prevail on the men in them to come nearer, but no entreaties could induce them to trust themselves within our reach. They kept eagerly pointing to the shore with their paddles, and calling on us to go thither; and several of their countrymen who stood upon the beach held up something white, which we considered also as an invitation to land. But I did not think proper to risk losing the advantage of a fair wind for the sake of examining an island which appeared to be of little consequence. For this reason I made sail to the north, but not without getting from them, during their vicinity to our ship, the name of their island, which they called Toobouai.

At daybreak, in the morning of the 12th, we saw the island of Maitea. Soon after, Otaheite made its appearance.

When we first drew near the island, several canoes came off to the ship, each conducted by two or three men. But as they were common fellows, Omai took no particular notice of them, nor they of him. At length, a chief, whom I had known before, named Ootee, and Omai's brother-in-law, who chanced to be now at this corner of the island, and three or four more persons, all of whom knew Omai, came on board. Yet there was nothing either tender or striking in their meeting; on the contrary, there seemed to be a perfect indifference on both sides, till Omai having taken his brother down into the cabin, opened the drawer where he kept his red feathers and gave him a few. This being presently known amongst the rest of the natives upon deck, the face of affairs was entirely turned; and Ootee, who would hardly speak to Omai before, now begged that they might be friends and exchange names. Omai accepted of the honour, and confirmed it with a present of red feathers; and Ootee, by way of return, sent ashore for a hog. But it was evident to every one of us that it was not the man, but his property they were in love with. Such was Omai's first reception among his countrymen. I own I never expected it would be otherwise; but still I was in hopes that the valuable cargo of presents, with which the liberality of his friends in England had loaded him, would be the means of raising him into consequence, and of making him respected, and even courted by the first persons throughout the extent of the Society Islands. This could not but have happened had he conducted himself with any degree of prudence. But instead of it, I am sorry to say that he paid too little regard to the repeated advice of those who wished him well, and suffered himself to be duped by every designing knave.

The important news of red feathers being on board our ships having been conveyed on shore by Omai's friends, day had no sooner begun to break next morning, than we were surrounded by a multitude of canoes, crowded with people bringing hogs and fruit to market. At first, a quantity of feathers, not greater than what might be got from a tom-tit, would purchase a hog of forty or fifty pounds weight. But as almost everybody in the ships was possessed of some of this precious article of trade, it fell in its value above five hundred per cent before night.

Soon after we had anchored, Omai's sister came on board to see him. I was happy to observe that, much to the honour of them both, their meeting was marked with expressions of the tenderest affection, easier to be conceived than to be described.

This moving scene having closed, and the ship being properly moored, Omai and I went on shore. My first object was to pay a visit to a man, whom my friend represented as a very extraordinary personage indeed, for he said that he was the god of Bolabola. We found him seated under one of those small awnings which they usually carry in their larger canoes. He was an elderly man, and had lost the use of his limbs, so that he was carried from place to place upon a hand-barrow. From Omai's account of this person, I expected to have seen some religious adoration paid to him; but excepting some young plantain-trees that lay before him, and upon the awning under which he sat, I could observe nothing by which he might be distinguished from their other chiefs. Omai presented to him a tuft of red feathers tied to the end of a small stick, but after a little conversation on indifferent matters with this Bolabola man, his attention was drawn to an old woman, the sister of his mother. She was already at his feet, and had bedewed them plentifully with tears of joy.

I left him with the old lady in the midst of a number of people who had gathered round him, and went to view a house, said to be built by strangers since I was here before. By an inscription, I found it was erected by some Spaniards that had been lately there in two ships from Lima.

When I returned, I found Omai holding forth to a large company, and it was with some difficulty that he could be got away to accompany me on board, where I had an important affair to settle, in regard to the stated allowance of spirituous liquors; and I had the satisfaction to find that the crews of both ships unanimously consented to an abridgment in the usual quantity while at this place, that they might not be under the necessity of being put to a short allowance in a cold climate.

The next day we began some necessary operations. I also put on shore the bull, cows, horses, and sheep, and appointed two men to look after them while grazing; for I did not intend to leave any of them at this part of the island.

During the two following days it hardly ever ceased raining. The natives, nevertheless, came to us from every quarter, the news of our arrival having rapidly spread. On the 17th, Omai and I went ashore to pay a formal visit to a young chief named Waheiadooa, who had come down to the beach. On this occasion Omai, assisted by some of his friends, dressed himself, not after the English fashion, nor that of Otaheite, nor that of Tongataboo, nor in the dress of any country upon earth, but in a strange medley of all that he was possessed of.

On our landing, Etary, or the god of Bolabola, carried on a hand-barrow, attended us to a large house, where he was set down, and we seated ourselves on each side of him. I caused a piece of Tongataboo cloth to be spread out before us, on which I laid the presents I intended to make. Presently the young chief came, attended by his mother and several principal men, who all seated themselves at the other end of the cloth facing us. Then a man who sat by me made a speech, consisting of short and separate sentences, part of which was dictated by those about him. He was answered by one from the opposite side near the chief. Etary spoke next, then Omai, and both of them were answered from the same quarter. These orations were entirely about my arrival and connections with them. The person who spoke last told me, amongst other things, that he was authorised to make a formal surrender of the province of Tiaraboo to me, and of everything in it, which marks very plainly that these people are no strangers to the policy of accommodating themselves to present circumstances. At length the young chief was directed by his attendants to come and embrace me, and by way of confirming this treaty of friendship we exchanged names. The ceremony being closed, he and his friends accompanied me on board to dinner.

Having taken in a fresh supply of water, and finished all our other necessary operations, on the 22nd I brought off the cattle and sheep, and made ready for sea.

On the 23rd, we got under sail, and steered for Matavai Bay, where the *Resolution* anchored the same evening. But the *Discovery* did not get in till the next morning.

About nine o'clock in the morning, Otoo, the king of the whole island, attended by a great number of canoes full of people, came from Oparre, his place of residence, and sent a message on board, expressing a desire to see me. Accordingly I landed, accompanied by Omai and some of the officers. We found a prodigious number of people assembled on this occasion, and in the midst of them was the king, attended by his father, his two brothers, and three sisters. I went up first and saluted him, followed by Omai, who kneeled and embraced his legs. He had prepared himself for this ceremony, by dressing in his very best suit of clothes, and behaved with a great deal of respect and modesty. Nevertheless, very little notice was taken of him. Perhaps envy had some share in producing this cold reception. He made the chief a present of a large piece of red feathers, and about two or three yards of gold cloth; and I gave him a suit of fine linen, a gold-laced hat, some tools, and, what was of more value than all the other articles, a quantity of red feathers, and one of the bonnets in use at the Friendly Islands.

After the hurry of this visit was over, the king and the whole royal family accompanied me on board, followed by several canoes laden with all kinds of provisions, in quantity sufficient to have served the companies of both ships for a week. Soon after the king's mother, who had not been present at the first interview, came on board, bringing with her a quantity of provisions and cloth, which she divided between me and Omai. For although he was but little noticed at first by his countrymen, they no sooner gained the knowledge of his riches, than they began to court his friendship. I encouraged this as much as I could; for it was my wish to fix him with Otoo. As I intended to leave all my European animals at this island, I thought he would be able to give some instruction about the management of them, and their use. Besides, I knew and saw that the farther he was from his native island, he would be the better respected. But unfortunately, poor Omai rejected my advice, and conducted himself in so imprudent a manner, that he soon lost the friendship of Otoo, and of every other person of note in Otaheite.

As soon as we had dined, a party of us accompanied Otoo to Oparre, taking with us the poultry with which we were to stock the island. These I left at Oparre in the possession of Otoo, and the geese and ducks began to breed before we sailed. We found there a gander, which the natives told us was the same that Captain Wallis had given to Oberea ten years before; several goats, and the Spanish bull which they kept tied to a tree near Otoo's house. I never saw a finer animal of his kind. He was now the property of Etary, and had been brought from Oheitepeha to this place, in order to be shipped for Bolabola. But it passes my comprehension how they can contrive to carry him in one of their canoes. If we had not arrived, it would have been of little consequence who had the property of him, as, without a cow, he could be of no use, and none had been left with him. Next day I put ashore three cows and a horse, a mare and sheep.

Having thus disposed of these passengers, I found myself lightened of a very heavy burthen. The trouble and vexation that attended the bringing this living cargo thus far, is hardly to be conceived. But the satisfaction that I felt in having been so fortunate as to fulfil his Majesty's humane design, in sending such valuable animals to supply the wants of two worthy nations, sufficiently recompensed me for the many anxious hours I had passed, before this subordinate object of my voyage could be carried into execution.

As I intended to make some stay here, we set up the two observatories on Matavai Point. Adjoining to them, two tents were pitched for the reception of a guard, and of such people as it might be necessary to leave on shore in different departments. At this station, I entrusted the command to Mr King, who, at the same time, attended the observations for ascertaining the going of the time-keeper, and other purposes.

On the 26th, I had a piece of ground cleared for a garden, and planted it with several articles. Some melons, potatoes, and two pineapple plants, were in a fair way of succeeding before we left the place. I had brought from the Friendly Islands several shaddock trees. These I also planted here, and they can hardly fail of success, unless their growth should be checked by the same premature curiosity which destroyed a vine planted by the Spaniards at Oheitepeha. A number of the natives got together to taste the first fruit it bore; but, as the grapes were still sour, they considered it as little better than poison, and it was unanimously determined to tread it under foot. In that state Omai found it by chance, and was overjoyed at the discovery, for he had a full confidence, that if he had but grapes, he could easily make wine. Accordingly he had several slips cut off from the tree to carry with him, and we pruned and put in order the remains of it. Probably, grown wise by Omai's instructions, they may now suffer the fruit to grow to perfection, and not pass so hasty a sentence upon it again.

We found here the young man whom we called Oedidee, but whose real name is Heete-heete. I had carried him from Ulietea in 1773, and brought him back in 1774; after he had visited the Friendly Islands, New Zealand, Easter Island, and the Marquesas, and been on board my ship in that extensive navigation, about seven months. He was tenacious of his good-breeding, and 'yes, Sir', or, 'if you please, Sir', were frequently repeated by him. Heete-heete, who is a native of Bolabola, had arrived in Otaheite about three months before, with no other intention that we could learn, than to gratify his curiosity, or perhaps some other favourite passion. It was evident, however, that he preferred the modes, and even garb of his countrymen, to ours. For though I gave him some clothes, which our Admiralty Board had been pleased to send for his use (to which I added a chest of tools, and a few other articles as a present from myself), he declined wearing them after a few days.

This instance may be urged as a proof of the strong propensity natural to man, of returning to habits acquired at an early age, and only interrupted by accident.

In the morning of the 27th, a man came from Oheitepeha, and told us that two Spanish ships had anchored in that bay the night before, and, in confirmation of this intelligence, he produced a piece of coarse blue cloth, which he said he got out of one of the ships, and which, indeed, to appearance was almost quite new. I despatched Lieutenant Williamson in a boat to look into Oheitepeha Bay, and, in the meantime, I put the ships into a proper posture of defence. For though England and Spain were in peace when I left Europe, for aught I knew, a different scene might by this time have opened. However, the fellow had imposed upon us, as was found by Williamson's report.

Hitherto the attention of Otoo and his people had been confined to us; but next morning a new scene of business opened, by the arrival of some messengers from Eimeo, with intelligence that the people in that island were in arms, and that Otoo's partisans there had been worsted, and obliged to retreat to the mountains. The quarrel between the two islands, which commenced in 1774, had, it seems, partly subsisted ever since. The formidable armament which I saw at that time, had sailed soon after I then left Otaheite; but the malcontents of Eimeo had made so stout a resistance, that the fleet had returned without effecting much, and now another expedition was necessary.

On the arrival of these messengers, all the chiefs who happened to be at Matavai, assembled at Otoo's house where I actually was at the time, and had the honour to be admitted into their council. One of the messengers opened the business of the assembly in a speech of considerable length, in order to excite the assembled chiefs of Otaheite to arm on the occasion. This opinion was combated by others who were against commencing hostilities. At length the party for war prevailed. Otoo during the whole debate remained silent. Those of the council who were for prosecuting the war applied to me for my assistance, and all of them wanted to know what part I would take. Omai was sent for to be my interpreter, but as he could not be found, I was obliged to speak for myself, and told them as well as I could, that as the people of Eimeo had never offended me, I could not think myself at liberty to engage in hostilities against them. With this declaration they seemed satisfied.

On our inquiring into the cause of the war, we were told that some years ago a brother of Waheadooa, of Tieraboo, was sent to Eimeo at the request of Maheine, a popular chief of that island, to be their king; but that he had not been there a week before Maheine having caused him to be killed, set up for himself in opposition to Tierataboonooe, his sister's son, who became the lawful heir; or else had been pitched upon by the people of Otaheite to succeed to the government on the death of the other.

Towha, a man of much weight in the island, happened not to be at Matavai at this time. It however appeared that he was no stranger to what was transacted, and that he entered with more spirit into the affair than any other chief. For, early in the morning of the 1st of September, a messenger arrived from him to acquaint Otoo that he had killed a man to be sacrificed to the *Eatooa* to implore the assistance of the god against Eimeo. This act of worship was to be performed at the great *morai* at Attahooroo, and Otoo's presence, it seems, was absolutely necessary on that solemn occasion.

I proposed to Otoo that I might be allowed to accompany him. To this he readily consented; and we immediately set out in my boat with my old friend Potatou, Mr Anderson, and Mr Webber; Omai following in a canoe.

As soon as we landed at Attahooroo, which was about two o'clock in the afternoon, Otoo expressed his desire that the seamen might be ordered to remain in the boat, and that Mr Anderson, Mr Webber, and myself, might take off our hats as soon as we should come to the *morai*, to which we immediately proceeded, attended by a great many men and some boys, but not one woman. We found four priests and their attendants or assistants waiting for us.

The ceremonies now began. One of the priest's attendants brought a young plantain tree and laid it down before Otoo. One of the priests seated at the *morai* now began a long prayer. During this prayer a man who stood by the officiating priest held in his hand two bundles, seemingly of cloth. In one of them, as we afterwards found, was the royal *maro*; and the other, if I may be allowed the expression, was the ark of the *Eatooa*. As soon as the prayer was ended, the priests at the *morai*, with their attendants, went and sat down by those upon the beach, carrying with them the two bundles. Here they renewed their prayers. The dead body was now taken out of a canoe and laid upon the beach, with the feet to the sea. The priests placed themselves around it, some sitting and others standing, and one or more of them repeated sentences for about ten minutes. It was now laid in a parallel direction with the sea-shore. One of the priests then standing at the feet of it pronounced a long prayer, in which he was at times joined by the others, each holding in his hand a tuft of red feathers. In the course of this prayer some hair was pulled off the head of the sacrifice, and the left eye taken out, both of which were presented to Otoo wrapped up in a green leaf. He did not, however, touch it, but gave to the man who presented it the tuft of feathers which he had received from Towha. This, with the hair and eye, was carried back to the priests. During some part of this last ceremony a kingfisher making a noise in the trees, Otoo turned to me, saying, 'That is the *Eatooa*!' and seemed to look upon it to be a good omen.

The body was then carried a little way with its head toward the *morai* and laid under a tree, near which were fixed three broad thin pieces of wood, differently but rudely carved. The bundles of cloth were laid on a part of the *morai*, and the tufts of red feathers were placed at the feet of the sacrifice, round which the priests took their stations, and we were now allowed to go as near as we pleased. He who seemed to be the chief priest sat at a small distance and spoke for a quarter of an hour, but with different tones and gestures, so that he seemed to expostulate with, or question the dead person, to whom he constantly addressed himself. He then chanted a prayer which lasted nearly half an hour, in a whining, melancholy tone, accompanied by two other priests, and in which Potatou and some others joined. In the course of this prayer some more hair was plucked by the priest from the head of the corpse and put upon one of the bundles. After this the chief priest prayed alone, holding in his hand the feathers which came from Towha. When he had finished he gave them to another, who prayed in like manner. Then all the tufts of feathers were laid upon the bundles of cloth, which closed the ceremony at this place.

The corpse was then carried up to the most conspicuous part of the *morai*, with the feathers, the two bundles of cloth, and the drums, the last of which beat slowly. The feathers and bundles were laid against the pile of stones, and the corpse at the foot of them.

The priests having again seated themselves round it, renewed their prayers while some of their attendants dug a hole about two feet deep, into which they threw the unhappy victim, and covered it over with earth and stones. While they were putting him into the grave a boy squeaked aloud, and Omai said to me that it was the *Eatooa*. During this time a fire having been made, a dog was produced and killed by twisting his neck and suffocating him. The hair was singed off, and the entrails taken out and thrown into the fire, where they were left to consume. The body of the dog, after being besmeared with blood and dried over the fire, was, with the liver and heart, carried and laid down before the priests, who sat praying round the grave. They continued their ejaculations over the dog for some time, while two men at intervals beat on two drums very loud, and a boy screamed as before in a loud shrill voice three different times. This, as we were told, was to invite *Eatooa* to feast on the banquet that they had prepared for him. As soon as the priests had ended their prayers, the carcass of the dog, with what belonged to it, was laid on a scaffold about six feet high, that stood close by, on which lay the remains of two other dogs and of two pigs which had lately been sacrificed, and at this time emitted an intolerable stench. This kept us at a greater distance than would otherwise have been required of us. When the dog was put upon the scaffold the priest and attendants gave a kind of shout, which closed the ceremonies for the present. The day being now also closed, we were conducted to a house belonging to Potatou, where we were entertained and lodged for the night. Some other religious rites were performed next day, but on this subject we think we have said enough to satisfy our readers – perhaps to disgust them.

The unhappy victim offered to the object of their worship upon this occasion seemed to be a middle-aged man, and as we were told was a *towtow* – that is, one of the lowest class of the people. But after all my inquiries, I could not learn that he had been pitched upon on account of any particular crime committed by him meriting death. Having had an opportunity of examining the appearance of the body of the poor sufferer now offered up, I could observe that it was bloody about the head and face, and a good deal bruised upon the right temple, which marked the manner of his being killed. And we were told that he had been privately knocked on the head with a stone.

Whenever any one of the great chiefs thinks a human sacrifice necessary on any particular emergency, he pitches upon the victim. Some of his trusty servants are then sent, who fall upon him suddenly and put him to death with a club or by stoning him. The king is next acquainted with it, whose presence at the solemn rites that follow is, as I was told, absolutely necessary; and indeed, on the present occasion, we could observe that Otoo bore a principal part.

It is much to be regretted that a practice so horrid in its own nature, and so destructive of that inviolable right of self-preservation which everyone is born with, should be found still existing. Though we should suppose that never more than one person is sacrificed on any single occasion at Otaheite, it is more than probable that these occasions happen so frequently as to make a shocking waste of the human race; for I counted no less than forty-nine skulls of former victims lying before the *morai*, where we saw one more added to the number. And as none of those skulls had as yet suffered any considerable change from the weather, it may hence be inferred that no great length of time had elapsed since at least this considerable number of unhappy wretches had been offered upon this altar of blood.

Human sacrifices, however, are not the only barbarous custom we find still prevailing amongst this benevolent humane people. For besides cutting out the jawbones of their enemies slain in battle, which they carry about as trophies, they in some measure offer their bodies as a sacrifice to the *Eatooa*. Soon after a battle in which they have been victors, they collect all the dead that have fallen into their hands and bring them to the *morai*, where, with a great deal of ceremony, they dig a hole and bury them all in it, as so many offerings to the gods; but their skulls are never after taken up.

Before we parted, we were asked if the solemnity at which we had been present answered our expectations; what opinion we had of its efficacy; and whether we performed such acts of worship in our own country? During the celebration of the horrid ceremony, we had preserved a profound silence, but as soon as it was closed had made no scruple in expressing our sentiments very freely about it to Otoo and those who attended him; of course, therefore, I could not conceal my detestation of it in a subsequent conversation with Towha. Omai was made use of as our interpreter, and he entered into our arguments with so much spirit that this chief seemed to be in great wrath, especially when he was told that if he had put a man to death in England as he had done here, his rank would not have protected him from being hanged for it. Upon this he exclaimed, *maeno! maeno!* (vile! vile!) and would not hear another word. During this debate many of the natives were present, chiefly the attendants and servants of Towha himself; and when Omai began to explain the punishment that would be inflicted in England upon the greatest man if he killed the meanest servant, they seemed to listen with great attention, and were probably of a different opinion from that of their master on this subject.

On the 4th a party of us dined ashore with Omai, who gave excellent fare, consisting of fish, fowls, pork, and puddings. After dinner I attended Otoo, who had been one of the party, back to his house, where I found all his servants very busy getting a quantity of provisions ready for me. Amongst other articles there was a large hog, which they killed in my presence. There was also a large pudding, the whole process in making which I saw. It was composed of breadfruit, ripe plantains, taro, and palm or pandanus nuts, each rasped, scraped, or beat up fine, and baked by itself. A quantity of juice, pressed from coconut kernels, was put into a large tray or wooden vessel. The other articles, hot from the oven, were deposited in this vessel, and a few hot stones were also put in to make the contents simmer. Three or four men made use of sticks to stir the several ingredients till they were incorporated one with another, and the juice of the coconut was turned to oil, so that the whole mass at last became of the consistency of a hasty-pudding. Some of these puddings are excellent, and few that we make in England equal them. Otoo's hog being baked, and the pudding which I have described being made, they, together with two living hogs and a quantity of breadfruit and coconuts, were put into a canoe and sent on board my ship, followed by myself and all the royal family.

In the evening of the 7th we played off some fireworks before a great concourse of people. Some were highly entertained with the exhibition, but by far the greater number of spectators were terribly frightened, insomuch that it was with difficulty we could prevail upon them to keep together to see the end of the show. A table-rocket was the last: it flew off the table and dispersed the whole crowd in a moment; even the most resolute among them fled with precipitation.

Otoo was not more attentive to supply our wants by a succession of presents, than he was to contribute to our amusement by a succession of diversions. A party of us having gone down to Oparre on the 10th, he treated us with what may be called a play. His three sisters were the actresses, and the dresses that they appeared in were new and elegant; that is, more so than we had usually met with at any of these islands.

In the evening we returned from Oparre, where we left Otoo and all the royal family, and I saw none of them till the 12th, when all but the chief himself paid me a visit. He, as they told me, was gone to Attahooroo to assist this day at another human sacrifice, which the chief of Tiaraboo had sent thither to be offered up at the *morai*. This second instance, within the course of a few days, was too melancholy a proof how numerous the victims of this bloody superstition are amongst this humane people. I would have been present at this sacrifice too, had I known of it in time, for now it was too late.

The following evening Otoo returned from exercising this most disagreeable of all his duties as sovereign; and the next day, being now honoured with his company, Captain Clerke and I, mounted on horseback, took a ride round the plain of Matavai, to the very great surprise of a great train of people who attended on the occasion, gazing upon us with as much astonishment as it we had been centaurs. Omai, indeed, had once or twice before this attempted to get on horseback, but he had as often been thrown off before he could contrive to seat himself, so that this was the first time they had seen anybody ride a horse. What Captain Clerke and I began was after this repeated every day while we stayed by one or another of our people; and yet the curiosity of the natives continued still unabated. They were exceedingly delighted with these animals after they had seen the use that was made of them; and, as far as I could judge, they conveyed to them a better idea of the greatness of other nations than all the other novelties put together that their European visitors had carried amongst them.

In the morning of the 18th, Mr Anderson, myself, and Omai went again with Otoo to Oparre, and took with us the sheep which I intended to leave upon the island, consisting of an English ram and ewe, and three Cape ewes, all which I gave to Otoo. After dining with Otoo we returned to Matavai, leaving him at

Oparre. This day and also the 19th we were very sparingly supplied with fruit. Otoo hearing of this, he and his brother, who had attached himself to Captain Clerke, came from Oparre between nine and ten o'clock in the evening with a large supply for both ships. This marked his humane attention more strongly than anything he had hitherto done for us. The next day all the royal family came with presents, so that our wants were not only relieved, but we had more provisions than we could consume.

Having got all our water on board, the ships being caulked, the rigging overhauled, and everything put in order, I began to think of leaving the island, that I might have sufficient time to spare for visiting the others in this neighbourhood. With this view we removed from the shore our observatories and instruments, and bent the sails.

Early in the morning of the 22nd, Otoo and his father came on board to know when I proposed sailing. For having been informed that there was a good harbour at Eimeo, I had told them that I should visit that island on my way to Huaheine, and they were desirous of taking a passage with me, and of their fleet sailing at the same time to reinforce Towha. As I was ready to take my departure, I left it to them to name the day, and the Wednesday following was fixed upon, when I was to take on board Otoo, his father, mother, and, in short, the whole family. These points being settled, I proposed setting out immediately for Oparre, where all the fleet, fitted out for the expedition, was to assemble this day and to be reviewed.

I had but just time to get into my boat when news was brought that Towha had concluded a treaty with Maheine, and had returned with his fleet to Attahooroo. This unexpected event made all farther proceedings in the military way quite unnecessary; and the war canoes, instead of rendezvousing at Oparre, were ordered home to their respective districts.

I now returned on board my ship, attended by Otoo's mother, his three sisters, and eight more women. At first I thought that this numerous train of females came into my boat with no other view than to get a passage to Matavai. But when we arrived at the ship they told me they intended passing the night on board for the express purpose of undertaking the cure of the disorder I had complained of, which was a pain of the rheumatic kind. I accepted the friendly offer, had a bed spread for them upon the cabin floor, and submitted myself to their directions. They began to squeeze me with both hands from head to foot, but more particularly on the parts where the pain was lodged, till they made my bones crack, and my flesh became a perfect mummy. In short, after undergoing this discipline about a quarter of an hour, I was glad to get away from them. However, the operation gave me immediate relief, which encouraged me to submit to another rubbing down before I went to bed, and it was so effectual that I found myself pretty easy all the night after. My female physicians repeated their prescription the next morning before they went ashore, and again in the evening when they returned on board; after which I found the pains entirely removed, and the cure being perfected, they took their leave of me the following morning. This they call *romee*; an operation which, in my opinion, far exceeds the flesh-brush or anything of the kind that we make use of externally. It is universally practised amongst these islanders, being sometimes performed by the men, but more generally by the women.

The war with Eimeo being finally closed, all our friends paid us a visit on the 26th; and as they knew that we were upon the point of sailing, brought with them more hogs than we could take off their hands. For, having no salt left to preserve any, we wanted no more than for present use.

Our friend Omai got one good thing at this island for the many good things he gave away. This was a very fine double-sailing canoe, completely equipped, and fit for the sea. Some time before I had made up for him a suit of English colours, but he thought these too valuable to be used at this time, and patched up a parcel of colours, such as flags and pendants, to the number of ten or a dozen, which he spread on different parts of his vessel, all at the same time, and drew together as many people to look at her as a man-of-war would, dressed in a European port. These streamers of Omai were a mixture of English, French, Spanish, and Dutch, which were all the European colours that he had seen.

Omai had also provided himself with a good stock of cloth and coconut oil, which are not only in greater plenty, but much better at Otaheite than at any of the Society Islands, insomuch that they are articles of trade. Omai would not have behaved so inconsistently and so much unlike himself as he did in many instances, but for his sister and brother-in-law, who, together with a few more of their acquaintance, engrossed him entirely to themselves, with no other view than to strip him of everything he had got. And they would undoubtedly have succeeded in their scheme if I had not put a stop to it in time, by taking the most useful articles of his property into my possession.

On the 28th, Otoo came on board and informed me that he had got a canoe, which he desired I would take with me and carry home, as a present from him to his Majesty the King of Great Britain, whom he called *Earee rahie no Pretane*; it being the only thing, he said, that he could send worth his acceptance. I was not a little pleased with Otoo for this mark of his gratitude. It was a thought entirely his own, not one of us having given him the least hint about it; and it showed that he fully understood to whom he was indebted for the most valuable presents he had received. As it was too large for me to take on board, I could only thank him for his good intention, but it would have pleased him much better if his present could have been accepted.

We were detained here some days longer than I expected by light breezes from the west. At length, at three o'clock in the afternoon of the 29th, the wind came at east, and we weighed anchor.

The frequent visits we had lately paid to this island seem to have created a full persuasion that the intercourse will not be discontinued. It was strictly enjoined to me by Otoo to request in his name the *Earee rahie no Pretane* to send him, by the next ships, red feathers, and the birds that produce them, axes, half a dozen muskets, with powder and shot, and by no means to forget horses

If I could have prevailed upon Omai to fix himself at Otaheite I should not have left it so soon as I did; for there was not a probability of our being better or cheaper supplied with refreshments at any other place than we continued to be here, even at the time of our leaving it. Besides, such a cordial friendship and confidence existed between us and the inhabitants as could hardly be expected anywhere else; and it was a little extraordinary that this friendly intercourse had never once been suspended by any untoward accident, nor had there been a theft committed that deserves to be mentioned.

When the Spanish ships which had some time before touched here left the island, four Spaniards remained behind. Two were priests, one a servant, and the fourth made himself very popular among the natives, who distinguish him by the name of Mateema. He seems to have been a person who had studied their language, or at least to have spoken it so as to be understood, and to have taken uncommon pains to impress the minds of the islanders with the most exalted ideas of the greatness of the Spanish nation, and to make them think meanly of the English. He even went so far as to assure them that we no longer existed as an independent nation; that Pretane was only a small island which they, the Spaniards, had entirely destroyed; and for me, that they had met with me at sea, and with a few shot had sent my ship and every soul in her to the bottom; so that my visiting Otaheite at this time was of course very unexpected.

With what design the priests stayed we cannot guess. If it was to convert the natives to the Roman Catholic faith, they have not succeeded in any one instance. When they had stayed ten months, two ships came to Oheitepeha, took them on board, and sailed again in five days. This hasty departure shows, that whatever design the Spaniards might have upon this island, they had now laid it aside; yet, before they went away, they would have the natives believe that they still meant to return, and to bring with them houses, all kinds of animals, and men and women, who were to settle, live and die on the island. Otoo said, if the Spaniards should return, he would not let them come to Matavai Fort, which he said was ours. It was easy to see that the idea pleased him; little thinking that the completion of it would at once deprive him of his kingdom and the people of their liberties. This shows with what facility a settlement might be made at Otaheite, which, grateful as I am for repeated good offices, I hope will never happen.

We had no sooner anchored at the neighbouring island of Eimeo than the ships were crowded with the inhabitants, whom curiosity alone brought on board, for they had nothing with them for the purposes of barter. But the next morning this deficiency was supplied, several canoes then arriving from more distant parts, which brought with them abundance of breadfruit, coconuts, and a few hogs. These they exchanged for hatchets, nails, and beads; for red feathers were not so much sought after here as at Otaheite.

In the morning of the 2nd of October, Maheine, the chief of the island, paid me a visit. He approached the ship with great caution, and it required some persuasion to get him on board.

This chief, who, with a few followers, had made himself in a manner independent of Otaheite, is between forty and fifty years old. He is bald-headed, which is rather an uncommon appearance in these islands at that age. He wore a kind of turban, and seemed ashamed to show his head. They had seen us shave the head of one of their people whom we had caught stealing, they therefore concluded that this was the punishment usually inflicted by us upon all thieves; and one or two of our gentlemen, whose heads were not overburthened with hair, we could observe, lay under violent suspicions of being *tetos*, or thieves.

'Having employed two or three days in getting up all our spirit casks to tar their heads, which we found necessary to save them from the efforts of a small insect to destroy them, we hauled the ship off into the stream on the 6th of October in the morning, intending to put to sea the next day, but an accident happened that prevented it. We had sent our goats ashore to graze, with two men to look after them; notwithstanding which precaution the natives had contrived to steal one of them this evening. The loss of this goat would have been of little consequence if it had not interfered with my views of stocking other islands with these animals; but this being the case, it became necessary to recover it if possible, and after much trouble we succeeded.

At Eimeo we abundantly supplied the ships with firewood. We had not taken in any at Otaheite, where the procuring this article would have been very inconvenient, there not being a tree at Matavai but what is useful to the inhabitants. We also got here good store of refreshments.

There is a very striking difference in the women of this island and those of Otaheite. Those of Eimeo are of low stature, have a dark hue, and, in general, forbidding features. If we met with a fine woman amongst them, we were sure, upon inquiry, to find that she had come from some other island.

We left Eimeo on the 12th of October, and the next morning we saw Huaheine. At noon we anchored at the north entrance of Owharre harbour, which is on the west side of the island.

Our arrival brought all the principal people of the island to our ships on the next morning, being the 13th. This was just what I wished, as it was high time to think of settling Omai; and the presence of these chiefs, I guessed, would enable me to do it in the most satisfactory manner. He now seemed to have an inclination to establish himself at Ulietea; and if he and I could have agreed about the mode of bringing that plan to bear, I should have had no objection to adopt it. His father had been dispossessed by the men of Bolabola, when they conquered Ulietea, of some land in that island; and I made no doubt of being able to get it restored to the son in an amicable manner. For that purpose it was necessary that he should be on good terms with those who now were masters of the island, but he was too great a patriot to listen to any such thing, and was vain enough to suppose that I would reinstate him in his forfeited lands by force. This made it impossible to fix him at Ulietea, and pointed out to me Huaheine as the proper place. I therefore resolved to avail myself of the presence of the chief men of the island, and to make this proposal to them.

After the hurry of the morning was over, we got ready to pay a formal visit to Taireetareea the sovereign, meaning then to introduce this business. Omai dressed himself very properly on the occasion, and prepared a handsome present for the chief himself, and another for his *Eatooa*. Indeed, after he had got clear of the gang that surrounded him at Otaheite, he behaved with such prudence as to gain respect. We waited some time for Taireetareea, as I would do nothing till the *Earee rahie* came; but when he appeared I found that his presence might have been dispensed with, as he was not above eight or ten years of age. Omai, who stood at a little distance from this circle of great men, began with making his offering to the gods, consisting of red feathers, cloth, etc. Each article was laid before one of the company, who I understood was a priest, and was delivered with a set speech or prayer, spoken by one of Omai's friends who sat by him, but mostly dictated by himself. In these prayers he did not forget his friends in England, nor those who had brought him safe back. The *Earee rahie no Pretane*, Lord Sandwich, Toote, Tatee,[1] were mentioned in every one of them. When Omai's offerings and prayers were finished, the priest took each article, in the same order in

1 Cook and Clerke.

which it had been laid before him, and after repeating a prayer, sent it to the *morai*, which, as Omai told us, was at a great distance, otherwise the offerings would have been made there.

These religious ceremonies having been performed, Omai sat down by me and we entered upon business. Omai's establishment was then proposed to the assembled chiefs.

He acquainted them 'That he had been carried by us into our country, where he was well received by the great king and his *earees*, and treated with every mark of regard and affection while he stayed amongst us; that he had been brought back again enriched by our liberality with a variety of articles which would prove very useful to his countrymen; and that, besides the two horses which were to remain with him, several new and valuable animals had been left at Otaheite, which would soon multiply and furnish a sufficient number for the use of all the islands in the neighbour-hood. He then signified to them that it was my earnest request, in return for all my friendly offices, that they would give him a piece of land to build a house upon, and to raise provisions for himself and servants; adding, that if this could not be obtained for him in Huaheine, either by gift or by purchase, I was determined to carry him to Ulietea and fix him there.'

One of the chiefs immediately expressed himself to this effect, 'That the whole Island of Huaheine and everything in it were mine; and that, therefore, I might give what portion of it I pleased to my friend.' Omai was greatly pleased to hear this, thinking, no doubt, that I should be very liberal, and give him enough. But to offer what it would have been improper to accept, I considered as offering nothing at all; and, therefore, I now desired that they would not only assign the particular spot, but also the exact quantity of land which they would allot for the settlement. And, after a short consultation among themselves, my request was granted by general consent; and the ground immediately pitched upon adjoining to the house where our meeting was held. The extent along the shore of the harbour, was about two hundred yards; and its depth, to the foot of the hill somewhat more; but a proportional part of the hill was included in the grant.

This business being settled to the satisfaction of all parties, I set up a tent ashore, established a post, and erected the observatories. The carpenters of both ships were also set to work to build a small house for Omai, in which he might secure the European commodities that were his property. At the same time, some hands were employed in making a garden for his use.

Omai now began seriously to attend to his own affairs, and repented heartily of his ill-judged prodigality while at Otaheite. He found at Huaheine, a brother, a sister, and a brother-in-law; the sister being married. But these did not plunder him, as he had lately been by his other relations. I was sorry, however, to discover, that though they were too honest to do him any injury, they were of too little consequence in the island to do him any positive good. They had neither authority nor influence to protect his person, or his property; and, in that helpless situation, I had reason to apprehend that he run great risk of being stripped of everything he had got from us, as soon as he should cease to have us within his reach.

A man who is richer than his neighbours, is sure to be envied by numbers who wish to see him brought down to their own level. But in countries, where civilisation, law, and religion, impose their restraints, the rich have a reasonable ground of security. It was very different with Omai. He was to live amongst those who are strangers, in a great measure, to any other principle of action besides the immediate impulse of their natural feelings. But, what was his principal danger, he was to be placed in the very singular situation of being the only rich man in the community to which he was to belong. And having, by a fortunate connection with us, got into his possession an accumulated quantity of a species of treasures which none of his countrymen could create by any art or industry of their own, while all coveted a share of this envied wealth, it was natural to apprehend that all would be ready to join in attempting to strip its sole proprietor.

To prevent this, if possible, I advised him to make a proper distribution of some of his moveables, to two or three of the principal chiefs; who, being thus gratified themselves, might be induced to take him under their patronage, and protect him from the injuries of others. He promised to follow my advice; and I heard, with satisfaction, before I sailed, that this very prudent step had been taken. Not trusting, however, entirely to the operations of gratitude, I had recourse to the more forcible motive of intimidation. With this view, I took every opportunity of notifying to the inhabitants, that it was my intention to return to their island

again, after being absent the usual time; and that if I did not find
Omai in the same state of security in which I was now to leave
him, all those whom I should then discover to have been his
enemies, might expect to feel the weight of my resentment.

While we lay in this harbour, we carried ashore the bread
remaining in the bread-room, to clear it of vermin. The number of
cockroaches that infested the ship at this time is incredible; the
damage they did us was very considerable; and every method
devised by us to destroy them proved ineffectual. According to Mr
Anderson's observations, they were of two sorts, the *Blatta orientalis*
and *germanica*. The first of these had been carried home in the ship
from her former voyage, where they withstood the severity of the
hard winter in 1776, though she was in dock all the time. The
others had only made their appearance since our leaving New
Zealand; but had increased so fast, that when a sail was loosened,
thousands of them fell upon the decks. The *orientalis*, though in
infinite numbers, scarcely came out but in the night, when they
made everything in the cabin seem as if in motion, from the
particular noise in crawling about.

The intercourse of trade and friendly offices was carried on
between us and the natives, without being disturbed by any one
accident, till the evening of the 22nd, when a man found means to
get into Mr Bayly's observatory, and to carry off a sextant
unobserved. As soon as I was made acquainted with the theft, I
went ashore, and got Omai to apply to the chiefs to procure
restitution. He did so; but they took no steps towards it, being
more attentive to a *heeva* that was then acting, till I ordered the
performers of the exhibition to desist. They were now convinced
that I was in earnest, and began to make some inquiry after the
thief who was sitting in the midst of them quite unconcerned,
insomuch, that I was in great doubt of his being the guilty person,
especially as he denied it. Omai, however, assuring me that he was
the man, I sent him on board the ship, and there confined him.
This raised a general ferment amongst the assembled natives; and
the whole body fled, in spite of my endeavours to stop them.
Having employed Omai to examine the prisoner, with some
difficulty he was brought to confess where he had hid the sextant;
but, as it was now dark, we could not find it till daylight the next
morning, when it was brought back unhurt. After this, the natives

recovered from their fright, and began to gather about us as usual. As the thief seemed to be a very hardened fellow, I punished him with some severity.

This, however, did not deter him, for in the night between the 24th and 25th a general alarm was spread, occasioned, as was said, by one of our goats being stolen by this very same man. On examination, we found that all was safe in that quarter. Probably the goats were so well guarded that he could not put his design in execution. But his hostilities had succeeded against another object; and it appeared that he had destroyed and carried off several vines and cabbage plants in Omai's grounds; and he publicly threatened to kill him and to burn his house, as soon as we should leave the island. To prevent the fellow's doing me and Omai any more mischief, I had him seized and confined again on board the ship, with a view of carrying him off the island; and it seemed to give general satisfaction to the chiefs that I meant thus to dispose of him.

Omai's house being nearly finished, many of his moveables were carried ashore on the 26th. Amongst a variety of other useless articles was a box of toys, which, when exposed to public view, seemed greatly to please the gazing multitude. But as to his pots, kettles, dishes, plates, drinking-mugs, glasses, and the whole train of our domestic accommodations, hardly any one of his country-men would so much as look at them. Omai himself now began to think that they were of no manner of use to him; that a baked hog was more savoury food than a boiled one; that a plantain leaf made as good a dish or plate as pewter; and that a coconut shell was as convenient a goblet as a black jack. And, therefore, he very wisely disposed of as many of these articles of English furniture for the kitchen and pantry, as he could find purchasers for, amongst the people of the ships: receiving from them in return, hatchets, and other iron tools, which had a more intrinsic value in this part of the world, and added more to his distinguishing superiority over those with whom he was to pass the remainder of his days.

Early in the morning of the 30th, the Bolabola man, whom I had in confinement, found means to make his escape out of the ship. Upon inquiry, it appeared that not only the sentry placed over the prisoner, but the whole watch upon the quarter-deck where he was confined, had laid themselves down to sleep. He seized the opportunity to take the key of the irons out of the binnacle drawer where he had seen it put, and set himself at liberty. I was not a little pleased to hear, afterward, that this fellow had transported himself to Ulietea.

As soon as Omai was settled in his new habitation, I began to think of leaving the island, and got everything off from the shore this evening, except the horse and mare, and a goat big with kid, which were left in the possession of our friend, with whom we were now finally to part. I also gave him a boar and two sows of the English breed; and he had got a sow or two of his own.

The history of Omai will, perhaps, interest a very numerous class of readers, more than any other occurrence of the voyage. Every circumstance, therefore, which may serve to convey a satisfactory account of the exact situation in which he was left, will be thought worth preserving, and the following particulars are added to complete the view of his domestic establishment. He had picked up at Otaheite four or five Toutous; the two New Zealand youths remained with him, and his brother, and some others joined him at Huaheine, so that his family consisted already of eight or ten persons, if that can be called a family, to which not a single female as yet belonged. At present Omai did not seem at all disposed to take unto himself a wife.

The house that we erected for him was twenty-four feet by eighteen, and ten feet high. It was settled that, immediately after our departure, he should begin to build a large house, after the fashion of his country, one end of which was to be brought over that which we had erected, so as to enclose it entirely for greater security. In this work, some of the chiefs promised to assist him, and, if the intended building should cover the ground which he marked out, it will be as large as most upon the island.

His European weapons consisted of a musket, bayonet, and cartouch box, a fowling-piece, two pair of pistols, and two or three swords or cutlasses. The possession of these made him quite happy, which was my only view in giving him such presents. For I was always of opinion that he would have been happier without firearms and other European weapons, than with them, as such implements of war, in the hands of one whose prudent use of them I had some grounds for mistrusting, would rather increase his dangers than establish his superiority. After he had got on shore everything that belonged to him, and was settled in his house, he had most of the officers of both ships two or three times to dinner, and his table was always well supplied with the very best provisions that the island produced.

Before I sailed, I had the following inscription cut upon the outside of the house:

Georgius Tertius, Rex. 2 Novembris, 1777.
Naves { Resolution, Jac. Cook, Pr.
       { Discovery, Car. Clerke, Pr.

On the 2nd of November, at four in the afternoon, I took the advantage of a breeze which then sprung up at east, and sailed out of the harbour. Most of our friends remained on board till the ships were under sail, when, to gratify their curiosity, I ordered five guns to be fired. They then all took their leave, except Omai, who remained till we were at sea. In an hour or two after he went ashore, taking a very affectionate farewell of all the officers. He sustained himself with a manly resolution till he came to me. Then his utmost efforts to conceal his tears failed, and Mr King, who went in the boat, told me that he wept all the time in going ashore.

It was no small satisfaction to reflect, that we had brought him safe back to the very spot from which he was taken. And yet, such is the strange nature of human affairs, that it is probable we left him in a less desirable situation than he was in before his connection with us.

Omai, from being much caressed in England, lost sight of his original condition, and never considered in what manner his acquisitions, either of knowledge or of riches, would be estimated by his countrymen at his return, which were the only things he could have to recommend him to them now more than before, and on which he could build his future greatness or happiness. Rank seems to be the very foundation of all distinction here, and of its attendant power; and, so pertinaciously, or rather blindly adhered to, that unless a person has some degree of it, he will certainly be despised and hated if he assumes the appearance of exercising any authority. This was really the case in some measure with Omai, though his countrymen were pretty cautious of expressing their sentiments while we remained amongst them. Had he made a proper use of the presents he brought with him from England, this, with the knowledge he had acquired by travelling so far, might have enabled him to form the most useful connections. But we have already given instances of his childish inattention to this obvious means of advancing his interest. His schemes seemed to be of a higher, though ridiculous nature, indeed, I may say meaner, for revenge rather than a desire of becoming great, appeared to actuate him from the beginning. This, however, may be excused, if we consider that it is common to his countrymen. His father was doubtless a man of considerable property in Ulietea, when that island was conquered by those of Bolabola, and, with many others, sought refuge in Huaheine, where he died, and left Omai with some other children, who, by that means, became totally dependent. In this situation he was taken up by Captain Furneaux, and carried to England. Whether he really expected, from his treatment there, that any assistance would be given him against the enemies of his father and his country, or whether he imagined that his own personal courage and superiority of knowledge, would be sufficient to dispossess the conquerors of Ulietea, is uncertain; but from the beginning of the voyage this was his constant theme. He would not listen to our remonstrances on so wild a determination, but flew into a passion, if more moderate and reasonable counsels were proposed for his advantage. As we advanced, however, on our voyage, he became more sensible of his error, and, by the time we reached the Friendly Islands, had even such apprehensions of his reception at home, that he would fain have stayed behind at Tongataboo, under Feenou's protection. At these islands he squandered away much of his European treasure very unnecessarily. At Matavai, he continued the same inconsiderate behaviour, till I absolutely put a stop to his profusion.

Whether the remains of his European wealth, which, after all his improvident waste, was still considerable, will be more prudently administered by him, or whether the steps I took, as already explained, to ensure him protection in Huaheine shall have proved effectual, must be left to the decision of future navigators of this ocean; with whom it cannot but be a principal object of curiosity to trace the future fortunes of our traveller.

Whatever faults belonged to Omai's character, they were more than overbalanced by his great good nature and docile disposition. During the whole time he was with me, I very seldom had reason to be seriously displeased with his general conduct. His grateful heart always retained the highest sense of the favours he had received in England, nor will he ever forget those who honoured him with their protection and friendship during his stay there. He had tolerable share of understanding, but wanted application and perseverance to exert it, so that his knowledge of things was very general, and in many instances imperfect. He was not a man of much observation. There were many useful arts as well as elegant amusements amongst the people of the Friendly Islands, which he might have conveyed to his own, where they probably would have been readily adopted as being so much in their own way. But I never found that he used the least endeavour to make himself master of any one. This kind of indifference is, indeed, the characteristic foible of his nation. We are not, therefore, to expect that Omai will be able to introduce many of our arts and customs amongst them, or much improve those to which they have been long habituated. I am confident, however, that he will endeavour to bring to perfection the various fruits and vegetables we planted, which will be no small acquisition. But the greatest benefit these islands are likely to receive from Omai's travels will be in the animals that have been left upon them, which, probably, they never would have got, had he not come to England. When these multiply, of which I think there is little doubt, Otaheite and the Society Islands will equal, if not exceed, any place in the known world for provisions.

Omai's return, and the substantial proofs he brought back with him of our liberality, encouraged many to offer themselves as volunteers to attend me to Pretane. I took every opportunity of expressing my determination to reject all such applications.

If there had been the most distant probability of any ship being again sent to New Zealand, I would have brought the two youths of that country home with me, as both of them were very desirous of continuing with us. Tiarooa, the eldest, was an exceedingly well-disposed young man, with strong natural sense, and capable of receiving any instruction. He seemed to be fully sensible of the inferiority of his own country to these islands, and resigned himself, though perhaps with reluctance, to end his days in ease and plenty in Huaheine. But the other was so strongly attached to us that he was taken out of the ship and carried ashore by force. He was a witty, smart boy, and on that account much noticed on board.

The boat which carried Omai ashore (never to join us again) having returned to the ship, we hoisted her in, and immediately stood over for Ulietea, where I intended to touch next.

On the 4th we arrived in the harbour of Ohamaneno, and were visited by Oreo, the chief of the island, with whom I interchanged civilities and presents.

On the 6th we set up the observatories and got the necessary instruments on shore.

Though we had separated from Omai, we were still near enough to have intelligence of his proceedings, and I had desired to hear from him. Accordingly, about a fortnight after our arrival at Ulietea, he sent two of his people in a canoe, who brought me the satisfactory intelligence that he remained undisturbed by the people of the island, and that everything went well with him, except that his goat had died in kidding. He accompanied this intelligence with a request that I would send him another goat and two axes. Being happy to have this additional opportunity of serving him, the messengers were sent back to Huaheine on the 18th with the axes and two kids, male and female, which were spared for him out of the *Discovery*.

On the 24th, I was informed that a midshipman and a seaman, both belonging to the *Discovery*, were missing. As the midshipman was known to have expressed a desire to remain at these islands, it seemed pretty certain that he and his companion had gone off with this intention, and Captain Clerke set out in quest of them, with two armed boats and a party of marines. His expedition proved fruitless, for he returned in the evening without having got any certain intelligence where they were. From the conduct of the natives, Captain Clerke seemed to think that they intended to conceal the deserters, and with that view had amused him with false information the whole day, and directed him to search for them in places where they were not to be found. The Captain judged right, for the next morning we were told that our runaways were at Otaha. As these two were not the only persons in the ship who wished to end their days at these favourite islands, in order to put a stop to any further desertion, it was necessary to get them back at all events; and that the natives might be convinced that I was in earnest, I resolved to go after them myself.

Accordingly, I set out the next morning with two armed boats, being accompanied by the chief himself. I proceeded, as he directed, without stopping anywhere, till we came to the middle of the east side of Otaha. But when we got to the place where we expected to find them, we were told that they had quitted this island, and gone over to Bolabola the day before. I did not think proper to follow them thither, but returned to the ships, fully determined, however, to have recourse to a measure which I guessed would oblige the natives to bring them back.

Soon after daybreak, the chief, his son, daughter, and son-in-law came on board the *Resolution*. The three last I resolved to detain till the two deserters should be brought back. With this view Captain Clerke invited them to go on board his ship, and as soon as they arrived there confined them in his cabin. The chief was with me when the news reached him. He immediately acquainted me with it, supposing that this step had been taken without my knowledge, and consequently without my approbation. I instantly undeceived him; and then he began to have apprehensions as to his own situation, and his looks expressed the utmost perturbation of mind. But I soon made him easy as to this, by telling him that he was at liberty to leave the ship whenever he pleased, and to take such measures as he should judge best calculated to get our two men back: that if he succeeded, his friends on board the *Discovery* should be delivered up; if not, that I was determined to carry them away with me.

Oreo himself did not give way to unavailing lamentations, but instantly began his exertions to recover our deserters, by despatching a canoe to Bolabola with a message to Opoony, the sovereign of that island, acquainting him with what had happened, and requesting him to seize the two fugitives and send them back. The messenger, who was no less a man than the father of Pootoe, Oreo's son-in-law, before he set out came to receive my commands.

The consequence, however, of the prisoners was so great, that the natives did not think proper to trust to the return of our people for their release, or at least their impatience was so great, that it hurried them to meditate an attempt which might have involved them in still greater distress, had it not been fortunately prevented. Between five and six o'clock in the evening I observed that all their canoes in and about the harbour began to move off, as if some sudden panic had seized them. I was ashore, abreast of the ship at the time, and inquired in vain to find out the cause, till our people called to us from the *Discovery*, and told us that a party of the natives had seized Captain Clerke and Mr Gore, who had walked out a little way from the ships. Struck with the boldness of this plan of retaliation, which seemed to counteract me so effectually in my own way, there was no time to deliberate. I instantly ordered the people to arm, and in less than five minutes a strong party, under the command of Mr King, was sent to rescue our two gentlemen. At the same time two armed boats, and a party under Mr Williamson, went after the flying canoes, to cut off their retreat to the shore. These several detachments were hardly out of sight before an account arrived that we had been misinformed, upon which I sent and called them all in.

It was evident, however, from several corroborating circumstances, that the design of seizing Captain Clerke had really been in agitation amongst the natives. Nay, they made no secret in speaking of it the next day. But their first and great plan of operations was to have laid hold of me. It was my custom every evening to bathe in the fresh water. Very often I went alone, and always without arms. Expecting me to go as usual this evening, they had determined to seize me, and Captain Clerke too if he had accompanied me. But I had, after confining Oreo's family, thought it prudent to avoid putting myself in their power, and had cautioned Captain Clerke and the officers not to go far from the ships. In the course of the afternoon, the chief asked me three several times if I would not go to the bathing place; and when he found at last that I could not be prevailed upon, he went off with the rest of his people in spite of all that I could do or say to stop him. But as I had no suspicion at this time of their design, I imagined that some sudden fright had seized them, which would, as usual, soon be over. Finding themselves disappointed as to me, they fixed on those who were more in their power. It was fortunate for all parties that they did not succeed; and not less fortunate that no mischief was done on the occasion. For not a musket was fired, except two or three to stop the canoes. To that firing, perhaps, Messrs Clerke and Gore owed their safety; for at that very instant a party of the natives, armed with clubs, were advancing towards them, and on hearing the report of the muskets they dispersed.

Oreo, the chief, being uneasy as well as myself that no account had been received from Bolabola, set out the evening of the 28th for that island, and desired me to follow down the next day with the ships. This was my intention, but the wind would not admit of our getting to sea. But the same wind which kept us in the harbour brought Oreo back from Bolabola with the two deserters. They had reached Otaha the same night they deserted, but finding it impossible to get to any of the islands to the eastward for want of wind, they had proceeded to Bolabola, and from thence to the small island Toobaee, where they were taken. As soon as they were on board the three prisoners were released. Thus ended an affair which had given me much trouble and vexation. Nor would I have exerted myself so resolutely on the occasion but for the reason before mentioned, and to save the son of a brother officer from being lost to his country.

The wind continuing contrary, confined us in the harbour till the morning of the 7th of December, when we took the advantage of a light breeze at north-west, and with the assistance of all the boats got out to sea.

As soon as we had got clear of the harbour we took our leave of Ulietea and steered for Bolabola. Oreo and six or eight men more took a passage with us. My sole object in visiting this island was to get possession of an anchor which M. Bougainville had lost at Otaheite; it was taken up there and sent to the chief of this place as a present. I wanted it to fabricate hatchets and other iron tools, which we had almost expended in exchange for refreshments, and we now wanted to create a new stock of trading articles.

We landed where the natives directed us, and soon after I was introduced to Opoony the chief, in the midst of a great concourse of people. Having no time to lose, as soon as the necessary formality of compliments was over, I asked the chief to give me the anchor, and produced the present I had prepared for him, consisting of a linen nightgown, a shirt, some gauze handkerchiefs, a looking-glass, some beads and other toys, and six axes. Upon the receipt of these presents he ordered it to be delivered. Having thus completed my negotiation I returned on board, hoisted in the boats, and made sail from the island to the north.

When we consider that this island is not more than eight leagues in compass, it is rather remarkable that its people should have attempted or have been able to achieve the conquest of Ulietea and Otaha, the former of which islands is of itself at least double its size.

How high the Bolabola men are now in estimation at Otaheite may be inferred from Monsieur Bougainville's anchor having been conveyed to them. To the same cause we must ascribe the intention of transporting to their island the Spanish bull; and they had already got possession of a ram, brought to Otaheite by the Spaniards. I carried ashore a ewe which we had brought from the Cape of Good Hope; and I hope that by this present I have laid the foundation for a breed of sheep at Bolabola. I also left at Ulietea, under the care of Oreo, an English boar and sow, and two goats; so that not only Otaheite, but all the neighbouring islands will, in a few years, have their race of hogs considerably improved, and probably be stocked with all the valuable animals which have been transported hither by their European visitors.

Captain Cook informs his readers that the following observations on these islands are written by Mr Anderson. 'Perhaps there is scarcely a spot in the universe that affords a more luxuriant prospect than the south-east part of Otaheite. The hills are high and steep, but they are covered to the very summits with trees and shrubs. The flat land, which bounds those hills toward the sea, and the interjacent valleys also, teem with various productions, that grow with the most exuberant vigour. Nature has been no less liberal in distributing rivulets, which are found in every valley. The habitations of the natives are scattered, without order, upon these flats; and many of them appearing toward the shore, presented a delightful scene viewed from our ships.

'The natural fertility of the country, combined with the mildness and serenity of the climate, renders the natives careless in their cultivation. The cloth-plant, which is raised by seeds brought from the mountains, and the ava, or intoxicating pepper, are almost the only things to which they seem to pay any attention.

'I have inquired very carefully into their manner of cultivating the breadfruit tree, but was always answered that they never planted it. This, indeed, must be evident to everyone who will examine the places where the young trees come up.

'Their chief trees beside are the coconut and the plantain; the latter only requires attention; in three months after it is planted it begins to bear, during which time it gives young shoots, which supply a succession of fruit. For the old stocks are cut down as the fruit is taken off.

'Curiosities of any kind are not numerous. Amongst these we may reckon a pond or lake of fresh water, at the top of one of the highest mountains; to go to, and to return from which, takes three or four days. It is remarkable for its depth, and has eels of an enormous size in it. This is esteemed one of the greatest natural curiosities in the country.

'The muscular appearance, so common amongst the Friendly islanders, and which seems a consequence of their being accustomed to much action, is lost here, where the superior fertility of their country enables the inhabitants to lead a more indolent life.

'Personal endowments being in great esteem amongst them, they have recourse to several methods of improving them, according to their notions of beauty. This is done by remaining a month or two in the house; during which time they wear a great quantity of clothes, and eat nothing but breadfruit, to which they ascribe a remarkable property in whitening them.

'Their common diet is made up of at least nine-tenths of vegetable food; and it is perhaps owing to this temperate course of life that they have so few diseases among them. They only reckon five or six, which might be called chronic or national disorders.

'Their behaviour, on all occasions, seems to indicate a great openness and generosity of disposition. I never saw them, in any misfortune, labour under the appearance of anxiety, after the critical moment was past. Neither does care ever seem to wrinkle their brow. On the contrary, even the approach of death does not appear to alter their usual vivacity.

'Such a disposition leads them to direct all their aims only to what can give them pleasure and ease. They delight in music, neither are they strangers to the soothing effects produced by particular sorts of motion; which, in some cases, seem to allay any perturbation of mind with as much success as music.

'The Otaheiteans express their notions of death very emphatically, by saying, that "the soul goes into darkness", or rather into night. Their language is so copious, that for the breadfruit alone, in its different states, they have above twenty names; as many for the taro root; and about ten for the coconut.

'Notwithstanding the extreme fertility of the island, a famine frequently happens, in which, it is said, many perish. In times of scarcity, after their breadfruit and yams are consumed, they have recourse to various roots, which grow without cultivation upon the mountains. The patarra, which is found in vast quantities, is what they use first. It is not unlike a very large potato or yam, and good when in its growing state.

'Of animal food, a very small portion falls at any time to the share of the lower class of people; and then it is either fish, sea-eggs, or other marine productions, for they seldom or never eat pork. The *eree* alone is able to furnish pork every day; and inferior chiefs, according to their riches, once a week, fortnight, or month.

'It is also amongst the better sort that the ava is chiefly used. But this beverage is prepared somewhat differently from that which we saw so much of at the Friendly Islands. They pour a very small quantity of water upon the root here; and sometimes roast or bake, and bruise the stalks without chewing it previously to its infusion. But its pernicious effects are very obvious; perhaps owing to the manner of preparing it, as we often saw instances of its intoxicating, or rather stupefying, powers. As an excuse for a practice so destructive, they allege that it is adopted to prevent their growing too fat; but it evidently enervates them, and in all probability shortens their days.

'The times of eating at Otaheite are very frequent. Their first meal is about two o'clock in the morning, after which they go to sleep; and the next is at eight. At eleven they dine, and again at two and at five, and sup at eight. The women have not only the mortification of being obliged to eat by themselves, and in a different part of the house from the men, but by a strange kind of policy, are excluded from a share of most of the better sorts of food. The women generally serve up their own victuals, for they would certainly starve before any grown man would do them such an office. When we inquired into the reasons of it, we could get no other answer but that it is right and necessary that it should be so.

'The women, indeed, are often treated with a degree of harshness or rather brutality, which one would scarcely suppose a man would bestow on an object for whom he had the least affection. Nothing, however, is more common than to see the men beat them without mercy; and unless this treatment is the effect of jealousy, which both sexes at least pretend to be sometimes infected with, it will be difficult to account for it.

'Their religious system is extensive, and in many instances singular, but few of the common people have a perfect knowledge of it, that being confined chiefly to their priests, who are pretty numerous. They do not seem to pay respect to one god, as possessing pre-eminence, but believe in a plurality of divinities, who are all very powerful.

'Their assiduity in serving their gods is remarkably conspicuous. Not only the *whattas*, or offering places of the *morais*, are commonly loaded with fruits and animals, but there are few houses where you do not meet with a small place of the same sort near them. Many of them are so religiously scrupulous, that they will not begin a meal without first laying aside a morsel for the *Eatooa*.

'They believe the soul to be both immaterial and immortal. They say that it keeps fluttering about the lips during the pangs of death, and that then it ascends and mixes with, or as they express it, is eaten by the deity. In this state it remains for some time; after which it departs to a certain place, destined for the reception of the souls of men, where it exists in eternal night. They have no idea of any permanent punishment after death, for the souls of good and of bad men are eaten indiscriminately by God.

'Some of their notions about the Deity are extravagantly absurd. They believe that he is subject to the power of those very spirits to whom he has given existence, and that, in their turn, they frequently eat or devour him, though he possess the power of recreating himself. When the moon is in its wane, it is said that they are then devouring their *Eatooa*, and that as it increases he is renewing himself.

'They have traditions concerning the creation which, as might be expected, are complex and clouded with obscurity. They say that a goddess, having a lump or mass of earth suspended in a cord, gave it a swing and scattered about pieces of land, thus constituting Otaheite and the neighbouring islands, which were all peopled by a man and woman originally fixed at Otaheite. The spots observed in the moon are supposed to be groves of a sort of trees which once grew in Otaheite, and being destroyed by some accident, their seeds were carried up thither by doves where they now flourish.'

Monday, December the 8th, after leaving Bolabola, I steered to the northward, with the wind generally eastward, till after we had crossed the line, and had got into north latitudes.

Seventeen months had now elapsed since our departure from England. With regard to the principal object of my instructions, our voyage was at this time only beginning; and therefore my attention to every circumstance that might contribute toward our safety and success, was now to be called forth anew. As soon as I had got beyond the extent of my former discoveries, I ordered a survey to be taken of all the stores that were in the ships, that I might know how to use them to the greatest advantage.

On the 24th, after passing the line, land was discovered. Upon a nearer approach it was found to be one of those low islands so common in this ocean — that is, a narrow bank of land enclosing the sea within. A few coconut trees were seen in two or three places, but in general the land had a very barren appearance.

At daybreak the next morning I sent two boats to search more accurately for a landing place, and at the same time two others to fish at a grappling near the shore. These last returned about eight o'clock with upward of two hundredweight of fish. Encouraged by this success, they were despatched again after breakfast.

On the 26th, and the following day, we caught a considerable number of turtles.

On the 28th I landed, in company with Mr Bayly, on the island which lies between the two channels, to prepare the telescopes for observing an approaching eclipse of the sun, which was one great inducement to my anchoring here.

On the morning of the 30th, the day when the eclipse was to happen, Mr King, Mr Bayly, and myself, went ashore to attend the observation, in which we had tolerable success.

In the afternoon, the boats and turtling party all returned on board, except a seaman belonging to the *Discovery*, who had been missing two days. There were two of them at first who had lost their way, but disagreeing about the most probable track to bring them back to their companions, they had separated, and one of them joined the party, after having been absent twenty-four hours, and been in great distress.

As soon as Captain Clerke knew that one of the stragglers was still in this awkward situation, he sent a party in search of him, who returned with their lost companion. This poor fellow must have suffered far greater distress than the other straggler, not only as having been lost a longer time, but as we found that he was too squeamish to drink turtle's blood, which the other did, as there was no water in the island.

Having some coconuts and yams on board in a state of vegetation, I ordered them to be planted here.

We got at this island, for both ships, about three hundred turtle, weighing, one with another, about ninety or a hundred pounds. They were all of the green kind, and perhaps as good as any in the world. We also caught, with hook and line, as much fish as we could consume during our stay. They consisted principally of cavallies, of different sizes, large and small snappers, and a few of two sorts of rock fish.

There were not the smallest traces of any human being having ever been here before us; and, indeed, should anyone be so unfortunate as to be accidentally driven upon the island, or left there, it is hard to say that he could be able to prolong existence. A ship touching here must expect nothing but fish and turtle, and of these an abundant supply may be depended upon.

As we kept our Christmas here, I called this discovery Christmas Island.

On the 2nd of January 1778, at daybreak, we weighed anchor, and resumed our course to the north. We discovered no land till daybreak in the morning of the 18th, when an island made its appearance, and soon after we saw more land, entirely detached from the former.

On the 19th, at sunrise, the island first seen bore east several leagues distant. This being directly to windward, which prevented our getting near it, I stood for the other, and not long after discovered a third island in the direction of west-north-west, as far distant as land could be seen. Soon after, we saw some canoes coming off from the shore toward the ships. I immediately brought to to give them time to join us. They had from three to six men each, and on their approach we were agreeably surprised to find that they spoke the language of Otaheite, and of the other islands we had lately visited. It required but very little address to get them to come alongside, but no entreaties could prevail upon any of them to come on board. I tied some brass medals to a rope, and gave them to those in one of the canoes, who, in return, tied some small mackerel to the rope as an equivalent. This was repeated, and some small nails, or bits of iron, which they valued more than any other article, were given them.

These people were of a brown colour, and though of the common size, were stoutly made. There was little difference in the casts of their colour, but a considerable variation in their features – some of their visages not being very unlike those of Europeans. They seemed very mild, and had no arms of any kind, if we except some small stones, which they had evidently brought for their own defence, and these they threw overboard, when they found that they were not wanted.

Seeing no signs of an anchoring place at this eastern extreme of the island, I ranged along the south-east side, at the distance of half a league from the shore. As soon as we made sail the canoes left us, but others came off as we proceeded along the coast, bringing with them roasting pigs, and some very fine potatoes, which they exchanged, as the others had done, for whatever was offered to them. Several small pigs were purchased for a sixpenny nail, so that we again found ourselves in a land of plenty.

The next morning we stood in for the land, and were met by several canoes filled with people, some of whom took courage and ventured on board.

In the course of my several voyages I never before met with the natives of any place so much astonished as these people were upon entering a ship. Their eyes were continually flying from object to object – the wildness of their looks and gestures fully expressing their entire ignorance about everything they saw, and strongly marking to us that till now they had never been visited by Europeans, nor been acquainted with any of our commodities except iron, which, however, it was plain they had only heard of, or had known it in some small quantity, brought to them at some distant period. They seemed only to understand that it was a substance much better adapted to the purposes of cutting or of boring holes than anything their own country produced. They asked for it by the name of *hamaite*, probably referring to some instrument, in the making of which iron could be usefully employed. For the same reason they frequently called iron by the name of *toe*, which, in their language, signifies a hatchet, or rather a kind of adze. When we showed them some beads, they asked first what they were, and then whether they should eat them. But on their being told that they were to be hung in their ears, they returned them as useless. They were equally indifferent as to a looking-glass which was offered them, and returned it for the same reason, but sufficiently expressed their desire for *hamaite* and *toe*, which they wished might be very large. They were in some respect naturally well-bred, or at least fearful of giving offence, asking where they should sit down, whether they might spit upon the deck, and the like. Some of them repeated a long prayer before they came on board, and others afterwards sung and made motions with their hands, such as we had been accustomed to see in the dances of the islands we had lately visited. There was another circumstance in which they also perfectly resembled those other islanders. At first on their entering the ship they endeavoured to steal everything they came near, or rather to take it openly, as what we either should not resent or not hinder. We soon convinced them of their mistake; and if they after some time became less active in appropriating to themselves whatever they took a fancy to, it was because they found that we kept a watchful eye over them.

At nine o'clock, being pretty near to the shore, I sent three armed boats, under the command of Lieutenant Williamson, to look for a landing-place and for fresh water. I ordered him that if he should find it necessary to land in search of the latter, not to suffer more than one man to go with him out of the boats.

While the boats were occupied in examining the coast, we stood on and off with the ships, waiting for their return. About noon Mr Williamson came back, and reported that he had seen a large pond near one of the villages which contained fresh water. He also reported that he had attempted to land in another place, but was prevented by the natives, who, coming down to the boats in great numbers, attempted to take away the oars, muskets, and in short everything that they could lay hold of, and pressed so thick upon him that he was obliged to fire, by which one man was killed. But this unhappy circumstance I did not know till after we had left the island, so that all my measures were directed as if nothing of the kind had happened.

Between three and four o'clock I went ashore with three armed boats to examine the water, and to try the disposition of the inhabitants, several hundreds of whom were assembled on the beach.

The very instant I leaped on shore the collected body of the natives all fell flat upon their faces, and remained in that very humble posture till, by expressive signs, I prevailed upon them to rise. They then brought a great many small pigs which they presented to me, with plantain trees, using much the same ceremonies that we had seen practised on such occasions at the Society and other islands; and a long prayer being spoken by a single person, in which others of the assembly sometimes joined, I expressed my acceptance of their proffered friendship by giving them in return such presents as I had brought with me from the ship for that purpose. When this introductory business was finished, I stationed a guard upon the beach, and got some of the natives to conduct me to the water, which proved to be very good, and in a proper situation for our purpose. Having satisfied myself about this very essential point, and about the peaceable disposition of the natives, I returned on board, and then gave orders that everything should be in readiness for landing and filling our water-casks in the morning, when again I went ashore.

As soon as we landed a trade was set on foot for hogs and potatoes, which the people of the island gave us in exchange for nails and pieces of iron, formed into something like chisels. We met with no obstruction in watering; on the contrary, the natives assisted our men in rolling the casks to and from the pool, and readily performed whatever we required.

Everything thus going on to my satisfaction, and considering my presence on the spot as unnecessary, I left the command to Mr Williamson, who had landed with me, and made an excursion into the country up the valley, accompanied by Mr Anderson and Mr Webber. A numerous train of natives followed us; and one of them, whom I had distinguished for his activity in keeping the rest in order, I made choice of as our guide. Everyone whom we met fell prostrate upon the ground, and remained in that position till we had passed. This, as I afterwards understood, is the mode of paying their respect to their own great chiefs. As we ranged down the coast from the east in the ships we had observed at every village one or more elevated white objects, like pyramids, or rather obelisks; and one of these, which I guessed to be at least fifty feet high, was very conspicuous from the ship's anchoring station, and seemed to be at no great distance up this valley. To have a nearer inspection of it was the principal object of my walk. The moment we got to it we saw that it stood in a burying-ground or *morai*, the resemblance of which, in many respects, to those we were so well acquainted with at other islands in this ocean could not but strike us; and we also soon found that the several parts that compose it were called by the same names.

After we had examined very carefully everything that was to be seen about the *morai*, we returned by a different route. At noon I went on board to dinner. having procured in the course of the day nine tuns of water; and by exchanges, chiefly for nails and pieces of iron, about seventy or eighty pigs and a few fowls. These people merited our best commendations, never once attempting to cheat us, either ashore or alongside the ships. Some of them, indeed, at first betrayed a thievish disposition; but they soon laid aside a conduct which we convinced them they could not persevere in with impunity.

Amongst the articles which they brought to barter this day, we could not help taking notice of a particular sort of cloak and cap. The first are nearly of the size and shape of the short cloaks worn by the women in England. The ground of them is a network, upon which the most beautiful red and yellow feathers are so closely fixed, that the surface might be compared to the thickest and richest velvet, which they resemble, both as to the feel and the glossy appearance.

The cap is made almost exactly like a helmet, with the middle part or crest sometimes of a hand's breadth, and it sits very close upon the head, having notches to admit the ears. It is a frame of twigs and osiers covered with a network, into which are wrought feathers in the same manner as upon the cloaks, though rather closer and less diversified. These probably complete the dress with the cloaks, for the natives sometimes appeared in both together.

We were at a loss to guess whence they could get such a quantity of these beautiful feathers, but were soon informed, for they afterwards brought great numbers of skins of small red birds for sale.

Next day one of our visitors, who offered some fish-hooks for sale, was observed to have a very small parcel tied to the string of one of them, which he separated with great care and reserved for himself when he parted with the hook. Being asked what it was, he pointed to his belly. It struck us that it might be human flesh. The question being put to him, he answered that the flesh was part of a man. Another of his countrymen who stood by him, was then asked whether it was their custom to eat those killed in battle, and he immediately answered in the affirmative.

After leaving Atooi, as this island was named, we proceeded to Oneeheow, on the coast of which we anchored.

Six or seven canoes had come off to us before we anchored, bringing some small pigs and potatoes, and a good many yams and mats. The people in them resembled those of Atooi, and seemed to be equally well acquainted with the use of iron, which they asked for also by the names of *hamaite* and *toe*, parting readily with all their commodities for pieces of this precious metal.

These visitors furnished us with an opportunity of agitating again the curious inquiry whether they were cannibals. One of the islanders, who wanted to get in at the gun-room port, was refused, and at the same time asked whether, if he should come in, we would kill and eat him. This gave a proper opening to retort the question as to this practice; and a person behind the other in the canoe, who paid great attention to what was passing, immediately answered that if we were killed on shore they would certainly eat us; but that their eating us would be the consequence of our being at enmity with them. I cannot see the least reason to hesitate in pronouncing it to be certain that the horrid banquet of human flesh is as much relished here amidst plenty as it is in New Zealand.

On the 30th, I sent Mr Gore ashore with a guard of marines, and a party to trade with the natives for refreshments. The weather soon became very unpropitious, and the sea ran so high that we had no manner of communication with our party on shore, and even the natives themselves durst not venture out to the ships in their canoes. In the evening of next day I sent the master in a boat up to the south-east head or point of the island to try if he could land under it. He returned with a favourable report, but it was too late now to send for our party till the next morning; and thus they had another night to improve their intercourse with the natives.

Encouraged by the master's report, I went myself with the

pinnace and launch up to the point to bring the party on board, taking with me a ram-goat and two ewes, a boar and sow-pig of the English breed, and the seeds of melons, pumpkins, and onions, being very desirous of benefiting these poor people by furnishing them with some additional articles of food. I found my party already there with some of the natives in company. To one of them, whom Mr Gore had observed assuming some command, I gave the goats, pigs, and seeds.

The ground through which I passed was in a state of nature, very stony, and the soil seemed poor. It was, however, covered with shrubs and plants, some of which perfumed the air with a more delicious fragrancy than I had met with at any other of the islands in this ocean. The habitations of the natives were thinly scattered about, and it was supposed that there could not be more than five hundred people upon the island. Our people had an opportunity of observing the method of living amongst the natives, and it appeared to be decent and cleanly. They did not, however, see any instance of the men and women eating together, and the latter seemed generally associated in companies by themselves. It was found that they burnt here the oily nuts of the *dooe dooe* for lights in the night, as at Otaheite, and that they baked their hogs in ovens. A particular veneration seemed to be paid here to owls, which they have very tame; and it was observed to be a pretty general practice amongst them to pull out one of their teeth, for which odd custom, when asked the reason, the only answer that could be got was, that it was *teeha*.

On Monday, the 2nd of February, we stood away to the northward, in prosecution of our voyage. Our ship procured from these islands provisions sufficient for three weeks at least; and Captain Clerke, more fortunate, obtained of their vegetable productions a supply that lasted his people upwards of two months.

It is worthy of observation, that the islands in the Pacific Ocean, which our late voyages have added to the geography of the globe, have been generally found lying in groups or clusters, the single intermediate islands, as yet discovered, being few in proportion to the others, though probably there are many more of them still unknown, which serve as steps between the several clusters. Of what number this newly-discovered archipelago consists must be left for future investigation. We saw five of them, whose names, as given to us by the natives, are Wohaoo, Atooi, Oneeheow, Oreehoua, and Tahoora.

The temperature of the climate may be easily guessed from the situation. Were we to judge of it from our experience, it might be said to be very variable, notwithstanding it was now the season of the year when the weather is supposed to be most settled, the sun being at his greatest annual distance. The heat was at this time very moderate, and few of those inconveniences which many of those tropical countries are subject to, either from heat or moisture, seem to be experienced here.

Besides the vegetable articles bought by us as refreshments, amongst which were at least five or six varieties of plantains, the island produces breadfruit, though it seems to be scarce, as we saw only one tree, which was large and had some fruit upon it.

The scarlet birds which were brought for sale were never met with alive; but we saw a single small one, about the size of a canary-bird, of a deep crimson colour, a large owl, two large brown hawks or kites, and a wild duck; and it is probable there are a great many sorts, judging by the quantity of fine yellow, green, and very small velvet like black feathers, used upon the cloaks, and other ornaments worn by the inhabitants.

Fish and other marine productions were, to appearance, not various.

The hogs, dogs, and fowls, which were the only tame or domestic animals that we found here, were all of the same kind that we met with at the South Pacific Islands.

The inhabitants are of a middling stature, firmly made. Their visage, especially amongst the women, is sometimes round; but we cannot say that they are distinguished as a nation by any general cast of countenance. Their colour is nearly of a nut-brown. The women are little more delicate than the men in their formation; and I may say that, with a very few exceptions, they have little claim to those peculiarities that distinguish the sex in other countries. There is, indeed, a more remarkable equality in the size, colour, and figure of both sexes, than in most places I have visited.

They are very expert swimmers. It was very common to see women with infants at the breast, when the surf was so high that they could not land in the canoes, leap overboard, and without endangering their little ones, swim to the shore through a sea that looked dreadful.

They seem to be blessed with a frank, cheerful disposition; they live very sociably in their intercourse with one another, and, except the propensity to thieving, which seems innate in most of the people we have visited in this ocean, they were exceedingly friendly to us. It was a pleasure to observe with how much affection the women manage their infants, and how readily the men lent their assistance to such a tender office, thus sufficiently distinguishing themselves from those savages who esteem a wife and child as things rather necessary than desirable, or worthy of their notice.

Though they seem to have adopted the mode of living in villages, there is no appearance of defence or fortification near any of them; and the houses are scattered about without any order. Some are large and commodious, from forty to fifty feet long, and twenty or thirty broad, while others of them are mere hovels. They are well thatched with long grass, which is laid on slender poles, disposed with some regularity. The entrance is made indifferently in the end or side, and is an oblong hole, so low, that one must rather creep than walk in. No light enters the house but by this opening; and though such close habitations may afford a comfortable retreat in bad weather, they seem but ill adapted to the warmth of the climate. Of animal food they can be in no want, as they have abundance of hogs, which run without restraint about the houses; and if they eat dogs, which is not improbable, their stock of these seemed to be very considerable. The great number of fishing-hooks found amongst them, showed that they derived no inconsiderable supply of animal food from the sea.

They bake their vegetable food with heated stones, in the same manner as the inhabitants of the southern islands. The only artificial dish we met with was a taro pudding, which, though a disagreeable mess, from its sourness, was greedily devoured by the natives.

In everything manufactured by these people, there appears to be an uncommon degree of neatness and ingenuity. Their cloth, which is the principal manufacture, is made from the *Morus papyrifera*, and, doubtless, in the same manner as at Otaheite and Tongataboo; in colouring or staining it, the people of Atooi display a superiority of taste, by the endless variation of figures which they execute.

They fabricate a great many white mats, which are strong, with many red stripes, rhombuses, and other figures interwoven on one side, and often pretty large.

They stain their gourd-shells prettily with undulated lines, triangles, and other figures of a black colour; instances of which we saw practised at New Zealand. Their wooden dishes and bowls, out of which they drink their ava, are of the etooa-tree, or cordia, as neat as if made in our turning-lathe, and perhaps better polished. A great variety of fishing-hooks are ingeniously made of pearl shell. One fishing-hook was procured, nine inches long, of a single piece of bone, which, doubtless, belonged to some large fish. The elegant form and polish of this could not certainly be outdone by any European artist, even if he should add all his knowledge in design to the number and convenience of his tools.

The only iron tools, or rather bits of iron, seen amongst them, and which they had before our arrival, were a piece of iron hoop, about two inches long, fitted into a wooden handle; and another edge-tool, which our people guessed to be made of the point of a broadsword. How they came by them I cannot account for.

Though I did not see a chief of any note, there were, however, several, as the natives informed us, who reside upon Atooi, and to whom they prostrate themselves as a mark of submission. After I had left the island, one of the chiefs made his appearance, and paid a visit to Captain Clerke on board the *Discovery*. His attendants helped him into the ship and placed him on the gangway. Their care of him did not cease then, for they stood round him, holding each other by the hands; nor would they suffer anyone to come near him but Captain Clerke himself. He was a young man, clothed from head to foot, accompanied by a young woman, supposed to be his wife. His name was said to be Tamahano. Captain Clerke made him some suitable presents, and received from him, in return, a large bowl, supported by two figures of men, the carving of which, both as to the design and the execution, showed some degree of skill.

In their language they had not only adopted the soft mode of the Otaheitans in avoiding harsh sounds, but the whole idiom of their language, using not only the same affixes and suffixes to their words, but the same measure and cadence in their songs, though in a manner somewhat less agreeable.

How happy would Lord Anson have been, and what hardships would he have avoided, if he had known that there was a group of islands, halfway between America and Tinian, where all his wants could have been effectually supplied.

On the 2nd of February we stood away to the northward, and without meeting with anything memorable, on the 7th of March the long-looked for coast of New Albion[1] was seen, extending from N.E. to S.E., distant ten or twelve leagues. The land appeared to be of a moderate height, diversified with hills and valleys, and almost everywhere covered with wood.

After coasting along and combating contrary winds, on the 29th we anchored in eighty-five fathoms water, so near the shore as to reach it with a hawser.

We no sooner drew near the inlet than we found the coast to be inhabited, and three canoes came off to the ship. In one of these were two men, in another six, and in the third ten. Having come pretty near us, a person in one of the two last stood up and made a long harangue, inviting us to land, as we guessed by his gestures. At the same time he kept strewing handfuls of feathers towards us, and some of his companions threw handfuls of red dust or powder in the same manner. The person who performed the office of orator wore the skin of some animal, and held in each hand something which rattled as he kept shaking it. After tiring himself with his repeated exhortations, of which we did not understand a word, he was quiet. After the tumultuous oration had ceased, one of them sung a very agreeable air, with a degree of softness and melody which we could not have expected. In a short time the canoes began to come off in great numbers; and we had at one time thirty-two of them near the ship, carrying from three to seven or eight persons each, both men and women. Several of these stood up in their canoes haranguing and making gestures, after the manner of our first visitors. One canoe was remarkable for a singular head, which had a bird's eye and bill of an enormous size painted on it; and a person who was in it, who seemed to be a chief, was no less remarkable for his uncommon appearance, having many feathers hanging from his head, and being painted in an extraordinary

---

1 This part of the west side of North America was so named by Sir Francis Drake.

manner. He held in his hands a carved bird of wood, as large as a pigeon, with which he rattled, as the person first mentioned had done; and was no less vociferous in his harangue, which was attended with some expressive gestures.

Though our visitors behaved very peaceably, and could not be suspected of any hostile intention, we could not prevail upon any of them to come on board. They showed great readiness, however, to part with anything they had, and took from us whatever we offered them in exchange; but were more desirous of iron than of any other of our articles of commerce, appearing to be perfectly acquainted with the use of that metal. Many of the canoes followed us to our anchoring place, and a group of about ten or a dozen of them remained alongside the *Resolution* most part of the night.

These circumstances gave us a reasonable ground of hope that we should find this a comfortable station to supply all our wants, and to make us forget the hardships and delays experienced during a constant succession of adverse winds and boisterous weather, almost continual since our arrival upon the coast of America.

Next morning I lost no time in endeavouring to find a commodious harbour where we might station ourselves during our continuance. I had very little trouble in finding what we wanted. On the north west of the arm we were now in, and not far from the ships, I met with a convenient, snug cove, well suited for our purpose.

A great many canoes, filled with the natives, were about the ships all day, and a trade commenced betwixt us and them, which was carried on with the strictest honesty on both sides. The articles which they offered to sale were skins of various animals, such as bears, wolves, foxes, deer, raccoons, polecats, martens; and in particular, the sea otters, which are found at the islands east of Kamtschatka. Besides the skins in their native shape, they also brought garments made of them, and another sort of clothing made of the bark of a tree, or some plant like hemp; weapons, such as bows, arrows, and spears; fish-hooks, and instruments of various kinds; wooden visors of many different monstrous figures; a sort of woollen stuff, blanketing; bags filled with red ochre, pieces of carved work, beads, and several other little ornaments of thin brass and iron, shaped like a horseshoe, which they hang at their noses, and several chisels or pieces of iron fixed to handles. From their possessing which metals, we could infer that they had either been visited by some civilised nation, or had connections with tribes on their continent who had communication with them. But the most extraordinary of all the articles which they brought to the ships for sale were human skulls, and hands not yet quite stripped of the flesh, which they made our people plainly understand they had eaten; and indeed, some of them had evident marks that they had been upon the fire. We had but too much reason to suspect, from this circumstance, that the horrid practice of feeding on their enemies was prevalent here. For the various articles which they brought they took in exchange knives, chisels, pieces of iron and tin, nails, looking-glasses, buttons, or any kind of metal. Glass beads they were not fond of, and cloth of every sort they rejected.

If they had any distrust or fear of us at first they now appeared to have laid it aside, for they came on board the ships and mixed with our people with the greatest freedom. We soon discovered that they were as light-fingered as any of our friends in the islands we had visited in the course of the voyage, and they were far more dangerous thieves; for, possessing sharp iron instruments, they could cut a hook from a tackle, or any other piece of iron from a rope, the instant that our backs were turned. If we missed a thing immediately after it had been stolen, we found little difficulty in detecting the thief, as they were ready enough to impeach one another. But the guilty person generally relinquished his prize with reluctance, and sometimes we found it necessary to have recourse to force.

A considerable number of the natives visited us daily, and every now and then we saw new faces. On their first coming they generally went through a singular mode of introducing themselves. They would paddle, with all their strength, quite round both ships, a chief, or other principal person in the canoe, standing up with a spear or some other weapon in his hand, and speaking, or rather hallooing, all the time. Sometimes the orator of the canoe would have his face covered with a mask, representing either a human visage or that of some animal; and instead of a weapon, would hold a rattle in his hand, as before described. After making this circuit round the ships, they would come alongside and begin to trade without further ceremony.

During these visits they gave us no other trouble than to guard against their thievish tricks. But in the morning of the 4th of April we had a serious alarm. Our party on shore, who were employed in cutting wood and filling water, observed that the natives all around them were arming themselves in the best manner they could, preparing sticks and collecting stones. On hearing this, I thought it prudent to arm also. However, our fears were ill-grounded; these hostile preparations were not directed against us, but against a body of their own countrymen, who were coming to fight them; and our friends of the Sound, on observing our apprehensions, used their best endeavours to convince us that this was the case. At length the difference, whatever it was, seemed to be compromised, but the strangers were not allowed to come alongside the ships, nor to have any trade or intercourse with us. Probably we were the cause of the quarrel.

We resumed our work in the afternoon, and continued the repairs of the vessels without interruption, and other necessary business.

Bad weather now came on, but that did not, however, hinder the natives from visiting us daily. They frequently brought us a tolerable supply of fish, either sardines, or what resembled them much, a small kind of bream, and sometimes small cod.

On the 18th, a party of strangers, in six or eight canoes, came into the cove, where they remained looking at us for some time, and then retired without coming alongside either ship. We supposed that our old friends, who were more numerous about us than these new visitors, would not permit them to have any intercourse with us. We also found that many of the principal natives who lived near us, carried on a trade with more distant tribes in the articles they had procured for us. For we observed that they would frequently disappear for four or five days at a time, and then return with fresh cargoes of skins and curiosities, which our people were so passionately fond of, that they always came to a good market. Nothing would go down with our visitors but metal; and brass had by this time supplanted iron, being so eagerly sought after, that, before we left this place, hardly a bit of it was left in the ships, except what belonged to our necessary instruments. Whole suits of clothes were stripped of every button; bureaus of their furniture, and copper kettles, tin canisters, candlesticks, and the like, all went to wreck.

After a fortnight's bad weather, the 19th proving a fair day, we availed ourselves of it to get up the topmasts and yards, and to fix up the rigging; and having now finished most of our heavy work, I set out next morning to take a view of the Sound. I first went to the west point, where I found a large village. The people received me very courteously. In most of the houses were women at work making dresses of the plant or bark before mentioned, which they executed exactly in the same manner that the New Zealanders manufacture their cloth. Others were occupied in opening and curing fish.

I now found, by traversing a few miles west of this village, what I had before conjectured, that the land under which the ships lay was an island, and that there were many smaller ones lying scattered in the Sound, on the west of it. Opposite the north end of our island, upon the mainland, I observed a village, and there I landed. The inhabitants of it were not so polite as those of the other. But this cold reception seemed owing to one surly chief, who would not let me enter their houses, following me wherever I went, and several times, by expressive signs, marking his impatience that I should be gone. Some of the young women, better pleased with us than was their inhospitable chief, dressed themselves expeditiously in their best apparel, and welcomed us, by joining in a song, which was far from disagreeable.

The day being now far spent, I proceeded for the ships. When I got on board I was informed that while I was absent, they had been visited by some strangers, who, by signs, made our people understand that they had come from the south-east, beyond the bay. They brought several skins, garments, and other articles, which they bartered. But what was most singular, two silver tablespoons were purchased from them, which, from their peculiar shape, we supposed to be of Spanish manufacture. One of these strangers wore them round his neck by way of ornament.

Captain Clerke and I went in the forenoon of next day with two boats to the village at the west point of the Sound. When I was there the day before, I had observed that plenty of grass grew near it; and it was necessary to lay in a quantity of this for the few goats and sheep which were still left on board. The inhabitants received us with the same demonstrations of friendship which I had experienced before; and the moment we landed, I ordered some of my people to begin their operation of cutting. I had not the least imagination that the natives could make any objection to our furnishing ourselves with what seemed to be of no use to them, but was necessary for us. However, I was mistaken, for the moment that our men began to cut, some of the inhabitants interposed, and would not permit them to proceed, saying they must *makook*; that is, must first buy it. I bargained with them for it, and thought that we were now at liberty to cut wherever we pleased. But here again I was under a mistake; for the liberal manner in which I had paid the first pretended proprietors, brought fresh demands upon me from others; and so many of them were to be satisfied, that I very soon emptied my pockets. When they found that I really had nothing more to give, their importunities ceased, and we were permitted to cut wherever we pleased, and as much as we chose to carry away.

Everything being now ready, in the morning of the 26th I intended to have put to sea, but both wind and tide being against us, was obliged to continue where we were. At four o'clock in the afternoon we had every forerunner of an approaching storm; this made me hesitate a little whether I should venture to sail, or wait till the next morning. But my anxious impatience to proceed upon the voyage, made me determine to put to sea at all events.

Our friends the natives attended us till we were almost out of the Sound; some on board the ships, and others in their canoes. To one of their chiefs, who had attached himself to me, I presented a new broadsword, with a brass hilt, the possession of which made him completely happy. I make no doubt that whoever comes after me to this place, will find the natives prepared with no inconsiderable supply of skins, an article of trade which they could observe we were eager to possess, and which we found could be purchased to great advantage.

On my arrival in this inlet, I had honoured it with the name of King George's Sound, but I afterwards found that it is called Nootka by the natives. The harbours and anchoring places within its circuit are numerous.

The land bordering upon the sea-coast is of a middling height and level, but within the Sound it rises almost everywhere into steep hills, which agree in their general formation, ending in round or blunted tops, with some sharp though not very prominent ridges on their sides. Some of these hills may be reckoned high.

The trees which chiefly compose the woods are the Canadian pine, white cypress, *Cypressus thyoides*, the wild pine, with two or three other sorts of pine less common.

As the season was advancing very fast, and our necessary repairs took up all our time, excursions of every kind, either on the land or by water, were never attempted. And as we lay in a cove on an island, no other animals were ever seen alive in the woods than two or three raccoons, martens, and squirrels. The account, therefore, that we can give of the quadrupeds is taken from the skins which the natives brought to sell.

Of these, the most common were bears, deer, foxes, and wolves. The bear skins were in great numbers, few of them very large, but in general of a shining black colour. The deer skins were scarcer, and they seem to belong to that sort called the fallow deer by the historians of Carolina, though Mr Pennant thinks it quite a different species from ours, and distinguishes it by the name of Virginian deer. The foxes are in great plenty, and of several varieties – some yellow, some red, some white, and some black. Besides the common sort of marten, the pine-marten is here, and the ermine is also found at this place. The raccoons and squirrels are of the common sort.

Hogs, dogs, and goats, have not as yet found their way to this place. Nor do the natives seem to have any knowledge of our brown rats, to which, when they saw them on board the ships, they applied the name they give to squirrels.

The sea animals seen off the coast were whales, porpoises, and seals. The last of these seem only of the common sort, judging from the skins which we saw here.

Sea-otters, which live mostly in the water, are found here. The fur of these animals, as mentioned in the Russian accounts, is certainly softer and finer than that of any others we know of, and therefore the discovery of this part of the continent of North America, where so valuable an article of commerce may be met with, cannot be a matter of indifference.

Birds, in general, are not only rare as to the different species, but very scarce as to numbers, and these few are so shy, that, in all probability, they are continually harassed by the natives, perhaps for food, certainly to get possession of their feathers, which they use as ornaments. Those which frequent the woods are crows and ravens, not at all different from our English ones; a bluish jay or magpie, common wrens, which are the only singing bird that we heard; the Canadian or emigrating thrush; and a considerable number of brown eagles, with white heads and tails, which, though they seem principally to frequent the coast, come into the Sound in bad weather, and sometimes perch upon the trees.

The birds which frequent the waters and the shores are not more numerous than the others. Quebrantahuessoses, gulls, and shags, were seen off the coast; and the two last also frequent the Sound; they are of the common sort. We observed wild ducks in considerable flocks; and the greater lumme, or diver, found in our northern countries. There were also seen, once or twice, some swans flying across the Sound.

Fish are more plentiful in quantity than birds, though the variety is not very great; and yet, from several circumstances, it is probable that even the variety is considerably increased at certain seasons.

As to the mineral substances in this country, though we found both iron and copper, there is little reason to believe that either of them belong to the place.

The persons of the natives are in general under the common stature, but not slender in proportion, being commonly pretty full or plump, though not muscular. The visage of most of them is round and full, and sometimes also broad, with high prominent cheeks; and above these the face is frequently much depressed, the nose also flattening at its base, with pretty wide nostrils, and a rounded point. The forehead rather low; the eyes small, black, and rather languishing than sparkling; the mouth round, with large round thickish lips; the teeth tolerably equal and well set, but not remarkably white. Their eyebrows are scanty, and always narrow; but the hair of the head is in great abundance, very coarse and strong, and without a single exception, black, straight, and lank, or hanging down over the shoulders.

Their colour we could never positively determine, as their bodies were encrusted with paint and dirt; though in particular cases, when these were well rubbed off, the whiteness of the skin appeared almost to equal that of Europeans.

The women are nearly of the same size, colour, and form, with the men, from whom it is not easy to distinguish them, as they possess no natural delicacies sufficient to render their persons agreeable.

Their common dress is a flaxen garment, or mantle, ornamented on the upper edge by a narrow strip of fur, and at the lower edge by fringes or tassels; it is tied over the shoulders. Over this, which reaches below the knees, is worn a small cloak of the same substance, likewise fringed at the lower part. In shape, this resembles a round dish cover, being quite close, except in the middle, where there is a hole just large enough to admit the head.

Besides the above dress, which is common to both sexes, the men frequently throw over their other garments the skin of a bear, wolf, or sea-otter, with the hair outward, and tie it as a cloak near the upper part, wearing it sometimes before, and sometimes behind. Their dress would by no means be inelegant were it kept clean. But as they rub their bodies constantly over with red paint, of a clayey or coarse ochre substance, mixed with oil, their garments by this means contract a rancid offensive smell, and a greasy nastiness, so that they make a very wretched dirty appearance.

The ears of many of them are perforated in the lobe, where they make a pretty large hole, and two others higher up on the outer edge. In these holes they hang bits of bone, quills fixed upon a leathern thong, small shells, bunches of woollen tassels, or pieces of thin copper, which our beads could never supplant. The septum of the nose in many is also perforated, through which they draw a piece of soft cord; and others wear at the same place small thin pieces of iron, brass, or copper, shaped almost like a horse-shoe, the narrow opening of which receives the septum, so that the two points may gently pinch it, and the ornament thus hangs over the upper lip. The rings of our brass buttons, which they eagerly purchased, were appropriated to this use.

Sometimes they wear carved wooden masks, or visors, applied on the face, or to the upper part of the head, or forehead. Some of these resemble human faces, furnished with hair, beards, and eyebrows; others the heads of birds, particularly of eagles and quebrantahuessoses; and many of the heads of land and sea animals, such as wolves, deer, porpoises, and others. So fond are they of these disguises, that I have seen one of them put his head into a tin kettle he had got from us, for want of another sort of mask. Whether they use these extravagant masquerade ornaments on any particular religious occasion or diversion, or whether they be put on to intimidate their enemies when they go to battle, by their monstrous appearance, or as decoys when they go to hunt animals, is uncertain.

Though there be but too much reason, from their bringing to sale human skulls and bones, to infer that they treat their enemies with a degree of brutal cruelty, this circumstance rather marks a general agreement of character with that of almost every tribe of uncivilised men in every age, and in every part of the globe, than that they are to be reproached with any charge of peculiar inhumanity. They seem to be a docile, courteous, good-natured people.

When displeased, they are exceedingly violent, but they are soon pacified. Their curiosity appears in some measure to lie dormant. For few expressed any desire to see or examine things wholly unknown to them; and which, to those truly possessed of that passion, would have appeared astonishing. They were always contented to procure the articles they knew and wanted, regarding everything else with great indifference; nor did our persons, apparel, and manners, so different from their own, or even the extraordinary size and construction of our ships, seem to excite admiration or even engage attention.

The only instruments of music (if such they may be called) which I saw amongst them, were a rattle, and a small whistle with one hole only. They use the rattle when they sing, but upon what occasions they use the whistle I know not; unless it be when they dress themselves like particular animals, and endeavour to imitate their howl or cry. I once saw one of them dressed in a wolf's skin, with the head over his own, and imitating that animal by making a squeaking noise with one of these whistles which he had in his mouth.

The houses are disposed in three ranges or rows, rising gradually behind each other, the largest being that in front and the others less. Though there be some appearance of regularity in this disposition, there is none in the single houses. The height of the sides and ends of these habitations is seven or eight feet; the back part is higher than the front, by which means the planks that compose the roof slant forward; they are laid on loose, and are moved to let out smoke and admit air or light. There are holes or windows in the sides of the houses to look out at, but without any regularity of shape or disposition; and these have bits of mat hung before them to prevent the rain getting in.

Their furniture consists chiefly of a great number of chests and boxes of all sizes, which are generally piled upon each other, close to the sides or ends of the house, and contain their spare garments, skins, masks, and other things which they set a value upon. Their other domestic utensils are mostly square and oblong pails or buckets to hold water and other things; round wooden cups and bowls, and small shallow wooden troughs about two feet long, out of which they eat their food; and baskets of twigs, bags of matting, fishing implements, etc.

The nastiness and stench of their houses are, however, at least equal to the confusion. But amidst all the filth and confusion that are found in the houses, many of them are decorated with images. These are nothing more than the trunks of very large trees, four or five feet high, set up singly or by pairs, at the upper end of the apartment, with the front carved into a human face, the arms and hands cut out upon the sides, and variously painted, so that the whole is a truly monstrous figure. The general name of these images is *klumna*; and the names of two particular ones, which stood abreast of each other, three or four feet asunder, in one of the houses, were Natchkoa and Matseeta. A mat, by way of curtain, for the most part hung before them, which the natives were not willing at all times to remove; and when they did unveil them, they seemed to speak of them in a very mysterious manner.

It was natural, from these circumstances, for us to think that they were representatives of their gods, and yet we had proofs of the little real estimation they were in; for, with a small quantity of iron or brass, I could have purchased all the gods in the place, and I actually got two or three of the very smallest sort.

The chief employment of the men is fishing and killing land or sea animals. The women are occupied in manufacturing their flaxen or woollen garments, and in preparing the sardines for drying. The young men appeared to be the most indolent or idle set in this community, for they were either sitting in scattered companies, to bask themselves in the sun, or lay wallowing in the sand upon the beach, like a number of hogs, for the same purpose, without any covering. But this disregard of decency was confined to the men. The women were always properly clothed, and

behaved with the utmost propriety; justly deserving all commend-
ation for a bashfulness and modesty becoming their sex, but more
meritorious in them, as the men seem to have no sense of shame.

Their weapons are bows and arrows, slings, spears, short trun-
cheons of bone, somewhat like the patoo patoo of New Zealand,
and a small pickaxe, not unlike the American tomahawk. The
tomahawk is a stone six or eight inches long, pointed at one end,
and the other end fixed into a handle of wood, which resembles
the head and neck of the human figure, and the stone is fixed in
the mouth, so as to represent an enormously large tongue.

From the number of stone weapons and others, we might almost
conclude that it is their custom to engage in close fight; and we had
too convincing proofs that their wars are both frequent and
bloody, from the vast number of human skulls which they brought
to sell.

Their manufactures and mechanic arts are far more extensive and
ingenious, whether we regard the design or the execution, than
could have been expected from the natural disposition of the people,
and the little progress that civilisation has made amongst them in
other respects. The garments with which they cover themselves
must necessarily engage their first care, and are the most material of
those that can be ranked under the head of manufactures. They are
made of the bark of a pine tree beat into a hempen state. It is not
spun; but, after being properly prepared, is spread upon a stick
which is fastened across to two others that stand upright. It is
disposed in such a manner that the manufacturer, who sits on her
hams at this simple machine, knots it across with small plaited
threads, at the distance of half an inch from each other. Though by
this method it be not so close or firm as cloth that is woven, the
bunches between the knots make it sufficiently impervious to the
air, by filling the interstices, and it has the additional advantage of
being softer and more pliable.

Their taste or design in working figures upon their garments,
corresponds with their fondness for carving in everything they
make of wood. The imitative arts being nearly allied, no wonder
that to their skill in working figures in their garments, and carving
them in wood, they should add that of drawing them in colours.
We have sometimes seen the whole process of their whale fishery
painted on the caps they wear. This, though rudely executed,

serves at least to show that they have some notion of a method of commemorating and representing actions in a lasting way.

Their canoes are of a simple structure, but to appearance well calculated for every useful purpose. Even the largest, which carry twenty people or more, are formed of one tree. Many of them are forty feet long, seven broad, and about three deep. For the most part they are without any ornament, but some have a little carving, and are decorated by setting seals' teeth on the surface like studs, as is the practice on their masks and weapons. A few have likewise a kind of additional head or prow, like a large cut-water, which is painted with the figure of some animal.

Their principal tools are the chisel and the knife. The chisel is a long flat piece fitted into a handle of wood. A stone serves for a mallet, and a piece of fish skin for a polisher. I have seen some of these chisels that were eight or ten inches long, and three or four inches broad, but in general they were smaller. The knives are of various sizes, some very large.

Iron, which they call *seekemaile* (which name they also give to tin, and all white metals) is familiar to them. Yet we never observed the least sign of their having seen ships like ours before, nor of their having traded with such people. They expressed no marks of surprise at seeing our ships; nor were they even startled at the report of a musket; till one day, upon their endeavouring to make us sensible that their arrows and spears could not penetrate the hide-dresses, one of our gentlemen shot a musket ball through one of them folded six times. At this they were so much staggered, that they plainly discovered their ignorance of the effect of fire-arms. This was very often confirmed afterward when we used them at their village, and other places, to shoot birds, the manner of which plainly confounded them.

The most probable way by which we can suppose that they get their iron, is by trading for it with the other Indian tribes, who either have immediate communication with European settlements upon that continent, or receive it, perhaps, through several inter-mediate nations. The same might be said of the brass and copper found amongst them.

We could observe that there are such men as chiefs, who are distinguished by the name or title of *acweek*, and to whom the others are in some measure subordinate. But I should guess the authority of each of these great men extends no farther than the family to which he belongs, and who own him as their head. These *acweeks* were not always elderly men; from which I concluded that this title came to them by inheritance.

Their language is by no means harsh or disagreeable, farther than proceeds from their using the *k* and *h* with more force, or pronouncing them with less softness, than we do.

On quitting the Sound, I bore away steering north-west; in which direction I supposed the coast to lie. At half-past one in the afternoon, it blew a perfect hurricane, so that I judged it highly dangerous to run any longer before it, and therefore brought the ships to. At this time the *Resolution* sprung a leak. It was no sooner discovered than the fish-room was found to be full of water, and the casks in it afloat; but this was in a great measure owing to the water not finding its way to the pumps through the coals that lay at the bottom of the room. For after the water was baled out, which employed us till midnight, and had found its way directly from the leak to the pumps, it appeared that one pump kept it under, which gave us no small satisfaction.

At seven in the evening on the 1st of May, we got sight of the land, which abounds with hills, but one considerably out-tops the rest; this I called Mount Edgcumbe. It was wholly covered with snow, as were also all the other elevated hills; but the lower ones, and the flatter spots bordering upon the sea, were free from it, and covered with wood.

On the 3rd, we saw a large inlet, distant six leagues, and the most advanced point of the land, lying under a very high peaked mountain, which obtained the name of Mount Fair Weather. The inlet was named Cross Sound, as being first on that day so marked in our calendar.

From the 4th to the 10th, nothing very interesting occurred. On the 10th, we found ourselves no more than three leagues from the coast of the continent, which extended as far as the eye could reach. To the westward of this last direction was an island that extended from north to south, distant six leagues. A point shoots out from the main toward the north-east end of the island, about five or six leagues distant. This point I named Cape Suckling.

On the 11th, I bore up for the island. At ten o'clock in the morning, I went in a boat and landed upon it, with a view of seeing what lay on the other side; but finding it farther to the hills than I expected, and the way being steep and woody, I was obliged to drop the design. At the foot of a tree, on a little eminence not far from the shore, I left a bottle with a paper in it, on which were inscribed the names of the ships, and the date of our discovery. And along with it I enclosed two silver twopenny pieces of his Majesty's coin, of the date 1772. These, with many others, were furnished me by the Revd Dr Kaye (now Dean of Lincoln), and, as a mark of my esteem and regard for that gentleman, I named the island after him, Kaye's Island. It is eleven or twelve leagues in length, but its breadth is not above a league or a league and a half in any part of it.

On this island there are a considerable number of pines, and the whole seems covered with a broad girdle of wood. In the passage from the ship to the shore we saw a great many fowls sitting upon the water, or flying about in flocks or pairs, the chief of which were a few quebrantahuessoses, divers, ducks, or large petrels, gulls, shags, and burres. At the place where we landed, a fox came from the verge of the wood, and eyed us with very little emotion, walking leisurely without any signs of fear. He was of a reddish-yellow colour, like some of the skins we bought at Nootka, but not of a large size.

We were now threatened with a fog and a storm, and I wanted to get into some place to stop the leak before we encountered another gale. These reasons induced me to steer for an inlet, which we had no sooner reached than the weather became so foggy that we could not see a mile before us, and it became necessary to secure the ships in some place, to wait for a clearer sky. With this view, I hauled close under a cape which I now called Cape Hinchinbroke, and anchored before a small cove a little within the cape, and about a quarter of a mile from the shore.

At some short intervals the fog cleared away, and gave us a sight of the lands around us. The westernmost point we had in sight on the north shore, bore north north-west half west, two leagues distant. Between this point and the shore, under which we were at anchor, is a bay about three leagues deep; on the south-east side of which there are two or three coves, such as that before in which we had anchored; and in the middle some rocky islands.

To these islands Mr Gore was sent in a boat, in hopes of shooting some eatable birds. But he hardly got to them before about twenty natives made their appearance in two large canoes; on which he thought proper to return to the ships, and they followed him. They would not venture alongside, but kept at some distance hallooing aloud and alternately clasping and extending their arms, and in a short time began a kind of song exactly after the manner of those at Nootka. Their heads were also powdered with feathers. One man held out a white garment, which we interpreted as a sign of friendship, and another stood up in the canoe quite naked for almost a quarter of an hour, with his arms stretched out like a cross, and motionless. Though we returned all their signs of friendship, and by every expressive gesture tried to encourage them to come alongside, we could not prevail.

At ten o'clock next morning we got under sail in order to look out for some place where we might search for and stop the leak; our present station being too much exposed for this purpose.

The natives who visited us the preceding evening came off again in the morning in five or six canoes, but not till we were under sail; and although they followed us for some time they could not get up with us. At eight o'clock the violence of the squalls obliged us to anchor in a bay.

The weather, bad as it was, did not hinder three of the natives from paying us a visit. The treatment these men met with induced many more to visit us between one and two the next morning, in both great and small canoes. A few ventured on board the ship, but not till some of our people had stepped into their boats. Amongst those who came on board was a good-looking middle-aged man, whom we afterwards found to be the chief. He was clothed in a dress made of the sea-otter's skin, and had on his head such a cap as is worn by the people of King George's Sound, ornamented with sky-blue glass beads, about the size of a large pea. He seemed to set a much higher value upon these than upon our white glass beads. Any sort of beads, however, appeared to be in high estimation with these people; and they readily gave whatever they had in exchange for them, even their fine sea-otter skins.

These people were also desirous of iron; but they wanted pieces eight or ten inches long at least, and of the breadth of three or four fingers. The points of some of their spears or lances were of that metal, others were of copper, and a few of bone, of which the points of their darts, arrows, etc., were composed. I could not prevail upon the chief to trust himself below the upper deck; nor did he and his companions remain long on board. But while we had their company, it was necessary to watch them narrowly, as they soon betrayed a thievish disposition. At length, after being about three or four hours alongside the *Resolution*, they all left her and went to the *Discovery*; where, after looking down the hatchways and seeing nobody but the officer of the watch, they no doubt thought they might plunder her with ease, especially as she lay at some distance from us. It was unquestionably with this view that they all repaired to her. Several of them, without any ceremony, went on board, drew their knives, made signs to the officer and people on deck to keep off, and began to look about them for plunder. The first thing they met with was the rudder of one of the boats, which they threw overboard to those of their party who had remained in their canoes. Before they had time to find another object that pleased their fancy, the crew were alarmed, and began to come on deck armed with cutlasses. On seeing this, the whole company of plunderers sneaked off in their canoes with as much deliberation and indifference as if they had done nothing amiss; and they were observed describing to those who had not been on board how much longer the knives of the ship's crew were than their own.

Just as we were going to weigh the anchor, to proceed farther up the bay, it began to blow and to rain as hard as before; so that we were obliged to veer away the cable again and lay fast. Toward the evening, finding that the gale did not moderate, and that it might be some time before an opportunity offered to get higher up, I came to a resolution to heel the ship where we were. In heaving the anchor out of the boat, one of the seamen, either through ignorance or carelessness, or both, was carried overboard by the buoy-rope, and followed the anchor to the bottom. It is remarkable, that in this very critical situation, he had presence of mind to disengage himself, and come up to the surface of the water, where he was taken up, with one of his legs fractured in a dangerous manner.

The leak being stopped, which was found to be in the seams, at four o'clock in the morning of the 17th we weighed, and steered to the north-westward with a light breeze at east north-east, thinking, if there should be any passage to the north through this inlet, that it must be in that direction. We were now upward of 520 leagues to the westward of any part of Hudson's Bay.

Next morning, at three o'clock, we weighed, and, with a gentle breeze at north, proceeded to the southward down the inlet, and met with the same broken ground as on the preceding day. However, we soon extricated ourselves from it. Next evening we were again in the open sea, and found the coast trending west by south, as far as the eye could reach.

To the inlet which we had now left I gave the name of Prince William's Sound.

The natives, who came to make us several visits while we were in the Sound, were generally not above the common height, though many of them were under it. They were square, or strong chested; and the most disproportioned part of their body seemed to be their heads, which were very large, with thick short necks, and large, broad, or spreading faces, which, upon the whole, were flat. Their eyes, though not small, scarcely bore a proportion to the size of their faces; and their noses had full round points, hooked or turned up at the tip. Their hair was black, thick, straight, and strong; and their beards, in general, thin or wanting. Very few of them have any pretensions to beauty, though their countenance commonly indicates a considerable share of vivacity, good nature, and frankness.

Their common dress (for men, women, and children are clothed alike) is a kind of close frock, or rather robe, reaching generally to the ankles, though sometimes only to the knees. At the upper part is a hole just sufficient to admit the head, with sleeves that reach to the wrist. These frocks are made of the skins of different animals; the most common of which are those of the sea-otter, gray fox, raccoon, and pine-marten, with many of seal skins; and in general they are worn with the hairy side outward. Some also have these frocks made of the skins of fowls, with only the down remaining on them, which they glue on other substances. A few have a kind of cape or collar; and some a hood; but the other is the most common form, and seems to be their whole dress in good weather. When it rains, they put over this another frock, ingeniously made from the intestines of whales, or some other large animal, prepared so skilfully as almost to resemble our gold-beaters' leaf.

In general they do not cover their legs or feet; but a few have a kind of skin stockings, which reach halfway up the thigh; and scarcely any of them are without mittens for the hands, made of the skins of bears' paws.

Both sexes have the ears perforated with several holes, about the outer and lower part of the edge, in which they hang little bunches of beads. The septum of the nose is also perforated, through which they frequently thrust the quill feathers of small birds, or little bending ornaments, made of shelly substances, strung on a stiff string or cord, three or four inches long, which give them a truly grotesque appearance. But the most uncommon and unsightly ornamental fashion, adopted by some of both sexes, is the having their under lip slit, or cut quite through in the direction of the mouth, a little below the swelling part. This incision, which is made even in the sucking children, is often above two inches long; and either by its natural retraction, when the wound is fresh, or by the repetition of some artificial management, assumes the true shape of lips, and becomes so large as to admit the tongue through. This happened to be the case when the first person, having this incision, was seen by one of the seamen, who called out that the man had two mouths; and, indeed, it does not look unlike it. In this artificial mouth they stick a flat narrow ornament, made chiefly out of a solid shell or bone, cut into little narrow pieces like small teeth.

The men frequently paint their faces of a bright red, and of a black colour, and sometimes of a blue or leaden colour; but not in any regular figure; and the women, in some measure, endeavour to imitate them, by puncturing or staining the chin with black that comes to a point in each cheek; a practice very similar to which is in fashion among the females of Greenland. Upon the whole, I have nowhere seen savages who take more pains than these people to ornament, or rather to disfigure, their persons.

For defensive armour, they have a kind of jacket, or coat of mail, made of thin laths, bound together with sinews, which make it quite flexible, though so close as not to admit an arrow or dart. It only covers the trunk of the body, and may not be improperly compared to a woman's stays.

Besides the animals which were seen at Nootka, there are some others in this place which we did not find there, such as the white bear; of whose skins the natives brought several pieces, and some entire skins of cubs, from which their size could not be determined. We also found the wolverine, or quickhatch, which had very bright colours; a larger sort of ermine than the common one, which is the same as at Nootka, varied with a brown colour, and with scarcely any black on its tail. The natives also brought the skin of the head of some very large animal; but it could not be positively determined what it was, though from the colour and shagginess of the hair, and its unlikeness to any land animal, we judged it might probably be that of the large male ursine seal or sea-bear. The number of skins we found here, points out the great plenty of these several animals just mentioned; but it is remarkable that we neither saw the skins of the moose nor of the common deer.

The beads and iron found amongst these people left no room to doubt that they must have received them from some civilised nation. We were pretty certain, from circumstances already mentioned, that we were the first Europeans with whom they had ever communicated directly; and it remains only to be decided from what quarter they had got our manufactures by intermediate conveyance. And there cannot be the least doubt of their having received these articles, through the intervention of the more inland tribes, from Hudson's Bay, or the settlement on the Canadian Lakes.

May the 21st, I steered to the south-west, and passed a lofty promontory. As the discovery of it was connected with the Princess Elizabeth's birthday, I named it Cape Elizabeth. Beyond it we could see no land, so that at first we were in hopes that it was the western extremity of the Continent; but not long after we found our mistake, for fresh land appeared in sight, bearing west south-west. We continued our course with little variation, observing many high mountains near the coast till the 30th, when we anchored in nineteen fathoms water under the eastern shore.

About noon two canoes, with a man in each, came off to the ship, from near a place where we had seen some smoke the preceding day. They laboured very hard in paddling across the strong tide, and hesitated a little before they would come quite close; but, upon signs being made to them, they approached. One of them talked a great deal to no purpose, for we did not understand a word he said. He kept pointing to the shore, which we interpreted to be an invitation to go thither. They accepted of a few trifles from me, which I conveyed to them from the quarter gallery.

When the flood made, we weighed, and stood over to the western shore with a fresh gale at north north-east. This, with the other on the opposite shore, contracted the channel to the breadth of four leagues. Through this channel ran a prodigious tide.

As we proceeded farther up the marks of a river displayed themselves. The water was found to be fresher, insomuch that I was convinced that we were in a large river, and not in a strait communicating with the Northern Seas. But I was desirous of having stronger proofs; and therefore weighed with the next flood, in the morning of the 31st, and plied higher up, or rather drove up with the tide, for we had but little wind.

About eight o'clock we were visited by several of the natives, in one large, and several small canoes. The latter carried only one person each; and some had a paddle with a blade at each end, after the manner of the Esquimaux.

Soon after we came to an anchor, about two leagues from the west shore. The weather was misty, with drizzling rain, and clear by turns. At the clear intervals, we saw an opening between the mountains on the eastern shore, bearing east from the station of the ships, with low land, which we supposed to be islands lying between us and the mainland. From these appearances we were in some doubt whether the inlet did not take an easterly direction through the above opening, or whether that opening was only a branch of it, and the main channel continued its northern direction through the low land now in sight.

To determine this point, and to examine the shoals, I despatched two boats under the command of the master; and as soon as the flood-tide made, followed with the ships. We had now many evident proofs of being in a great river.

Early next morning, being the 1st of June, the master returned and reported that he found the inlet, or rather river, contracted to the breadth of one league, by low land on each side, through which it took a northerly direction He proceeded three leagues through this narrow part, which he found navigable for the largest ships. While the ebb or stream ran down, the water was perfectly fresh, but after the flood made, it became brackish, and towards high water very much so, even as high up as we went.

All hopes of finding a passage were now given up. However, I despatched two boats, under the command of Lieutenant King, to examine the tides, and to make such other observations as might give us some insight into the nature of the river, which I shall distinguish by the name of River Turnagain. By means of this river, and its several branches, a very extensive inland communication seems to lie open. We had traced it seventy leagues or more from its entrance, without seeing the least appearance of its source.

If the discovery of this great river, which promises to vie with the most considerable ones already known to be capable of extensive inland navigation, should prove of use either to the present or to any future age, the time we spent in it ought to be less regretted. But to us, who had a much greater object in view, the delay thus occasioned was an essential loss. The season was advancing apace. We knew not how far we might have to proceed to the south, and we were now convinced that the continent of North America extended farther to the west than, from the most modern reputable charts, we had reason to expect. This made the existence of a passage into Hudson's Bay less probable, or at least showed it to be of greater extent. It was a satisfaction to me, however, to reflect that, if I had not examined this very considerable inlet, it would have been assumed by speculative fabricators of geography as a fact, that it communicated with the sea to the north, or with Hudson's Bay to the east.

In the afternoon I sent Mr King again, with two armed boats, with orders to land on the northern point of the low land, on the south east side of the river, there to display the flag; to take possession of the country and river in his Majesty's name, and to bury in the ground a bottle, containing some pieces of English coin of the year 1772, and a paper, on which was inscribed the names of our ships, and the date of our discovery.

We weighed anchor as soon as it was high-water, and with a faint breeze southerly, stood over to the west shore, where the return of the flood obliged us to anchor early next morning. Soon after several large and some small canoes, with natives, came off, who bartered their skins; after which they sold their garments, till many of them were quite naked.

In plying down the river, a good many of the natives came off. Their company was very acceptable; for they brought with them a large quantity of very fine salmon, which they exchanged for such trifles as we had to give them. Most of it was split ready for drying; and several hundredweight of it was procured for the two ships.

In the afternoon of the 2nd of June, the mountains, for the first time since our entering the river, were clear of clouds; and we discovered a volcano in one of those on the west side. It did not make any striking appearance, emitting only a white smoke, but no fire.

The wind remaining southerly, we continued to tide it down the river. Before we left this place, six canoes came off from the east shore – some conducted by one, and others by two men. They remained at a little distance from the ships, viewing them with a kind of silent surprise, at least half an hour, without exchanging a single word with us, or with one another. At length they took courage and came alongside, began to barter with our people, and did not leave us till they had parted with everything they brought with them, consisting of a few skins and some salmon.

Most of the skins which we purchased here were made up into garments. However, some of these were in good condition, but others were old and ragged enough. But as these poor people make no other use of skins but for clothing themselves, it cannot be supposed that they are at the trouble of dressing more of them than are necessary for this purpose. And perhaps this is the chief use for which they kill the animals, for the sea and the rivers seem to supply them with their principal articles of food. It would probably be much otherwise were they once habituated to a constant trade with foreigners.

Nothing interesting happened till the 18th, when, having occasion to send a boat on board the *Discovery*, one of the people in her shot a very beautiful bird of the hawk kind. It is somewhat less than a duck, and of a black colour, except the fore part of the head, which is white, and from above and behind each eye arises an elegant yellowish white crest, revolved backward as a ram's horn. The bill and feet are red. We had for some days seen these birds in large flocks.

On the 19th, being near the shore, the *Discovery* fired three guns, brought to, and made the signal to speak with us. A boat was immediately sent to her, and in a short time returned with Captain Clerke. I now learned from him that some natives, in three or four canoes, who had followed the ship for some time, at length got under his stern. One of them then made many signs, taking off his cap and bowing after the manner of Europeans. A rope being handed down from the ship, to this he fastened a small thin wooden case or box; and having delivered this safe, and spoken something, and made some more signs, the canoes dropped astern and left the *Discovery*. No one on board her had any suspicion that the box contained anything, till after the departure of the canoes, when it was accidentally opened and a piece of paper was found folded up carefully, upon which something was written in Russian language, as was supposed. The date 1778 was prefixed to it, and in the body of the written note there was a reference to the year 1766. Not learned enough to decipher the alphabet of the writer, his numerals marked sufficiently that others had preceded us in visiting this dreary part of the globe, who were united to us by other ties besides those of our common nature; and the hopes of soon meeting with some of the Russian traders could not but give a sensible satisfaction to those who had for such a length of time been conversant with the savages of the Pacific Ocean, and of the continent of North America.

Captain Clerke was at first of opinion that some Russians had been shipwrecked here; and that these unfortunate persons seeing our ships pass, had taken this method to inform us of their situation. Impressed with humane sentiments on such an occasion, he was desirous of stopping till they might have time to join us. But no such idea occurred to me. I rather thought that the paper contained a note of information, left by some Russian trader who had lately been amongst these islands, to be delivered to the next visitors. Fully convinced of this, I did not stay to inquire any further into the matter, but made sail, and stood away to the westward.

We continued to run all night, with a gentle breeze at north-east; and at two o'clock next morning some breakers were seen within us, at the distance of two miles.

The breakers forced us so far from the continent that we had but a distant view of the coast. Over some adjoining islands we could see the mainland covered with snow, but particularly some hills whose elevated tops were seen towering above the clouds to a most stupendous height. The most south-westerly of these hills was discovered to have a volcano, which continually threw up vast columns of black smoke. It stands not far from the coast. It is also remarkable from its figure, which is a complete cone, and the volcano is at the very summit.

In the afternoon, having three hours' calm, our people caught upward of a hundred halibuts, some of which weighed a hundred pounds. This was a very seasonable refreshment to us. In the height of our fishing a small canoe, conducted by one man, came to us from the large island. On approaching the ship he took off his cap and bowed. It was evident that the Russians must have a communication and traffic with these people, not only from their acquired politeness but from the note before mentioned. But we had now a fresh proof of it, for our present visitor wore a pair of green cloth breeches, and a jacket of black cloth or stuff, under the gut-shirt of his own country. He had nothing to barter except a grey fox skin, and some fishing implements or harpoons, the heads of the shafts of which were neatly made of bone.

The weather was cloudy and hazy, with now and then sunshine, till the afternoon of the 22nd, when the wind came round to the south-east, and, as usual, brought thick, rainy weather. Before the fog came on, no part of the mainland was in sight except the volcano, and another mountain close by it. We made but little progress for some days, having the wind variable, and but little of it.

On the morning of the 25th we got a breeze easterly, and, what was uncommon with this wind, clear weather, so that we not only saw the volcano but other mountains, both to the east and west of it, and all the coast of the mainland under them, much plainer than at any time before.

The weather in the afternoon became gloomy, and at length turned to a mist, so thick that we could not see a hundred yards before us. We were now alarmed at hearing the sound of breakers on our larboard bow. On heaving the lead, we found twenty-eight fathoms water. I immediately brought the ship to, and anchored over a bottom of coarse sand.

A few hours after, the fog having cleared a little, it appeared that we had escaped very imminent danger. We found ourselves three-quarters of a mile from the north-east side of an island. Two elevated rocks were about half a league each from us, and about the same distance from each other. There were several breakers about them, and yet Providence had, in the dark, conducted the ships through between these rocks, which I should not have ventured in a clear day, and to such an anchoring place that I could not have chosen a better.

On a point which bore west from the ship, three-quarters of a mile distant, were several natives and their habitations. To this place we saw them tow in two whales, which we supposed they had just killed. A few of them now and then came off to the ships and bartered a few trifling things with our people, but never remained above a quarter of an hour at a time. On the contrary, they rather seemed shy, and yet we could judge that they were no strangers to vessels something like ours. They behaved with a degree of politeness uncommon to savage tribes.

At daybreak on the 28th, we weighed with a light breeze at south, which was succeeded by variable light airs from all directions. But as there ran a rapid tide in our favour, we got through before the ebb made. We came to anchor in twenty-eight fathoms water, pretty near the southern shore.

While we lay here several of the natives came off to us, and bartered a few fishing implements for tobacco. One of them, a young man, overset his canoe while alongside of one of our boats. Our people caught hold of him, but the canoe went adrift. The youth, by this accident, was obliged to come into the ship, and he went down into my cabin upon the first invitation, without expressing the least reluctance or uneasiness. His own clothes being wet, I gave him others, in which he dressed himself with as much ease as I could have done. From his behaviour, and that of some others, we were convinced that these people were no strangers to Europeans, and to some of their customs. But there was something in our ships that greatly excited their curiosity; for such as could not come off in canoes assembled on the neighbouring hills to look at them.

Soon after we anchored, a native of the island brought on board such another note as had been given to Captain Clerke. He presented it to me, but it was written in the Russian language, which, as already observed, none of us could read. As it could be of no use to me, and might be of consequence to others, I returned it to the bearer, and dismissed him with a few presents, for which he expressed his thanks by making several low bows as he retired.

Thick fogs and a contrary wind detained us till the 2nd of July, which afforded an opportunity of acquiring some knowledge of the country and of its inhabitants.

It is called by the natives Samganoodha. Great plenty of good water may be easily got, but nothing else.

Having now put to sea, we steered to the north, meeting with nothing to obstruct us in this course, but made very little progress for many successive days, nor met with anything remarkable.

In the morning of the 16th we found ourselves nearer the land than we expected. Here, between two points, the coast forms a bay, in some parts of which the land was hardly visible from the masthead. I sent Lieutenant Williamson, with orders to land, and see what direction the coast took, and what the country produced; for, from the ships, it had but a barren appearance.

Soon after, Mr Williamson returned, and reported that he had landed on the point, and having climbed the highest hill, found that the farthest part of the coast in sight bore nearly north. He took possession of the country in his Majesty's name, and left on the hill a bottle, in which was inscribed on a piece of paper, the names of the ships and the date of the discovery. The promontory, to which he gave the name of Cape Newenham, is a rocky point of tolerable height. The hills are naked, but on the lower grounds grew grass and other plants. He saw no other animal but a doe and her fawn, and a dead sea-horse or cow, upon the beach.

From the 16th to the 21st nothing material occurred. On the 21st we were obliged to anchor, to avoid running upon a shoal, which had only a depth of five feet. While we lay here, twenty-seven men of the country, each in a canoe, came off to the ships, which they approached with great caution, hallooing and opening their arms as they advanced. This we understood was to express their pacific intentions. At length some approached near enough to receive a few trifles that were thrown to them. This encouraged the rest to venture alongside, and a traffic presently commenced between them and our people. They resembled the other natives of the coast, and appeared to be wholly unacquainted with people like us; they knew not the use of tobacco, nor was any foreign article seen in their possession, unless a knife may be looked upon as such. This indeed was only a piece of common iron, fitted in a wooden handle, so as to answer the purpose of a knife.

The canoes were made of skins, like all the others we had lately seen, only with this difference, that these were broader, and the hole in which the man sits was wider than in any I had before met with.

Variable winds, with rain, prevailed till the 3rd of August. Mr Anderson, my surgeon, who had been lingering under a consumption for more than twelve months, expired between three and four this afternoon. He was a sensible young man, an agreeable companion, well skilled in his own profession, and had acquired considerable knowledge in other branches of science. The reader of this journal will have observed how useful an assistant I had found him in the course of the voyage; and, had it pleased God to have spared his life, the public, I make no doubt, might have received from him such communications, on various parts of the natural history of the several places we visited, as would have abundantly shown that he was not unworthy of this commend-ation. Soon after he had breathed his last, land was seen to the westward, twelve leagues distant. It was supposed to be an island, and to perpetuate the memory of the deceased, for whom I had a very great regard, I named it Anderson's Island.

At ten in the morning of the 5th, with the wind at S.W., we ran down and anchored between an island and the continent in seven fathoms water. This island, which was named Sledge Island, is about four leagues in circuit. I landed here, but saw neither shrub nor tree, either upon the island or on the continent. That people had lately been on the island was evident, from the marks of their feet. We found, near where we landed, a sledge, which occasioned this name being given to the island. It seemed to be such an one as the Russians in Kamtschatka make use of over the ice or snow. It was ten feet long, twenty inches broad, and had a kind of rail work on each side, and was shod with bone. The construction of it was admirable, and all the parts neatly put together.

After several observations from the 6th to the 9th, I was satisfied that the whole was a continued coast. I tacked and stood away for its north-west part, and came to an anchor near a point of land, which I named Cape Prince of Wales. It is the western extremity of all America hitherto known.

At daybreak in the morning of the 10th, we resumed our course to the west, and about ten o'clock we anchored in a large bay, two miles from the shore.

As we were standing into this bay we perceived the north shore, a village, and some people, whom the sight of the ships seemed to have thrown into confusion or fear. At these habitations I proposed to land, and accordingly went, with three armed boats, accompanied with some of the officers. About thirty or forty men, each armed with a spontoon, a bow and arrows, stood drawn up on a rising ground close by the village. As we drew near, three of them came down toward the shore, and were so polite as to take off their caps and make us low bows. We returned the civility, but this did not inspire them with sufficient confidence to wait for our landing; for the moment we put the boats ashore they retired. I followed them alone, and by signs and gestures prevailed on them to stop and receive some trifling presents. In return they gave me two fox-skins and a couple of sea-horse teeth.

They seemed very cautious, expressing their desire, by signs, that no more of our people should be permitted to come up. A few beads distributed to those about us soon created a kind of confidence, and by degrees a sort of traffic between us commenced. In exchange for knives, beads, tobacco, and other articles, they gave us some of their clothing and a few arrows. But nothing that we had to offer could induce them to part with a spear or a bow. These they held in constant readiness, never once quitting them, except at one time, when four or five persons laid theirs down while they gave us a song and a dance.

The arrows were pointed either with bone or stone, but very few of them had barbs, and some of them had a round blunt point. What use these may be applied to I cannot say, unless it be to kill small animals without damaging the skin. The bows were such as we had seen on the American coast, and like those used by the Esquimaux. The spears or spontoons were of iron or steel, and of European or Asiatic workmanship; in which no little pains had been taken to ornament them with carving and inlayings of brass and of a white metal.

Several other things, and in particular their clothing, showed that they were possessed of a degree of ingenuity far surpassing what one could expect to find among so northern a people. All the Americans we had seen since our arrival on that coast were rather low of stature, with round chubby faces and high cheek bones. The people we now were amongst, far from resembling them, had long visages, and were stout and well made. In short, they appeared to be a quite different nation. We saw neither women nor children of either sex, nor any aged except one man, who was bald headed, and he was the only one who carried no arms. All of them had their ears bored, and some had glass beads hanging to them. These were the only fixed ornaments we saw about them, for they wear none to the lips.

Their clothing consisted of a cap, a frock, a pair of breeches, a pair of boots, and a pair of gloves, all made of leather, or of the skins of deer, dogs, seals, etc., extremely well dressed, some with the hair or fur on, but others without it.

We found the village composed both of their summer and winter habitations. The latter are exactly like a vault, the floor of which is sunk a little below the surface of the earth. One of them which I examined was of an oval form, about twenty feet long, and twelve or more high.

The summer huts were pretty large and circular, being brought to a point at the top. The framing was of slight poles and bones, covered with the skins of sea animals. I examined the inside of one. There was a fireplace just within the door, where lay a few wooden vessels, all very dirty. Their bed-places were close to the side, and took up about half the circuit. The bed and bedding were of deer skins, and most of them were dry and clean.

At first we supposed some land visible to the westward to be a part of the island of Alaschka, laid down in Mr Staehlin's map, but from the figure of the coast, the situation of the opposite shore of America, and from the longitude, we soon began to think that it was more probably the eastern extremity of Asia, explored by Behring in 1728.

After a stay of between two and three hours with these people we returned to our ships, and soon after we weighed anchor and stood out of the bay. From this station we steered east, in order to get nearer the American coast.

On Monday the 7th, before noon, we perceived a brightness in the northern horizon like that reflected from ice, commonly called the blink. About an hour after, the sight of a large field of ice left us no longer in doubt about the cause of the brightness of the horizon. At half-past two we tacked close to the edge of the ice, in twenty-two fathoms water, not being able to stand on any farther, for the ice was quite impenetrable, and extended from west to south to east by north, as far as the eye could reach. Here were abundance of sea-horses.

On the 18th, at noon, we were near five leagues farther to the eastward. We were at this time close to the edge of the ice, which was as compact as a wall, and seemed to be ten or twelve feet high at least; but farther north it appeared much higher.

We now stood to the southward, and after running six leagues, shoaled the water to seven fathoms, but it soon deepened to nine fathoms. At this time we saw land extending from south to south-east by east, about three or four miles distant. The eastern extreme forms a point which was much encumbered with ice, for which reason it obtained the name of Icy Cape. The other extreme of the land was lost in the horizon, so that there can be no doubt of its being a continuation of the American continent.

Our situation was now more and more critical. We were in shoal water, upon a lee shore, and the main body of the ice to windward driving down upon us. I therefore made the signal for the *Discovery* to tack, and tacked myself at the same time.

Next day we had a good deal of drift ice about us, and the main ice was about two leagues to the north. It was too close and in too large pieces to attempt forcing the ships through it. On the ice lay a prodigious number of sea-horses, and as we were in want of fresh provisions the boats from each ship were sent to get some.

Their fat at first is as sweet as marrow, but in a few days it grows rancid unless it be salted, in which state it will keep much longer. The lean flesh is coarse, black, and has rather a strong taste; and the heart is nearly as well tasted as that of a bullock. The fat, when melted, yields a good deal of oil, which burns very well in lamps, and their hides, which are very thick, were very useful about our rigging. The teeth or tusks of most of them were at this time very small; even some of the largest and oldest of these animals had them not exceeding six inches in length. From this we concluded that they had lately shed their old teeth.

They lie in herds of many hundreds upon the ice, huddling one over the other like swine, and roar or bray very loud, so that in the night or in foggy weather they gave us notice of the vicinity of the ice before we could see it. We never found the whole herd asleep – some being always upon the watch. These, on the approach of the boat, would wake those next to them; and the alarm being thus gradually communicated, the whole herd would be awake presently. They did not appear to us to be that dangerous animal some authors have described, not even when attacked. They are rather more so to appearance than in reality. Vast numbers of them would follow and come close up to the boats; but the flash of a musket in the pan, or even pointing one at them, would send them down in an instant. The female, however, will defend the young one to the very last, and at the expense of her own life, whether in the water or upon the ice. Nor will the young one quit the dam, though she be dead.

Why they should be called sea-horses is hard to say, unless the word be a corruption of the Russian name *morse*, for they have not the least resemblance of a horse. This is without doubt the same animal that is found in the Gulf of St Lawrence, and there called sea-cow. It is certainly more like a cow than a horse; but this likeness consists in nothing but the snout. In short, it is an animal like a seal, but incomparably larger, weighing sometimes more than one thousand pounds, and measuring ten feet from the snout to the tail.

By the time that we had got our sea-horses on board, we were in a manner surrounded with the ice, and had no way left to clear it but by standing to the southward, which was done till three o'clock next morning. At two in the afternoon we fell in with the main ice, along the edge of which we kept, being partly directed by the roaring of the sea-horses, for we had a very thick fog. Thus we continued sailing till near midnight, when we got in amongst the loose ice, and heard the surge of the sea upon the main ice.

Next morning the fog clearing away, we saw the continent of America, extending from south by east to east by south; and at noon from south-west half south to east; the nearest part five leagues distant.

I continued to steer in for it until eight o'clock, in order to get a nearer view of it and to look for a harbour, but seeing nothing like one I stood again to the north.

The ice obliged us to change our course frequently till the 27th, when we tacked and stood to the west, and at seven in the evening we were close in with the edge of the ice, which lay east from north-east, and west south-west, as far each way as the eye could reach. Having but little wind I went with the boats to examine the state of the ice. I found it consisting of loose pieces of various extent, and so close together that I could hardly enter the outer edge with a boat; and it was as impossible for the ships to enter it, as if it had been so many rocks.

A thick fog which came on while I was thus employed with the boats, hastened me aboard rather sooner than I could have wished, with one sea-horse to each ship. We had killed more, but could not wait to bring them with us. The number of these animals, on all the ice that we had seen, is almost incredible. By this time our people began to relish them. We now stretched to the south-east.

On the 29th, the weather, which had been hazy, cleared up. This enabled us to have a pretty good view of the Asiatic coast, which in every respect is like the opposite one of America; that is, low land next the sea with elevated land farther back. It was perfectly destitute of wood and even snow, but was probably covered with a mossy substance that gave it a brownish cast. In the low ground, lying between the high land and the sea, was a lake extending to the south-east further than we could see.

The season was now so far advanced, and the time when the frost was expected to set in so near at hand, that I did not think it consistent with prudence to make any farther attempts to find a passage into the Atlantic this year in any direction, so little was the prospect of succeeding. My attention was now directed toward finding out some place where we might supply ourselves with wood and water; and the object uppermost in my thoughts was, how I should spend the winter so as to make some improvements in geography and navigation, and at the same time be in a condition to return to the north in farther search of a passage the ensuing summer.

After standing off till we got into eighteen fathoms water, I bore up to the eastward along the coast of Asia. At daybreak on the 30th we made sail, and steered such a course as I thought would bring us in with the land; for the weather was as thick as ever, and it snowed incessantly. At ten we got sight of the coast, bearing south-west, four miles distant.

The inland country hereabout is full of hills, some of which are of a considerable height. The land was covered with snow.

September 2nd, we had now fair weather and sunshine; and as we ranged along the coast at the distance of four miles, we saw several of the inhabitants, and some of their habitations, which looked like little hillocks of earth. None of them, however, attempted to come off to us, which seemed a little extraordinary. These people must be the Tschutski, a nation that, at the time Mr Muller wrote, the Russians had not been able to conquer.

The more I was convinced of my being now upon the coast of Asia, the more I was at a loss to reconcile Mr Staehlin's map of the

New Northern Archipelago with my observations, and I had no way to account for the great difference, but by supposing that I had mistaken some part of what he calls the Island of Alaschka for the American continent, and had missed the channel that separates them. Admitting even this, there would still have been a considerable difference. It was with me a matter of some consequence to clear up this point the present season, that I might have but one object in view the next. And as the northern isles are represented by him as abounding with wood, I was in hopes, if I should find them, of getting a supply of that article, which we now began to be in great want of on board.

With these views, I steered over for the American coast, and on the 6th we got sight of it.

Pursuing our course, on the 9th we found ourselves upon a coast covered with wood, an agreeable sight, to which of late we had not been accustomed. Next morning, being about a league from the west shore, I took two boats and landed, attended by Mr King, to seek wood and water. Here we observed tracks of deer and foxes on the beach, on which also lay a great quantity of driftwood, and there was no want of fresh water. I returned on board with an intention to bring the ships to an anchor here, but the wind then veering to north-east, I stretched over to the opposite shore, in hopes of finding wood there also, and anchored at eight o'clock in the evening, but next morning we found it to be a peninsula united to the continent by a low neck of land, on each side of which the coast forms a bay, which obtained the name of Cape Denbigh.

Several people were seen upon the peninsula, and one man came off in a small canoe. I gave him a knife and a few beads, with which he seemed well pleased. Having made signs to him to bring us something to eat, he immediately left us and paddled towards the shore, but meeting another man coming off, who happened to have two dried salmon, he got them from him, and, on returning to the ship, would give them to nobody but me. Some of our people thought that he had asked for me under the name of Capitane; but in this they were probably mistaken.

Lieutenant Gore being now sent to the peninsula, reported that there was but little fresh water, and that wood was difficult to be got at, by reason of the boats grounding at some distance from the beach. This being the case I stood back to the other shore, and at eight o'clock the next morning, sent all the boats and a party of men, with an officer, to get wood from the place where I had landed two days before.

Next day a family of the natives came near to our wooding party. I know not how many there were at first but I saw only the husband, the wife, and their child, and a fourth person, who bore the human shape and that was all, for he was the most deformed cripple I had ever seen or heard of. The other man was almost blind and neither he nor his wife were such good-looking people as we had sometimes seen amongst the natives of this coast. The under lips of both were bored, and they had in their possession some such glass beads as I had met with before amongst their neighbours. But iron was their beloved article. For four knives, which we had made out of an old iron hoop, I got from them near four hundred pounds weight of fish, which they had caught on this or the preceding day. I gave the child, who was a girl, a few beads, on which the mother burst into tears, then the father, then the cripple, and at last, to complete the concert, the girl herself. But this music continued not long. Before night we had got the ships amply supplied with wood, and had carried on board above twelve tuns of water to each.

Some doubts being still entertained whether the coast we were now upon belonged to an island or the American continent, and the shallowness of the water putting it out of our power to determine this with our ships, I sent Lieutenant King with two boats under his command, to make such searches as might leave no room for a variety of opinions on the subject.

This officer returned from his expedition on the 16th, and reported that he proceeded with the boats about three or four leagues farther than the ships had been able to go, that he then landed on the west side; that from the heights he could see the two coasts join, and the inlet terminate in a small river or creek, before which were banks of sand or mud, and everywhere shoal water.

From the elevated spot on which Mr King surveyed the Sound, he could distinguish many extensive valleys with rivers running through them, well wooded, and bounded by hills of a gentle ascent and moderate height.

In honour of Sir Fletcher Norton, speaker of the House of Commons, and Mr King's near relation, I named this inlet Norton's Sound.

It was now high time to think of leaving these northern regions, and to retire to some place during the winter, where I might procure refreshments for my people, and a small supply of provisions. No place was so conveniently within our reach where we could expect to have our wants relieved as the Sandwich Islands. To them, therefore, I determined to proceed.

On the 2nd of October, at daybreak, we saw the island of Oonalashka, bearing south-east. But as this was to us a new point of view, and the land was obscured by a thick haze, we were not sure of our situation till noon, when the observed latitude determined it. But as all harbours were alike to me, provided they were equally safe and convenient, I hauled into a bay that lies ten miles to the westward of Samganoodha, known by the name of Egoochshac; but we found very deep water, so that we were glad to get out again. The natives, many of whom lived here, visited us at different times, bringing with them dried salmon and other fish, which they exchanged with the seamen for tobacco. But a few days before, every ounce of tobacco that was in the ship had been distributed among them; and the quantity was not half sufficient to answer their demands Notwithstanding this, so improvident a creature is an English sailor, that they were as profuse in making their bargains, as if we had arrived at a port in Virginia.

In the afternoon of the 3rd, we anchored in Samganoodha harbour; and the next morning the carpenters of both ships were set to work to overhaul and repair the ships.

There were great quantities of berries found ashore In order to avail ourselves as much as possible of this useful refreshment, one-third of the people by turns had leave to go and pick them. Considerable quantities of them were also procured from the natives. If there were any seeds of the scurvy in either ship, these berries, and the use of spruce beer which they had to drink every other day, effectually eradicated them.

We also got plenty of fish; at first mostly salmon, both fresh and dried, which the natives brought us. Some of the fresh salmon was in high perfection; we caught a good many salmon trout, and once a halibut that weighed two hundred and fifty-four pounds. The fishery failing, we had recourse to hooks and lines. A boat was sent out every morning, and seldom returned without eight or ten halibut, which were more than sufficient to serve all our people.

On the 8th, I received by the hands of an Oonalashka man, named Derramoushka, a very singular present, considering the place. It was a rye loaf, or rather a pie made in the form of a loaf, for it enclosed some salmon highly seasoned with pepper. This man had the like present for Captain Clerke, and a note for each of us, written in a character which none of us could read. It was natural to suppose that this present was from some Russians now in our neighbourhood, and therefore we sent by the same hand to these our unknown friends, a few bottles of rum, wine, and porter. I also sent along with Derramoushka, Corporal Lediard, of the marines, an intelligent man, in order to gain some farther information, with orders that, if he met with any Russians, he should endeavour to make them understand that we were English, the friends and allies of their nation.

On the 10th, Lediard returned with three Russian seamen, or furriers, who with some others resided at Egoochshac, where they had a dwelling-house, some store-houses, and a sloop of about thirty tons burthen. They were all three well-behaved intelligent men, and very ready to give me all the information I could desire. But for want of an interpreter, we had some difficulty to understand each other.

On the 14th, in the evening, while Mr Webber and I were at a village, at a small distance from Samganoodha, a Russian landed there, who I found was the principal person amongst his countrymen in this and the neighbouring islands. His name was Erasim Gregorioff Sin Ismyloff. He arrived in a canoe carrying three persons, attended by twenty or thirty other canoes, each conducted by one man. I took notice that the first thing they did after landing was to make a small tent for Ismyloff, of materials which they brought with them; and then they made others for themselves of their canoes and paddles, which they covered with grass, so that the people of the village were at no trouble to find them lodging. Ismyloff, having invited us into his tent, set before us some dried salmon and berries, which I was satisfied was the best cheer he had. He appeared to be a sensible, intelligent man, and I felt no small mortification in not being able to converse with him unless by signs, assisted by figures and other characters, which, however, were a very great help. I desired to see him on board the next day, and accordingly he came with all his attendants.

I found that he was very well acquainted with the geography of these parts, and with all the discoveries that had been made in them by the Russians. On seeing the modern maps, he at once pointed out their errors.

From what we could gather from Ismyloff and his countrymen, the Russians have made several attempts to get a footing upon that part of the continent that lies contiguous to Oonalashka and the adjoining islands, but have always been repulsed by the natives, whom they describe as a very treacherous people. They mentioned two or three captains or chief men who had been murdered by them, and some of the Russians showed us wounds which they said they had received there.

He would fain have made me a present of a sea-otter skin which he said was worth eighty roubles at Kamtschatka. However, I thought proper to decline it, but I accepted of some dried fish, and several baskets of the lily or saranne root, which is described at large in the History of Kamtschatka. Next day Mr Ismyloff left us with all his retinue, promising to return in a few days. Accordingly, on the 19th, he made us another visit, and remained with us till the 21st, in the evening, when he took his final leave. To his care I entrusted a letter to the Lords Commissioners of the Admiralty, in which was enclosed a chart of all the northern coasts I had visited. Mr Ismyloff seemed to have abilities that might entitle him to a higher station in life than that in which we found him.

In the morning of the 22nd we made an attempt to get to sea, with the wind at south-east, which miscarried. The following afternoon we were visited by one Jacob Ivanovitch Soposnicoff, a Russian, who commanded a small vessel at Oomanak. This man had a great share of modesty and intelligence.

After we became acquainted with these Russians, some of our gentlemen, at different times, visited their settlement on the island, where they always met with a hearty welcome. This settlement consisted of a dwelling-house and two store-houses. And, besides the Russians, there was a number of the Kamtschadales, and of the natives, as servants or slaves to the former. Some others of the natives, who seemed independent of the Russians, lived at the same place. They all dwell in the same house, the Russians at the upper end, the Kamtschadales in the middle, and the natives at the lower end, where is fixed a large boiler for preparing their food, which consists chiefly of what the sea produces, with the addition of wild roots and berries.

As the island supplies them with food, so it does, in a great measure, with clothing. This consists chiefly of skins, and is perhaps the best they could have. The upper garment is made like our waggoner's frock, and reaches as low as the knee. Besides this, they wear a waistcoat or two, a pair of breeches, a fur cap, and a pair of boots, the soles and upper leathers of which are of Russian leather, but the legs are made of some kind of strong gut.

There are Russians settled upon all the principal islands between Oonalashka and Kamtschatka, for the sole purpose of collecting furs. Their great object is the sea beaver or otter. I never heard them inquire after any other animal, though those whose skins are of inferior value are also made part of their cargo.

It is now time to give some account of the native inhabitants. To all appearance they are the most peaceable, inoffensive people I ever met with. And as to honesty, they might serve as a pattern to the most civilised nation upon earth. But, from what I saw of their neighbours, with whom the Russians have no connection, I doubt whether this was their original disposition, and rather think that it has been the consequence of their present state of subjection.

These people are rather low of stature, but plump and well shaped, with rather short necks, swarthy chubby faces, black eyes, small beards, and long, straight, black hair, which the men wear loose behind, and cut before; but the women tie up in a bunch.

Both sexes wear the same in fashion; the only difference is in the materials. The women's frock is made of seal-skin, and that of the men of the skins of birds, both reaching below the knee. This is the whole dress of the women. But over the frock the men wear another made of gut, which resists water, and has a hood to it, which draws over the head. Some of them wear boots, and all of them have a kind of oval-snouted cap, made of wood, with a rim to admit the head.

They make use of no paint, but the women puncture their faces slightly; and both men and women bore the under lip, to which they fix pieces of bone.

Their food consists of fish, sea animals, birds, roots, and berries, and even of seaweed. They eat almost everything raw. Boiling and broiling were the only methods of cookery that I saw them make use of, and the first was probably learnt from the Russians.

I was once present when the Chief of Oonalashka made his dinner on the raw head of a large halibut, just caught, which he swallowed with as much satisfaction as we should do raw oysters. When he had done, the remains of the head were cut in pieces, and given to the attendants, who tore off the meat with their teeth, and gnawed the bones like so many dogs.

Their method of building is as follows. They dig in the ground an oblong square pit, the length of which seldom exceeds fifty feet, and the breadth twenty; but in general the dimensions are smaller. Over this excavation they form the roof of wood, which the sea throws ashore. This roof is covered first with grass, and then with earth, so that the outward appearance is like a dunghill. In the middle of the roof, towards each end, is left a square opening, by which the light is admitted: one of these openings being for this purpose only, and the other being also used to go in and out by, with the help of a ladder. Round the sides and ends of the huts, the families (for several are lodged together) have their separate apartments, where they sleep and sit at work, not upon benches, but in a kind of concave trench, which is dug all round the inside of the house, and covered with mats, so that this part is kept tolerably decent. But the middle of the house, which is common to all the families, is far otherwise; for, although it be covered with dry grass, it is a receptacle for dirt of every kind.

Their household furniture consists of bowls, spoons, buckets, piggins or cans, matted baskets, and perhaps a Russian kettle or pot. All these utensils are very neatly made, and well formed, and yet we saw no other tools among them but the knife and the hatchet. There are few, if any of them, that do not smoke, chew tobacco, and take snuff; a luxury that bids fair to keep them always poor.

I saw not a fireplace in any one of their houses. They are lighted, as well as heated, by lamps, which are simple, and yet answer the purpose very well. They are made of a flat stone, hollowed on one side like a plate, and about the same size, or rather larger. In the hollow part they put the oil, mixed with a little dry grass, which serves the purpose of a wick.

They produce fire both by collision and by attrition; the former by striking two stones one against another, on one of which a good deal of brimstone is first rubbed. The latter method is with two pieces of wood, one of which is a stick of about eighteen inches in length, and the other a flat piece. The pointed end of the stick they pressed upon the other, whirling it nimbly round as a drill, thus producing fire in a few minutes.

Their canoes are built nearly after the manner of those used by the Greenlanders and Esquimaux, the framing being of slender laths, and the covering of seal-skins. They are about twelve feet long, a foot and a half broad in the middle, and twelve or fourteen inches deep. Upon occasion, they can carry two persons, one of whom is stretched at full length in the canoe, and the other sits in the seat, or round hole, which is nearly in the middle.

Their fishing and hunting implements are all made in great perfection of wood and bone, and differ very little from those used by the Greenlanders, as they are described by Crantz. These people are very expert in striking fish, both in the sea and in rivers. They also make use of hooks and lines, nets and weirs. The hooks are composed of bone, and the lines of sinews.

The fishes which are common to other northern seas are found here, such as whales, grampuses, porpoises, swordfish, halibut, cod, salmon, trout, soles, flat fish, several other sorts of small fish, and there may be many more that we had no opportunity of seeing. Sea-horses are, indeed, in prodigious numbers about the ice; and the sea-otter is, I believe, nowhere found but in this sea. We sometimes saw an animal, with a head like a seal's, that blew after the manner of whales. It was larger than a seal, and its colour was white, with some dark spots. Probably this was the sea-cow or manati.

I think I may venture to assert that sea and water fowls are neither in such numbers, nor in such variety, as with us in the northern parts of the Atlantic Ocean.

The few land birds that we met with are the same with those in Europe; but there may be many others which we had no opportunity of knowing. A very beautiful bird was shot in the woods at Norton Sound, which, I am told, is sometimes found in England, and known by the name of chatterer.

As our excursions and observations were confined wholly to the sea-coast, it is not to be expected that we could know much of the animals or vegetables of the country. There are no deer upon Oonalashka, or upon any other of the islands. Nor have they any domestic animals, not even dogs. Foxes and weasels were the only quadrupeds we saw.

There is a great variety of plants at Oonalashka, and most of them were in flower the latter end of June. The principal one is the saranne, or lily root, which is about the size of a root of garlic; the taste is not disagreeable and we found means to make some good dishes with it.

We must reckon, amongst the food of the natives, some other wild roots; the stalk of a plant resembling angelica; and berries of several different sorts, such as bramble-berries; cranberries; hurtle-berries; heath-berries; a small red berry which, in Newfoundland, is called partridge-berry; and another brown berry unknown to us. This has somewhat of the taste of a sloe, but it is unlike it in every other respect. It is very astringent, if eaten in any quantity. Brandy might be distilled from it.

On the low ground, and in the valleys, is plenty of grass, which grows very thick, and to a great length. I am of opinion that cattle might subsist at Oonalashka all the year round, without being housed.

What their notions are of the Deity, and of a future state, I know not. I am equally unacquainted with their diversions, nothing having been seen that could give us an insight into either.

They are remarkably cheerful and friendly. They do not seem to be long-lived. I nowhere saw a person, man or woman, whom I could suppose to be sixty years of age, and but very few who appeared to be above fifty.

I have frequently remarked how nearly the natives, on this north-west side of America, resemble the Greenlanders and Esquimaux, in various particulars of person, dress, weapons, canoes, and the like. However, I was much less struck with this than with the affinity which we found subsisting between the dialects of the Greenlanders and Esquimaux, and those of Norton's Sound and Oonalashka. From which there is great reason to believe that all these nations are of the same extraction; and if so, there can be little doubt of there being a northern communication of some sort, by sea, between this west side of America and the east side, through Baffin's Bay; which communication, however, may be effectually shut up against ships by ice and other impediments. Such, at least, was my opinion at this time.

In the morning of Monday, the 26th of October, we put to sea from Samganoodha harbour. My intention was now to proceed to the Sandwich Islands, there to spend a few of the winter months, in case we should meet with the necessary refreshments, and then to direct our course to Kamtschatka, so as to endeavour to be there by the middle of May the ensuing summer. In consequence of this resolution, I gave Captain Clerke orders how to proceed in case of separation: appointing the Sandwich Islands for the first place of rendezvous, and the harbour of Petropaulowska in Kamtschatka for the second.

Nothing remarkable happened during our course. At daybreak on the 26th of November, land was seen extending from south south-east to west. We were now satisfied that the group of the Sandwich Islands had been only imperfectly discovered, as those which we had visited in our progress northward all lie to the leeward of our present station.

I bore up and ranged along the coast to the westward. It was not long before we saw people on several parts of the shore, and some houses and plantations. The country seemed to be both well wooded and watered.

At noon, seeing some canoes coming off to us, I brought to. We got from our visitors a quantity of cuttlefish for nails and pieces of iron. They brought very little fruit and roots; but told us that they had plenty of them on their island, as also hogs and fowls. Having no doubt that the people would return to the ships next day with the produce of their country, I kept plying off all night, and in the morning stood close in shore. At first only a few of the natives visited us; but toward noon we had the company of a good many, who brought with them breadfruit, potatoes, taro, or eddy roots, a few plantains, and small pigs; all of which they exchanged for nails and iron tools.

In the afternoon of the 30th, being off the north-east end of the island, several canoes came off to the ships. Most of these belonged to a chief named Terreeoboo, who came in one of them. He made me a present of two or three small pigs; and we got by barter from the other people a little fruit. After a stay of about two hours they all left us, except six or eight of their company, who chose to remain on board. A double sailing canoe came soon after to attend upon them, which we towed astern all night. In the evening we discovered another island to windward, which the natives call Owhyhee.

On the 1st of December, at eight in the morning, finding that we could fetch Owhyhee, I stood for it; and our visitors from another island, called Mowee, not choosing to accompany us, embarked in their canoe, and went ashore.

Next morning we were surprised to see the summits of the mountains on Owhyhee covered with snow. As we drew near the shore, some of the natives came off to us. They were a little shy at first, but we soon enticed some of them on board, and at last prevailed upon them to return to the island and bring off what we wanted.

Having procured a quantity of sugar-cane, and finding a strong decoction of it produced a very palatable beer, I ordered some more to be brewed for our general use. But when the cask was now broached, not one of my crew would even so much as taste it. I myself and the officers continued to make use of it whenever we could get materials for brewing it. A few hops, of which we had some on board, improved it much. It has the taste of new malt beer; and I believe no one will doubt of its being very wholesome. Yet my inconsiderate crew alleged that it was injurious to their health.

Every innovation whatever on board a ship, though ever so much to the advantage of seamen, is sure to meet with their highest disapprobation. Both portable soup and sauerkraut were at first condemned as stuff unfit for human beings. Few commanders have introduced into their ships more novelties, as useful varieties of food and drink, than I have done. It has, however, been in a great measure owing to various little deviations from established practice that I have been able to preserve my people, generally speaking, from that dreadful distemper, the scurvy, which has perhaps destroyed more of our sailors in their peaceful voyages than have fallen by the enemy in military expeditions.

I kept at some distance from the coast till the 13th, when I stood in again; and, after having had some trade with the natives who visited us, returned to sea.

At daybreak a dreadful surf breaking upon the shore, which was not more than half a league distant, it was evident that we had been in the most imminent danger. Nor were we yet in safety, the wind veering more easterly, so that for some time we did but just keep our distance from the coast.

In the afternoon of the 20th, some of the natives came off in their canoes, bringing with them a few pigs and plantains. We continued trading with the people till four in the afternoon, when having got a pretty good supply, we made sail and stretched off to the northward.

I had never met with a behaviour so free from reserve and suspicion in my intercourse with any tribes of savages, as we experienced in the people of this island. It was very common for them to send up into the ship the several articles they brought off for barter; afterward, they would come in themselves, and make their bargains on the quarter-deck. The people of Otaheite, even after our repeated visits, do not care to put so much confidence in us.

On the 23rd, we tacked to the southward, and had hopes of weathering the island. We should have succeeded if the wind had not died away, and left us to the mercy of a great swell which carried us fast toward the land, which was not two leagues distant. At length some light puffs of wind which came with showers of rain, put us out of danger. While we lay as it were becalmed, several of the islanders came off with hogs, fowls, fruit, and roots.

At four in the afternoon, after purchasing everything that the natives had brought off, which was full as much as we had occasion for, we made sail and stretched to the north. At midnight we tacked and stood to the south-east. Upon a supposition that the *Discovery* would see us tack, the signal was omitted; but she did not see us, as we afterwards found, and continued standing to the north; for at daylight next morning she was not in sight. At six in the evening the southernmost extreme of the island bore south-west, the nearest shore seven or eight miles distant, so that we had now succeeded in getting to the windward of the island, which we had aimed at with so much perseverance.

The *Discovery*, however, was not yet to be seen. But the wind as we had it, being very favourable for her to follow us, I concluded that it would not be long before she joined us.

We began to be in want of fresh provision on the 30th. At ten o'clock next morning we were met by the islanders with fruit and roots; but in all the canoes were only three small pigs.

Before daybreak the atmosphere was again loaded with heavy clouds; and the new year was ushered in with very hard rain, which continued at intervals till past ten o'clock. We lay to, trading with the inhabitants till three o'clock in the afternoon; when, having a tolerable supply, we made sail with a view of proceeding to look for the *Discovery*.

The three following days were spent in running down the south-east side of the island.

On the 5th January 1779, in the morning, we passed the south point of the island. On this there stands a pretty large village, the inhabitants of which thronged off to the ship with hogs and women. It was not possible to keep the latter from coming on board. This part of the country, from its appearance, did not seem capable of affording any vegetables. Marks of it having been laid waste by the explosion of a volcano, everywhere presented themselves: the devastation that it had made in this neighbourhood was visible to the naked eye.

Between ten and eleven next morning we saw with pleasure the *Discovery* coming round the south point of the island; and at one in the afternoon she joined us. Captain Clerke then coming on board, informed me that he had cruised four or five days where we were separated, and then plied round the east side of the island; but that, meeting with unfavourable winds, he had been carried to some distance from the coast. He had one of the islanders on board all this time, who had remained there from choice, and had refused to quit the ship, though opportunities had offered.

For several days we kept as usual standing off and on with occasional visits from the natives. At daybreak on the 16th, seeing the appearance of a bay, I sent Mr Bligh with a boat from each ship to examine it, being at this time three leagues off. Canoes now began to arrive from all parts, so that before ten o'clock, there were not fewer than a thousand about the two ships, most of them crowded with people, and well laden with hogs and other productions of the island. One of our visitors took out of the ship a boat's rudder. He was discovered, but too late to recover it. I thought this a good opportunity to show these people the use of firearms, and two or three muskets, and as many four-pounders were fired over the canoe which carried off the rudder. As it was not intended that any of the shot should take effect, the surrounding multitude of natives seemed rather more surprised than frightened. In the evening Mr Bligh returned, and reported that he had found a bay, in which was good anchorage and fresh water. Here I resolved to carry the ships to refit, and supply ourselves with every refreshment the place could afford. Numbers of our visitors requested permission to sleep on board. Curiosity was not the only motive, at least with some; for the next morning several things were missing, which determined me not to entertain so many another night.

At eleven o'clock in the forenoon we anchored in the bay, which is called by the natives Karakakooa. The ships continued to be much crowded with natives, and were surrounded by a multitude of canoes. I had nowhere, in the course of my voyages, seen so numerous a body of people assembled at one place. For besides those in canoes, all the shore was covered with spectators, and many hundreds were swimming round the ships like shoals of fish. We could not but be struck with the singularity of this scene; few now lamented our having failed in our endeavours to find a northern passage homeward last summer. To this disappointment we owed our having it in our power to revisit the Sandwich Islands, and to enrich our voyage with a discovery which, though the last, seemed in many respects to be the most important that had hitherto been made by Europeans throughout the extent of the Pacific Ocean.

While Captain Cook seems to have enjoyed the idea of this discovery, little did he imagine that his labours were so soon to be terminated at this disastrous place, which will ever derive a disgraceful immortality from his sad fate. Here his journal ends; and as we have recorded the principal events of his useful life, we shall detail the melancholy circumstances that led to his lamented death, preserving as nearly as possible the words of his amiable coadjutor Captain King, whose account of the voyage now commences.

Karakakooa Bay is situated on the west side of the island of Owhyhee, in a district called Akona. It is about a mile in depth, and bounded by two low points of land at the distance of half a league from each other. On the north point, which is flat and barren, stands the village of Kowrowa; and in the bottom of the bay, near a grove of tall coconut trees, there is another village of a more considerable size called Kakooa. This bay appearing to Captain Cook a proper place to refit the ships, and lay in an additional supply of water and provisions, we moored on the north side.

As soon as the inhabitants perceived our intention of anchoring in the bay, they came off from the shore in astonishing numbers, and expressed their joy by singing and shouting, and exhibiting a variety of wild and extravagant gestures.

Among the chiefs that came on board the *Resolution* was a young man called Pareea, whom we soon perceived to be a person of great authority. On presenting himself to Captain Cook, he told him that he was *jakanee* to the king of the island, who was at that time engaged on a military expedition at Mowee, and was expected to return within three or four days. A few presents from Captain Cook attached him entirely to our interests, and he became exceedingly useful to us in the management of his countrymen, as we had soon occasion to experience; for we had not been long at anchor, when it was observed that the *Discovery* had such a number of people hanging on one side, as occasioned her to heel considerably; and that the men were unable to keep off the crowds which continued pressing into her. Captain Cook being apprehensive that she might suffer some injury, pointed out the danger to Pareea, who immediately went to their assistance, cleared the ship of its encumbrances, and drove away the canoes that surrounded her.

The authority of the chiefs over the inferior people appeared, from this incident, to be of the most despotic kind. A similar instance of it happened the same day on board the *Resolution*, where the crowd being so great as to impede the necessary business of the ship, we were obliged to have recourse to the assistance of Kaneena, another of their chiefs, who had likewise attached himself to Captain Cook. The inconvenience we laboured under being made known, he immediately ordered his countrymen to quit the vessel; and we were not a little surprised to see him jump overboard without a moment's hesitation.

Both these chiefs were men of strong and well-proportioned bodies, and of countenances remarkably pleasing; Kaneena, especially, was one of the finest men I ever saw. He was about six feet high, had regular and expressive features, with lively dark eyes; his carriage was easy, firm, and graceful.

The inhabitants had hitherto behaved with great fairness and honesty, but we now found the case exceedingly altered. The immense crowd of islanders which blocked up every part of the ships, not only afforded frequent opportunity of pilfering, without risk of discovery, but our inferiority in number held forth a prospect of escaping with impunity in case of detection. Another circumstance to which we attributed this alteration in their behaviour, was the presence and encouragement of their chiefs; for generally tracing the booty into the possession of some men of consequence, we had the strongest reason to suspect that these depredations were commited at their instigation.

Soon after the *Resolution* had got into her station, our two friends Pareea and Kaneena brought on board a third chief, named Koah, who, we were told, was a priest, and had been in his youth a distinguished warrior. He was a little old man, of an emaciated figure; his eyes exceedingly sore and red, and his body covered with a white leprous scurf, the effects of an immoderate use of the ava. Being led into the cabin, he approached Captain Cook with great veneration, and threw over his shoulders a piece of red cloth which he had brought along with him. Then stepping a few paces back, he made an offering of a small pig, which he held in his hand, whilst he pronounced a discourse that lasted for a considerable time.

When this ceremony was over, Koah dined with Captain Cook, eating plentifully of what was set before him; but, like the rest of the inhabitants of the islands in these seas, could scarcely be prevailed on to taste a second time our wine or spirits. In the evening Captain Cook, attended by Mr Bayly and myself, accompanied him on shore. We landed at the beach, and were received by four men who carried wands tipped with dog's hair, and marched before us, pronouncing with a loud voice a short sentence, in which we could only distinguish the word *Orono*.[1] The crowd which had been collected on the shore retired at our approach, and not a person was to be seen except a few lying prostrate on the ground, near the huts of the adjoining village.

Before I proceed to relate the adoration that was paid to Captain Cook, and the peculiar ceremonies with which he was received on this fatal island, it will be necessary to describe a *morai*, or burying-

1 Captain Cook generally went by this name amongst the natives of Owhyhee; but we could never learn its precise meaning, though it was certainly a title of religious veneration.

place, situated at the south side of the beach at Kakooa. It was a square solid pile of stones, about forty yards long, twenty broad, and fourteen in height. The top was flat and well paved, and surrounded by a wooden rail, on which were fixed the skulls of the captives sacrificed on the death of their chiefs. In the centre of the area stood a ruinous old building of wood, connected with the rail on each side by a stone wall, which divided the whole space into two parts. On the side next the country were five poles, upwards of twenty feet high, supporting an irregular kind of scaffold; on the opposite side, toward the sea, stood two small houses, with a covered communication.

We were conducted by Koah to the top of this pile, by an easy ascent. At the entrance we saw two large wooden images, with features violently distorted, and a long piece of carved wood, of a conical form inverted, rising from the top of their heads; the rest was without form, and wrapped round with red cloth. We were here met by a tall young man with a long beard, who presented Captain Cook to the images; and after chanting a kind of hymn, in which he was joined by Koah, they led us to that end of the *morai* where the five poles were fixed. At the foot of them were twelve images, ranged in a semicircular form, and before the middle figure stood a high stand or table, on which lay a putrid hog, and under it pieces of sugar-cane, coconuts, breadfruit, plantains, and sweet potatoes. Koah having placed the Captain under this stand, took down the hog, and held it toward him; and after having a second time addressed him in a long speech, pronounced with much vehemence and rapidity, he let it fall on the ground, and led him to the scaffolding, which they began to climb together, not without great risk of falling. At this time we saw, coming in solemn procession, at the entrance of the top of the *morai*, ten men carrying a live hog, and a large piece of red cloth. Being advanced a few paces, they stopped, and prostrated themselves; and Kaireekeea, the young man above mentioned, went to them, and receiving the cloth, carried it to Koah, who wrapped it round the Captain, and afterward offered him the hog, which was brought by Kaireekeea with the same ceremony.

Whilst Captain Cook was aloft, in this awkward situation, swathed round with red cloth, and with difficulty keeping his hold amongst the pieces of rotten scaffolding, Kaireekeea and Koah began their office, chanting sometimes in concert, and sometimes alternately. This lasted a considerable time; at length Koah let the hog drop, when he and the Captain descended together. He then led him to the images before mentioned, and having said something to each in a sneering tone, snapped his fingers at them as he passed, he brought him to that in the centre, which, from its being covered with red cloth, appeared to be in greater estimation than the rest. Before this figure he prostrated himself and kissed it, desiring Captain Cook to do the same, who suffered himself to be directed by Koah throughout the whole of this ceremony.

We were now led back into the other division of the *morai*, where there was a space ten or twelve feet square, sunk about three feet below the level of the area. Into this we descended, and Captain Cook was seated between two wooden idols, Koah supporting one of his arms, while I was desired to support the other. At this time arrived a second procession of natives carrying a baked hog and a pudding, some breadfruit, coconuts, and other vegetables which were presented as before.

When this offering was concluded, the natives sat down, fronting us, and began to cut up the baked hog, to peel the vegetables, and break the coconuts, whilst others employed themselves in brewing the ava, which is done by chewing it in the same manner as at the Friendly Islands. Kaireekeea then took part of the kernel of a coconut which he chewed, and wrapped it in a piece of cloth, rubbed with it the captain's face, head, hands, arms, and shoulders. The ava was then handed round, and after we had tasted it, Koah and Pareea began to pull the flesh of the hog in pieces, and to put it into our mouths. I had no great objection to be fed by Pareea, who was very cleanly in his person; but Captain Cook, who was served by Koah, recollecting the putrid hog, could not swallow a morsel; and his reluctance, as may be supposed, was not diminished, when the old man, according to his own mode of civility, had chewed it for him.

When this last ceremony was finished, which Captain Cook put an end to as soon as he decently could, we quitted the *morai*, after distributing amongst the people some pieces of iron and other trifles, with which they seemed highly gratified. The men with wands conducted us to the boats, repeating the same words as before. The people again retired, and the few that remained, prostrated themselves as we passed along the shore. We immediately went on board, our minds full of what we had seen, and extremely well satisfied with the good dispositions of our new friends, whose respect to the person of Captain Cook seemed approaching to adoration.

The next morning I went on shore with a guard of eight marines, including the corporal and lieutenant, having orders to erect the observatory in such a situation as might best enable me to super-intend and protect the waterers and the other working parties that were to be on shore. As we were viewing a spot conveniently situated for this purpose in the middle of the village, Pareea offered to pull down some houses that would have obstructed our observa-tions. However, we thought it proper to decline this offer, and fixed on a field of sweet potatoes adjoining to the *morai*, which was readily granted us; and the priests, to prevent the intrusion of the natives, immediately consecrated the place by fixing their wands round the wall by which it was enclosed.

No canoes ever presumed to land near us; the natives sat on the wall, but none offered to come within the tabooed space, till he had obtained our permission. But though the men at our request would come across the field with provisions, yet not all our endeavours could prevail on the women to approach us. This circumstance afforded no small matter of amusement to our friends on board, where the crowds of people, and particularly of women that continued to flock thither, obliged them almost every hour to clear the vessel, in order to have room to do the necessary duties of the ship.

From the 19th to the 24th, when Pareea and Koah left us to attend Terreeoboo, who had landed on some other part of the island, nothing very material happened on board.

We had not been long settled at the observatory before we discovered in our neighbourhood the habitations of a society of priests, whose regular attendance at the *morai* had excited our curiosity. Their huts stood round a pond of water, and were surrounded by a grove of coconut trees, which separated them from the beach and the rest of the village, and gave the place an air of religious retirement. On my acquainting Captain Cook with these circumstances, he resolved to pay them a visit; and, as he expected, was received in the same manner as before.

During the rest of the time we remained in the bay, whenever

Captain Cook came on shore he was attended by one of these priests, who went before him, giving notice that the *Orono* had landed, and ordering the people to prostrate themselves. The same person also constantly accompanied him on the water, standing in the bow of the boat with a wand in his hand, and giving notice of his approach to the natives who were in canoes, on which they immediately left off paddling, and lay down on their faces till he had passed.

The civilities of this society were not, however, confined to mere ceremony and parade. Our party on shore received from them every day a constant supply of hogs and vegetables, more than sufficient for our subsistence; and several canoes loaded with provisions were sent to the ships with the same punctuality. No return was ever demanded, or even hinted at in the most distant manner. Their presents were made with a regularity more like the discharge of a religious duty than the effect of mere liberality.

As everything relating to the character and behaviour of this people must be interesting to the reader, on account of the tragedy that was afterwards acted here; it will be proper to acquaint him, that we had not always so much reason to be satisfied with the conduct of the warrior chiefs, or *earees*, as with that of our priests. In all our dealings with the former, we found them sufficiently attentive to their own interests; and besides their habit of stealing, which may admit of some excuse from the universality of the practice amongst the islanders of these seas, they make use of other artifices equally dishonourable.

On the 24th we were a good deal surprised to find that no canoes were suffered to put off from the shore, and that the natives kept close to their houses. After several hours' suspense, we learned that the bay was tabooed, and all intercourse with us interdicted, on account of the arrival of Terreeoboo. In the afternoon of next day, Terreeoboo visited the ships in a private manner, attended only by one canoe, in which were his wife and children. He stayed on board till near ten o'clock, when he returned to the village of Kowrowa.

The next day about noon, the king in a large canoe, attended by two others, set out from the village, and paddled toward the ship in great state. Their appearance was grand and magnificent. In the first canoe was Terreeoboo and his chiefs, dressed in their rich feathered cloaks and helmets, and armed with long spears and daggers; in the second came the venerable Kaoo, the chief of the priests and his brethren, with their idols displayed on red cloth. The third canoe was filled with hogs and various sorts of vegetables. As they went along, the priests in the centre canoe sung their hymns with great solemnity; and, after paddling round the ships, instead of going on board as we expected, they made toward the shore at the beach where we were stationed.

As soon as I saw them approaching, I ordered out our little guard to receive the king; and Captain Cook perceiving that he was going on shore, followed him, and arrived nearly at the same time. We conducted them into the tent, where they had scarcely been seated when the king rose up, and in a very graceful manner threw over the captain's shoulders the cloak he himself wore, put a feathered helmet upon his head, and a curious fan into his hand. He also spread at his feet five or six other cloaks, all exceedingly beautiful, and of the greatest value. His attendants then brought four very large hogs, with sugar-canes, coconuts, and breadfruit; and this part of the ceremony was concluded by the king's exchanging names with Captain Cook, which, amongst all the islanders of the Pacific Ocean, is esteemed the strongest pledge of friendship. A procession of priests with a venerable old personage at their head, now appeared, followed by a long train of men leading large hogs, and others carrying plantains, sweet potatoes, etc. By the looks and gestures of Kaireekeea, I immediately knew the old man to be the chief of the priests on whose bounty we had so long subsisted. He had a piece of red cloth in his hands which he wrapped round Captain Cook's shoulders, and afterward presented him with a small pig in the usual form.

As soon as the formalities of the meeting were over, Captain Cook carried Terreeoboo, and as many chiefs as the pinnace could hold, on board the *Resolution*. They were received with every mark of respect that could be shown them; and Captain Cook in return for the feathered cloak, put a linen shirt on the king, and girt his own hanger round him. The ancient Kaoo, and about half a dozen more old chiefs remained on shore, and took up their abode at the priests' houses. During all this time not a canoe was seen in the bay, and the natives either kept within their huts, or lay prostrate on the ground.

The quiet and inoffensive behaviour of the natives having taken away every apprehension of danger, we did not hesitate to trust ourselves amongst them at all times, and in all situations. The officers of both ships went daily up the country in small parties, or even singly, and frequently remained out the whole night. It would be endless to recount all the instances of kindness and civility which we received upon those occasions. Wherever we went, the people flocked about us, eager to offer every assistance in their power, and highly gratified if their services were accepted.

The satisfaction we derived from their gentleness and hospitality was, however, frequently interrupted by that propensity to stealing which they have in common with all the other islanders of these seas. This circumstance was the more distressing, as it sometimes obliged us to have recourse to acts of severity, which we should willingly have avoided, if the necessity of the case had not absolutely called for them.

On the 28th, Captain Clerke, whose ill health confined him for the most part on board, paid Terreeoboo his first visit at his hut on shore. He was received with the same formalities as were observed with Captain Cook; and on his coming away, though the visit was quite unexpected, he received a present of thirty large hogs, and as much fruit and roots as his crew could consume in a week.

As we had not yet seen anything of their sports or athletic exercises, the natives, at the request of some of our officers, entertained us this evening with a boxing-match. Though these games were much inferior, as well in point of solemnity and magnificence, as in the skill and powers of the combatants, to what we had seen exhibited at the Friendly Islands, yet, as they differed in some particulars, it may not be improper to give a short account of them. We found a vast concourse of people assembled on a level spot of ground, at a little distance from our tents. A long space was left vacant in the midst of them, at the upper end of which sat the judges, under three standards, from which hung slips of cloth of various colours, the skins of two wild geese, a few small birds, and bunches of feathers. When the sports were ready to begin, the signal was given by the judges, and immediately two combatants appeared. They came forward slowly, lifting up their feet very high behind and drawing their hands along the soles. As they approached, they frequently eyed each other from head to foot in a contemptuous manner, casting several arch looks at the spectators, straining their muscles, and using a variety of affected gestures. Being advanced within reach of each other, they stood with both arms held out straight before their faces, at which part all their blows were aimed. They struck in what appeared to our eyes an awkward manner, with a full swing of the arm, made no attempt to parry, but eluded their adversary's attack by an inclination of the body, or by retreating. The battle was quickly decided, for if either of them was knocked down, or even fell by accident, he was considered as vanquished, and the victor expressed his triumph by a variety of gestures, which usually excited, as was intended, a loud laugh among the spectators. As these games were given at our desire, we found it was universally expected that we should have borne our part in them; but our people, though much pressed by the natives, turned a deaf ear to their challenge, remembering full well the blows they got at the Friendly Islands.

This day died William Watman, a seaman of the gunner's crew, who, with the sincerest attachment, had followed Captain Cook's fortunes for a number of years.

At the request of the king of the island, he was buried on the *morai*, and the ceremony was performed with as much solemnity as our situation permitted. Old Kaoo and his brethren were spectators, and preserved the most profound silence and attention whilst the service was reading. When we began to fill up the grave, they approached it with great reverence, threw in a dead pig, some coconuts and plantains, and for three nights afterwards they surrounded it, sacrificing hogs, and performing their usual ceremonies of hymns and prayers, which continued till daybreak.

The ships being in great want of fuel, the Captain desired me, on the 2nd of February, to treat with the priests for the purchase of the rail that surrounded the top of the *morai*. I must confess I had at first some doubt about the decency of this proposal, and was apprehensive that even the bare mention of it might be considered by them as a piece of shocking impiety. In this, however, I found myself mistaken. Not the smallest surprise was expressed at the application, and the wood was readily given, even without stipulating for anything in return.

Terreeoboo and his chiefs had, for some days past, been very inquisitive about the time of our departure. This circumstance had excited in me a great curiosity to know what opinion this people had formed of us, and what were their ideas respecting the cause and objects of our voyage. I took some pains to satisfy myself on these points, but could never learn anything farther than that they imagined we came from some country where provisions had failed, and that our visit to them was merely for the purpose of filling our bellies. Indeed, the meagre appearance of some of our crew, the hearty appetites with which we sat down to their fresh provisions, and our great anxiety to purchase and carry off as much as we were able, led them naturally enough to such a conclusion. It was ridiculous enough to see them stroking the sides and patting the bellies of the sailors (who were certainly much improved in the sleekness of their looks during our short stay in the island), and telling them, partly by signs and partly by words, that it was time for them to go, but if they would come again the next breadfruit season, they should be better able to supply their wants. On our telling Terreeoboo we should leave the island the next day but one, we observed that a sort of proclamation was immediately made through the villages, to require the people to bring in their hogs and vegetables for the king to present to the *Orono* on his departure.

The next day being fixed for our departure, Terreeoboo invited Captain Cook and myself to attend him on the 3rd, to the place where Kaoo resided. On our arrival, we found the ground covered with parcels of cloth, a vast quantity of red and yellow feathers tied to the fibres of coconut husks, and a great number of hatchets and other pieces of ironware that had been got in barter from us. At a little distance from these lay an immense quantity of vegetables of every kind, and near them was a very large herd of hogs. At first we imagined the whole to be intended as a present for us, till Kaireekeea informed me that it was a gift, or tribute from the people of that district to the king; and accordingly, as soon as we were seated, they brought all the bundles, and laid them severally at Terreeoboo's feet, who gave all the hogs and vegetables, and two-thirds of the cloth, to Captain Cook and myself. We were astonished at the value and magnitude of this present, which far exceeded everything of the kind we had seen, either at the Friendly or Society Islands.

The same day we quitted the *morai*, and got the tents and

astronomical instruments on board. The charm of the taboo was now removed; and here I hope I may be permitted to relate a trifling occurrence, in which I was principally concerned. Having had the command of the party on shore, during the whole time we were in the bay, I had an opportunity of becoming well acquainted with the natives.

I spared no endeavours to conciliate their affections and gain their esteem; and had the good fortune to succeed so far, that, when the time of our departure was made known, I was strongly solicited to remain behind, not without offers of the most flattering kind. When I excused myself by saying that Captain Cook would not give his consent, they proposed that I should retire into the mountains, where they said they would conceal me, till after the departure of the ships; and on my farther assuring them that the Captain would not leave the bay without me, Terreeoboo and Kaoo waited upon Captain Cook, whose son they supposed I was, with a formal request that I might be left behind. The Captain, to avoid giving a positive refusal to an offer so kindly intended, told them that he could not part with me at that time, but that he should return to the island next year, and would then endeavour to settle the matter to their satisfaction.

Early in the morning of the 4th of February, we unmoored and sailed out of the bay, and were followed by a great number of canoes. Captain Cook's design was to finish the survey of Owhyhee before he visited the other islands, in hopes of meeting with a road better sheltered than the bay we had just left.

We had calm weather this and the following day, which made our progress to the northward very slow. In the morning of the 6th, having passed the westernmost point of the island, we found ourselves abreast of a deep bay, called by the natives Toe-yah-yah. We had great hopes that this bay would furnish us with a safe and commodious harbour, as we saw to the north-east several fine streams of water. On examination, however, it was found unfit for our purpose.

After encountering some gales of wind with immaterial damage, on the 8th, at daybreak, we found that the foremast had given way. This accident induced Captain Cook to return to Karakakooa Bay. On the 10th, the weather became moderate, and a few canoes came off to us, from which we learnt that the late storm had done much mischief, and that several large canoes had been lost. During the remainder of the day we kept beating to windward, and before night we were within a mile of the bay; but not choosing to run on while it was dark, we stood off and on till daylight next morning, when we dropped anchor nearly in the same place as before.

We were employed the whole of the 11th, and part of the 12th, in getting out the foremast, and sending it, with the carpenters, on shore. As these repairs were likely to take up several days, Mr Bayly and myself got the astronomical apparatus on shore the 12th, and pitched our tents on the *morai*, having with us a guard of a corporal and six marines. We renewed our friendly correspondence with the priests, who, for the greater security of the workmen and their tools, tabooed the place where the mast lay, sticking their wands round it as before. The sailmakers were also sent on shore, to repair the damages which had taken place in their department during the late gales.

Upon coming to anchor, we were surprised to find our reception very different from what it had been on our first arrival; no shouts, no bustle, no confusion; but a solitary bay, with only here and there a canoe stealing close along the shore. The impulse of curiosity, which had before operated to so great a degree, might now, indeed, be supposed to have ceased, but the hospitable treatment we had invariably met with, and the friendly footing on which we parted, gave us some reason to expect that they would again have flocked about us with great joy on our return.

We were forming various conjectures upon the occasion of this extraordinary appearance, when our anxiety was at length relieved by the return of a boat which had been sent on shore, and brought us word that Terreeoboo was absent, and had left the bay under the taboo. Though this account appeared very satisfactory to most of us, yet others were of opinion that the interdiction of all intercourse with us, on pretence of the king's absence, was only to give him time to consult the chiefs in what manner it might be proper to treat us. Whether these suspicions were well founded, or the account given by the natives was the truth, we were never able to ascertain. For though it is not improbable that our sudden return, for which they could see no apparent cause, and the necessity of which we afterwards found it very difficult to make them comprehend, might occasion some alarm; yet the unsuspicious conduct of Terreeoboo, who, on his supposed arrival the next morning, came immediately to visit Captain Cook, and the consequent return of the natives to their former friendly intercourse with us, are strong proofs that they neither meant nor apprehended any change of conduct.

Toward the evening of the 13th, however, the officer who commanded the watering party of the *Discovery* came to inform me that several chiefs had assembled at the well near the beach, driving away the natives, whom we had hired to assist the sailors in rolling down the casks to the shore. He told me at the same time that he thought their behaviour extremely suspicious, and that they meant to give him some farther disturbance. At his request, therefore, I sent a marine along with him, but suffered him to take only his side-arms. In a short time the officer returned, and on his acquainting me that the islanders had armed themselves with stones, and were grown very tumultuous, I went myself to the spot, attended by a marine, with his musket. Seeing us approach, they threw away their stones, and on my speaking to some of the chiefs, the mob were driven away, and those who chose it were suffered to assist in filling the casks.

Soon after our return to the tents, we were alarmed by a continued fire of muskets from the *Discovery*, which we observed to be directed at a canoe that we saw paddling toward the shore in great haste, pursued by one of our small boats. We immediately concluded that the firing was in consequence of some theft, and Captain Cook ordered me to follow him with a marine armed, and to endeavour to seize the people as they came on shore. Accordingly we ran toward the place where we supposed the canoe would land, but were too late; the people having quitted it, and made their escape into the country before our arrival; but the goods stolen had been recovered.

During our absence a difference of a more serious and unpleasant nature had happened. The officer who had been sent in the small boat, and was returning on board with the goods, which had been restored, observing Captain Cook and me engaged in the pursuit of the offenders, thought it his duty to seize the canoe, which was left drawn up on the shore. Unfortunately this canoe belonged to Pareea, who arriving at the same moment from on board the *Discovery*, claimed his property with many protestations of his innocence. The officer refusing to give it up, and being joined by the crew of the pinnace, a scuffle ensued, in which Pareea was knocked down by a violent blow upon his head with an oar. The natives, who were collected about the spot, and had hitherto been peaceable spectators, immediately attacked our people with such a shower of stones as forced them to retreat with great precipitation, and swim off to a rock at some distance from the shore. The pinnace was immediately ransacked by the islanders; and but for the timely interposition of Pareea, who seemed to have recovered from the blow, and forgot it at the same instant, would soon have been entirely demolished. Having driven away the crowd, he made signs to our people that they might come and take possession of the pinnace, and that he would endeavour to get back the things which had been taken out of it. After their departure he followed them in his canoe with a midshipman's cap, some other trifling articles of the plunder, and with much apparent concern at what had happened, asked if the *Orono* would kill him, and whether he would permit him to come on board next day? On being assured that he should be well received, he joined noses (as their custom is) with the officers, in token of friendship, and paddled over to the village of Kowrowa.

When Captain Cook was informed of what had passed, he expressed much uneasiness at it, and, as we were returning on board, 'I am afraid,' said he, 'that these people will oblige me to use some violent measures; for (he added) they must not be left to imagine that they have gained an advantage over us.'

Next morning, the 14th, at daylight, I went on board the *Resolution* for the time-keeper, and in my way was hailed by the *Discovery*, and informed that their cutter had been stolen during the night from the buoy where it was moored.

When I arrived on board I found the marines arming, and Captain Cook loading his double-barrelled gun. It had been his usual practice whenever anything of consequence was lost at any of the islands in this ocean, to get the king or some of the principal *earees* on board, and to keep them as hostages till it was restored. This method, which had been always attended with success, he meant to pursue on the present occasion.

It was between seven and eight o'clock when we quitted the ship together; Captain Cook in the pinnace, having Mr Phillips and nine marines with him, and myself in the small boat. The last orders I received from him were, to quiet the minds of the natives on our side of the bay, by assuring them they should not be hurt; to keep my people together, and to be on my guard. We then parted; the Captain went toward Kowrowa, where the king resided, and I proceeded to the beach. My first care on going ashore was, to give strict orders to the marines to remain within the tent, to load their pieces with ball, and not to quit their arms. Afterwards I took a walk to the huts of old Kaoo and the priests, and explained to them as well as I could the object of the hostile preparations, which had exceedingly alarmed them. I found that they had already heard of the cutter's being stolen, and I assured them, that though Captain Cook was resolved to recover it, and to punish the authors of the theft, yet that they, and the people of the village on our side, need not be under the smallest apprehension of suffering any evil from us. Kaoo asked me with great earnestness if Terreeoboo was to be hurt. I assured him he was not; and both he and the rest of his brethren seemed much satisfied with this assurance.

In the meantime Captain Cook having called off the launch, which was stationed at the north point of the bay, and taken it along with him, proceeded to Kowrowa, and landed with the lieutenant and nine marines. He immediately marched to the village, where he was received with the usual marks of respect, the people prostrating themselves before him, and bringing their accustomed offerings of small hogs. Finding that there was no suspicion of his design, his next step was to inquire for Terreeoboo, and the two boys, his sons, who had been his constant guests on board the *Resolution*. In a short time the boys returned along with the natives, who had been sent in search of them, and immediately led Captain Cook to the house where the king had slept. They found the old man just awoke from sleep; and after a short conversation about the loss of the cutter, from which Captain Cook was convinced that he was in nowise privy to it, he invited him to return in the boat, and spend the day on board the *Resolution*. To this proposal the king readily consented, and immediately got up to accompany him.

Things were in this prosperous train; the two boys being already in the pinnace, and the rest of the party having advanced near the waterside, when an elderly woman, called Kanee-kaba-reea, the mother of the boys, and one of the king's favourite wives, came after him, and with many tears and entreaties, besought him not to go on board. At the same time two chiefs, who came along with her, laid hold of him, and insisting that he should go no farther, forced him to sit down. The natives, who were collecting in prodigious numbers along the shore, and had probably been alarmed by the firing of the great guns, and the appearances of hostility in the bay, began to throng round Captain Cook and their king. In this situation, the lieutenant of marines observing that his men were huddled close together in the crowd, and thus incapable of using their arms, if any occasion should require it, proposed to the Captain to draw them up along the rocks close to the water's edge; and the crowd readily making way for them to pass, they were drawn up in a line at the distance of about thirty yards from the place where the king was sitting.

All this time the old king remained on the ground with the strongest marks of terror and dejection in his countenance; Captain Cook, not willing to abandon the object for which he had come on shore, continuing to urge him in the most pressing manner to proceed, whilst on the other hand, whenever the king appeared inclined to follow him, the chiefs, who stood round him, interposed, at first with prayers and entreaties, but afterwards having recourse to force and violence, insisted on his staying where he was. Captain Cook therefore finding that the alarm had spread too generally, and that it was in vain to think any longer of getting him off without bloodshed, at last gave up the point, observing to Mr Phillips, that it would be impossible to compel him to go on board without running the risk of killing a great number of the inhabitants.

Though the enterprise, which had carried Captain Cook on shore, had now failed and was abandoned, yet his person did not appear to have been in the least danger, till an accident happened which gave a fatal turn to the affair. The boats, which had been stationed across the bay, having fired at some canoes that were attempting to get out, unfortunately had killed a chief of the first rank. The news of his death arrived at the village where Captain Cook was, just as he had left the king and was walking slowly toward the shore. The ferment it occasioned was very conspicuous; the women and children were immediately sent off, and the men put on their war mats, and armed themselves with spears and stones. One of the natives, having in his hands a stone and a long iron spike (which they called a *pahooa*), came up to the Captain, flourishing his weapon by way of defiance, and threatening to throw the stone. The Captain desired him to desist, but the man persisting in his insolence, he was at length provoked to fire a load of small shot. The man having his mat on, which the shot was not able to penetrate, this had no other effect than to irritate and encourage them. Several stones were thrown at the marines, and one of the *earees* attempted to stab Mr Phillips with his *pahooa*, but failed in the attempt, and received from him a blow with the butt-end of his musket. Captain Cook now fired his second barrel loaded with ball, and killed one of the foremost of the natives. A general attack with stones immediately followed, which was answered by a discharge of musketry from the marines and the people in the boats. The islanders, contrary to the expectations of everyone, stood the fire with great firmness; and before the marines had time to reload, they broke in upon them with dreadful shouts and yells. What followed was a scene of the utmost horror and confusion.

Four of the marines were cut off amongst the rocks in their retreat, and fell a sacrifice to the fury of the enemy; three more were dangerously wounded, and the lieutenant, who had received a stab between the shoulders with a *pahooa*, having fortunately reserved his fire, shot the man who had wounded him just as he was going to repeat his blow. Our unfortunate commander, the last time he was seen distinctly, was standing at the water's edge, and calling out to the boats to cease firing and to pull in. Whilst he faced the natives none of them had offered him any violence, but having turned about to give his orders to the boats, he was stabbed in the back and fell with his face into the water. On seeing him fall, the islanders set up a great shout, and his body was immediately dragged on shore and surrounded by the enemy, who, snatching the dagger out of each other's hands, showed a savage eagerness to have a share in his destruction.

Thus fell our great and excellent commander! After a life of so much distinguished and successful enterprise, his death, as far as regards himself, cannot be reckoned premature, since he lived to finish the great work for which he seems to have been designed, and was rather removed from the enjoyment, than cut off from the acquisition of glory. How sincerely his loss was felt and lamented by those who had so long found their general security in his skill and conduct, and every consolation under their hardships in his tenderness and humanity, it is neither necessary nor possible for me to describe, much less shall I attempt to paint the horror with which we were struck, and the universal dejection and dismay which followed so dreadful and unexpected a calamity.

It has been already related that four of the marines who attended Captain Cook were killed by the islanders on the spot. The rest, with Mr Phillips their lieutenant, threw themselves into the water and escaped, under cover of a small fire from the boats. On this occasion a remarkable instance of gallant behaviour, and of affection for his men, was shown by that officer. For he had scarcely got into the boat, when seeing one of the marines, who was a bad swimmer, struggling in the water, and in danger of being taken by the enemy, he immediately jumped into the sea to his assistance, though much wounded himself, and after receiving a blow on the head from a stone, which had nearly sent him to the bottom, he caught the man by the hair and brought him safe off.

As soon as the general consternation which the news of this calamity occasioned throughout both crews had a little subsided, their attention was called to our party at the *morai*, where the mast and sails were on shore, with a guard of only six marines. It is impossible for me to describe the emotions of my own mind, during the time these transactions had been carrying on at the other side of the bay. Being at the distance only of a short mile from the village of Kowrowa, we could see distinctly an immense crowd collected on the spot where Captain Cook had just before landed. We heard the firing of the musketry, and could perceive some extraordinary bustle and agitation in the multitude. We afterwards saw the natives flying, the boats retire from the shore, and passing and repassing, in great stillness, between the ships. I must confess that my heart soon misgave me. Where a life so dear and valuable was concerned, it was impossible not to be alarmed by appearances both new and threatening.

My first care, on hearing the muskets fired, was to assure the people, who were assembled in considerable numbers round the wall of our consecrated field, and seemed equally at a loss with ourselves how to account for what they had seen and heard, that they should not be molested; and that, at all events, I was desirous of continuing on peaceable terms with them. We remained in this posture till the boats had returned on board, when Captain Clerke, observing through his telescope that we were surrounded by the natives, and apprehending they meant to attack us, ordered two four-pounders to be fired at them. Fortunately these guns, though well aimed, did no mischief, and yet gave the natives a convincing proof of their power. One of the balls broke a coconut tree in the middle, under which a party of them were sitting; and the other shivered a rock that stood in an exact line with them. As I had just before given them the strongest assurances of their safety, I was exceedingly mortified at this act of hostility, and, to prevent a repetition of it, immediately despatched a boat to acquaint Captain Clerke that at present I was on the most friendly terms with the natives, and that, if occasion should hereafter arise for altering my conduct toward them, I would hoist a jack as a signal for him to afford us all the assistance in his power.

We expected the return of the boat with the utmost impatience, and after remaining a quarter of an hour under the most torturing anxiety and suspense, our fears were at length confirmed by the arrival of Mr Bligh with orders to strike the tents as quickly as possible, and to send the sails that were repairing on board. Just at the same moment, our friend Kaireekeea, having also received intelligence of the death of Captain Cook from a native who had arrived from the other side of the bay, came to me with great sorrow and dejection in his countenance to inquire if it was true.

Our situation was at this time extremely critical and important. Not only our own lives, but the event of the expedition, and the return of at least one of the ships, being involved in the same common danger. We had the mast of the *Resolution* and the greatest part of our sails on shore, under the protection of only six marines – their loss would have been irreparable; and though the natives had not as yet shown the smallest disposition to molest us, yet it was impossible to answer for the alteration which the news of the transaction at Kowrowa might produce. I therefore thought it prudent to dissemble my belief of the death of Captain Cook, and to desire Kaireekeea to discourage the report, lest either the fear of our resentment, or the successful example of their countrymen, might lead them to seize the favourable opportunity which at this time offered itself of giving us a second blow.

Having placed the marines on the top of the *morai*, which formed a strong and advantageous post, and left the command with Mr Bligh, giving him the most positive directions to act entirely on the defensive, I went on board the *Discovery*, in order to represent to Captain Clerke the dangerous situation of our affairs. As soon as I quitted the spot the natives began to annoy our people with stones, and I had scarcely reached the ship before I heard the firing of the marines. I therefore returned instantly on shore, where I found things growing every moment more alarming. The natives were arming and putting on their mats, and their numbers increased very fast. I could also perceive several large bodies marching towards us along the cliff which separates the village of Kakooa from the north side of the bay, where the village of Kowrowa is situated.

They began at first to attack us with stones from behind the walls of their enclosures, and finding no resistance on our part they soon grew more daring. A few resolute fellows having crept along the beach under cover of the rocks, suddenly made their appearance at the foot of the *morai* with a design, as it seemed, of storming it on the side next the sea, which was its only accessible part, and were not dislodged till after they had stood a considerable number of shot, and seen one of their party fall.

About this time, a strong reinforcement from both ships having landed, the natives retreated behind their walls; which giving me access to our friendly priests, I sent one of them to endeavour to bring their countrymen to some terms, and to propose to them that if they would desist from throwing stones I would not permit our men to fire. This truce was agreed to, and we were suffered to launch the mast and carry off the sails and our astronomical apparatus unmolested. As soon as we had quitted the *morai* they took possession of it and some of them threw a few stones, but without doing us any mischief.

It was half an hour past eleven o'clock when I got on board the *Discovery*, where I found no decisive plan had been adopted for our future proceedings. The restitution of the boat, and the recovery of the body of Captain Cook, were the objects which, on all hands, we agreed to insist on, and it was my opinion that some vigorous steps should be taken, in case the demand of them was not immediately complied with. However, after mature deliberation, it was determined to accomplish these points by conciliatory measures if possible.

In pursuance of this plan, it was determined that I should proceed toward the shore with the boats of both ships, well manned and armed, with a view to bring the natives to a parley, and, if possible, to obtain a conference with some of the chiefs.

I left the ships about four o'clock in the afternoon, and as we approached the shore I perceived every indication of a hostile reception. The whole crowd of natives was in motion, the women and children retiring, the men putting on their war-mats, and arming themselves with long spears and daggers. Concluding, therefore, that all attempts to bring them to a parley would be in vain unless I first gave them some ground for mutual confidence, I ordered the armed boats to stop, and went on in the small boat alone, with a white flag in my hand, which, by a general cry of joy from the natives, I had the satisfaction to find was instantly understood. The women immediately returned from the side of the hill whither they had retired, the men threw off their mats, and all sat down together by the water-side, extending their arms, and inviting me to come on shore.

Though this behaviour was very expressive of a friendly disposition, yet I could not help entertaining some suspicions of its sincerity. But when I saw Koah with a boldness and assurance altogether unaccountable, swimming off toward the boat with a white flag in his hand, I thought it necessary to return this mark of confidence, and therefore received him into the boat, though armed; a circumstance which did not tend to lessen my suspicions. I must confess I had long harboured an unfavourable opinion of this man. I told him that I had come to demand the body of Captain Cook, and to declare war against them unless it was instantly restored. He assured me that this should be done as soon as possible, and that he would go himself for that purpose; and after begging of me a piece of iron, with as much assurance as if nothing extraordinary had happened, he leaped into the sea and swam ashore, calling out to his countrymen that we were all friends again.

We waited near an hour with great anxiety for his return; during which time the rest of the boats had approached so near the shore as to enter into conversation with a party of the natives at some distance from us; by whom they were plainly given to understand that the body had been cut to pieces, and carried up the country; but of this circumstance I was not informed till our return to the ships.

After various delays, negotiations, and hostile preparations, about eight o'clock, it being very dark, a canoe was heard paddling toward the ship; and as soon as it was seen, both the sentinels on deck fired into it. There were two persons in the canoe, and they immediately roared out 'Tinnee' (which was the way in which they pronounced my name), and said they were friends, and had something for me belonging to Captain Cook. When they came on board, they threw themselves at our feet, and appeared exceedingly frightened. Luckily neither of them was hurt, notwithstanding the balls of both pieces had gone through the canoe. One of them was the person who constantly attended Captain Cook with the circumstances of ceremony already described: and who, though a man of rank in the island, could scarcely be hindered from performing for him the lowest offices of a menial servant. After lamenting with abundance of tears the loss of the *Orono*, he told us that he had brought us a part of his body. He then presented to us a small bundle wrapped up in cloth, which he brought under his arm; and it is impossible to describe the horror which seized us on finding in it a piece of human flesh about nine or ten pounds weight. This, he said, was all that remained of the body; that the rest was cut to pieces and burnt; but that the head and all the bones, except what belonged to the trunk, were in the possession of Terreeoboo and the other *earees*; that what we saw had been allotted to Kaoo, the chief of the priests, to be made use of in some religious ceremony, and that he had sent it as a proof of his innocence and attachment to us.

This afforded an opportunity of informing ourselves whether they were cannibals, and we did not neglect it. They immediately showed as much horror at the idea as any European would have done, and asked, very naturally, if that was the custom amongst us. They afterwards asked us, with great earnestness and apparent apprehension, When the *Orono* would come again, and what he would do to them on his return? The same inquiry was frequently made afterwards by others; and this idea agrees with the general tenor of their conduct towards him, which showed that they considered him as a being of a superior nature.

We pressed our two friendly visitors to remain on board till morning, but in vain. They told us that if this transaction should come to the knowledge of the king or chiefs it might be attended with the most fatal consequences to their whole society; in order to prevent which, they had been obliged to come off to us in the dark, and the same precaution would be necessary in returning on shore. They informed us farther that the chiefs were eager to revenge the death of their countrymen, and particularly cautioned us against trusting Koah, who, they said, was our mortal and implacable enemy, and desired nothing more ardently than an opportunity of fighting us.

We learned from these men that seventeen of their countrymen were killed in the first action at Kowrowa, of whom five were chiefs; and that Kaneena and his brother, our very particular friends, were unfortunately of that number. Eight, they said, were killed at the observatory, three of whom were also of the first rank.

During the remainder of this night, we heard loud howling and lamentations. Early in the morning we received another visit from Koah. I must confess I was a little piqued to find that, notwithstanding the most evident marks of treachery in his conduct, and the positive testimony of our friends the priests, he should still be permitted to carry on the same farce, and to make us appear to be the dupes of his hypocrisy. Indeed our situation was become extremely awkward and unpromising; none of the purposes for which this pacific course of proceeding had been adopted having hitherto been in the least forwarded by it.

This day a man had the audacity to come within musket-shot, ahead of the ship, and after flinging several stones at us, he waved Captain Cook's hat over his head, whilst his countrymen on shore were exulting and encouraging his boldness. Our people were all in a flame at this insult, and coming in a body on the quarter-deck, begged they might no longer be obliged to put up with these repeated provocations, and requested me to obtain permission for them from Captain Clerke to avail themselves of the first fair occasion of revenging the death of their commander. On my acquainting him with what was passing, he gave orders for some great guns to be fired at the natives on shore, and promised the crew, that if they should meet with any molestation at the watering-place the next day, they should then be left at liberty to chastise them.

It is somewhat remarkable, that before we could bring our guns to bear, the islanders had suspected our intentions from the stir they saw in the ship, and had retired behind their houses and walls. We were therefore obliged to fire in some measure at random; notwithstanding which, our shot produced all the effects that could have been desired. For soon after, we saw Koah paddling towards us with extreme haste, and on his arrival we learned that some people had been killed, and amongst the rest Maiha-maiha, a principal chief, and a near relation to the king.

At night the usual precautions were taken for the security of the ships; and as soon as it was dark, our two friends, who had visited us the night before, came off again. They assured us, that though the effect of our great guns this afternoon had terrified the chiefs exceedingly, they had by no means laid aside their hostile intentions, and advised us to be on our guard.

The next morning the boats of both ships were sent ashore for water; and the *Discovery* was warped close to the beach, in order to cover that service. We soon found that the intelligence which the priests had sent us was not without foundation, and that the natives were resolved to take every opportunity of annoying us, when it could be done without much risk.

Throughout all this group of islands, the villages, for the most part, are situated near the sea, and the adjacent ground is enclosed with stone walls, about three feet high. They consist of loose stones, and the inhabitants are very dexterous in shifting them with great quickness to such situations as the direction of the attack may require. In the sides of the mountain which hangs over the bay, they have also little holes or caves, of considerable depth, the entrance of which is secured by a fence of the same kind. From behind both these defences the natives kept perpetually harassing our waterers with stones; nor could the small force we had on shore, with the advantage of muskets, compel them to retreat.

In this exposed situation our people were so taken up in attending to their own safety, that they employed the whole forenoon in filling only one tun of water. As it was therefore impossible to perform this service till their assailants were driven to a greater distance, the *Discovery* was ordered to dislodge them with her great guns; which being effected by a few discharges, the men landed without molestation. However, the natives soon after made their appearance again in their usual mode of attack; and it was now found absolutely necessary to burn down some straggling houses near the wall, behind which they had taken shelter. In executing these orders, I am sorry to add, that our people were hurried into acts of unnecessary cruelty and devastation.

Their orders were only to burn a few straggling huts which afforded shelter to the natives. We were therefore a good deal surprised to see the whole village on fire; before a boat, that was sent to stop the progress of the mischief, could reach the shore, the houses of our old and constant friends, the priests, were all in flames. I cannot enough lament the illness that confined me on board this day. The priests had always been under my protection.

Several of the natives were shot in making their escape from the flames; and our people cut off the heads of two of them and brought them on board. The fate of one poor islander was much lamented by us all. As he was coming to the well for water, he was shot at by one of the marines. The ball struck his calibash, which he immediately threw from him and fled. He was pursued into one of the caves I have before described, and no lion could have defended his den with greater courage and fierceness, till at last, after having kept two of our people at bay for a considerable time, he expired covered with wounds.

Soon after the village was destroyed, we saw, coming down the hill, a man, attended by fifteen or twenty boys, holding pieces of white cloth, green boughs, plantains, etc., in their hands. As they approached nearer, it was found to be our much esteemed friend Kaireekeea, who had fled on our first setting fire to the village, and had now returned, and desired to be sent on board the *Resolution*.

When he arrived we found him exceedingly grave and thoughtful. We endeavoured to make him understand the necessity we were under of setting fire to the village, by which his house, and those of his brethren, were unintentionally consumed. He expostulated a little with us on our want of friendship, and on our ingratitude. And, indeed, it was not till now that we learnt the whole extent of the injury we had done them. He told us that, relying on the promises I had made them, and the assurances they had afterwards received from the men who had brought us the remains of Captain Cook, they had not removed their effects back into the country, with the rest of the inhabitants, but had put everything that was valuable of their own, as well as what they had collected from us, into a house close to the *morai*, where they had the mortification to see it all set on fire by ourselves.

On coming on board he had seen the heads of his countrymen lying on the deck, at which he was exceedingly shocked, and desired with great earnestness that they might be thrown overboard. This request Captain Clerke instantly ordered to be complied with.

In the evening the watering party returned on board, having met with no farther interruption. We passed a gloomy night, the cries and lamentations we heard on shore being far more dreadful than ever. Our only consolation was, the hope that we should have no occasion in future for a repetition of such severities.

The natives being at last convinced that it was not the want of ability to punish them which had hitherto made us tolerate their provocations, desisted from giving us any further molestation; and in the evening, a chief called Eappo, who had seldom visited us, but whom we knew to be a man of the very first consequence, came with presents from Terreeoboo to sue for peace. These presents were received, and he was dismissed with the same answer which had before been given, that until the remains of Captain Cook should be restored, no peace would be granted. We learned from this person, that the flesh of all the bodies of our people, together with the bones of the trunks, had been burnt; that the limb bones of the marines had been divided amongst the inferior chiefs; and that those of Captain Cook had been disposed of in the following manner: the head to a great chief called Kahoo-opeon, the hair to Maia-maia, and the legs, thighs, and arms to Terreeoboo.

Between ten and eleven o'clock on the 20th, we saw a great number of people descending the hill which is over the beach, in a kind of procession, each man carrying a sugar-cane or two on his shoulders, and breadfruit, taro, and plantains in his hand. They were preceded by two drummers, who, when they came to the waterside, sat down by a white flag, and began to beat their drums, while those who had followed them advanced one by one; and having deposited the presents they had brought, retired in the same order. Soon after, Eappo came in sight, in his long feathered cloak, bearing something with great solemnity in his hands; and having placed himself on a rock, he made signs for a boat to be sent him.

Captain Clerke, conjecturing that he had brought the bones of Captain Cook, which proved to be the fact, went himself in the pinnace to receive them; and ordered me to attend him in the cutter. When we arrived at the beach Eappo came into the pinnace, and delivered to the Captain the bones wrapped up in a large quantity of fine new cloth, and covered with a spotted cloak of black and white feathers. He afterward attended us to the *Resolution*, but could not be prevailed upon to go on board; probably not choosing, from a sense of decency, to be present at the opening of the bundle. We found in it both the hands of Captain Cook entire, which were well known from a remarkable scar on one of them, that divided the thumb from the forefinger, the whole length of the metacarpal bone; the skull, but with the scalp separated from it, and the bones that form the face wanting, the scalp with the hair upon it cut short, and the ears adhering to it; the bones of both arms, with the skin of the forearms hanging to them; the thigh and leg bones joined together, but without the feet. The ligaments of the joints were entire; and the whole bore evident marks of having been in the fire, except the hands, which had the flesh left upon them, and were cut in several places, and crammed with salt, apparently with an intention of preserving them. The scalp had a cut in the back part of it, but the skull was free from any fracture. The lower jaw and feet, which were wanting, Eappo told us had been seized by different chiefs, and that Terreeoboo was using every means to recover them.

The next morning Eappo and the king's son came on board, and brought with them the remaining bones of Captain Cook; the barrels of his gun, his shoes, and some other trifles that belonged to him. Eappo took great pains to convince us that Terreeoboo, Maiha-maiha, and himself, were most heartily desirous of peace; that they had given us the most convincing proof of it in their power; and that they had been prevented from giving it sooner by the other chiefs, many of whom were still our enemies. We found the cutter had been broken up.

Nothing now remained but to perform the last offices to our great and unfortunate commander. Eappo was dismissed with orders to taboo all the bay; and in the afternoon, the bones having been put into a coffin, and the service read over them, they were committed to the deep with the usual military honours. What our feelings were on this occasion, I leave the world to conceive; those who were present know that it is not in my power to express them.

During the forenoon of the 22nd, not a canoe was seen paddling in the bay; the taboo, which Eappo had laid on it the day before, at our request, not being yet taken off. At length Eappo came off to us. We assured him that we were now entirely satisfied; and that as the *Orono* was buried, all remembrance of what had passed was buried with him. We afterwards desired him to take off the taboo and to make it known that the people might bring their provisions as usual. The ships were soon surrounded with canoes, and many of the chiefs came on board, expressing great sorrow at what had happened, and their satisfaction at our reconciliation. Several of our friends, who did not visit us, sent presents of large hogs and other provisions. Amongst the rest came the old treacherous Koah, but was refused admittance.

As we had now everything ready for sea, about eight o clock this evening we dismissed all the natives; Eappo, and the friendly Kaireekeea, took an affectionate leave of us. We immediately weighed and stood out of the bay. The natives were collected on the shore in great numbers; and as we passed along, received our last farewells with every mark of affection and good-will.

As every minute particular regarding the death of Captain Cook, and of the events which led to it, is of the deepest interest, the editor, at the risk of repetition, subjoins an extract from the remarks of Captain Clerke, who succeeded to the command of the expedition, written at the time on board the Resolution, and obtained from the Records of the Admiralty. They will be found to corroborate the account given of this lamentable transaction by Captain King.

REMARKS ON BOARD HIS MAJESTY'S SLOOP RESOLUTION, AT OIOHY'HE

Sunday, 14th February 1779

Ever since our arrival here, upon this our second visit, we have observed in the natives a stronger propensity to theft than we had reason to complain of during our former stay; every day produced more numerous and more audacious depredations. Today they behaved so ill on board the

Discovery, that I was obliged to order them all out of the ship, which I find was likewise the case on board the *Resolution*. None but the principal people were suffered on board. However, we let them lay alongside in their canoes, and amuse themselves as they thought proper. In the afternoon, I had a present of a cloak and a hog from Terre'aboo, who, with his retinue, made me a visit. In the evening they left the ship, and soon after a principal *aree*, whose name was Ter'rare, called on board. During my stay in the cabin with them a rascal by some means got up the ship's side, ran across the deck in the face of everybody there, snatched the armourer's tongs, together with a chisel, and jumped overboard. This was done so instantaneously, that the fellow was in the water before our people well saw what the fellow was about. A canoe immediately took him in, and made for shore. I heard the alarm, ran upon deck, and, being made acquainted with the business, ordered the people to fire at them. At the same time, Mr Edgar, the master, put off in the small cutter in chase of the canoe, which was presently out of the reach of our muskets. However, as I saw the *Resolution*'s pinnace join the chase, and Captain Cook run along shore to intercept the fellow's landing, I concluded it impossible for him to escape all; and the closing of the evening preventing a farther prospect of the business, I was very easy, expecting soon to have the boat back, with the tongs, etc.; but it was near eight before Mr Edgar returned, and then with such a story as I was a good deal hurt at. In the first place, Captain Cook was led altogether out of the way by those who undertook to be his guides. The pinnace and cutter pursued and ran the canoe where the culprit had taken refuge on shore, when the stolen goods were brought off and returned them; but Mr Edgar, thinking some punishment ought to be inflicted for such infamous conduct, he seized the canoe which brought off the thief. The boat happened to be that of Per'rare's, that had brought him on board, and was waiting his pleasure, whilst he was with me in the cabin. This looks very suspicious in Mr Per'rare, but if he did give countenance to these thefts, he added shameful ingratitude to his perfidy, for I had at various times been very attentive and liberal to him. However, he left me soon after the theft had been committed, with a promise of a speedy return with the plunder, which, to do him justice, he had frequently in these cases retrieved for me. He reached the shore as soon as our boat, when, finding his own canoe in danger, he strenuously opposed the seizure, and soon raised too numer- ous a mob for our boat's crew to deal with; who not readily giving up their capture, were warmly attacked by Per'rare and his gang he had mustered, with stones, clubs, etc. It unfortunately happened that both the boats were destitute of fire-arms (our friendly connections having lulled us into too great security), and of course had nothing more than equal weapons to repel this attack, the consequence of which was a defeat, being overpowered by numbers; and after receiving many hard thumps, were glad to get their own boats off, with half their oars broke, lost, etc. This was an unfortunate stroke as matters now stood, as it increased the confidence of these people, which before was too much bordering upon insolence.

In the morning, at daybreak, Lieutenant Burney, who was the officer of the watch, acquainted me that the large cutter was taken from the buoy where we had moored aud sunk her, to prevent the heat of the sun, which is very powerful, from renting the plank. Upon examining part of her moorings that was left upon the buoy, and was a four inch rope, I found plainly that it had been cut by some instrument or other, which clearly evinced she must have been taken away by the Indians, with which circumstance I directly waited upon Captain Cook, and made him acquainted, and, after some conversation on the subject, he proposed that his boats should go to the N.W. point of the bay, and mine to the S.E. point, to prevent any canoe going away, and if any attempted it to drive them on shore; for he said he would seize them all, and made no doubt but to redeem them they would very readily return the boat again. It was now between six and seven o'clock in the morning. I returned on board to put these orders into execution, and sent Lieutenant Rickman with the launch and small cutter, with their crews and some marines, well armed, to the station Captain Cook had assigned them. I soon after took the jolly boat (which now was the only boat I had left), and came to the *Resolution*, with an intention of having some more discourse with Captain Cook upon this business; but when I came near the ship, Lieutenant Gore told me that Captain Cook was gone with his pinnace, launch, and small cutter, to a town situated just within the N.W. point, where King Terre'aboo and the major part of the people of consequence then resided, upon which I returned to my ship, concluding, as Captain Cook was gone to the king, matters would soon be settled, for we were as yet by no mean on bad terms either with *arees* or anybody else. There were at this time many small canoes trading about the ships. Soon after I got on board, I observed some muskets discharged from my launch and small cutter, upon which I sent the jolly boat to know how matters went, and orders to Lieutenant Rickman, if he had made any seizures of canoes, to send them to the ship by the jolly boat.

It was now just eight o'clock, when we were alarmed by the discharge of a volley of small arms from Captain Cook's people, and a violent shout of the Indians. With my glass I clearly saw that our people were drove off to their boats, but I could not distinguish persons in that confused crowd. The pinnace and launch, however, continued the fire, and the *Resolution*, who was near enough to throw her shot on shore, fired her cannon among them. Thus circumstanced, without any boat to go to their assistance, and, consequently, destitute of all means of rendering them any kind of service, I was obliged to wait the return of these engaged boats to hear the event of these unhappy differences. The crews having fired away their ammunition, returned to the *Resolution*, and Lieutenant Williamson, who commanded them upon this duty, soon after came on board the *Discovery* with the melancholy account that Captain Cook and four marines had fallen in this confounded fray and that the rest of the marines who were on shore were with difficulty saved, three of whom were much wounded, particularly Mr Phillips, the lieutenant, who was a good deal bruised by blows of stones, and had received a deep stab with an iron pike in his shoulder. I immediately went on board the *Resolution*, sent a strong party of people to protect the astronomers at their tents, and carpenters who were at work upon the mast on the eastern side of the bay, and received from Lieutenant Phillips, who, with his marines, was on shore and present throughout the whole with Captain Cook, the following account:

Captain Cook landed at the town situated within the N.W. point with his pinnace and launch, leaving the small cutter off the point to prevent the escape of any canoes that might be disposed to get off. At his landing, he ordered nine marines, which he had in the boats, and myself on shore to attend him, and immediately marched into the town, where he inquired for Terre'aboo and the two boys (his sons, who had lived principally with Captain Cook on board the *Resolution* since Terre'aboo's first arrival among us). Messengers were immediately dispatched, and the two boys soon came, and conducted us to their father's house. After waiting some time on the outside, Captain Cook doubted the old gentleman being there, and sent me in that I might inform him. I found our old acquaintance just awoke from sleep; when, upon my acquainting him that Captain Cook was at the door, he very readily went with me to him. Captain Cook, after some little conversation, observed that Terre'aboo was quite innocent of what had happened, and proposed to the old gentleman to go on board with him, which he readily agreed to, and we accordingly proceeded toward the boats, but having advanced near to the water side, an elderly woman, whose name was Kar'na'cub'ra, one of his wives, came to him, and with many tears and entreaties, begged he would not go on board; at the same time, two chiefs laid hold of him, and insisting that he should not, made him sit down: the old man now appeared dejected and frightened. It was at this period we first began to suspect that they were not very well disposed towards us, and the marines being huddled together in the midst of an immense mob, composed of at least two or three thousand people, I proposed to

Captain Cook that they might be arranged in order along the rocks by the water side, which he approving of, the crowd readily made way for them, and they were drawn up accordingly. We now clearly saw they were collecting their spears, etc., but an awful rascal of a priest was singing and making a ceremonious offering to the Captain and Terre'aboo, to divert their attention from the manoeuvres of the surrounding multitude. Captain Cook now gave up all thoughts of taking Terre'aboo on board, with the following observations to me – 'We can never think of compelling him to go on board without killing a number of these people' – and I believe was just going to give orders to embark, when he was interrupted by a fellow armed with a long iron spike, which they call a *pah'hoo'ah*, and a stone. This man made a flourish with his *pah'hoo'ah*, and threatened to throw his stone, upon which Captain Cook discharged a load of small shot at him, but he having his mat on, the small shot did not penetrate it, and had no other effect than farther to provoke and encourage them. I could not observe the least fright it occasioned. Immediately upon this an *aree*, armed with a *pah'hoo'ah*, attempted to stab me, but I foiled his attempt by giving him a severe blow with the butt end of my musket. Just at this time they began to throw stones, and one of the marines was knocked down. The Captain then fired a ball and killed a man. They now made a general attack, and the Captain gave orders to the marines to fire and afterwards called out, 'Take to the boats.' I fired just after the Captain, and loaded again whilst the marines fired. Almost instantaneously upon my repeating the orders to take to the boats, I was knocked down by a stone, and in rising received a stab with a *pah'hoo'ah* in the shoulder; my antagonist was upon the point of seconding his blow, when I shot him dead. The business now was a most miserable scene of confusion. The shouts and yells of the Indians far exceeded all the noise I ever came in the way of. These fellows, instead of retiring upon being fired upon, as Captain Cook and I believe most people concluded they would, acted so very contrary a part, that they never gave the soldiers time to reload their pieces, but immediately broke in upon and would have killed every man of them, had not the boats by a smart fire kept them a little off, and picked up those who were not too much wounded to reach them. After being knocked down I saw no more of Captain Cook. All my people I observed were totally vanquished, and endeavouring to save their lives by getting to the boats. I therefore scrambled as well as I could into the water, and made for the pinnace, which I fortunately got hold of, but not before I received another blow from a stone just above the temple, which, had not the pinnace been very near, would have sent me to the bottom.

This is the substance of Lieutenant Phillips' relation of this most unfortunate event, to which I must add one circumstance more in justice to his gallantry and attention. He had not been many minutes in the boat, and of course scarcely recovered from the disagreeable sensations occasioned by the *pah'hoo'ah* and stones, when he saw one of his marines, who was but a very poor swimmer, and now farther disabled by wounds, just upon the point of sinking. He immediately jumped overboard again, caught the man by his hair, and brought him to the boat. Far the major part of these *pah'hoo'ahs,* with which many of the *arees* are now armed, and is their most deadly weapon, were furnished them by ourselves. The *arees* always seemed very desirous of them, and we troubled ourselves very little about the use they proposed for them. Old Terre'aboo got two from Captain Cook, and one from me, no longer than yesterday evening. Some time before the attack was made, intelligence was brought from the other side of the bay that the boats there, under the command of Lieutenant Rickman, had killed a man who was somewhat of an *aree*, which our people observed in some degree to disconcert them, but this was some time before they proceeded to violent measures. How the unhappy business was brought about is very hard to determine; to all appearance it was by no means a premeditated plan. On the part of Terre'aboo, if we consider his conduct throughout, we must acquit him of any bad intentions. His son, the young Prince Ka'oo'ah, was sitting in the pinnace with Mr Roberts, one of the mates (who then commanded her), with intention of coming off to the ship at the time the first gun was fired by Captain Cook. The poor boy then said he was frightened, and begged to be put on shore, which was immediately complied with. As to their being armed with their *pah'hoo'ahs* it was always the case; those who had them were so proud of the acquisition, that they never went anywhere without them, and as to their stones, nature has furnished them most abundantly in every part of their country. Upon the whole, I firmly believe matters would not have been carried to the extremities they were, had not Captain Cook attempted to chastise a man in the midst of this multitude, firmly believing, as his last resource in case of necessity, that the fire of his marines would undoubtedly disperse them. This idea was certainly founded upon great experience among various nations of Indians, in different parts of the world, but the unhappy event of today proved it in this case, however, fallacious. One very strong argument that they would not have proceeded thus had not Captain Cook first unfortunately fired, is, that but a very few minutes before the fray began, they readily cleared a way for the marines to march down to the water side, just by where the boats lay (as I have observed), had Captain Cook then been disposed to go off. Mr Phillips is of opinion, from all appearance at that time, they would have given him no interruption. Now, had they been previously determined upon the ensuing business, the attack upon the marines would have been made with more safety to themselves, and efficacy to their cause, when in the midst of the mob than when they were properly drawn up; this was too obvious an advantage to escape their sagacity. As to their collecting their spears, etc., as Mr Phillips observed, some time previous to the attack, he is of opinion, and I think very justly, that this arose from an apprehension that some force might be used in getting Terre'aboo to the ship, which I believe they were determined to oppose to the last extremity. However, be these matters as they may, the unfortunate business was now done, and it behoved me to take the most effectual method I could suggest to prevent more. As I before observed, I sent a strong party of people, which were commanded by Lieutenant King, to the eastern side of the bay to defend the astronomers and the carpenters at work upon the foremast. I soon observed a vast concourse of the natives assembling near them, when by a spring upon the *Discovery*'s cable, I was enabled to throw her four-pounders about their quarters, being well within distance, which in a great measure dispersed the association; but I could not do it effectually, they had such retreats behind a number of stone walls with which their villages and all the parts adjacent abound, and which I now suppose are purposed as a place of retirement when annoyed by the enemy. The vast numbers of people I observed collecting in various parts of the bay, and the resolution they had displayed in the attack, as represented by the Lieutenants Williamson and Phillips, rendered them, I thought, rather a formidable enemy, and that the safest and best method we could take would be to get everything from the shore to the ships, where we could work at our leisure, and they could not possibly annoy us without inevitable destruction to themselves. I therefore ordered the observatories and foremast to be got off with all expedition. I make no doubt but we might have protected these matters on shore with a good stout party, but they would have been continually harassed, and the work impeded, and had any unlucky accident gained them the possession of the foremast, though only for a few minutes, we should have been totally ruined in respect to another Northern campaign, which is certainly now my principal object to forward. Our party on shore, under Lieutenant King, were arranged on an eminence that the natives had thrown up for a *morai*, which gave them great advantages, as they commanded everything around them; the Indians, however, made two or three attacks with stones thrown from slings, but they were immediately repulsed with the loss, in the whole, of ten or twelve men; indeed they could not collect themselves to a formidable body for the fire of the *Discovery*. By noon we had got all our men and other matters on board, and the foremast alongside; with our glasses we could clearly see the Indians busied in conveying the dead bodies over a hill up the country. I cannot here help lamenting my own unhappy state of health, which is sometimes so bad as hardly to suffer me to keep the deck, and of course, farther incapacitates me for the succeeding so able a navigator as my honoured friend and predecessor; however, here are very able officers, and I trust, with a firm dependence upon Providence, that with their assistance I may be able to prosecute the remaining part of their Lordships' instructions with that zeal and alacrity as may procure me the honour of their approbation. The marines who fell with Captain Cook were Corporal Thomas, Theophilus Hinks, John Allen, and Thomas Flabchett; the lieutenant, sergeant, and two others wounded.

Monday, 15th February 1779
As there was still a vast concourse of people where this unfortunate fray happened, I had some notion of taking a stout party on shore, make what destruction I could among them, then burn the town, canoes, etc., for I have no doubt but firearms must drive everything before them when you take room for action; but the officers who had been present at the fray observed, that though our muskets must in the end prove effectual, such were their numbers, resolution, and advantageous retreats behind these walls, that the attempt would doubtless cost us some, and probably many men; that we laboured under great disadvantages in landing, which we were there obliged to do upon slippery rocks, where our people with shoes could hardly stand, and they having the fair use of the foot, were perfectly masters of themselves; upon these considerations, as the loss of a very few men would now be most severely felt by us, I thought it would be improper and probably injurious to the expedition to risk farther loss of the people. I therefore determined to turn all endeavours towards forwarding the equipment of the *Resolution* as we were now nearly in a tattered condition, and as soon as we were in any tolerable order, if they did not conduct themselves with some degree of propriety, to warp her within a proper distance of the town, and by landing under our own guns, thoroughly convince them that it was to our lenity, not our imbecility, that they owed their safety, so we got our fore-mast into the ship, placed it fore and aft upon the forecastle and quarter deck, and set the carpenters of both ships to work upon it. In the evening I sent the boats of the two ships, well manned and armed, under the command of Lieutenants King and Burney, with a flag of truce, with orders by no means whatever to land, but advance near enough to hold conversation and demand the bodies of our people, particularly Captain Cook's. Upon Mr King's arrival near the shore, and making known his demands, they appeared quite elate with joy at the prospect of a reconciliation, threw away their slings and mats which were their weapons and armour, extended their arms, and in short seemed happy in suggesting every mode of demonstrating their

satisfaction. An old fellow, whose name is Co'ah'ah, with whom we had all along been acquainted, with a white flag in his hand, swam off to the small cutter where our flag was, and promised we should have the body of Captain Cook tomorrow, but that it was carried too far up the country to be brought down tonight. These assurances Mr King likewise received from many other people with whom he conversed by the water side.

Mr Burney was some little distance from Mr King and talked with different people. He says he clearly understood from some of them that the body was cut up; however, from their fair promises, I hoped the morrow would produce it in some state or the other. That we might be as safe as possible from the machinations of these people, I ordered guard boats to row round the ships during the darkness of the night, being under some apprehensions of attempts upon our cables.

Tuesday, 16th February, 1779

In the morning old Co'ah'ah made several trips to us in a small canoe with his white flag flying, assisted by only one man, and made many fair promises of the bodies being returned; he brought off two or three little pigs at different times, which, as he professed so much friendship, and seemed to confide so much in us, I accepted.

This evening, just after dark, a priest, whose name was Car'na'care, a friend of Mr King's, came on board and brought with him a large piece of flesh, which we soon saw to be human, and which he gave us to understand was part of the corpse of our late unfortunate Captain; it was clearly a part of the thigh, about six or eight pounds, without any bone at all. The poor fellow told us that all the rest of the flesh had been burnt at different places with some peculiar kind of ceremony, that this had been delivered to him for that purpose, but as we appeared anxious to recover the body, he had brought us all that he could get of it; he likewise added, that the bones, which was all that now remained, were in the possession of King Terre'aboo. The extraordinary friendship and attention of these priests, since our first arrival amongst them, has been such as we never before met with nor could expect from any Indians, or indeed I believe I may say from any nation of people in the world. They abound in the riches of the country, which they deal out with a most liberal hand. Our astronomers and people on shore were fairly kept by them, and they were continually sending presents of hogs, fish, fruit, etc., to both Captain Cook and myself, at the same time were so perfectly disinterested, that it was with difficulty we got them to accept of any return at all adequate to their donations. The latter end of January a party was sent up the country to look a little about them. They set out in the evening, and where they halted for the night were overtaken and joined by a man from old Ca'ha'ha's, who was the chief-priest, or as we termed him, the bishop.

This good old gentleman hearing that some people were gone upon an expedition about the isle, sent this man after them with a general order that they should be supplied with whatever they wanted, wherever they thought proper to travel. This honest fellow, Car'na'care, who I believe is son to the bishop, certainly brought off this flesh with a most friendly intention; he begs we will put no kind of trust in the social aspects and promises of his countrymen, for that they do mean and are determined to do us farther mischief if they possibly can. Old Co'ah'ah, he says, they make use of as a spy to examine our condition of defence, etc., having some notion of attacking the ships. Here are clearly party matters subsisting between the laity and the clergy, and in these cases a strict attention to the representation of either, I believe, is generally wide of the truth; however, we must take care not to lay ourselves so open as to render it possible for any plan of treachery to reach us; and as to their attack upon the ships, I should imagine it must turn out to them the most unhappy expedition they ever experienced. After staying on board about two hours, Car'na'care returned to the shore, observing that regard to his safety obliged him to make his visit in the dark, for should it be publicly known they would immediately destroy him. As the command of course now devolved to me, I appointed myself to the *Resolution*; Mr Gore, the first lieutenant of that ship, to the command of the *Discovery*; Mr King the first, Mr Williamson the second, and Mr William Harvey, who is now upon his third trip with Captain Cook, to be the third lieutenant of the *Resolution*. I know nothing of any particular commands of their Lordships in case of vacancies, but have often heard Captain Cook, in private conversation, declare his intention of making Mr Harvey a lieutenant; and as I am perfectly ignorant of their Lordships' pleasure upon that head, I hope they will approve of my attention and respect to the memory of that great navigator, in acting consistently with his avowed purposes.

Wednesday, 17th February 1779

Early this afternoon an impudent rascal came off from the town, on the north west point, and having advanced to within 200 yards of the ship, waved a hat to us, which I could clearly distinguish to have been it of Captain Cook's. He then put it upon his head and flung some stones from a sling towards the ship, whilst the vast concourse of people upon the shore were shouting and laughing. This was too gross an insult to bear with any degree of patience. The rascal in his canoe, being right ahead of the ship, soon perceived the people getting into the boat, and made for the shore with too much celerity for us to come near him. I did not fire at him, as it's great odds but he was missed, which would farther show them the fallibility of our arms. However, as he was undoubtedly set on by the people on shore, who were still upon the rocks by the water side, though the ship was too far off to throw the shot with the exactitude I could wish, still we were not quite out of reach, and this multitude being a fine large mark, I fired several of the four-pounders at them, when they dispersed in a great hurry. In the evening two *arees* came off, and begged we would fire at them no more, and expressed their wishes for peace. I found the great shot had frightened them confoundedly, some having fell among the crowd and wounded a nephew of Terre'aboo's, whose name was Ky'mare'mare (an old friend of mine), and three or four others, by scattering the splinters of stones among them. We now learnt there were four *arees* with thirteen men killed, and many others badly wounded in the fray with Captain Cook. In the morning, as I wanted some water, I ordered the *Discovery* as near as convenient to the shore to cover the watering party, and sent the boats of the two ships properly equipped upon that duty, under the commands of the Lieutenants Rickman and Harvey, with orders not to let any of the natives come near them, but by no means to molest them if they did not first give provocation by acting offensively. Very soon after their landing, such was the strange infatuation of these people, notwithstanding they saw everything was clearly against them, they began to throw stones at the party. They, however, had the discretion in general to get behind some houses of a town that was built all along the head of the beach, or upon a high hill under which the well was situate, and from thence roll them down. Some were daring enough to come upon the open beach for the greater convenience of discharging their stones, but five or six of these being killed, put an end to this beach fighting, and they all retired behind the houses, from whence they continued to throw without ceasing, but to very little effect, for there was such a distance that, by a good look-out, they were easily avoided. At noon the boats returned.

Thursday, 18th February 1779
In the afternoon the boats returned to the watering business, and, as the natives continued troublesome, we burnt down the town that was at the head of the beach, which deprived them of their principal shelter. The rogues upon the hill continued to roll down stones, and their situation was so elevated we could not possibly annoy them. However, they did us no other harm than somewhat to retard the business, as the people were under a necessity of keeping some look-out to avoid the stones. In the evening they were tired of the business; many of them came to the watering party with green boughs and white flags (emblems of peace), and begged we would be friends, promising to give us no farther molestation. They were socially received, and assured of our good offices, if they would conduct themselves properly. In the morning the parties returned to the watering duty, the natives were civil and attentive, supplying them with fruits, etc.

Friday, 19th February 1779

Our good friends the priests still continue their extraordinary attention and benevolence. They send us many presents of hogs, fruits, etc. By the assistance of these good people, and some poor fellows who came off in the dark and traded, being, as they say, afraid to be seen to hold connection with us, we have all along, except one day, been able to collect roots enough for our own necessary consumption. As to pork, we have abundance.

Saturday, 20th February 1779

An *aree* of distinction came off with two hogs and a large quantity of roots, which he said was a present from Terre'aboo, who, he gave me to understand, was very desirous of peace. I told him I had very little objection to peace, but insisted they should first return the remains of Captain Cook, which he promised heartily to do. He took his leave and returned to the shore. About noon E'ar'po came to the beach with abundance of attendants, laden with roots and some hogs. I went in the pinnace, and took Mr King in the cutter, near enough to the shore to hold conversation, and demanded the remains of Captain Cook, which he delivered to me very decently wrapped up. I then took him on board, and treated him, with three *arees*, his friends, socially. I asked him for the remains of the other four people; but he told me that Captain Cook, being the principal man, he of course became the property of king Terre'aboo; that the others were taken by various *arees*, who were now dispersed in different parts of the isle, and that it would be impossible to collect them. I thought this so probable an account, that I said no more upon the subject.

Sunday, 21st February 1779

In the evening E'ar'po and his friends returned to the shore, apparently very happy. They gave me an account of their loss of men in our various skirmishes, which amounts to four *arees* killed and six wounded; of their people, twenty-five killed and fifteen wounded. This is the same as I have before heard, and as it is corroborated, I suppose it is the fact. Upon examining the remains of my late honoured and much-lamented friend, I found all his bones, excepting those of the back, jaw, and feet – the two latter articles E'ar'po brought me in the morning – the former, he declared, had been reduced to ashes with the trunk of the body. As Car'na'care had told us, the flesh was taken from all the bones, excepting those of the hands, the skin of which they had cut through in many places, and salted, with an intention, no doubt, of preserving them. E'ar'po likewise brought this morning the two barrels of Captain Cook's gun – the one beat flat, with intention of making a cutting instrument of it; the other a good deal bent and bruised, together with a present of thirteen hogs from Terre'aboo. The day before it on which this miserable business happened, during the old gentleman's visit, I made him a present of a red cloth cloak, which he desired might be edged with green cloth, and left it on board with me for that purpose, proposing to come for it the next morning; but these unhappy circumstances falling out, it still remained in my possession, and he now desired E'ar'po to ask me for it, which of course I sent him, with a proper return for his present. I mention this circumstance among many others, to evince how little idea there was of this miserable breach that has happened between us. During the forenoon, I had a visit from the young prince Ka'oo'ah, who, as I have before observed, is a son of Terre'aboo's, and of course paid great attention and respect to here by all ranks of people.

Monday, 22nd February 1779
This afternoon we have an abundant market for hogs and fruit. Both arees and people now put themselves in our power, without any kind of apprehension. They appear exceedingly desirous of resuming our former confidence and intercourse, and that with so much appearance of sincerity, that had I any point to carry I think I might put some degree of confidence in them with great safety; but my business is now to get to sea, and quit this group of islands as soon as circumstances will admit me.

In the evening I had the remains of Captain Cook committed to the deep, with all the attention and honour we could possibly pay in this part of the world.

We now continue the narrative of Captain King.

On the 22nd we got clear of the land about ten o'clock, and hoisting in the boats, stood to the northward.

After touching at Woahoo, where it was found watering would have been inconvenient, Captain Clerke determined, without farther loss of time, to proceed to Atooi. On the 28th we bore away for that island, which we were in sight of by noon; and about sunset, were off its eastern extremity.

We had no sooner anchored in our old station, than several canoes came alongside of us; but we could observe that they did not welcome us with the same cordiality in their manner, and satisfaction in their countenances, as when we were here before.

Our principal object here was to water the ships with the utmost expedition; and I was sent on shore early in the afternoon. We found a considerable number of people collected upon the beach, who received us at first with great kindness; but as soon as we had got the casks on shore, began to be exceedingly troublesome. It was with great difficulty I was able to form a circle, according to our usual practice, for the convenience of our trading party, and had no sooner done it, than I saw a man laying hold of the bayonet of one of the soldier's muskets, and endeavouring with all his force to wrench it out of his hand. This fray was occasioned by the latter's having given the man a slight prick with his bayonet, in order to make him keep without the line.

I now perceived that our situation required great circumspection and management, and accordingly gave the strictest orders that no one should fire, nor have recourse to another act of violence, without positive commands. As soon as I had given these directions, I was called to the assistance of the watering party, where I found the natives equally inclined to mischief. They had demanded from our people a large hatchet for every cask of water, and this not being complied with, they would not suffer the sailors to roll them down to the boats.

I had no sooner joined them, than one of the natives advanced up to me with great insolence, and made the same claim. I told him that as a friend, I was very willing to present him with a hatchet, but that I should certainly carry off the water without paying anything for it: and I immediately ordered the pinnace men to proceed in their business, and called three marines from the traders to protect them.

Though the natives continued for the most part to pay great deference and respect to me, yet they did not suffer me to escape without contributing my share to their stock of plunder. One of them came up to me with a familiar air, and with great management diverted my attention, whilst another, wrenching the hanger, which I held carelessly in my hand, from me, ran off with it like lightning.

It was in vain to think of repelling this insolence by force; guarding therefore against its effects in the best manner we were able, we had nothing to do but to submit patiently to it. My apprehensions were, however, a little alarmed by the information I soon after received from the sergeant of marines, who told me that, turning suddenly round, he saw a man behind me holding a dagger in the position of striking. In case of a real attack, our whole force, however advantageously disposed, could have made but a poor resistance. On the other hand, I thought it of some consequence to show the natives we were under no fears.

At last we got everything into the boats, and only the gunner, a seaman of the boat's crew, and myself, remained on shore. As the pinnace lay beyond the surf, through which we were obliged to swim, I told them to make the best of their way to it, and that I should follow them.

With this order I was surprised to find them both refuse to comply, and the consequence was a contest amongst us who should be the last on shore. It seems that some hasty words I had just before used to the sailor, which he thought reflected on his courage, was the cause of this odd fancy in him; and the old gunner finding a point of honour started, thought he could not well avoid taking a part in it. In this ridiculous situation we might have remained some time, had not our dispute been soon settled by the stones that began to fly about us, and by the cries of the people from the boats to make haste, as the natives were following us into the water with clubs and spears. I reached the side of the pinnace first, and finding the gunner was at some distance behind, and not yet entirely out of danger, I called out to the marines to fire one musket. In the hurry of executing my orders they fired two, and when I got into the boat I saw the natives running away, and one man with a woman sitting by him, left behind on the beach. The man made several attempts to rise without being able, and it was with much regret I perceived him to be wounded in the groin.

During our absence Captain Clerke had been under the greatest anxiety for our safety. And these apprehensions were considerably increased from his having entirely mistaken the drift of the conversation he had held with some natives who had been on board. The frequent mention of the name of Captain Cook, with other strong and circumstantial descriptions of death and destruction, made him conclude that the knowledge of the unfortunate events at Owhyhee had reached them, and that these were what they alluded to, whereas, all they had in view was to make known to him the wars that had arisen in consequence of the goats that Captain Cook had left at Oneeheow, and the slaughter of the poor goats themselves, during the struggle for the property of them.

The next morning, March 2, I was again ordered on shore with the watering party. The risk we had run the preceding day determined Captain Clerke to send a considerable force from both ships for our guard, amounting in all to forty men under arms. This precaution, however, was now unnecessary, for we found the beach left entirely to ourselves, and the ground between the landing place and the lake tabooed with small white flags. We concluded from this appearance, that some of the chiefs had certainly visited this quarter, and that, not being able to stay, they had kindly and considerately taken this step for our greater security and convenience.

The next day we completed our watering without meeting with any material difficulty. On our return to the ships, we found that several chiefs had been on board, and had made excuses for the behaviour of their countrymen, attributing their riotous conduct to the quarrels which subsisted at that time amongst the principal people of the island. The quarrel had arisen about the goats we had left at Oneeheow the last year, the right of property in which was claimed by Toneoneo, on the pretence of that island's being a dependency of his.

On the 7th we were surprised with a visit from Tonconeo. When he heard the dowager princess was in the ship, it was with great difficulty we could prevail on him to come on board, not from any apprehension that he appeared to entertain of his safety, but from an unwillingness to see her. Their meeting was with sulky and lowering looks on both sides. He stayed but a short time, and seemed much dejected; but we remarked, with some surprise, that the women, both at his coming and going away, prostrated themselves before him; and that he was treated by all the natives on board with the respect usually paid to those of his rank. Indeed it must appear somewhat extraordinary that a person who was at this time in a state of actual hostility with the opposite party, and was even prepared for another battle, should trust himself almost alone within the power of his enemies.

On the 8th, at nine in the morning, we weighed and sailed toward Oneeheow, and at three in the afternoon, anchored in twenty fathoms water, nearly on the same spot as in the year 1778.

On the 12th, the weather being moderate, the master was sent to the north-west side of the island to look for a more convenient place for anchoring. He returned in the evening, having found a fine bay with good anchorage; also to the eastward were four small wells of good water, the road to them level, and fit for rolling casks.

Being now about to leave the Sandwich Islands it may be proper to make a few remarks. This group consists of eleven islands. They are called by the natives: 1. Owhyhee; 2. Mowee; 3. Ranai, or Ornai; 4. Morotinnee, or Morokinne; 5. Kahowrowee, or Tahoorowa; 6. Morotoi, or Morokoi; 7. Woahoo, or Oahoo; 8. Atooi, Atowi, or Towi, and sometimes Kowi; 9. Neeheehow, or Oneeheow; 10. Oreehoua, or Reehoua; and 11. Tahoora; and are all inhabited excepting Morotinnee and Tahoora. Besides the islands above enumerated, we were told by the Indians that there is another called Modoopapapa, or Komodoopapapa, which is low and sandy, and visited only for the purpose of catching turtle and sea-fowl.

They were named by Captain Cook the Sandwich Islands, in honour of the Earl of Sandwich, under whose administration he had enriched geography with so many splendid and important discoveries.

The inhabitants of the Sandwich Islands are undoubtedly of the same race with those of New Zealand, the Society and Friendly Islands, Easter Island, and the Marquesas. This fact, which, extraordinary as it is, might be thought sufficiently proved by the striking similarity in their manners and customs, and the general resemblance of their persons, is established beyond all controversy by the absolute identity of their language.

From what continent they originally emigrated, and by what steps they have spread through so vast a space, those who are curious in disquisitions of this nature may perhaps not find it very difficult to conjecture. It has been already observed, that they bear strong marks of affinity to some of the Indian tribes that inhabit the Ladrones and Caroline Islands; and the same affinity may again be traced amongst the Battas and the Malays. When these events happened is not so easy to ascertain; it was probably not very lately, as they are extremely populous, and have no tradition of their own origin but what is perfectly fabulous.

The natives of these islands are in general above the middle size, and well made. Their complexion is rather darker than that of the Otaheiteans, and they are not altogether so handsome a people.

However, many of both sexes had fine open countenances, and the women in particular had good eyes and teeth, and a sweetness and sensibility of look, which rendered them very engaging. Their hair is of a brownish black, and neither uniformly straight, like that of the Indians of America, nor uniformly curling, as amongst the African negroes, but varying in this respect like the hair of Europeans.

The same superiority that is observable in the persons of the *earees*, through all the other islands, is found also here. Those whom we saw were, without exception, perfectly well formed; whereas the lower sort, besides their general inferiority, are subject to all the variety of make and figure that is seen in the populace of other countries.

They seem to have few native diseases among them, but many of the *earees* suffer dreadfully from the immoderate use of the ava. There is something very singular in the history of this pernicious drug. When Captain Cook first visited the Society Islands, it was very little known among them. On his second voyage, he found the use of it very prevalent at Ulietea, but it had still gained very little ground at Otaheite. When we were last there, the dreadful havoc it had made was beyond belief, insomuch that the Captain scarcely knew many of his old acquaintances. At the Friendly Islands it is also constantly drunk by the chiefs, but so much diluted with water that it does not appear to produce any bad effects. At Atooi also it is used with great moderation, and the chiefs are, in consequence a much finer set of men there than in any of the neighbouring islands. Our good friends, Kaireekeea and old Kaoo, were persuaded by us to refrain from it; and they recovered amazingly during the short time we afterward remained in the island.

Notwithstanding the irreparable loss we suffered from the sudden resentment and violence of these people, yet, in justice to their general conduct, it must be acknowledged that they are of the most mild and affectionate disposition, equally remote from the extreme levity and fickleness of the Otaheiteans, and the distant gravity and reserve of the inhabitants of the Friendly Islands. They appear to live in the utmost harmony and friendship with one another. The women who had children were remarkable for their tender and constant attention to them; and the men would often lend their assistance in those domestic offices with a willingness that does credit to their feelings.

The inhabitants of these islands differ from those of the Friendly Isles, in suffering, almost universally, their beards to grow. There were indeed a few, amongst whom was the old king, that cut it off entirely, and others that wore it only upon the upper lip. The same variety in the manner of wearing the hair is also observable here as among the other islanders of the South Sea; besides which they have a fashion, as far as we know, peculiar to themselves. They cut it close on each side of the head down to the ears.

Both sexes wear necklaces made of strings of small variegated shells, and an ornament, in the form of the handle of a cup, about two inches long, and half an inch broad, made of wood, stone, or ivory, finely polished, which is hung about the neck by fine threads of twisted hair, doubled sometimes a hundred fold. Instead of this ornament, some of them wear on their breast a small human figure made of bone, suspended in the same manner.

The custom of tattooing the body they have in common with the rest of the natives of the South Sea islands, but it is only at New Zealand and the Sandwich Islands that they tattoo the face. They have a singular custom amongst them, the meaning of which we could never learn – that of tattooing the tip of the tongues of the females.

The dress of the men generally consists only of a piece of thick cloth, called the maro, about ten or twelve inches broad, which they pass between the legs, and tie round the waist. This is the common dress of all ranks of people Their mats, some of which are beautifully manufactured, are of various sizes, but mostly about five feet long and four broad. These they throw over their shoulders, and bring forward before; but they are seldom used, except in time of war, for which purpose they seem better adapted than for ordinary use, and capable of breaking the blow of a stone, or any blunt weapon.

The common dress of the women bears a close resemblance to that of the men. They wrap round the waist a piece of cloth that reaches half way down the thighs, and sometimes in the cool of the evening they appear with loose pieces of fine cloth thrown over their shoulders, like the women of Otaheite. The *pau* is another dress very frequently worn by the younger part of the sex. It is made of the thinnest and finest sort of cloth, wrapped several times round the waist, and descending to the leg, so to have the appearance of a full short petticoat.

'The way of spending their time appears to be very simple, and to admit of little variety. They rise with the sun, and after enjoying the cool of the evening, retire to rest a few hours after sunset. The making of canoes and mats forms the occupation of the *earees*; the women are employed in manufacturing cloth, and the *towtows* are principally engaged in the plantations and fishing.

Their music is of a rude kind, having neither flutes nor reeds, nor instruments of any other sort that we saw, except drums of various sizes. But their songs, which they sung in parts, and accompany with a gentle motion of the arms, in the same manner as the Friendly Islanders, had a very pleasing effect.

The people of these islands are manifestly divided into three classes. The first are the *earees*, or chiefs of each district, one of whom is superior to the rest, and is called at Owhyhee *earee-taboo* and *earee-moee*. By the first of these words they express his absolute authority, and by the latter all are obliged to prostrate themselves (or put themselves to sleep, as the word signifies) in his presence. The second class are those who appear to enjoy a right of property without authority. The third are the *towtows,* or servants, who have neither rank nor property.

The chiefs exercise their power over one another in the most haughty and oppressive manner. Of this I shall give two instances. A chief of the lower order had behaved with great civility to one of our officers, and in return I carried him on board and introduced him to Captain Cook, who invited him to dine with us. While we were at table Pareea, who was chief of a superior order, entered, whose face but too plainly manifested his indignation at seeing our guest in so honourable a situation. He immediately seized him by the hair of the head, and was proceeding to drag him out of the cabin when the Captain interfered, and, after a deal of altercation, all the indulgence we could obtain, without coming to a quarrel with Pareea, was that our guest should be suffered to remain, being seated upon the floor, whilst Pareea filled his place at the table. At another time, when Terreeoboo first came on board the *Resolution*, Maiha–maiha, who attended him, finding Pareea on deck, turned him out of the ship in the most ignominious manner.

The religion of these people resembles, in most of its principal features, that of the Society and Friendly Islands. Their *morais*, their *whattas*, their idols, their sacrifices, and their sacred songs, all of which they have in common with each other, are convincing proofs that their religious notions are derived from the same source.

It has been mentioned that the title of *Orona*, with all its honours, was given to Captain Cook; and il is also certain that they regarded us generally as a race of people superior to themselves, and used often to say that the great *Eatooa* dwelled in our country.

Human sacrifices are more frequent here, according to the account of the natives themselves, than in any other islands we visited. These horrid rites are not only had recourse to upon the commencement of war, and preceding great battles, and other signal enterprises, but the death of any considerable chief calls for a sacrifice of one or more *towtows*, according to his rank; and we were told that men were destined to suffer on the death of Terreeoboo.

To this class of their customs may also be referred that of knocking out their fore-teeth, as a propitiatory sacrifice to the *Eatooa* to avert any danger or mischief to which they might be exposed.

On the 15th of March, at seven in the morning, weighed anchor, and passing to the north of Tahoora stood on to the south-west. On the 23rd the wind, which had been moderate for some time, freshened and increased to a strong gale, which split some of our old sails, and made the running rigging very frequently give way. This gale lasted twelve hours; it then became more moderate, and continued so till the 25th at noon, when we entirely lost it, and had only a very light air.

On the 30th, the winds and unsettled state of the weather induced Captain Clerke to alter his plan, and at six in the evening we began to steer north-west, which we continued till the 6th of April, when we lost the trade wind.

The standing orders, established by Captain Cook, of airing the bedding, placing fires between decks, washing them with vinegar, and smoking them with gunpowder, were observed without any intermission. For some time past, even the operation of mending the sailors' old jackets had risen into a duty both of difficulty and importance. It may be necessary to inform those who are unacquainted with the habits of seamen, that they arc so accustomed in ships of war to be directed in the care of themselves by their officers, that they lose the very idea of foresight, and contract the thoughtlessness of infants. I am sure that if our people had been left to their discretion alone, we should have had the whole crew naked before the voyage had been half finished. It was natural to expect that their experience during our voyage to the north last year would have made them sensible of the necessity of paying some attention to these matters; but if such reflections ever occurred to them, their impression was so transitory that, upon our return to the tropical climates, their fur jackets, and the rest of their cold country clothes, were kicked about the decks as things of no value, though it was generally known in both ships that we were to make another voyage towards the pole. They were of course picked up by the officers, and being put into casks, restored about this time to the owners.

On the 12th the wind came gradually round to the east, and increased to a strong gale. Ever since we left the Sandwich Islands we had been incommoded by a leak, which made twelve inches of water every hour; but as we had always been able to keep it under with the hand-pumps, it gave us no great uneasiness till the 13th, when we were greatly alarmed by a sudden inundation that deluged the whole space between decks. The water which had lodged in the coal-hole, not finding a sufficient vent into the well, had forced up the platforms over it, and in a moment set everything afloat. Our situation was indeed exceedingly distressing, nor did we immediately see any means of relieving ourselves. As soon as a passage was made for it, the greatest part of the water emptied itself into the well and enabled us to get out the rest with buckets. But the leak was now so much increased that we were obliged to keep one half of the people constantly pumping and baling till the noon of the 15th. Our men bore, with great cheerfulness, this excessive fatigue, which was much increased by their having no dry place to sleep in, and on this account we began to serve their full allowance of grog.

As we were now approaching the place where a great extent of land is said to have been seen by de Gama, we were glad of the opportunity which the course we were steering gave, of contributing to remove the doubts, if any should be still entertained, relative to this pretended discovery. After standing off and on the whole of this day without seeing anything of the land, we again steered to the northward, not thinking it worth our while to lose time in search of an object, the opinion of whose existence had been already pretty generally exploded.

The sudden alteration from the sultry heat which we felt the beginning of this month to the extreme cold which we now experienced, was attended with great inconvenience to us.

On the 21st we saw a whale and a land-bird, and in the afternoon the water looking muddy, we sounded, but got no ground with a hundred and forty fathoms of line. During the three preceding days we saw large flocks of wildfowl of a species resembling ducks. This is usually considered as a proof of the vicinity of land, but we had no other signs of it since the 16th, in which time we had run upwards of a hundred and fifty leagues.

On the 22nd the cold was exceedingly severe, and the ropes were so frozen that it was with difficulty we could force them through the blocks.

On the 23rd, at six in the morning, the land appeared in mountains covered with snow, and extending from north-east to south-west, a highly conical rock, bearing south-west, at three or four leagues' distance. We had no sooner taken this imperfect view than we were covered with a thick fog. As soon as the weather cleared up we stood in to make a nearer view of the land, and a more dismal and dreary prospect I never beheld. The coast appears straight and uniform, having no inlets or bays; the ground from the shore rises in hills of a moderate elevation, behind which are ranges of mountains, whose summits were lost in the clouds. The whole scene was entirely covered with snow, except the sides of some of the cliffs, which rose too abruptly from the sea for the snow to lie upon them.

The wind continued blowing very strong from the north-east, with thick hazy weather and sleet, from the 24th till the 28th. The ship appeared to be a complete mass of ice; the shrouds were so encrusted with it as to measure in circumference more than double their usual size; and, in short, the experience of the oldest seaman among us had never met with anything like the continued showers of sleet and the extreme cold which we now encountered.

On the 28th, in the morning, the weather at last cleared, and the wind fell to a light breeze from the same quarter as before. We had a fine warm day, and as we now began to expect a thaw, the men were employed in breaking the ice from off the rigging, masts, and sails, in order to prevent its falling on our heads. About three in the afternoon a fair wind sprung up from the southward, with which we stood in for Awatska Bay.

Having passed the mouth of the bay, which is about four miles long, we opened a large circular basin of twenty-five miles in circumference, and at half-past four came to an anchor in six fathoms water. We examined every corner of the bay with our glasses in search of the town of St Peter and St Paul, which, according to the accounts given us at Oonalashka, we had conceived to be a place of some strength and consideration. At length we discovered, on a narrow point of the land to the north-east, a few miserable log-houses and some conical huts, raised on poles, amounting in all to about thirty, which, from their situation, notwithstanding all the respect we wished to entertain for a Russian ostrog, we were under the necessity of concluding to be Petro-paulowska. However, in justice to the generous and hospitable treatment we found here, I shall beg leave to anticipate the reader's curiosity, by assuring him that our disappointment proved to be more of a laughable than a serious nature. For in this wretched extremity of the earth, barricaded with ice, and covered with summer snow, in a poor miserable port, we met with feelings of humanity, joined to a greatness of mind, which would have done honour to any nation or climate.

During the night much ice drifted by us with the tide, and at daylight I was sent with the boats to examine the bay, and deliver the letters we had brought from Oonalashka to the Russian commander.

As we approached, we observed a few men hurrying backward and forward, and presently after, a sledge drawn by dogs, with one of the inhabitants in it, came down to the sea-side opposite to us. Whilst we were gazing at this unusual sight, and admiring the great civility of this stranger, which we imagined had brought him to our assistance, the man, after viewing us for some time very attentively, turned short round, and went off with great speed towards the ostrog. We were not less chagrined than disappointed at this abrupt departure, as we began to find our journey over the ice attended not only with great difficulty, but even with danger.

When we were within a quarter of a mile of the ostrog, we perceived a body of armed men marching towards us, consisting of about thirty soldiers, headed by a decent looking person with a cane in his hand. He halted within a few yards of us, and drew up his men in a martial and good order. I delivered to him Ismyloff's letters, and endeavoured to make him understand as well as I could (though I afterwards found in vain), that we were English, and had brought them papers from Oonalashka. After having examined us attentively, he began to conduct us towards the village in great silence and solemnity, frequently halting his men to form them in different manners, and make them perform several parts of their manual exercise.

At length we arrived at the house of the commanding officer of the party, into which we were ushered; and after no small stir in giving orders, and disposing of the military without doors, our host made his appearance, accompanied by another person, whom we understood to be the secretary of the port. One of Ismyloff's letters was now opened, and the other sent off by a special messenger to Bolcheretsk, a town on the west side of the peninsula of Kamtschatka where the Russian commander of this province usually resides.

The officer in whose house we were at present entertained was a sergeant, and the commander of the ostrog. Nothing could exceed the kindness and hospitality of his behaviour, after he had recovered from the alarm occasioned by our arrival. We found the house insufferably hot, but exceedingly neat and clean. After I had changed my wet clothes, which the sergeant's civility enabled me to do, by furnishing me with a complete suit of his own, we were invited to sit down to dinner, which I have no doubt was the best he could procure; and, considering the shortness of time he had to provide it, was managed with some ingenuity. The sergeant's wife brought in several dishes herself, and was not permitted to sit down at table. Having finished our repast, during which it is hardly necessary to remark that our conversation was confined to a few bows, and other signs of mutual respect, we endeavoured to open to our host the cause and objects of our visit to this port. As Ismyloff had probably written to them on the same subject in the letters we had before delivered, he appeared very readily to conceive our meaning; but as there was unfortunately no one in the place that could talk any other language except Russian or Kamtschadale, we found the utmost difficulty in comprehending the information he meant to convey to us. After some time spent in these endeavours to understand one another, we conceived the sum of the intelligence we had procured, to be, that though no supply either of provisions or naval stores were to be had at this place, yet that these articles were in great plenty at Bolcheretsk. That the commander would most probably be very willing to give us what we wanted, but that till the sergeant had received orders from him, neither he nor his people, nor the natives, could even venture to go on board the ship.

It was now time for us to take our leave; and a sledge, drawn by five dogs, with a driver, was immediately provided for each of our party. The sailors were highly delighted with this mode of conveyance; and what diverted them still more was, that the two boat-hooks had also a sledge appropriated to themselves. These sledges are so light, and their construction so well adapted to the purposes for which they are intended, that they went with great expedition and perfect safety over the ice, which it would have been impossible for us, with all our caution, to have passed on foot.

On our return, we found the boats towing the ship toward the village; and at seven we got close to the ice and moored. Next morning the carpenters were set to work to stop the leak, which had given us so much trouble during our last run. Several of our gentlemen paid their visits to the sergeant, by whom they were received with great civility; and Captain Clerke sent him two bottles of rum, which he understood would be the most acceptable present he could make him, and received in return some fine fowls of the grouse kind, and twenty trouts.

The following morning, on our observing two sledges drive into the village, Captain Clerke sent me on shore, to inquire whether any message was arrived from the commander of Kamtschatka, which, according to the sergeant's account, might now be expected, in consequence of the intelligence that had been sent of our arrival. Bolcheretsk, by the usual route, is about 135 English miles from St Peter and St Paul's. Our despatches were sent off in a sledge drawn by dogs, on the 29th, about noon. And the answer arrived, as we afterwards found, early this morning; so that they were only a little more than three days and a half in performing a journey of 270 miles.

The return of the commander's answer was, however, concealed from us for the present; and I was told on my arrival at the sergeant's, that we should hear from him the next day.

About ten o'clock next forenoon, we saw several sledges driving down to the edge of the ice, and sent a boat to conduct the persons who were in them on board. One of these was a Russian merchant from Bolcheretsk, named Fedositsch, and the other a German, called Port, who had brought a letter from Major Behm, the commander of Kamtschatka, to Captain Clerke. When they got to the edge of the ice, and saw distinctly the size of the ships, which lay within about 200 yards from them, they appeared to be exceedingly alarmed; and before they would venture to embark, desired two of our boat's crew might be left on shore as hostages for their safety. We afterwards found that Ismyloff, in his letter to the commander, had misrepresented us, for what reason we could not conceive, as two small trading boats; and that the sergeant, who had only seen the ships at a distance, had not in his despatches rectified the mistake.

When they arrived on board, we still found, from their cautious and timorous behaviour, that they were under some unaccountable apprehensions; and an uncommon degree of satisfaction was visible in their countenances on the German's finding a person amongst us with whom he could converse. This was Mr Webber, who spoke that language exceedingly well. Mr Port being introduced to Captain Clerke, delivered to him the commander's letter, which was written in German, inviting him and his officers to Bolcheretsk. Mr Port at the same time acquainted him that the major had conceived a very wrong idea of the size of the ships, and of the service we were engaged in; Ismyloff, in his letter, having represented us as two small English packet boats, and cautioned him to be on his guard, insinuating that he suspected us to be no better than pirates.

Being now enabled to converse with the Russians by the aid of our interpreter, our first inquiries were directed to the means of procuring a supply of fresh provisions and naval stores, from the want of which we had been for some time in great distress. On inquiry, it appeared that the whole stock of live cattle which the country about the bay could furnish amounted only to two heifers; and these the sergeant very readily promised to procure us. Our applications were next made to the merchant, but we found the terms upon which he offered to serve us so exorbitant, that Captain Clerke thought it necessary to send an officer to visit the commander at Bolcheretsk, and to inquire into the price of stores at that place.

Captain Clerke having thought proper to fix on me for this service, I received orders, together with Mr Webber, who was to accompany me as an interpreter, to be ready to set out the next day.

Captain Gore was now added to our party, and we were attended by Messrs Port and Fedositsch, with two Cossacks, and were provided by our conductors with warm furred clothing, a precaution which we soon found very necessary, as it began to snow briskly just after we set out.

On the morning of the second day, we were met by the Toion, or Chief of Karatchin, who had been apprised of our coming, and had provided canoes that were lighter, and better contrived for navigating the higher parts of the river Awatska. We now went on very rapidly, the toion's people being both stout and fresh, and remarkable for their expertness in this business. At ten we got to the ostrog, the seat of his command, where we were received at the waterside by the Kamtschadale men and women, and some Russian servants belonging to Fedositsch, who were employed in making canoes. They were all dressed out in their best clothes.

This ostrog was pleasantly situated by the side of the river. We were conducted to the dwelling of the toion, who was a plain decent man, born of a Russian woman by a Kamtschadale father. His house, like all the rest in this country, was divided into two apartments. A long narrow table, with a bench round it, was all the furniture we saw in the outer; and the household stuff of the inner, which was the kitchen, was not less simple and scanty. But the kind attention of our host, and the hearty welcome we received, more than compensated for the poverty of his lodgings.

Whilst we were at dinner in this miserable hut, the guests of a people with whose existence we had before been scarcely acquainted, and at the extremity of the habitable globe, a solitary half-worn pewter spoon, whose shape was familiar to us, attracted our attention; and on examination we found it stamped on the back with the word London. I cannot pass over this circumstance in silence, out of gratitude for the many pleasant thoughts, the anxious hopes and tender remembrances it excited in us. Those who have experienced the effects that long absence and extreme distance from their native country produce on the mind, will readily conceive the pleasure such trifling incidents can give.

We were now to quit the river, and perform the next part of our journey on sledges.

After walking about the village, which contained nothing remarkable, we returned to supper, and afterwards took a short repose; but we were soon awakened by the melancholy howlings of the dogs, which continued all the time our baggage was lashing upon the sledges; but as soon as they were yoked, and we were all prepared to set out, this changed into a light cheerful yelping, which entirely ceased the instant they marched off. These dogs are in shape somewhat like the Pomeranian breed, but considerably larger.

As we did not choose to trust to our own skill, we had each of us a man to drive and guide the sledge, which, from the state the roads were now in, proved a very laborious business. I had a very good-humoured Cossack to attend me, who was, however, so very unskilful in his business, that we were overturned almost every minute, to the great entertainment of the rest of the company. Our party consisted in all of ten sledges. That in which Captain Gore was carried was made of two lashed together, and abundantly provided with furs and bear skins; it had ten dogs, yoked four abreast; as had also some of those that were heavy laden with baggage.

When we had proceeded about four miles it began to rain; which, added to the darkness of the night, threw us all into confusion. It was at last agreed that we should remain where we were till daylight; and, accordingly, wrapping ourselves up in our furs, we waited patiently for morning. About three o'clock we were called on to set out, our guides being apprehensive that if we waited longer we might be stopped by the thaw, and neither be able to proceed nor to return. After encountering many difficulties, which were principally occasioned by the bad condition of the road, at two in the afternoon we got safe to an ostrog called Natcheekin.

We were received here in the same hospitable manner as at Karatchin, and in the afternoon we went to visit a remarkable hot spring which is near this village. We saw at some distance, the steam rising from it as from a boiling cauldron; and as we approached, perceived the air had a strong sulphureous smell. The main spring forms a basin of about three feet in diameter, besides which there are a number of lesser springs of the same degree of heat in the adjacent ground; so that the whole spot, to the extent of near an acre, was so hot that we could not stand two minutes in the same place. The water flowing from these springs is collected in a small bathing pond, and afterward forms a little rivulet; which, at the distance of about a hundred and fifty yards, falls into the river. The bath, they told us, had wrought great cures in several disorders, such as rheumatism, swelled and contracted joints, and scorbutic ulcers.

The next morning we embarked on the Bolchoireka in canoes. The country on each side was very romantic but unvaried; the river running between mountains of the most craggy and barren aspect, where there was nothing to diversify the scene, but now and then the sight of a bear, and the flights of wildfowl.

At daylight on the 12th, we found we had got clear of the mountains, and were entering a low extensive plain, covered with shrubby trees. About nine in the forenoon we arrived at an ostrog called Opatchin, which is computed to be fifty miles from Natcheekin, and is nearly of the same size as Karatchin. We found here a sergeant with four Russian soldiers, who had been two days waiting for our arrival, and who immediately despatched a light boat to Bolcheretsk with intelligence of our approach. The remainder of our passage was performed with great facility and expedition, the river growing more rapid as we descended, and less obstructed by shoals.

As we approached the capital, we were sorry to observe, from an appearance of much stir and bustle, that we were to be received in form. Decent clothes had been for some time a scarce commodity amongst us; and our travelling dresses were made up of a burlesque mixture of European, Indian, and Kamtschadale fashions. The manner in which we were received by the commander was the most engaging that could be conceived, and increased my mortification at finding that he had almost entirely forgotten the French language, so that the satisfaction of conversing with him was wholly confined to Mr Webber, who spoke the German, his native tongue.

In company with Major Behm was Captain Shmaleff, the second in command, and another officer, with the whole body of the merchants of the place. They conducted us to the commander's house, where we were received by his lady with great civility, and found tea and other refreshments prepared for us.

About seven o'clock the commander, conceiving we might be fatigued with our journey, and desirous of taking some repose, begged he might conduct us to our lodgings. In our way we passed by two guard-houses, where the men were turned out under arms in compliment to Captain Gore; and were afterward brought to a very neat and decent house, which the major gave us to understand was to be our residence during our stay. Two sentinels were posted at the door, and in a house adjoining there was a sergeant's guard. Here the major took his leave, with a promise to see us next day.

Early in the morning we received the compliments of the commander, of Captain Shmaleff, and of the principal inhabitants of the town, who all honoured us with visits soon after. The two first having sent for Port, after we were gone to rest, and inquired of him what articles we seemed to be most in want of on board the ships, we found them prepared to insist on our sharing with the garrison under their command, in what little stock of provisions they had remaining.

We agreed to accept the liberality of these hospitable strangers with the best grace we could, but on condition that we might be made acquainted with the price of the articles we were to be supplied with, and that Captain Clerke should give bills to the amount upon the Victualling Office in London. This the major positively refused; and whenever it was afterwards urged, stopped us short by telling us he was certain that he could not oblige his mistress more than in giving every assistance in his power to her good friends and allies the English.

In return for such singular generosity we had little to bestow but our admiration and our thanks. Fortunately, however, Captain Clerke had sent by me a set of prints and maps belonging to the last voyage of Captain Cook, which he desired me to present in his name to the commander, who, being an enthusiast in everything relating to discoveries, received it with a satisfaction which showed that, though a trifle, nothing could have been more acceptable. Captain Clerke had likewise entrusted me with a discretionary power of showing him a chart of the discoveries made in the present voyage, and as I judged that a person in his situation, and of his turn of mind, would be exceedingly gratified by a communication of this sort, I made no scruple to repose in him a confidence of which his whole conduct showed him to be deserving.

I had the pleasure to find that he felt this compliment as I hoped he would, and was much struck at seeing in one view the whole of that coast, as well on the side of Asia as on that of America, of which his countrymen had been so many years employed in acquiring a partial and imperfect knowledge.

We dined this day at the commander's, who, studious on every occasion to gratify our curiosity, had, besides a number of dishes dressed in our own way, prepared a great variety of others after the Russian and Kamtschadale manner. The afternoon was employed in taking a view of the town and of the adjacent country. Bolcheretsk is situated in a low swampy plain that extends to the sea of Okotsk, being about forty miles long, and of a considerable breadth. It lies on the north side of the *Bolchoi-reka* (or great river). Below the town the river is from six to eight feet deep, and about a quarter of a mile broad. There is no corn of any species cultivated in this part of the country; and Major Behm informed me that his was the only garden that had yet been planted. I saw about twenty or thirty cows, and the major had six stout horses. These, and their dogs, are the only tame animals they possess.

The houses in Bolcheretsk are all of one fashion, being built of logs and thatched. That of the commander is much larger than the rest, consisting of three rooms of a considerable size, neatly papered, and which might have been reckoned handsome, if the talc, with which the windows were covered, had not given them a poor and disagreeable appearance. The inhabitants, taken all together, amount to between five and six hundred.

The next morning we applied privately to the merchant Fedositsch to purchase some tobacco for the sailors, who had been upward of a twelvemonth without this favourite commodity. However, this, like all our other transactions of the same kind, came immediately to the major's knowledge, and we were soon after surprised to find in our house four bags of tobacco, weighing upward of a hundred pounds each, which he begged might be presented in the name of himself and the garrison under his command, to our sailors. At the same time they had sent us twenty loaves of fine sugar, and as many pounds of tea, being articles they understood we were in great want of, which they begged to be indulged in presenting to the officers. Along with these, Madame Behm had also sent a present for Captain Clerke, consisting of fresh

butter, honey, figs, rice, and some other little things of the same
kind, attended with many wishes that in his infirm state of health
they might be of service to him. It was in vain we tried to oppose
this profusion of bounty, which I was really anxious to restrain,
being convinced that they were giving away, not a share, but
almost the whole stock of the garrison.

We dined this day with Captain Shmaleff, and in the afternoon,
in order to vary our amusements, he treated us with an exhibition
of the Russian and Kamtschadale dancing. No description can
convey an adequate idea of this rude and uncouth entertainment.
The figure of the Russian dance was much like those of our
hornpipes, and was performed either single, or by two or four
persons at a time. Their steps were short and quick, with the feet
scarce raised from the ground. But if the Russian dance was
ridiculous, the Kamtschadale was the most whimsical idea that ever
entered into any people's heads. It is intended to represent the
awkward and clumsy gestures of the bear. The body was always
bowed, and the knees bent, whilst the arms were used in imitating
the tricks and attitudes of that animal.

As our journey to Bolcheretsk had taken up more time than we
expected, and were told that our return might prove still more
difficult and tedious, we were under the necessity of acquainting
the commander this evening with our intention of setting out the
next day. We were most agreeably surprised when the major told
us that if we could stay one day longer he would accompany us, as
he should feel great pleasure in returning with us to St Peter and St
Paul's, that he might himself be a witness of everything done for us
that it was in their power to do.

We afterwards dined with the commander, who, in order to let
us see as much of the manners of the inhabitants, and of the
customs of the country, as our time would permit, invited the
whole of the better sort of people in the village to his house this
evening. All the women appeared very splendidly dressed, after the
Kamtschadale fashion. The whole was like some enchanted scene
in the midst of the wildest and most dreary country in the world.
Our entertainment again consisted of dancing and singing.

The next morning being fixed for our departure, we retired early
to our lodgings, when the first things we saw were three travelling
dresses, made after the fashion of the country, which the major had

provided for us. Indeed, what with his liberal presents, and the kindness of Captain Shmaleff, and many other individuals, who all begged to throw in their mite, together with the ample stock of provisions he had sent us for our journey, we had amassed no inconsiderable load of baggage.

During the course of our journey, we were much pleased with the great goodwill with which the *toions* and their Kamtschadales afforded us their assistance at the different ostrogs through which we passed; and I could not but observe the pleasure that appeared on their countenances on seeing the major, and their strong expressions of sorrow on hearing he was so soon going to leave them.

We had despatched a messenger to Captain Clerke, from Bolcheretsk, with an account of our reception, and of the major's intention of returning with us; at the same time apprising him of the day he might probably expect to see us. The major was much struck at the robust and healthy appearance of the boats' crews, and still more at seeing most of them without any other covering than a shirt and trousers, although at the very moment it actually snowed.

When Major Behm arrived, he was saluted with thirteen guns, and received with every other mark of distinction that it was in our power to pay him.

After visiting Captain Clerke, and taking a view of both the ships, he returned to dinner on board the *Resolution*; and in the afternoon the various curiosities we had collected in the course of our voyage were shown him, and a complete assortment of every article presented to him by the Captain. On this occasion I must not pass over an instance of great generosity and gratitude in the sailors of both ships, who, when they were told of the handsome present of tobacco that was made them by the major, desired, entirely of their own accord, that their grog might be stopped, and their allowance of spirits presented, on their part, to the garrison of Bolcheretsk. We could not but admire so extraordinary a sacrifice; and that they might not suffer by it, Captain Clerke and the rest of the officers substituted, in the room of the very small quantity the major could be prevailed on to accept, the same quantity of rum. This, with a dozen or two of Cape wine for Madame Behm, and such other little presents as were in our power to bestow, were accepted in the most obliging manner.

Major Behm having resigned the command of Kamtschatka, intended to have set out in a short time for Petersburg; and he now offered to charge himself with any despatches we might trust to his care. This was an opportunity not to be neglected; and Captain Clerke being persuaded that the whole account of our discoveries might safely be trusted to a person who had given such striking proof both of his public and private virtues, and considering that we had a very hazardous part of the voyage still to undertake, determined to send by him the whole of the journal of our late commander, with that part of his own which completed the period from Captain Cook's death till our arrival at Kamtschatka, together with a chart of all our discoveries, to be delivered to our ambassador at the Russian court.

During the three following days the major was entertained alternately in the two ships in the best manner we were able. On the 25th he took his leave, and was saluted with thirteen guns; and the sailors, at their own desire, gave him three cheers.

Short as our acquaintance had been with Major Behm, his noble and disinterested conduct had inspired us with the highest respect and esteem for him. The intrinsic value of the private presents we received from him, exclusive of the stores, must have amounted to upwards of two hundred pounds. But this generosity was far exceeded by the delicacy with which all his favours were conferred. 'The service in which you are employed,' he would often say, 'is for the general advantage of mankind, and therefore gives you a right, not merely to the offices of humanity, but to the privileges of citizens, in whatever country you may be thrown. I am sure I am acting agreeably to the wishes of my mistress in affording you all the relief in our power, and I cannot forget either her character, or my own honour, so much as to barter for the performance of a duty.'

During the time that the ships lay in the harbour of St Peter and St Paul, Captain Clerke's health continued daily to decline, notwithstanding the salutary change of diet which the country of Kamtschatka afforded him.

On the 1st of June we got on board nine thousand pounds weight of rye flour, with which we were supplied from the stores of St Peter and St Paul, and the *Discovery* had a proportional quantity. The men were immediately put on full allowance of bread, which they had not been indulged in since our leaving the Cape of Good Hope.

June 4th we had fresh breezes and hard rain, which disappointed us in our design of dressing the ships, and obliged us to content ourselves with firing twenty-one guns in honour of the day, and celebrating it in other respects in the best manner we were able.

On the 6th, twenty head of cattle, of a moderate size, were sent us by the commander's orders, from the Verchnei ostrog, which is near a hundred miles from this place in a direct line. They arrived in good condition. The eight following days were employed in making ready for sea.

Before daylight on the 15th, we were surprised with a rumbling noise resembling distant hollow thunder; and when the day broke we found the decks and sides of the ships covered with a fine dust like emery near an inch thick. The air at the same time continued loaded and darkened with this substance, and, toward the volcano mountain, situated to the north of the harbour, it was so thick and black that we could not distinguish the body of the hill. Along with the cinders fell several small stones which had undergone no change from the action of fire. In the evening we had dreadful thunder and lightning, which, with the darkness of the atmosphere, and the sulphureous smell of the air, produced altogether a most awful and terrifying effect. We were at this time about eight leagues from the foot of the mountain.

The aspect of the country was now very different from what it had been on our first arrival. The snow had disappeared, and the sides of the hills were covered with a beautiful verdure.

As it was Captain Clerke's intention to keep as much in sight of the coast of Kamtschatka as the weather would permit, the volcano was still seen throwing up immense volumes of smoke; and we had no soundings with one hundred and fifty fathoms at the distance of four leagues from the shore.

At noon, on the 6th of July, we passed a considerable number of large masses of ice; and, observing that it still adhered in several places to the shore on the continent of Asia, we were not much surprised to fall in, at three in the afternoon, with an extensive body of it stretching away to the westward. This sight gave great discouragement to our hopes of advancing much farther northward this year than we had the preceding.

Having little wind in the afternoon, we hoisted out the boats in pursuit of the sea-horses, which were in great numbers upon the detached pieces of ice; but they soon returned without success, these animals being exceedingly shy, and before they could come within gunshot, always making their retreat into the water.

We had sailed by the 9th near forty leagues ro the westward, along the edge of the ice, without seeing any openings or a clear sea to the northward beyond it, and had therefore no prospect of advancing farther north for the present.

On the 10th we hoisted out the boats again and sent them in pursuit of the sea-horses, which were in great numbers on the pieces of ice that surrounded us. Our people were more successful than they had been before, returning with three large ones and a young one, besides killing and wounding several others. The gentlemen who went on this party were witnesses of several remarkable instances of parental affection in those animals. On the approach of our boats toward the ice, they all took their cubs under their fins and endeavoured to escape with them into the sea.

At eight in the evening a breeze sprung up to the eastward, with which we still continued our course to the southward, and at twelve fell in with numerous large bodies of ice. We endeavoured to push through them with an easy sail, for fear of damaging the ship; and having got a little further to the southward, nothing was to be seen but one compact field of ice, stretching to the south-west, south-east, and north-east, as far as the eye could reach.

We continued to steer northward, with a moderate southerly breeze and fair weather, till the 13th, at ten in the forenoon, when we again found ourselves close in with a solid field of ice, to which we could see no limits from the masthead. This at once dashed all our hopes of penetrating farther.

Captain Clerke now resolved to make one more and final attempt on the American coast for Baffin's or Hudson's Bay, since we had been able to advance the farthest on this side last year. Accordingly, we kept working the remaining part of the day to the windward with a fresh easterly breeze.

On the 16th, in the forenoon, we found ourselves embayed, the ice having taken a sudden turn to the south-east, and in one compact body surrounding us on all sides, except on the south quarter. We therefore hauled our wind to the southward, being at this time in twenty-six fathoms water, and, as we supposed, about twenty-five leagues from the coast of America.

On the 18th, in the morning, we passed some small logs of drift-wood, and saw abundance of sea-parrots, and the small ice-birds, and likewise a number of whales. About nine in the evening a white bear was seen swimming close by the *Discovery*; it afterwards made to the ice, on which were also two others.

On the 19th, at one in the morning, the weather clearing up, we were so completely embayed, that there was no opening left but to the south, to which quarter we accordingly directed our course, returning through a remarkably smooth water. We were never able to penetrate farther north than at this time, and this was five leagues short of the point to which we advanced last season.

In the afternoon we saw two white bears in the water, to which we immediately gave chase in the jolly boat, and had the good fortune to kill them both. The larger, which probably was the dam of the younger, being shot first, the other would not quit it, though it might easily have escaped on the ice while the men were reloading, but remained swimming about, till after being fired upon several times, it was shot dead. The weight of the largest was 436 pounds.

These animals afforded us a few excellent meals of fresh meat. The flesh had indeed a strong fishy taste, but was in every respect infinitely superior to that of the sea horse; which, nevertheless, our people were again persuaded, without much difficulty, to prefer to their salted provisions.

At eight in the morning of the 21st, the wind freshening and the fog clearing away, we saw the American coast to the south-east, at the distance of eight or ten leagues, and hauled in for it, but were again stopped by the ice, and obliged to bear away to the westward along the edge of it.

Thus a connected solid field of ice, rendering every effort we could make to a nearer approach to the land fruitless, and joining, as we judged, to it, we took a farewell of the north-east passage to Old England.[1] I shall beg leave to give, in Captain Clerke's own words, the reasons of this his final determination, as well as of his

1 The highest latitude attained by Captain Clerke appears to have been 71° 56' N., which is to the northward of Icy Cape.

future plans; and this the rather, as it is the last transaction his health permitted him to write down.

It is now impossible to proceed the least farther to the north-ward upon this coast (America); and it is equally as improbable that this amazing mass of ice should be dissolved by the few remaining summer weeks which will terminate this season; but it will continue, it is to be believed, as it now is, an insurmountable barrier to every attempt we can possibly make. I therefore think it the best step that can be taken for the good of the service, to trace the sea over to the Asiatic coast, and to try if I can find any opening that will admit me farther north; if not, to see what more is to be done upon that coast, where I hope, yet cannot much flatter myself, to meet with better success, for the sea is now so choked with ice, that a passage, I fear, is totally out of the question.

Captain Clerke having determined, for the reasons just assigned, to give up all further attempts on the coast of America, and to make his last efforts in search of a passage on the coast of the opposite continent, we continued during the afternoon of the 21st of July to steer to the west north-west, through much loose ice.

In the morning of the 23rd, the clear water in which we continued to stand to and fro did not exceed a mile and a half, and was every instant lessening. At length, after using our utmost endeavours to clear the loose ice, we were driven to the necessity of forcing a passage to the southward, which at half past seven we accomplished, but not without subjecting the ship to some very severe shocks. The *Discovery* was less successful, for at eleven, when they had nigh got clear out, she became so entangled by several large pieces that her way was stopped, and immediately dropping to leeward, she fell broadside foremost on the edge of a considerable body of ice; and having at the same time an open sea to windward, the surf caused her to strike violently upon it. This mass at length either so far broke or moved as to set them at liberty to make another trial to escape; but, unfortunately, before the ship gathered way enough to be under command, she again fell to leeward on another fragment, and the swell making it unsafe to lie to wind-ward, and finding no chance of getting clear, they pushed into a small opening, furled their sails, and made fast with ice-hooks.

In this dangerous situation we saw them at noon about three miles from us, a fresh gale driving more ice to the north-west, and increasing the body that lay between us. To add to the gloomy apprehensions which began to force themselves on us, at half past four in the afternoon, the weather becoming thick and hazy, we lost sight of the *Discovery*. Our apprehensions for her safety did not cease till nine, when we heard her guns in answer to ours; and soon after, being hailed by her, were informed that upon the change of wind the ice began to separate, and that, setting all their sails, they forced a passage through it, though with considerable damage.

On the 24th, we had fresh breezes from south-west, with hazy weather, and kept running to the south-east till eleven in the forenoon, when a large body of loose ice, to which we could see no end, again obstructed our course.

As it was now necessary to come to some determination with respect to the course we were next to steer, Captain Clerke sent a boat with the carpenters on board the *Discovery*, to inquire into the particulars of the damage she had sustained. They returned in the evening with the report, that the damages they had received would require three weeks to repair.

Thus, finding a farther advance to the northward, as well as a nearer approach to either continent, obstructed by a sea blocked up with ice, we judged it both injurious to the service, as well as fruitless with respect to the design of our voyage, to make any farther attempts toward a passage. This, added to the representations of Captain Gore, determined Captain Clerke to sail for Awatska Bay, to repair our damages there; and, before the winter should set in, to explore the coast of Japan.

I will not endeavour to conceal the joy that brightened the countenances of every individual, as soon as Captain Clerke's resolutions were made known. We were all heartily sick of a navigation full of danger, and in which the utmost perseverance had not been repaid with the smallest probability of success. We therefore turned our faces home, after an absence of three years, with a delight and satisfaction which, notwithstanding the tedious voyage we had still to make, and the immense distance we had to run, were as freely entertained, and perhaps as fully enjoyed, as if we had been already in sight of the Land's End.

Captain Clerke was now no longer able to get out of his bed; he therefore desired that the officers would receive their orders from me, and directed that we should proceed with all speed to Awatska Bay. The wind continuing westerly, we stood on to the south till early on the morning of the 19th, when, after a few hours' rain, it blew from the eastward and freshened to a strong gale. We accordingly made the most of it while it lasted, by standing to the westward under all the sail we could carry. On the 21st, at half past five in the morning, we saw a very high peaked mountain on the coast of Kamtschatka, called Cheepoonskoi Mountain, twenty-five or thirty leagues distant.

On the 22nd of August 1779, at nine o'clock in the morning, departed this life, Captain Charles Clerke, in the thirty-eighth year of his age. He died of a consumption which had evidently commenced before he left England, and of which he had lingered during the whole voyage. His very gradual decay had long made him a melancholy object to his friends; yet the equanimity with which he bore it, the constant flow of good spirits, which continued to the last hour, and a cheerful resignation to his fate, afforded them some consolation. It was impossible not to feel a more than common degree of compassion for a person whose whole life had been a continued scene of those difficulties and hardships to which a seaman's occupation is subject, and under which he at last sunk. He was brought up to the navy from his earliest youth, and had been in several actions during the war which began in 1756; particularly in that between the *Bellona* and *Courageux*, where, being stationed in the mizzen-top, he was carried overboard with the mast, but was taken up without having received any hurt. He was midshipman in the *Dolphin*, commanded by Commodore Byron, on her first voyage round the world, and afterwards served on the American station. In 1768, he made his second voyage round the world in the *Endeavour*, as master's mate, and, by the promotion which took place during the expedition, he returned a lieutenant. His third voyage round the world was in the *Resolution*, of which he was appointed the second lieutenant; and soon after his return in 1775, he was promoted to the rank of master and commander. When the present expedition was ordered to be fitted out, he was appointed to the *Discovery*, to accompany Captain Cook, and by the death of the latter, succeeded as has been already mentioned, to the chief command.

It would be doing his memory extreme injustice not to say, that during the short time the expedition was under his direction, he was most zealous and anxious for its success. His health, about the time the principal command devolved upon him, began to decline very rapidly, and was every way unequal to encounter the rigours of a high northern climate. But the vigour and activity of his mind had in no shape suffered by the decay of his body, and though he knew that, by delaying his return to a warmer climate, he was giving up the only chance that remained for his recovery, yet careful and jealous to the last degree, that a regard to his own situation should never bias his judgment to the prejudice of the service, he persevered in the search of a passage till it was the opinion of every officer in both ships that it was impracticable, and that any farther attempts would not only be fruitless but dangerous.

Next day we anchored in the harbour of St Peter and St Paul, when our old friend the sergeant, who was still the commander of the place, came on board with a present of berries, intended for our poor deceased captain. He was exceedingly affected when we told him of his death, and showed him the coffin that contained his body. He signified his intention of sending off an express to the commander of Bolcheretsk, to acquaint him with our arrival, and Captain Gore availed himself of that occasion of writing him a letter, in which he requested that sixteen head of black cattle might be sent with all possible expedition.

In the morning of the 25th, Captain Gore made out the new commissions, in consequence of Captain Clerke's death; appointing himself to the command of the *Resolution*, and me to the command of the *Discovery*, and Mr Lanyan, master's mate of the *Resolution*, who had served in that capacity on board the *Adventure* in the former voyage, was promoted to the vacant lieutenancy. These promotions produced several other arrangements of course. The artificers were now busily employed in the necessary repairs. On Sunday afternoon, August the 29th, we paid the last offices to Captain Clerke. The officers and men of both ships walked in procession to the grave, whilst the ships fired minute guns; and the service being ended, the marines fired three volleys. He was interred under a tree, which stands on a rising ground in the valley to the north-side of the harbour, where the hospital and store-houses are situated. All the Russians in the garrison were assembled, and attended with great respect and solemnity.

The next day an ensign arrived from Bolcheretsk with a letter from the commander to Captain Gore, by which we understood that orders had been given about the cattle and that they might be expected here in a few days; and moreover, that Captain Shmaleff, the present commander, would himself pay us a visit immediately on the arrival of a sloop which was daily expected from Okotsk.

On the 15th we had finished the repairs, got on board all our food and water, and were ready to put to sea at a day's notice; but the cattle were not yet arrived, and as fresh provisions were the most important article of our wants, we could not think of taking our departure without them. We therefore thought this a favourable opportunity of taking some amusement on shore. Accordingly Captain Gore proposed a party of bear-hunting, which we all very readily came into; but we had but indifferent sport.

The 22nd being the anniversary of his Majesty's coronation, twenty-one guns were fired, and the handsomest feast our situation would allow of was prepared in honour of the day. As we were sitting down to dinner, the arrival of Captain Shmaleff was announced. He acquainted us, that our not having received the sixteen head of black cattle we had desired might be sent down, was owing to the very heavy rains at Verchnei, which had prevented their setting out. Specimens of all our curiosities were presented to him, and Captain Gore added to them a gold watch and a fowling-piece. Next morning he took his leave.

The next day I set on foot another hunting party, and put myself under the direction of the clerk of the parish, who was a celebrated bear-hunter. We arrived by sunset at the side of one of the larger lakes. The next step was to conceal ourselves as much as possible, and this we were able to do very effectually among some long grass and brushwood that grew close to the water's edge. We had not lain long in ambush before we had the pleasure to hear the growling of bears in different parts round about us, and our expectations were soon gratified by the sight of one of them in the water, which seemed to be swimming directly to the place where we lay hid. The moon at this time gave a considerable light; and when the animal had advanced about fifteen yards, three of us fired at it pretty nearly at the same time. The beast immediately turned short on one side, and made a noise which could not properly be called roaring, nor growling, nor yelling, but was a mixture of all three, and horrible beyond description. It retreated to some thick bushes at a little distance, and continued to make the same terrible noise; and though the Kamtschadales were persuaded it was mortally wounded, they thought it most advisable not to rouse it again for the present. It was at this time past nine o'clock, and the night threatening a change of weather, we returned home, and deferred the gratification of our curiosity till morning, when we found the bear dead in the place to which it had been watched. It proved to be a female, and beyond the common size.

The Kamtschadales very thankfully acknowledged their obligations to the bears for what little advancement they had hitherto made, either in the sciences or polite arts. They confess that they owe to them all their skill, both in physic and surgery; that, by remarking with what herbs these animals rub the wounds they have received, and what they have recourse to when sick and languid, they have become acquainted with most of the simples in use among them, either in the way of internal medicine or external application; they acknowledge the bears likewise for their dancing masters. Indeed, the evidence of one's senses puts this out of dispute; for the bear-dance of the Kamtschadales is an exact counterpart of every attitude and gesture peculiar to this animal through its various functions; and this is the foundation and groundwork of all their other dances, and what they value themselves most upon.

No occurrence worth mentioning took place till the 30th, when Captain Gore went to Paratounca to put up, in the church there, an escutcheon, prepared by Mr Webber, with an inscription upon it, setting forth Captain Clerke's age and rank, and the object of the expedition in which he was engaged at the time of his decease. We also affixed to the tree, under which he was buried, a board with an inscription upon it to the same effect.

On the 2nd of October both ships warped out of the harbour the day before the cattle arrived from Verchnei; and that the men might receive the full benefit of this much longed-for supply by consuming it fresh, Captain Gore came to a determination of staying five or six days longer.

At four in the afternoon of the 9th we unmoored, and now took our leave of this place.

Kamtschatka is the name of a peninsula situated on the eastern coast of Asia, running nearly north and south.

It is bounded on the north by the country of the Koriacks; to the south and east by the North Pacific Ocean: and to the west by the Sea of Okotsk. A chain of high mountains stretches the whole length of the country from north to south, dividing it nearly into two equal parts, whence a great number of rivers take their rise, and empty themselves on each side into the Pacific Ocean and the Sea of Okotsk.

If I may judge of the soil from what I saw of its vegetable productions, I should not hesitate in pronouncing it barren in the extreme. The whole bore a more striking resemblance to New-foundland than to any other part of the world I had ever seen.

It is natural to suppose that the severity of the climate must be in due proportion to the general sterility of the soil, of which it is probably the cause. The first time we saw this country was in the beginning of May 1779, when the whole face of it was covered with snow from six to eight feet deep. On our return, the 24th of August, the foliage of the trees, and all sorts of vegetation, seemed to be in the utmost state of perfection; but at the beginning of October, the tops of the hills were again covered with new fallen snow.

The real riches of this country must always consist in the number of wild animals it produces; and no labour can ever be turned to so good an account as what is employed upon their furrieries. Their animals are the common fox; the stoat or ermine; the zibeline or sable; the isatis or arctic fox; the varying hare; the mountain rat or earless marmot; the weasel; the glutton or wolverine; the argali or wild sheep; reindeer; bears; wolves; dogs.

The Russian government established over this country is mild and equitable, considered as a military one, in a very high degree. The natives are permitted to choose their own magistrates from among themselves, in the way, and with the same powers, they had ever been used. One of these, under the title of *toion*, presides over each ostrog; is the referee in all differences; imposes fines, and inflicts punishments for all crimes and misdemeanours; referring to the governor of Kamtschatka such only as he does not choose, from their intricacy or heinousness, to decide upon himself. The *toion* has likewise the appointment of a civil officer, called a corporal, who assists him in the execution of his office, and in his absence acts as his deputy.

By an edict of the present empress, no crime whatsoever can be punished with death. But we were informed that in cases of murder (of which there are very few), the punishment of the knout is administered with such severity that the offender for the most part dies under it.

Our instructions from the Board of Admiralty, having left a discretionary power with the commanding officer of the expedition, in case of failure in the search of a passage from the Pacific into the Atlantic Ocean, to return to England by whatever route he should think best for the farther improvement of geography, Captain Gore demanded of the principal officers their sentiments in writing respecting the manner in which these orders might most effectually be obeyed. The result of our opinions, which he had the satisfaction to find unanimous, and entirely coinciding with his own, that the condition of the ships, of the sails and cordage, made it unsafe to attempt, at so advanced a season of the year, to navigate the sea between Japan and Asia, which would otherwise have afforded the largest field for discovery; that it was therefore advisable to keep to the eastward of that island, and in our way thither to run along the Kuriles, and examine more particularly the islands that lie nearest the northern coast of Japan, which are represented as of a considerable size, and independent of the Russian and Japanese governments. Should we be so fortunate as to find in these any safe and commodious harbours, we conceived they might be of importance, either as places of shelter for any future navigators who may be employed in exploring these seas, or as the means of opening a commercial intercourse among the neighbouring dominions of the two empires. Our next object was to survey the coast of the Japanese Islands, and afterwards to make the coast of China, as far to the northward as we were able, and run along it to Macao.

This plan being adopted, I received orders from Captain Gore, in case of separation, to proceed immediately to Macao; and, at six o'clock in the evening of the 9th of October, having cleared the entrance of Awatska Bay, we steered to the south-east, with the wind north-west and by west. At midnight we had a dead calm, which continued till noon of the 10th. Being in soundings of sixty and seventy fathoms water, we employed our time very profitably in catching cod, which were exceedingly fine and plentiful; in the afternoon a breeze sprung up from the west, with which we stood along the coast to the southward.

After experiencing very blowing weather and adverse winds, which put us out of the course originally intended, at daybreak of the 26th we had the pleasure of descrying high land to the westward, which proved to be Japan.

We stood on till nine, when we were within two leagues of the land, and saw the smoke of several towns or villages, and many houses near the shore, in pleasant and cultivated situations.

On the 29th, at nine o'clock, the wind shifting to the southward, and the sky lowering, we tacked and stood off to the east, and soon after saw a vessel close in with the land, standing along the shore to the northward; and another in the offing, coming down on us before the wind. Objects of any kind, belonging to a country so famous, and yet so little known, it will be easily conceived must have excited a general curiosity, and accordingly every soul on board was upon deck in an instant to gaze at them. As the vessel to windward approached us, she hauled farther off shore; upon which, fearing that we should alarm them by the appearance of a pursuit, we brought the ships to, and she passed ahead of us, at the distance of about half a mile. It would have been easy for us to have spoken with them; but perceiving by their manoeuvres that they were much frightened, Captain Gore was not willing to augment their terrors; and, thinking that we should have many better opportunities of communication with this people, suffered them to go off without interruption.

At noon the wind freshened, and brought with it a good deal of rain; by three it had increased so much that the sea ran as high as anyone on board ever remembered to have seen it.

At eight in the evening the gale shifted to the west, without abating the least in violence, and, by raising a sudden swell in a contrary direction to that which prevailed before, occasioned the ships to strain and labour exceedingly. During the storm several of the sails were split on board the *Resolution*.

From the 29th of October to the 5th of November, we continued our course to the south-east, having very unsettled weather, attended with much lightning and rain. On both days we passed great quantities of pumice stone, several pieces of which we took up and found to weigh from one ounce to three pounds. We conjectured that these stones had been thrown into the sea by eruptions of various dates, as many of them were covered with barnacles, and others quite bare.

On the 15th we saw three islands, and bore away for the south point of the largest, upon which we observed a high barren hill, flattish at the top, and when seen from the west south-west, presents an evident volcanic crater. The earth, rock, or sand, for it was not easy to distinguish of which its surface is composed, exhibited various colours, and a considerable part we conjectured to be sulphur, both from its appearance to the eye, and the strong sulphureous smell which we perceived as we approached the point. Some of the officers on board the *Resolution*, which passed nearer the land, thought they saw steam rising from the top of the hill. From these circumstances Captain Gore gave it the name of Sulphur Island.

Captain Gore now directed his course to the west south-west for the Bashee Islands, hoping to procure at them such a supply of refreshments as would help to shorten his stay at Macao; but unfortunately he overshot them, from an inaccuracy in the chart to which he trusted.

In the forenoon of the 29th we passed several Chinese fishing boats, who eyed us with great indifference. Being now nearly in the latitude of the Lema Islands, we bore away west by north, and, after running twenty-two miles, saw one of them nine or ten leagues to the westward.

In the morning of the 30th we ran along the Lema Isles. At nine o'clock a Chinese boat, which had been before with the *Resolution*, came alongside, and wanted to put on board us a pilot, which, however, we declined, as it was our business to follow our consort.

We rejoiced to see the *Resolution* soon after fire a gun, and hoist her colours as a signal for a pilot. On repeating the signal, we saw an excellent race between four Chinese boats; and Captain Gore, having engaged with the man who arrived first to carry the ship to the Typa for thirty dollars, sent me word that as we could easily follow, that expense might be saved to us. Soon after a second pilot, getting on board the *Resolution*, insisted on conducting the ship, and, without farther ceremony, laid hold of the wheel, and began to order the sails to be trimmed. This occasioned a violent dispute, which at last was compromised by agreeing to go shares in the money.

In obedience to the instructions given to Captain Cook by the Board of Admiralty, it now became necessary to demand of the officers and men their journals, and what other papers they might have in their possession, relating to the history of our voyage. The execution of these orders seemed to require some delicacy as well as firmness. As soon, therefore, as I had assembled the ship's company on deck, I acquainted them with the orders we had received, and the reasons which I thought ought to induce them to yield a ready obedience. At the same time I told them that any papers which they were desirous not to have sent to the Admiralty should be sealed up in their presence, and kept in my own custody, till the intentions of the Board, with regard to the publication of the history of the voyage, were fulfilled, after which they should faithfully be restored back to them.

It is with the greatest satisfaction I can relate that my proposals met with the approbation and the cheerful compliance both of the officers and men; and I am persuaded that every scrap of paper containing any transactions relating to the voyage were given up. Indeed, it is doing bare justice to the seamen of this ship to declare, that they were the most obedient and the best disposed men I ever knew, though almost all of them were very young, and had never before served in a ship of war.

We kept working to windward till six in the evening, when we came to anchor on the 1st of December.

In the evening of the 2nd, Captain Gore sent me on shore to visit the Portuguese Governor, and to request his assistance in procuring refreshments for our crews. At the same time I took a list of the naval stores, of which both vessels were greatly in want, with an intention of proceeding immediately to Canton and applying to the servants of the East India Company, who were at that time resident there. On my arrival at the citadel, the fort-major informed me that the governor was sick, and not able to see company; on my acquainting the major with my desire of proceeding immediately to Canton, he told me that they could not venture to furnish me with a boat till leave was obtained from the hoppo or officer of the customs, and that the application for this purpose must be made to the Chinese government at Canton.

The mortification I felt at meeting with this unexpected delay could only be equalled by the extreme impatience with which we had so long waited for an opportunity of receiving intelligence from Europe. It often happens that, in the eager pursuit of an object, we overlook the easiest and most obvious means of attaining it. This was actually my case at present, for I was returning under great dejection to the ship, when the Portuguese officer who attended me, asked me if I did not mean to visit the English gentlemen at Macao. I need not add with what transport I received the information this question conveyed to me; nor the anxious hopes and fears, the conflict between curiosity and apprehension, which passed in my mind, as we walked toward the house of one of our countrymen.

In this state of agitation, it was not surprising that our reception, though no way deficient in civility or kindness, should appear cold and formal. In our inquiries, as far as they related to objects of private concern, we met, as was indeed to be expected, with little or no satisfaction; but the events of a public nature, which had happened since our departure, now, for the first time, burst all at once upon us, overwhelmed every other feeling, and left us for some time almost without the power of reflection.

On the 9th, Captain Gore received an answer from the Committee of the English supercargoes at Canton, in which they assured him that their best endeavours should be used to procure the supplies we stood in need of as expeditiously as possible, and that a passport should be sent for one of his officers.

The following day an English merchant, from one of our settlements in the East Indies, applied to Captain Gore for the assistance of a few hands to navigate a vessel he had purchased at Macao, up to Canton. Captain Gore judging this a good opportunity for me to proceed to that place, gave orders that I should take along with me my second lieutenant, the lieutenant of marines, and ten seamen. Though this was not precisely the mode in which I could have wished to visit Canton, yet, as it was very uncertain when the passport might arrive, and my presence might contribute materially to the expediting of our supplies. I did not hesitate to put myself on board.

I reached Canton on the 18th, a little after it was dark, and landed at the English factory, where, though my arrival was very unexpected, I was received with every mark of attention and civility. Wishing to make my stay as short as possible, I requested the gentlemen to procure boats for me the next day to convey the stores; but I was soon informed that a business of that kind was not to be transacted so rapidly in this country, that many forms were to be complied with, and, in short, that patience was an indispensable virtue in China.

I waited several days for the event of our application, without understanding that the matter was at all advanced toward a conclusion. Whilst I was doubting what measures to pursue, the commander of a country ship brought me a letter from Captain Gore, in which he acquainted me that he had engaged him to bring us down from Canton, and to deliver the stores we had procured at his own risk in the Typa.

As Canton was likely to be the most advantageous market for furs, I was desired by Captain Gore to carry with me about twenty sea-otters' skins, chiefly the property of our deceased commanders, and to dispose of them at the best price I could procure; a commission which gave me an opportunity of becoming a little acquainted with the genius of the Chinese for trade. Having acquainted some of the English supercargoes with these circumstances, I desired them to recommend me to some Chinese merchant of credit who would offer me a fair price. Having laid my goods before him, he examined them with great care, and told me that he could not venture to offer more than three hundred dollars for them. As I knew from the price our skins had sold for in Kamtschatka, that he had not offered me one half their value, I found myself under the necessity of driving a bargain. In my turn I therefore demanded one thousand; my Chinese then advanced to five hundred; then offered me a private present of tea and porcelain, amounting to one hundred more; then the same sum in money; and lastly rose to seven hundred dollars, on which I fell to nine hundred. At last, being tired of the contest, I consented to and received eight hundred.

During my stay at Canton I was carried by one of the English gentlemen to visit a person of the first consequence in the place. We were received in a long room or gallery, at the upper end of which stood a table with a large chair behind it, and a row of chairs extending from it on each side of the room. Being previously instructed that the point of civility consisted in remaining as long unseated as possible, I readily acquitted myself of this piece of etiquette; after which we were entertained with tea and some preserved and fresh fruits. Our host was very fat, with a heavy dull countenance, and of great gravity in his deportment. He spoke a little broken English and Portuguese; and, after we had taken our refreshment, he carried us about his house and garden, and having showed us all the improvements he was making, we departed.

In the evening of the 26th I took my leave of the supercargoes, having thanked them for their many obliging favours, amongst which I must not forget to mention a handsome present of tea for the use of the ships' companies, and a large collection of English periodical publications. The latter we found a valuable acquisition, as they both served to amuse our impatience during our tedious voyage home, and enabled us to return not total strangers to what had been transacting in our native country. At one o'clock the next morning we left Canton, and arrived at Macao about the same hour the day following, having passed down a channel which lies to the westward of that by which we had come up.

During our absence a brisk trade had been carrying on with the Chinese for the sea otter skins which had every day been rising in their value. One of our seamen sold his stock alone for eight hundred dollars; and a few prime skins, which were clean and had been well preserved, were sold for one hundred and twenty each. The whole amount of the value in specie and goods that was got for the furs in both ships, I am confident did not fall short of £2,000 sterling: and it was generally supposed that at least two-thirds of the quantity we had originally got from the Americans were spoiled and worn out, or had been given away and otherwise disposed of in Kamtschatka.

The rage with which our seamen were possessed to return to Cook's River, and by another cargo of skins to make their fortunes at one time, was not far short of mutiny.

The barter which had been carrying on with the Chinese for our sea-otter skins, had produced a very whimsical change in the dress of all our crew. On our arrival here nothing could exceed the ragged appearance both of the younger officers and seamen, for as our voyage had already exceeded, by near a twelvemonth, the time it was at first imagined we should remain at sea, almost the whole of our original stock of European clothes had been long worn out, or patched up with skins, and the various manufactures we had met with in the course of our discoveries. These were now again mixed and eked out with the gaudiest silks and cottons of China.

On the 12th of January 1780, at noon, we unmoored and scaled the guns, which on board my ship now amounted to ten; so that, by means of four additional ports, we could, if occasion required, fight seven on a side.

We thought it our duty to provide ourselves with these means of defence, though we had some reason to believe, from the public prints last received at Canton, that the generosity of our enemies had in a great measure rendered them superfluous. As this intelligence was farther confirmed by the private letters of several of the supercargoes, Captain Gore thought himself bound, in return for the liberal exceptions made in our favour, to refrain from availing himself of any opportunities of capture which these might afford, and to preserve throughout his voyage the strictest neutrality.

At two in the afternoon on the 13th, having got under sail, the *Resolution* saluted the fort of Macao with eleven guns, which was returned with the same number.

In the morning of the 20th we steered for Pulo Condore; and at half-past twelve we got sight of the island. As soon as we were come to anchor, Captain Gore fired a gun with a view of apprising the natives of our arrival, and drawing them towards the shore, but without effect. Early in the morning of the 21st, parties were sent to cut wood, which was Captain Gore's principal motive for coming hither.

None of the natives having yet made their appearance, notwithstanding a second gun had been fired, Captain Gore thought it advisable to land and go in search of them. We proceeded through a thick wood, up a steep hill, to the distance of a mile, when, after descending, we arrived at some huts; I ordered the party to stay without, lest the sight of so many armed men should terrify the inhabitants, whilst I entered and reconnoitred alone. I found in one of the huts an elderly man who was in a great fright, and preparing to make off with the most valuable effects. However, a few signs, particularly that most significant one of holding out a handful of dollars, and then pointing to a herd of buffaloes, and the fowls that were running about the huts in great numbers, left him without any doubts as to the objects of our visit. He pointed towards a place where the town stood, and made us comprehend that, by going thither, all our wants would be supplied. He ordered a young man to conduct us to the town as soon as an obstacle should be removed, of which we were not aware. On our first coming out of the wood, a herd of buffaloes, to the number of twenty at least, came running towards us, tossing up their heads, snuffing the air, and roaring in a hideous manner. They had followed us to the huts, and stood drawn up in a body at a little distance; and the old man made us understand that it would be exceedingly dangerous for us to move till they were driven into the woods; but so enraged were the animals grown at the sight of us, that this was not effected without a good ideal of time and difficulty. The men not being able to accomplish it, we were surprised to see them call to their assistance a few little boys, who soon drove them out of sight. Afterwards, we had occasion to observe, that in driving these animals, and securing them, which is done by putting a rope through a hole which is made in their nostrils, little boys were always employed, who could stroke and handle them with impunity at times when the men durst not approach them.

We were now conducted to the town, which consists of between twenty and thirty houses, built close together.

By means of my money, and pointing at different objects in sight, I had no difficulty in making a man who seemed to be the principal person of the company to which we were introduced, comprehend the main business of our errand, and I as readily understood from him that the chief or captain was absent, but would soon return; and that, without his consent, no purchases of any kind could be made.

Having at last procured a supply of buffaloes and some fat hogs, on the 28th of January 1780 we unmoored; and, as soon as we were clear of the harbour, steered south south-west.

On the 2nd of February, at eight in the morning, we tried for soundings, continuing to do the same every hour, till we had passed the Straits of Sunda, and found the bottom with twenty-three fathoms of line.

On the 5th we approached the coast of Sumatra. The country is covered with wood down to the water's edge, and the shores are so low, that the sea overflows the land, and washes the trunks of the trees. To this flat and marshy situation of the shore, we may attribute those thick fogs and vapours which we perceived every morning, not without dread and horror, hanging over the island, till they were dispersed by the rays of the sun. The shores of Banca, which are opposite, are much bolder; and the country inland rises to a moderate height, and appears to be well wooded throughout.

In the morning of the 9th, I received orders from Captain Gore to make sail towards a Dutch ship which now hove in sight to the southward, and which we supposed to be from Europe; and, according to the nature of the intelligence we could procure from her, either to join him at Cracatoa, where he intended to stop for the purpose of supplying the ships with arrack, or to proceed to the south-east end of Prince's Island, and there take in our water and wait for him.

I accordingly bore down towards the Dutch ship, which soon after came to an anchor to the eastward; and having got as near her as the tide would permit, we also dropped anchor.

Next morning Mr Williamson got on board the ship, and learnt that she had been seven months from Europe, and three from the Cape of Good Hope; that, before she sailed, France and Spain had declared war against Great Britain; and that she left Sir Edward Hughes with a squadron of men of war and a fleet of East India ships at the Cape. I immediately sent a boat to acquaint Captain Gore with the intelligence we had received.

At three o'clock in the morning of the 12th we stood over for Prince's Island, and came to an anchor within half a mile of the shore. Lieutenant Lanyan, who had been here before with Captain Cook, in the year 1770, was sent along with the master to look for the watering-place.

The natives, who came to us soon after we anchored, brought a plentiful supply of large fowls and some turtles; but the last, for the most part, were very small.

On the 19th, being favoured by a breeze from the north-west, we broke ground, and the next day had entirely lost sight of this place.

Of this island I shall only observe, that we were exceedingly struck with the great general resemblance of the natives, both in figure, colour, manners, and even language, to the nations we had been so much conversant with in the South Seas.

From the time of our entering these Straits, we began to experience the powerful effects of this pestilential climate. Two of our people fell dangerously ill of malignant putrid fevers, which, however, we prevented from spreading, by putting the patients apart from the rest in the most airy berths; and we had the singular satisfaction of escaping from these fatal seas, without the loss of a single life; probably owing to the vigorous health of the crews, and the strict attention now become habitual in our men, to the salutary regulations introduced amongst us by Captain Cook.

It had hitherto been Captain Gore's intention to proceed directly to St Helena, without stopping at the Cape, but the rudder of the *Resolution* having been reported to be in a dangerous state, he resolved to steer immediately for the Cape, as the most eligible place both for the recovery of the sick and for the repair of the rudder.

In the forenoon of the 10th of April, a snow was seen bearing down to us, which proved to be an English East-India packet, that had left Table Bay three days before, and was cruising with orders for the China fleet and other India ships.

The next morning we stood into Simon's Bay. We found lying here the *Nassau* and *Southampton* East Indiamen, waiting for convoy for Europe. The *Resolution* saluted the fort with eleven guns, and the same number was returned.

Mr Brandt, the governor of this place, came to visit us as soon as we had anchored. He appeared much surprised to see our crew in so healthy a condition, as the Dutch ship that had left Macao on our arrival there, and had touched at the Cape some time before, reported that we were in a most wretched state, having only fourteen hands left on board the *Resolution*, and seven on board the *Discovery* It is not easy to conceive the motive these people could have had for propagating so wanton and malicious a falsehood.

On the 15th I accompanied Captain Gore to Cape Town, and the next morning we waited on Baron Pletenberg, the governor, by whom we were received with every possible attention and civility. Both he and Mr Brandt had conceived a great personal affection for Captain Cook, as well as the highest admiration of his character, and heard the recital of his misfortune with many expressions of unaffected sorrow.

During our stay at the Cape we met with every proof of the most friendly disposition towards us, both in the governor and principal persons of the place, as well Africans as Europeans.

Having completed our victualling, and furnished ourselves with the necessary supply of naval stores, we sailed out of the bay on the 9th of May.

On the 12th of June we passed the equator for the fourth time during this voyage.

On the 12th of August we made the western coast of Ireland; and, after a fruitless attempt to get into Port Galway, from whence it was Captain Gore's intention to have sent the journals and maps of our voyage to London, we were obliged, by strong southerly winds, to steer to the northward. Our next object was to put into Lough Swilly; but the wind continuing in the same quarter, we stood on to the northward of Lewis Island; and on the 22nd of August, at eleven in the morning, both ships came to an anchor at Stromness. From hence I was despatched by Captain Gore, to acquaint the Board of Admiralty with our arrival; and on the 4th day of October the ships arrived safe at the Nore, after an absence of four years two months and twenty-two days.

On quitting the *Discovery* at Stromness, I had the satisfaction of leaving the whole crew in perfect health, and, at the same time, the number of convalescents on board the *Resolution* did not exceed two or three, of whom only one was incapable of service. In the course of our voyage the *Resolution* lost but five men by sickness, three of whom were in a precarious state of health at our departure from England; the *Discovery* did not lose a man. An unremitting attention to the regulations established by Captain Cook, with which the world is already acquainted, may be justly considered as the principal cause, under the blessing of Divine Providence, of this singular success. But the baneful effects of salt provisions might, perhaps, in the end have been felt, notwithstanding these salutary precautions, if we had not assisted them, by availing ourselves of every substitute our situation at various times afforded. These frequently consisting of articles, which our people had not been used to consider as food for men, and being sometimes exceedingly nauseous, it required the joint aid of persuasion, authority, and example, to conquer their prejudices and disgust.

The preventives we principally relied on were sauerkraut and portable soup. As to the anti-scorbutic remedies, with which we were amply supplied, we had no opportunity of trying their effects, as there did not appear the slightest symptoms of the scurvy in either ship during the whole voyage. Our malt and hops had also been kept as a resource in case of actual sickness; and on examination at the Cape of Good Hope were found entirely spoiled.

About the same time were opened some casks of biscuit, flour, pease, oatmeal, and groats, which, by way of experiment, had been put up in small casks, lined with tin-foil, and found all, except the pease, in a much better state than could have been expected in the usual manner of package.

I cannot neglect this opportunity of recommending to the consideration of government the necessity of allowing a sufficient quantity of Peruvian bark to such of His Majesty's ships as may be exposed to the influence of unwholesome climates. It happened very fortunately in the *Discovery*, that only one of the men, who had fevers in the Straits of Sunda, stood in need of this medicine, as he alone consumed the whole quantity usually carried out by surgeons in such vessels as ours. Had more been affected in the same manner, they would probably all have perished from the want of the only remedy capable of affording them effectual relief.

Another circumstance attending this voyage, which, if we consider its duration and the nature of the service in which we were engaged, will appear scarcely less singular than the extraordinary healthiness of the crews, was, that the two ships never lost sight of each other for a day together, except twice, which was owing, the first time, to an accident that happened to the *Discovery* off the coast of Owhyhee, and the second, to the fogs we met with at the entrance of Awatska Bay. A stronger proof cannot be given of the skill and vigilance of our subaltern officers, to whom this share of merit almost entirely belongs.

Thus ended a voyage distinguished by the extent and importance of its discoveries. Besides other inferior islands, it added that fine group called the Sandwich Islands, to the former known limits of the terraqueous globe, and ascertained the proximity of the two great continents of Asia and America.

This enterprise proved fatal to its principal conductors — Captains Cook and Clerke, as we have seen, never returned. Captain King, with a constitution broken by climate and fatigue, lived indeed to publish the voyage which will immortalise his name; but he soon after fell a martyr to what he had undergone in the service of his country. He died at Nice, whither he had retired for the mild salubrity of the air, in the autumn of 1784; and though cut off in the bloom of life, left a name covered with honour and remembered with regret. He was the fourth son of the Dean of Raphoe in Ireland, but of an English family.

Having come to a conclusion of the voyages in which the genius and talents of that great navigator Captain Cook are so pre-eminently displayed, we cannot omit the opportunity of gratifying a propensity which our readers must naturally feel of being made acquainted with what family he left behind him, and how the dispensations of Providence may have disposed of them; but in doing this, sorry are we to say, that we impose on ourselves a very painful duty, for we are unfortunately compelled to relate a tale of woe, melancholy and distressing in the extreme.

When he set out on his last voyage, Captain Cook's family consisted of his wife and three sons, the second of whom was lost on board the Thunderer *man of war, about six months after the unfortunate death of his father. The eldest son, who was appointed master and commander of the* Spitfire *sloop of war, while she lay off Poole waiting for hands, in attempting to get on board, was driven to sea in a boat during the night in a heavy gale of wind, and he and every person in the boat perished. But what considerably aggravates this misfortune is, as was afterwards disclosed by one of the sailors on board the vessel, that in their distress they were met by a revenue cutter, the hands of which threw them a rope, and lay to till they could bale their boat, or the fury of the wind should cease. But the master of the cutter, who was then in bed, was no sooner made acquainted with these circumstances, and that it was a king's boat, than, with an oath, he ordered his men immediately to set them adrift, and in that situation they were left to be overwhelmed by a tempestuous sea.*

His body was afterwards found, and conveyed to Spithead on board his own vessel, whence it was conveyed to Cambridge, and buried by the side of the youngest brother, who had suddenly died of a fever, and whose funeral he had attended only about six weeks before.

Thus was a tender mother prematurely deprived of her husband and children, and left to mourn their untimely fates, which had so powerful an effect upon her mind as to reduce Mrs Cook to a mere shadow of what she was formerly.

WORDSWORTH CLASSICS
OF WORLD LITERATURE

REQUESTS FOR INSPECTION COPIES   Lecturers wishing to obtain copies of Wordsworth Classics, Wordsworth Poetry Library or Wordsworth Classics of World Literature titles on inspection are invited to contact: Dennis Hart, Wordsworth Editions Ltd, Crib Street, Ware, Herts SG12 9ET; E-mail: dennis.hart@wordsworth-editions.com. Please quote the author, title and ISBN of the titles in which you are interested; together with your name, academic address, E-mail address, the course on which the books will be used and the expected enrolment.

Teachers wishing to inspect specific core titles for GCSE or A level courses are also invited to contact Wordsworth Editions at the above address.

Inspection copies are sent solely at the discretion of Wordsworth Editions Ltd.

APULEIUS
The Golden Ass

ARISTOTLE
The Nicomachean Ethics

MARCUS AURELIUS
Meditations

FRANCIS BACON
Essays

JAMES BOSWELL
The Life of Samuel Johnson
(UNABRIDGED)

JOHN BUNYAN
The Pilgrim's Progress

BALDESAR CASTIGLIONE
The Book of the Courtier

CATULLUS
Poems

CERVANTES
Don Quixote

CARL VON CLAUSEWITZ
On War
(ABRIDGED)

CONFUCIUS
The Analects

CAPTAIN JAMES COOK
The Voyages of Captain Cook

DANTE
The Inferno

CHARLES DARWIN
The Origin of Species
The Voyage of the Beagle

RENÉ DESCARTES
Key Philosophical Writings

FYODOR DOSTOEVSKY
The Devils

ERASMUS
Praise of Folly

SIGMUND FREUD
The Interpretation of Dreams

EDWARD GIBBON
The Decline and Fall of the Roman Empire
(ABRIDGED)

GUSTAVE FLAUBERT
A Sentimental Journey

KAHLIL GIBRAN
The Prophet

JOHANN WOLFGANG VON GOETHE
Faust

HERODOTUS
Histories

HOMER
The Iliad and The Odyssey

HORACE
The Odes

BEN JONSON
Volpone and Other Plays

KENKO
Essays in Idleness

WILLIAM LANGLAND
Piers Plowman

LAO TZU
Tao Te Ching

T. E. LAWRENCE
Seven Pillars of Wisdom